Economic Growth

How it works and how it transformed the world

Edward A. Hudson

Vernon Press

www.vernonpress.com

In the Americas:
Vernon Press
1000 N West Street,
Suite 1200, Wilmington,
Delaware 19801
United States

In the rest of the world
Vernon Press
C/Sancti Espiritu 17,
Malaga, 29006
Spain

Library of Congress Control Number: 2014958349

ISBN 978-1-62273-021-6

Preface

I spent my childhood in New Zealand. As a youngster in the 1950s I was amazed at the ever expanding stream of new products which appeared on the market and which made life easier, for my parents, and more fun, for me. The washing machine and the refrigerator, I remember, transformed my mother's life. The automobile transformed my life. I was aware, as was everyone in New Zealand, that this wave of plenty flowed "from the sheep's back", as the saying went. New Zealand's farms grew sheep and cows, exporting wool, meat and cheese to Britain and to the United States. I was also aware of the corollary – this prosperity depended on the prosperity and growth of Britain and the United States.

I moved to the United States in the 1960s. I was struck by the even greater prosperity I found there. I was equally struck by the attitude of Americans – friendly, helpful, optimistic and, above all, striving to improve themselves and their economic position. This was, it seemed to me, a dynamic country like no other. America was (and is) a land of plenty, partly because it is so blessed with natural resources but mainly because of its people. America is a land of change as its people work to improve their lot and, in so doing, move everyone forward in opportunity and prosperity. My story, of moving to America in search of opportunity, and of working and investing to grasp those opportunities, is also the story of America.

I studied at Harvard and got a Ph.D. in Economics. My thesis was on economic growth, applying a mathematical growth model to investigate the properties of the so called "turnpike". The feature of the turnpike is that, like the highway, there is just one efficient growth path and, if the planning horizon is long enough, efficient growth always travels along this one path, no matter what the beginning point and the target destination. This research was intensive in mathematics and computation. One thing I took from this research was not so much about economic growth but rather the value of systematically working towards a defined target. In addition I learned from Dale Jorgenson, my thesis adviser, and from three other Harvard professors – Otto Eckstein, Hendrik Houthakker and Wassily Leontief – that the answer to most questions comes from careful analysis of the FACTS. One implication for understanding the world is – look for the theory that fits the facts, not the facts that fit the theory. This is the philosophy that I have applied in this book.

I chose not to go into academia; I was interested instead in working on practical problems and trying to improve practical outcomes. This began with some heavy duty modeling. Working with Dale Jorgenson, I operationalized Dale's 9 sector (later expanded to 36 sector) general equilibrium growth model. This was the time of the first "energy crisis" (the price of oil went up) and we applied the model to investigating energy-economy interactions. Public opinion was shocked – the price of gasoline had doubled! Politicians, eager to be seen to be doing something, did something and transformed a normal economic adjustment into an ongoing problem. The problem was not solved until the 1980s when President Ronald Reagan removed Federal controls on petroleum and also by which time the normal economic forces of supply (expanding supply in response to higher prices) and demand (reducing demand due to higher prices) were starting to come into full play.

President Reagan said: "The nine most terrifying words in the English language are: 'I'm from the government and I'm here to help'". There is a certain amount of truth in this. So, disillusioned with governments I began a new career in management consulting. I have been doing this, mainly in strategy consulting, ever since. I have always kept an interest in economic growth but, until now, I have focused my work on strategy. During my career I was working on, observing and analyzing business - how businesses work, what makes them succeed, what makes them decline. And, all the time I was accumulating facts which, with my thinking framework as a highly trained economist, led to an understanding of how economies work – how they grow or, in the opposite case, how they stagnate.

Now that I have retired and have a little time to do other things, I have returned not so much to thinking about economic growth but to distilling everything I have learned and observed and analyzed about economic growth into a coherent system. I started active research and writing about four years ago. I knew my target end point, a book about economic growth, but I didn't know what would end up in the book. I was surprised. Analyzing the facts brought me to the realization that there was a clear logical framework concerning growth – what happens and how it happens. This framework is what I have tried to set out in this book.

Economists have dabbled for decades in thinking about economic growth. This dabbling turned into serious theory in the 1950s when Robert Solow (1956) led the development of so called "neoclassical growth models". Academic thinking since then has pretty much stayed within the framework initiated by Solow. These models attribute growth to increases in inputs of capital, labor and everything else – the residual, often characterized as technical change. This type of model does broadly describes the results of U.S. growth although it does less well for many other countries. Fundamentally, though, this approach describes the result but not the causes or the processes of growth. The approach set out in the present book has a different objective - to find the mechanisms of growth, how growth works, how economic growth comes about. My approach extends the academic model into causes rather than just effects.

The analysis of the mechanisms and processes of growth set out in this book can be applied to forecasting the future. These forecasts are separate to my analysis of growth itself but it is irresistible not to try to look into the future. I think that the outlook for continuing economic growth is reasonably good; I am optimistic. This optimism comes down to the character of the American people and the nature of the capitalist system. There is no reason to think that all the new products that can be developed have been developed; to the contrary, there is every reason to think that there is no shortage of desirable new products which can be developed even though we do not know today what these will be. The dynamism of the American people surely sets the stage for continued development of new and better products. The dynamism of American business similarly sets the stage for improvements in production efficiency, development of new production technologies, new management tools and other things which reduce costs/increase productivity, sustaining the growth in demand and generating increasing incomes.

There are serious risks though. First, there is the risk that governments will interfere with trade, restrict change, diminish incentives and add to costs, thereby threatening the human drivers of growth. Second, there are non-economic risks which currently are not being managed. I am thinking here of global environmental dangers from the loss of the world's fisheries, from the contamination of the oceans and, in particular, from climate change resulting from ever-increasing emissions of greenhouse gasses. Third, there are the risks of armed conflict and religion-fuelled terrorism. Our institutions are not up to the task of effectively managing these risks. Economically, the future looks bright but humankind faces the challenge of managing the global physical and security environment so that everyone on Earth can benefit from this bright economic future. I wish I could be as optimistic about these matters as I am about efficacy of the market/capitalist system.

My purpose in writing this book has been to clarify the practical features, processes and effects of economic growth. I hope that this view of economic growth will be of interest to economists, public policy-makers and those in the population in general who are concerned about how the world operates and how lives can be improved. I hope that these people find this book informative and, most of all, stimulating.

Contents

Chapter 1
Introduction

1.1 If there had been no growth

Most things about our day-to-day lives are due to economic growth. Without growth we would be living in the manner of people in England in 1700. A few would live in large houses, be looked after by servants, dress in fine clothes and eat high protein diets. Most, though, would work on the land, live in one or two room houses with no water supply or sewerage system, be illiterate and have no teeth. Women would cook, clean and have children; men would labor. Diet would be dominated by grains and beer. Mobility would be by walking. People would live and die in the village in which they were born. As life expectancy was less than 40 years there would be no concern about retirement. Food supply was so limited and death rates from infectious diseases were so high that most of us would simply not be here – populations would be a small fraction of what they are today.

Today, most people in high income countries are educated and in good health, have a life expectancy of around 80 years, live in comfortable houses with energy supply, water and sewerage systems, eat well (or even too well), be in paid work for less than half of their waking hours, have machines which drastically reduce the time and effort needed for household tasks, and have machines which provide entertainment, communication and mobility. And there are more of us – food supply, sanitation and health care are such that populations are many times greater than in 1700. These changes are all due to sustained increases in production (and its dual, income) over the past three centuries; in short, these changes are due to economic growth.

1.2 What is economic growth?

Economic growth is the continuing increase in per capita incomes or purchasing power.

These are increases continuing for many decades or for centuries. Economic growth has now been going on for 300 years. Some countries in earlier eras achieved rising per capita incomes but, when the source of the rise had been played out, were unable to continue the increase. The central feature of economic growth is that the increase is ongoing – once one source of growth has been played out another source emerges to take per capita incomes forward again, and so on and so on.

Increasing production which is totally absorbed in population increase is expansion but not growth; this is simply more people living the same way and doing the same things. Economic growth is about increasing average incomes. This allows people to increase their material standard of living, to enjoy more of more things, to be better educated, have better health, more leisure time, more entertainment and so on. Economic growth is about increasing the range and depth of choice available for people's consumption.

Economic growth always involves change. New goods and services are introduced, patterns of spending and consumption change, production expands, new production processes are developed, production takes place in new locations, people choose to live in new locations and so on. The pre-growth world featured static economies, or economies which increased in scale or extent but not structure, whereas growth economies involve continuing structural change. In a growth economy, the only constant is change.

1.3 Measuring growth

Economic growth conventionally is measured by the growth rate of constant price Gross Domestic Product (GDP) per capita. Constant price means that production is valued in different years in the prices of the base year; this takes inflation out of account, thereby indicating movements in the overall quantity of production of goods and services.

GDP is a measure of the value created in the production of traded goods and services. (Some non-traded production also is included such as the value of accommodation services from owner-occupied residential property.) This value added is the total income generated in an economy. This income is then spent on finished goods and services. Most of this final demand spending is by people consuming finished goods and services, some is by governments on producing public goods, some is directed to investment to provide increased productive capacity for the future and some (exports less imports) is spending by people in other countries. The value added in production, net incomes and final demand spending are different ways of looking at the same thing; numerically they are equal.

GDP is part of a measurement system called the National Accounts. GDP and related measures in the United States are also referred to as the National Economic Accounts. Table 1.1 shows the broad spending and income indicators of the National Economic Accounts for the United States for 2010. Total spending is Gross Domestic Expenditure (GDE), total income is Gross Domestic Income (GDI) and the value added (income created) in production is GDP. Numerically, GDE is equal to GDI and also to GDP. (The values in this Table are in current dollars, the dollars actually spent or received. For considering economic growth, production, expenditure and income are measured in constant dollars.)

Table 1.1 U.S. Economic Aggregates, 2010

Gross Domestic Expenditure (GDE)	$ billion	% of GDE
Personal consumption expenditures	10,246	71%
Gross private domestic investment	1,795	12%
Exports	1,840	13%
less Imports	-2,357	-16%
Government purchases	3,003	21%
Gross Domestic Expenditure	14,527	100%

Gross Domestic Income (GDI)	$ billion	% of GDI
Compensation of employees	7,981	55%
Net operating surplus, private enterprises + Current surplus, government enterprises	3,674	25%
Consumption of fixed capital	1,875	13%
Taxes on production and imports less subsidies	997	7%
Gross Domestic Income	14,527	100%

Gross Domestic Product (GDP)	$ billion	% of GDP
Agriculture, forestry, fishing, and hunting	157	1%
Mining	240	2%
Utilities	265	2%
Construction	512	4%
Durable manufactured goods	915	6%
Nondurable manufactured goods	787	5%
Retail and wholesale trade	1,682	12%
Transportation and warehousing	403	3%
Publishing, broadcasting, telecommunications, information	623	4%
Finance and insurance	1,242	9%
Real estate and rental and leasing	1,765	12%
Professional and business services	1,783	12%
Educational services, health care, and social assistance	1,272	9%
Arts, entertainment, recreation, accommodation and food services	556	4%
Other services except government	357	2%
Government	1,969	14%
Gross Domestic Product	14,527	100%

Source: U.S. Bureau of Economic Analysis, National Economic Accounts.

These different views also show the structure of economic activity. For example, final demand is dominated by personal consumption, labor income is greater than capital income, and spending is dominated by services.

GDP growth can also be separated into its sources in terms of productive inputs – labor, capital and everything else, the productivity of converting factor inputs (factor inputs are labor and capital) into outputs. This is called "growth accounting". Growth accounting typically finds that most growth in GDP per capita is due to more and better capital per worker along with increases in productivity.

1.4 A history of income

As England, part of the United Kingdom, was the birthplace of economic growth, we show in Figure 1.1 the graph of U.K. per capita GDP for the past 2,000 years.

Figure 1.1 GDP per capita, U.K.
GDP per capita in year 1 CE = 1

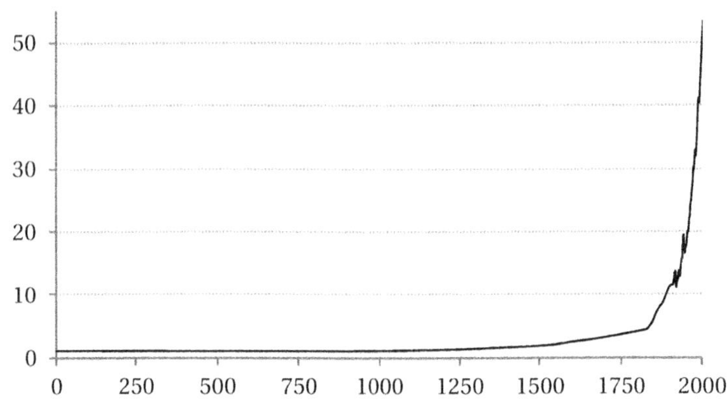

Source: Data from Maddison (2006b).

Average income today is more than 50 times larger than in the first millenium. Incomes did not change for a thousand years then very slowly began to rise. The rise accelerated in the 16th century, following the Black Death and coinciding with the European Renaissance and the Reformation. However, people were still doing the same thing, just doing it a little better, until the first half of the 18th century. This was the start of the "Industrial Revolution", the application of capital to the production of manufactured goods. Growth rates slowly accelerated. There are only two significant blips in the growth curve – disruptions associated with the aftermath of World War I and with the Great Depression of the 1930s. Economic growth has been going on now for 300 years.

1.5 A broad history of economic growth

Economic growth started in England in the early 18th century. Agricultural productivity had been rising for some time, leading to increasing production of food and, as food accounted for most of the household budget, to increasing incomes. This began to create some discretionary income – income left over after buying the basics of life (mainly food and shelter) and so available for non-basic purchases. People wanted in particular to buy cotton goods such as underclothes, shirts, dresses, towels and sheets. The rising demand for cotton goods running up against the restricted supply of costly, hand-made cottons stimulated the invention and development of mechanical ways of cleaning, spinning and weaving cotton. The machine age was born. Mechanical power initially was obtained from muscles and from water wheels. The new machines were made out of iron; this stimulated the development of low cost iron-making based on coke made from plentiful coal (in place of earlier, high cost iron using charcoal made from scarce wood). Steam engines were adapted from running mine pumps to powering machines. Mechanical power was most efficiently applied at scale so the factory was born. Conglomerations of factories gave rise to the new industrial cities. Steam engines were later applied to mobile uses – the railway and steamship ushered in the age of mobility. Low cost ways were developed for making steel and steel replaced iron in most uses. Growth was underway.

The locus of new products and processes went from cotton spinning to iron to the steam engine to the locomotive to weaving to the steamship then to steel. These changes took time. It took more than 100 years to go from the first mechanization of cotton spinning to the full mechanization of cotton weaving. It took around 100 years to go from Arkwright's cotton mill, which made low cost thread, to Bessemer's converter, which made low cost steel. But, by the 1870s, the age of the machine, the industrial age, had well and truly arrived.

The breakthrough into industrial growth took place in Britain. However, economic leadership gradually passed to the United States, based on a new set of growth industries such as electricity, household appliances and the automobile. These drove America forward until the 1970s. Different products then took over as growth drivers – the computer, health care, entertainment and recently the internet. The United States passed from the age of agriculture to the age of heavy industry and then to the age of services.

Economic growth continued by means of a succession of new products which found growing and ultimately massive demand. Some of the new products were goods, some were services, most involved new technologies but it was not the novel technologies which made the difference as much as the creation of new products which satisfied a previously unmet, or even unknown, consumer demand. This growth in demand was sustained by a growth in supply as more capital and increasing productivity expanded production capacity.

The growth process was so gradual and complex that there is no clear starting date. The initial impetus to growth was increasing agricultural productivity. Two indicative dates are 1701 when Jethro Tull invented his seed drill, and the 1730s when Charles Townshend introduced to England the four-field crop rotation system using wheat, barley, turnips and clover. The age of the machine might be said to start with Richard Arkwright's water frame, patented in 1769, which spun cotton into yarn. The age of the factory might be dated from the first cotton mill, also created by Arkwright, the Cromford Mill, which opened in 1771. Efficient mechanical power might be related to the high pressure boiler, introduced by Richard Trevithick in the early 1800s. Effective mobile mechanical power started with Robert Stephenson's locomotive, the *Planet*, built in 1830. The Bessemer converter, making low cost steel, was introduced from the 1860s. Electricity was introduced late in the 19th century, the landmark being when George Westinghouse opened the first alternating current system, from generation through transmission to customers. The age of the automobile really began with Henry Ford's low-priced car, the Model T, introduced in 1908. Modern commercial entertainment began in the 1930s while modern health care began in the 1950s. Modern computers and consumer electronics date from the 1960s with the internet starting in the 1990s.

This sequence illustrates one crucial feature of economic growth – the succession of new products which met huge consumer demand, creating growth industries which pull the economy forward. The enabling side of this process is the ongoing increase in production capability with more physical capital, more human capital and more efficient production processes allowing the increasing spending to be sustained and allowing incomes to increase.

A different feature of economic growth has been the increasing role of government. From the traditional roles of law and order and defense, government activity first expanded to encompass transportation and sanitation infrastructure, public health and education. More recently, governments have moved into income redistribution. People, through the political process rather than the market process, have chosen to devote a considerable part of the fruits of economic growth to government activities and to providing support for those at the lower end of the income distribution.

But government activity has been grafted onto the market system. A central feature of economic growth in Britain and the United States has been its decentralized nature, based on individual initiative operating within the market system. Economic growth has flourished only when the market system remains dominant and economic decisions are made by individual people and businesses, not by governments.

1.6 The growth leaders

The leading countries since 1850, in terms of GDP per capita, are shown in Figure 1.2.

Figure 1.2 Leading countries since 1850
GDP per capita in 1990 dollars

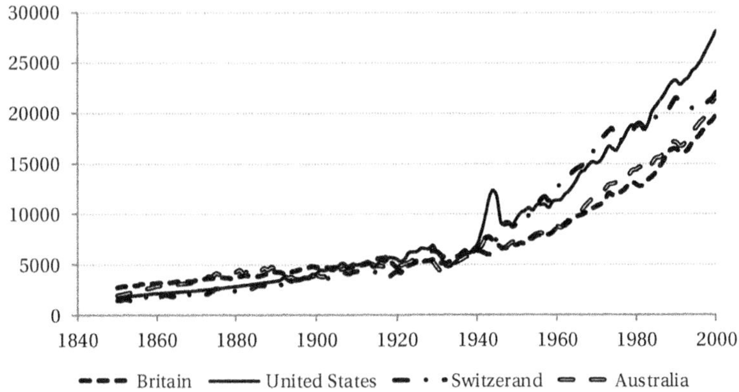

Source: Data from Maddison (2006b).

Britain led the way until early in the 20th century. World War I then brought Britain's leadership to a close. Australia led for a few years but rode on Britain's coat-tails, supplying agricultural products to the British market. The United States took the lead early in the century and has held it ever since. Switzerland showed higher GDP per capita for some years but this was due to supplying specialist goods and services to high income European and American customers. The United States has been the engine of growth for the past century.

1.7 Growth rates

Growth rates of the two leading countries, Britain and the United States, are shown in Table 1.2.

Table 1.2 Growth in Britain and the United States
Average annual growth of GDP per capita

	Britain	United States
1 - 1700	0.1%	
1700 - 1820	0.3%	0.7%
1820 - 1890	1.2%	1.4%
1890 - 2000	1.5%	2.0%

Source: Data from Maddison (2006b).

We note first that growth rates for each country accelerated as the growth process got underway. Also, growth rates in the United States have been more rapid than those in Britain. The United States early in the 20th century surpassed Britain in terms of the level of incomes; since then, United States growth has further accelerated.

But the main feature of this Table is the magnitude of the growth rates. All these growth trends are numerically low, in the range 1% to 2%. However, economic growth operates over long periods of time. Over these long periods, compound interest works its magic. Britain's growth, averaging 1.4% a year since 1820, doubled GDP per capita every 50 years. For the United States, with growth at 2.0% a year since 1890, GDP per capita doubles over just 35 years. 2.0% growth over 120 years (such as 1890 to 2010) will increase GDP per capita by a factor of 11. It is by continuing growth operating over the long run that economic growth has created huge increases in average incomes and has transformed the world.

1.8 The conventional theory of growth

People have long recognized the importance of economic performance. In the first century and a half of the Industrial Revolution attention was focused on how the economy worked, in particular how markets worked. This was understandable since, in the buzzing economies of western Europe and the United States, markets and the capitalist system seemed to generate ever rising incomes. World War I and its aftermath followed by the Great Depression brought this confidence to a halt; attention turned to the question of economic stability. World War II and the adoption of Keynesian ideas on the management of aggregate spending appeared to solve the stability problem. Attention then turned to trying to understand economic growth and to transplant growth from western Europe and North America to the low income countries of the world.

Today's conventional theory of growth started with the work of Robert Solow (1956). Solow-type models view the economy as a single entity and explain GDP in terms of the inputs of labor, capital and the remainder, labor effectiveness (often referred to simply as productivity). In these models, GDP growth results from increasing inputs of labor and capital and from increases in productivity.

Solow-type models have been expressed in compact mathematical form, allowing elegant examination of the properties of the predicted growth path. The economy is predicted to converge to a steady growth path on which GDP per capita increases at the steady rate "g", the rate of growth of labor effectiveness. Investing a greater share of GDP raises the level of the growth path but not the growth rate; the steady state growth rate is determined entirely by increases in productivity.

Although this conventional theory describes the outcome of GDP growth it does not really explain the growth process. As the steady state growth rate, "g", is external to the model, Solow models in effect describe growth after it happens. These models do not reveal the mechanisms of growth, the nature of the changes which create growth and result from growth. And, by focussing on supply or production potential these models do not look at consumers or spending, the demand side of growth. This conventional theory of growth represents a huge achievement in describing economic growth but it is not the whole story. This theory calls out for extension to cover the processes rather than just the results of growth.

1.9 Our objective

Our aim in understanding growth is to pick up where the conventional theory leaves off, to extend the theory of economic growth to encompass more of the processes and mechanisms of growth. In particular, we will look at:

- The role of spending and demand;
- The structure of the economy;
- The nature of change and innovation;
- The human features that drive the growth process.

We approach economic growth from a practical point of view. To do this we look at the history of growth to work out the causes and mechanisms of continuing growth. We then systematize these mechanisms so as to extend the conventional theory.

We start by going back 2,000 years. There were successful civilizations in Rome, China and later in western Europe. These leading countries expanded by exploiting their natural resources and their particular technologies. However, they could not break through these limits; they could not break away from their agricultural and trading foundations; they did not achieve economic growth. These countries went as far as they could go with their particular products and technologies but did not develop new products and new industries to move into sustained growth.

England achieved the breakthrough to growth. England's growth followed from agricultural advances which increased incomes sufficiently that people started to demand more manufactured goods. Supply of these manufactures, based on hand crafting, was severely limited. Some people, today we would call them entrepreneurs, responded to these economic opportunities by seeking and eventually finding ways of producing these goods in volume and at low cost. They did this by using machines. Physical capital embodied the changes. In time, additions to human capital - resulting from experience, training and education - accelerated the growth in production capability. Demand increased as people spent their rising incomes. New products were to the fore in attracting spending from the rising level of incomes. The result was introduction and adoption of a sequence of new products. These new products started off small but, tapping the huge potential markets created by rising discretionary income, grew rapidly. This process created the growth industries that pulled the economy forwards. Economic growth took place at the product and industry level; growth was driven by demand and enabled by supply expansion.

The United States adopted the British breakthroughs. Then, the United States grew in exactly the same way as Britain - by developing a sequence of successful new products, creating new markets and new industries. As one growth industry matured, essentially as its market became saturated, another growth industry emerged. Simultaneously, increases in production capability, from investment and from more productive management and processes, sustained the growth in spending and generated rising incomes. At a high level, this process saw the economy move from agriculture to manufacturing to services. At the industry level this process went, for example, from cotton, tobacco and wheat through railroads and automobiles, household appliances and electrical goods, to entertainment, computers, health care and the internet. The structure of the economy kept changing as productivity gains and market saturation slowed employment in old industries and resources followed spending into new industries. Employment and location followed this evolution, industry by industry.

This record shows how economic growth operates. Clearly, growth processes operate at the market level, not the economy-wide level. This requires us to look at growth industry by industry. It also requires us to look at spending (or demand) industry by industry, as economic growth is characterized by continuing introduction of new products, emergence of growth industries and slowing of mature industries. At the same time production capability increases through investment and productivity gains, allowing supply to expand to sustain the growing demand and to generate increasing net incomes. The structure of the economy keeps changing as spending patterns change, as industries move through their life cycle and as production effectiveness increases. Two kinds of innovation are always associated with these changes - product innovation (on the demand side) and process innovation (on the supply side). Economic growth proceeds through the interaction of demand changes (the driving force) and supply changes (the sustaining force). The key players on the demand side are creative, bold, driven individuals seeking to increase their incomes by creating new products and, on the supply side, individuals and businesses seeking to increase their incomes by improving production effectiveness.

This leads to important extensions to the conventional theory of economic growth. These extensions are first, to introduce demand (whereas the present theory focuses on supply) and second, to bring the analysis down to the industry level (whereas the present theory looks just at the economy as a whole). This theoretical extension is not mathematical but rather a systematic, logical summary of the causes and mechanisms of growth, based on careful interpretation of how growth actually works.

The extended theory focuses on markets and industries and shows how new products pull the economy along a continuing growth path. Demand features – product design, marketing, credit and the consumer society - are central to this process. Demand drives growth while supply expansion (from investment and productivity gains) permits growth. As in the rest of economics, demand and supply both are vital and both must be considered. And, by operating at the industry level, the extended theory allows the changing structure of the economy to be explained.

Then, looking at actual growth recorded by different countries in the past century, we distinguish three types of growth. "Frontier growth", typified by the United States, keeps pushing out the economic boundaries with new products, new production and new processes.

Next, "coat-tail growth" is where countries with fortunate resource endowments, such as oil or in food production, grow by supplying these products into the markets of the leading economies. And "catch-up growth" is where a country applies existing technologies and exploits its low costs to export to the high income countries, thereby growing rapidly until either it saturates the markets for these particular goods or it loses its cost advantage to another catch-up country. The extended theory of growth applies to frontier economies; rapid growth in other countries is due simply to the coat-tail process or the catch-up process.

We spend most of our time on GDP growth, and its industry and spending composition, rather than growth of GDP per capita. This is because the processes involved operate at the industry level. Then, once we understand GDP growth it is straightforward to convert this to growth in average incomes, or GDP per capita.

Chapter 2

The world before economic growth

2.1 The Roman Empire

2.1.1 Course of the Empire

Rome was the dominant force in the western world for more than 500 years. Rome was founded, supposedly in 753BCE, as a settlement on the banks of the Tiber River in central Italy. It expanded geographically, in population and economically to a zenith around 14CE, the end of the reign of the first emperor, Augustus. The Roman Empire remained strong and wealthy until 164CE when a smallpox pandemic killed a sixth of the population; the Empire then entered into a slow decline. The Empire in 330CE was split into two administrative regions – the west, based in Rome, and the east, based in Constantinople (modern Istanbul). Both empires disintegrated over the course of the following two centuries.

Rome expanded from the original settlement by military force. At its peak, the Roman Empire encompassed some 45 million people in the lands surrounding the Mediterranean. Rome conquered the Italian peninsular relatively early. To the west, Rome conquered the Iberian Peninsula and then expanded north. This expansion stopped at Hadrian's Wall, the northern border of Britannia (approximately England and Wales), and at the Rhine. The lands of northern England and of Germany were of marginal economic value to Rome and the cost of defending the frontiers was significant. These frontiers in effect represented an equilibrium – the line along which the net benefit from territorial expansion became zero. The zero net benefit boundary went along the Rhine, through the Balkans and the Danubian provinces, along the eastern boundary of what is now Turkey and across the deserts of north Africa.

Why did Rome embark on empire? After all, expansion by conquest is costly – armed force must be used, infrastructure must be constructed, colonial governments must be maintained and the imperial territories must be policed and defended. The answer is that Rome gained economically from empire. In fact, exploitation of conquered lands and peoples was the basis of the Roman economy.

2.1.2 Innovations

The expansion of Rome and its Empire was based on three key innovations – in military organization, governmental organization and civil engineering.

It appears that the Roman military had comparable equipment (in arms and protection) and comparable resources (in men, horses and ships) to contemporary states such as Carthage (based in what today is Tunis in north Africa) and the Gauls (in France). However, the Roman management system was superior. This system covered the organization of the infantry into effective fighting units, the introduction of an effective command structure, the organization of cavalry into effective forces, the coordination of infantry and cavalry, and the maintenance of a professional standing army which was well trained and highly disciplined. In addition, logistics were well organized with movement of troops along an extensive network of all-weather roads, movement of supply trains along these same roads, and a network of well-resourced and secure camps. The Roman military was almost invincible. The ultimate overrunning of the Empire by hordes from the north did not reflect Roman military defeat so much as the fact that the Empire gave up trying seriously to defend itself.

Government in republican Rome was structured so as to limit the power of the leaders. Two elected Consuls headed the government; each Consul was limited to serving a one year term and each had veto power. A Senate of 300 leading citizens, each appointed for life, had advisory power. An Assembly approved or rejected legislation. Officials in the administration of the government were elected. The provinces were led by governors in a decentralised administrative system. This system brought the rule of law, property rights, a judicial system, widespread literacy and a reasonable degree of personal security.

However, the political ambitions of Julius Caesar in the first century BCE ushered in a period of civil war which ended with the establishment of imperial government. The rule of the first emperor, Augustus, which ended in 14CE, saw Rome reach the height of its power and income. Rome added new provinces after this time but income per capita levelled off, never again to increase. Whether coincidentally or not, incomes ceased to increase after the establishment of imperial government.

In technology, the Romans excelled in civil engineering. The key innovations were knowledge of structural design, the arch and waterproof cement. These were used for structures – buildings, roads, bridges, ports, aqueducts and freshwater systems, stormwater systems and sewerage systems. This allowed Rome to construct and operate cities and also provided the transportation and communications infrastructure for the Empire.

2.1.3 Production

The provinces supplied Rome with wheat and other foodstuffs (such as wine and olive oil), metals and minerals, cloth, utensils and precious metals. The provinces paid Rome annual tributes (taxes) of grain. Egypt was the most valuable province with agricultural output per hectare some 2.5 times as large as in Italy because of watering and soil renewal by the Nile. Its annual tribute was around 135,000 tonnes, corresponding to 70% of the grain consumption of the city of Rome.

Large numbers of slaves were taken from conquered territories. For example, the 50,000 survivors from the defeated city of Carthage were sold into slavery in Rome and some 500,000 slaves were captured in Caesar's Gallic Wars. Slaves from Greece were highly valued because their education made them good in teaching and administrative tasks. Slaves provided a large part of labor input. Angus Maddison (2007) estimates that in 14CE, slaves provided 55% of labor input in peninsular Italy and 40% for the Empire as a whole.

Maddison estimates that consumption in 14CE absorbed around 87% of the output of the economy with investment accounting for only 6.5%. He estimates that this investment was almost entirely in structures, infrastructure and shipping. This suggests highly labor-intensive methods of production. This is not surprising in view of the relatively large supply of low-cost slave labor. Furthermore, what we know about Roman production techniques suggests that there was little equipment used in the productive processes.

The highest incomes were in peninsular Italy. Maddison estimates that average disposable income per capita in 14CE was $857 (in 1990 dollars) while the average income in the rest of the Empire was $516. This Italian income level was surpassed by the western European countries only after the Renaissance some 1,500 years later. Similarly, the urbanization ratio in Italy was reached again only after the Renaissance.

The high incomes in Italy and particularly the city of Rome were substantially the result of the transfer systems implemented by the government. Surplus production in the provinces was expropriated and moved to Rome. Basic living standards in Rome were in effect guaranteed by the public provision of housing and grain. Roman politicians as early as 140BCE began distributing free bread. The practice was continued by the emperors as a means of keeping the masses quiescent. In addition, the government provided entertainment in the form of libraries, theaters and games. The events held in the Roman Coliseum, seating capacity 50,000, and Circus Maximus, capacity 250,000, are examples of public entertainment. The policies of slavery, food handouts, public housing and organized free entertainment suggest that a significant part of the surplus expropriated by Rome was used to support leisure for its citizens.

2.1.4 Economic growth

The Romans early on made substantial advances in organizational and engineering technologies. However, Rome did not keep improving; its technologies were static. Once the original state of Rome had exploited these capabilities the only way forward was to expand into other areas, applying Rome's advantages to new territories, and to expropriate their productive surpluses. Rome's economy expanded in breadth but not depth. Rome's income peaked when Rome had exploited all the as yet independent areas in the region. The income of the citizens (and only some of the population were citizens) of Rome increased to unprecedented levels but consumption was devoted first to purchases of traditional goods and services and then to leisure and leisure activities.

Rome exhibited the classic behavior of empires – it exploited its strength to expand in breadth. The center grew rich on the back of the surpluses extracted from its conquered peoples. The conquests stopped when the net benefit from further expansion fell to zero – when the costs of defeating and occupying new lands matched the surplus which could be extracted from these lands. When the conquests stopped, the empire moved into a steady state or, more bluntly, it stagnated.

Incomes remained high for around 150 years but then started to decline. With the end of conquest, the supply of new slaves ceased and, with low reproduction rates of the slave population, the labor supply diminished. The Antonine plague which killed around a sixth of the population around 165CE greatly weakened the Empire. Trying to deal with attacks on the northern and eastern borders absorbed further resources. Both the western empire and the newly formed eastern empire entered into gradual, and ultimately terminal, decline.

Rome grew from tiny beginnings in the eighth century BCE to a major power in the first and second centuries CE before declining into oblivion 400 years later. The time scale of these developments is large – more than 1,000 years in total. The Roman civilization achieved unprecedented (in the western world) size in terms of population and extent. And its economic development was similarly impressive – the Roman Empire grew to sustain per capita incomes which were not seen again in Europe until after the Renaissance more than 1,000 years later. However, Rome did not achieve economic growth. Rome exploited its superior technologies but did not develop new technologies or new products. Rome increased its per capita income by exploiting its conquered territories, not by increasing its productive potential. Rome expanded but did not grow.

2.2 The Renaissance

2.2.1 The Italian states

The Italian states, in particular Venice, Florence and Rome, were the most prosperous in Europe for much of the 14th, 15th and 16th centuries. This was also a time of a blossoming in creative work in literature, architecture, painting and sculpture; a time called the Renaissance. Renaissance means rebirth and in a sense it was a rebirth of European creativity 1,000 years after the previous peaks reached during the Roman Empire. However, the Renaissance was not so much the rediscovery of Roman and Greek knowledge as it was the development of creative activities in new directions. There is no question that the Renaissance epoch saw real creative advances but there is a question as to whether this epoch saw comparable economic advances.

2.2.2 Venice

Venice, a port situated at the northern end of the Adriatic, had traditionally been a trading city. In particular, Venice had looked to the east, developing trading links with the Byzantine Empire and the Muslim world. And its trade with Asia was well established, both by ship and along the famous “silk road”. Marco Polo, one of a long line of Venetian traders, became famous not for trading with Asia but for writing of his travels and so introducing Europeans to the concept of the civilizations of China and Asia. The republic of Venice reached its zenith in the late 13th century when, with some 3,000 ships, it dominated Mediterranean commerce. In the 15th century, though, Venice lost its possessions in the eastern Mediterranean to the Ottomans and was weakened by the rise of Portugal as a trading nation. With more efficient ships, Portugal and later Spain out-competed Venice and came to dominate Europe's trade with Asia.

Venice developed a merchant culture and, with the best transportation technology of the day, grew wealthy on the basis of trade. Ultimately, though, its single form of advantage was competed away and Venice was unable to replace it. Venice did not achieve economic growth.

2.2.3 The Black Death

The Black Death (bubonic plague) arrived in Italy from Asia in 1347. Over the next five years the plague killed more than one third of Europe's population; the death rate in Italy is thought to have been more than 50%. Less catastrophic episodes of the plague occurred several more times in the 14th Century and then intermittently until the end of the 17th Century.

The Black Death had profound economic effects. The loss of half the population made labor scarce relative to land and capital. The power of landowners plummeted. This sent into terminal decline the feudal system/serfdom wherein laborers were tied to the land and in effect were the property of the lords/landowners. Wages increased, labor mobility began, markets for labor began to emerge. (Interestingly, the plague had a smaller impact in eastern Europe so the labor/land ratio in Russia remained high and serfdom continued.) The power of the Catholic Church increased as the Church portrayed the Black Death as God's vengeance on sinners and people gave treasure to the Church in an effort to be spared the plague.

A simple production function indicates the effects of losing half the population. Say output is $A \times K^{0.3} \times L^{0.7}$ where A is Total Factor Productivity, K is the input of capital and land and L is the input of labor. Halving labor input leads to GDP declining by 38%, wages (the marginal product of labor) increasing by 23% and per capita income also increasing by 23%.

The Black Death changed the nature of the economies of Europe. The power of landowners was reduced and the power of the individual increased. Higher incomes led to more spending on new types of goods. The new flexibility for workers allowed these new goods to be produced. The market system and capitalism were strengthened. The Black Death did not create economic growth but it did help diminish some of the obstacles to growth.

2.2.4 The Renaissance

The Renaissance began in Venice and then blossomed in Florence and Rome. The burgeoning of creative works was due to the sponsorship of wealthy patrons – the Doges (leaders) of Venice, the Medici and other wealthy families of Florence, and the Catholic Church. These wealthy individuals and families spent huge sums on high living and on conspicuous consumption of fine arts. Wealthy families such as the Medici, Borgia and Borghese exploited the Church as a route to power and, to this end, sponsored vast works of religious construction and decoration.

The highlights of the early Renaissance in Venice are the buildings around *Piazza San Marco* including the *Basilica*, with its distinct Byzantine influence, the *Ducal Palace*, the *Campanile* and the *Piazza* itself. The focus then moved to Florence. The main church, generally called *Il Duomo di Firenze*, was begun in 1296 and completed structurally in 1436. The dome was designed by Filippo Brunelleschi, sponsored by Cosimo de Medici. The bronze doors of the *Baptistery* were designed by Lorenzo Ghiberti. Lorenzo de Medici was a major patron, encouraging and sponsoring art from people including Leonardo da Vinci, Sandro Botticelli, and Michelangelo Buonarroti. Michelangelo carried out many works in Florence and, later, in Rome. Among his Florentine work was the sculpture *David*, completed in 1504.

Rome, meanwhile, was the seat of the Catholic Church, and the beneficiary of many works sponsored by leading families or commissioned directly. The *Sistine Chapel* was opened in 1483 but decoration continued with Michelangelo completing the ceiling in 1512 and the altar wall, featuring *The Last Judgment*, in 1541. The outstanding architectural work of the Renaissance was *Saint Peter's Basilica*. Construction began in 1506. Several people contributed to the design including the facade by Carlo Maderno, the dome by Michelangelo and the *Piazza* by Gian Lorenzo Bernini.

Two leading examples of the written word are the works of Dante and Machiavelli. Durante degli Alighieri (known today as Dante) wrote the epic poem *Divine Comedy* (written in the 14th century, first published in

1555) which describes Dante's journey through Hell (Inferno), Purgatory and Paradise. As well as being a major work of literature, the *Divine Comedy* helped stabilize Italian and establish it as an important literary language. Niccolò di Bernardo dei Machiavelli's *The Prince* is a treatise on the nature and practice of political power and government, written in the early 16th century. *The Prince* is famous not only for its analysis of the art of exercising political power but also for establishing the study of government as a legitimate intellectual discipline.

The Renaissance saw the beginning of exploration of the physical world, such as Leonardo da Vinci's investigations into human anatomy and mechanical devices and, a century later, Galileo Galilei's explorations in astronomy and physics. The main achievement of these natural philosophers was not so much their discoveries but their push to base thinking on observation and analysis rather than on religious doctrine.

2.2.5 Economic performance

Italy's relative economic performance is summarized in Table 2.1. (The Italian peninsular had been governed by separate states. The nation of Italy was created only in 1861 under the leadership of Giuseppe Garibaldi. By considering all of the Italian peninsular as one, this Table understates the achievements of the leading Italian states of Venice, Florence and Rome.)

Table 2.1 Incomes in Renaissance Europe

GDP per capita, 1990 dollars.

	1	1000	1500	1600
GDP per capita				
Italy	809	450	1,100	1,100
Netherlands	425	425	761	1,381
Spain	498	450	661	853
Western Europe (1)	599	425	798	907
Growth rates				
Italy		-0.1%	0.2%	0.0%
Netherlands		0.0%	0.1%	0.6%
Spain		0.0%	0.1%	0.3%
Western Europe (1)		0.0%	0.1%	0.1%

Note (1) 12 western European countries, excluding Spain.

Source: Data from Maddison (2006b).

In the year 1000, Italy and Spain were the highest income countries in Europe but by 1500 Italy had pulled ahead and was clearly in the top position. The leading Italian states had, for more than 200 years, the highest incomes in Europe.

These states grew wealthy from trade and through finance. But their surplus was spent on conventional consumption – of food and clothing – and conspicuous consumption of the arts and spending for the Catholic Church. In only one area did design and production advance – in architecture, literature and the fine arts. These artistic achievements doubtless improved the human spirit but they did little to grow the economy. There was no fundamental change leading to ongoing growth. Income growth, averaging 0.2% a year, was only slightly more rapid than Europe's overall growth rate of 0.1%. After 1500, Italy's average incomes did not grow at all. The Italian states enjoyed their surpluses while they lasted but did not make the transition to economic growth. The Italian states finally lost their trading advantage to Portugal, Spain and the Netherlands and it was these countries which took over economic leadership in Europe.

The Italian states experienced some of the changes that contributed to economic growth in Europe in later centuries. The Black Death broke the power of landowners, leading to the demise of the feudal system/serfdom, beginning the functioning of labor markets and allowing some flexibility in spending and production. The rise of trade and the growing interest in learning started to move the focus of life from the Church to the individual. However, the Catholic Church was a formidable obstacle to change. In Italy and later in Spain, the Church fought to maintain its power and, in so doing, to deny the role of reason and the primacy of the individual. Economic growth could not take root in these conditions.

2.3 The Spanish Empire

2.3.1 Course of the Empire

The Iberian Peninsula was part of the Roman Empire before being conquered by Moors in the 8th century. The Moors established independent Muslim states; these continued for around 700 years until Christian kingdoms emerged, gradually gaining supremacy. In 1492, these kingdoms defeated the last of the Moorish states and combined to form the kingdom of Spain. 1492 was also the year of the first voyage of Christopher Columbus to the New World, leading to the development of the Spanish Empire over the course of the 16th century. The Spanish Empire at its peak around 1700 covered much of the Americas, what today is the Philippines, part of Italy, the Low Countries of northwest Europe, and parts of modern-day France and Germany. Spain gradually lost its Empire in Europe to attack by other countries; Spain itself was occupied by Napoleonic France; the Empire in the Americas collapsed early in the 19th century. Spain was a world power for almost 300 years before returning to its roots on the Iberian Peninsula.

2.3.2 Economic performance

Spain's relative economic performance is summarized in Table 2.2.

Table 2.2 Growth in population and income

	1000-1500	1500-1600	1600-1700	1700-1820
Population				
Spain	0,1%	0,2%	0,1%	0,3%
Europe (1)	0,2%	0,3%	0,1%	0,4%
Spanish America (2), (3)	0,1%	-0,7%	0,3%	0,3%
GDP per capita				
Spain	0,1%	0,3%	0,0%	0,1%
Europe (1)	0,1%	0,1%	0,1%	0,2%
Spanish America (2)	0,0%	0,0%	0,2%	0,3%

Note (1) 12 western European countries, excluding Spain.
Note (2) 16 Spanish American countries excluding Caribbean, including Mexico.
Note (3) Population growth 1000-1500 is for Mexico.
Source: Data from Maddison (2006b).

Spanish income grew slightly more rapidly than the rest of Europe in the 16th century but lagged subsequently. Its population growth was slower than Europe's. Spain did not move onto an economic growth path. Whatever happened gave Spain a century of slightly more rapid economic expansion before the country faded into economic stagnation.

The consequences for the Spanish imperial territories were more striking. These territories saw growth in per capita incomes although this might have reflected their population declines after Spanish conquest. Due partly to military defeat but mainly to the effects of introduced diseases, the population of the Americas plummeted after the arrival of the Spaniards.

2.3.3 Reasons for this performance

How did Spain achieve a century of economic expansion and why was it unable to convert this expansion into real growth?

The policy of Spain was directed to expanding the country's power, not to increasing its prosperity. The pursuit and use of power had three strands – colonization abroad, expansion in Europe by force of arms, and promotion of the Catholic Church. These aims reflected the interests of the monarchy and the overarching power of the monarchy. The monarchy was not interested in economic objectives and there was no business class in Spain to pursue economic expansion. Instead, the monarchy was closely aligned with the Catholic Church and vigorously promoted the interests of the Church.

The colonization of the Americas was easy – Spanish military organization and technology were so superior to those of the indigenous peoples that Spain rapidly gained control of vast territories. Susceptibility to imported diseases then decimated the local populations. Governance of the new territories was driven by two objectives – spread of the Catholic Church and exploitation of local resources, especially precious metals.

The most sought after import from the New World was of silver and gold. Part of the import of treasure went to expand the money supply in Spain. Spending increased accordingly. We estimate that total spending rose over the course of the 16th century by 1.7% a year. This spending drew forth some increase in production, by greater use of existing capacity, but its main effect was to drive up prices. There was a long inflation, covering the whole century. (The link between treasure and inflation is strong - the correlation coefficient between the price level and cumulative imports of treasure is 0.87.) Only a small part of this increased spending, 0.3% a year, resulted in higher per capita incomes, as shown in Table 2.3.

Table 2.3 Growth in Spain in the 16th Century

Average annual rates of growth

Spending	1.7%
Prices	1.3%
Constant price GDP	0.4%
Population	0.2%
Real GDP per capita	0.3%

Sources: Data from Hamilton (1934) and Maddison (2006b).

Much of the increase in spending was by the government, the monarchy. This spending was directed mainly to military adventures and to expanding the facilities and personnel of the Catholic Church. The Spanish monarchy embarked on a long sequence of military adventures – it waged an 80 year war to try to subdue the Netherlands, it endeavored to defeat England (for example with the famous but ill-fated armada of 1588), it tried to defend its territorial possessions in Italy, Belgium and Germany, it conquered but then lost Portugal, and it warred with the Muslim Ottoman empire. These military efforts were costly to Spain and in the end futile.

Meanwhile, at home, the monarchy and the Catholic Church launched the Inquisition, an organized effort to stamp out religions other than Catholicism and even to purge those Catholics thought to exhibit insufficient zeal. The Tribunal of the Holy Office of the Inquisition was established in 1480 and was active for at least 150 years (although it was not formally disbanded until 1834) in seeking to impose Catholic orthodoxy. The Inquisition involved persecution of minorities, censorship of the written word and even censorship of the spoken word. Banishment and capital punishment were among the remedies available to the Inquisition. There is no doubt that the Inquisition discouraged free thinking and inhibited change in Spain.

Spain's experience shows that neither empire nor treasure is sufficient to move a country into sustainable economic growth. Spain did enjoy an increase in real incomes but this was limited to exploiting the surplus of conquered territories and to the fuller use of existing productive capacity. Spain made no effort to improve its economy. Instead, Spanish policies were dominated by religion and attempts at territorial expansion. These policies were antithetical to change. Economic growth never even started in Spain.

2.4 The Netherlands

2.4.1 Growth of trade

Venice had pioneered European trade with Asia. Then, the journey of the Portuguese explorer Vasco da Gama in 1497 began contact between western Europe and Asia. Spain was already colonizing the lands with relatively small and technologically primitive populations in the Americas. In contrast, Asia was densely populated with technologically sophisticated peoples. The most appealing way for Europe to interact with Asia was on a trading basis, not on an occupation and exploitative basis.

Portugal, with superior marine technology, superseded Venice as the leader in trading between Europe and Asia. The Netherlands initially focused inside Europe, exploiting its location to develop its local trade. There, the Netherlands was developing the basis for a trading economy with skill in shipbuilding and navigation, and with a commercial system including property rights, enforceable contracts, business organizations and credit arrangements. The Netherlands steadily expanded its trading activities until the Dutch Far East Company (VOC), founded in 1602, was granted a monopoly on Netherlands-Asian trade. The VOC rapidly grew its trade with Asia. Over the next two centuries, the VOC sent almost one million Europeans to work in its Asian operations. The VOC and its English counterpart, the East India Company, by a combination of better business practices and brute force, forced the Portuguese out of the Asian trade. Portugal refocused its attentions onto its colony in Brazil. The English then focused on India, leaving the VOC as the leading trader with what was known as the Far East.

European-Asian shipping movements are shown in Table 2.4. This shows the rise of the Netherlands, particularly in the 17th century.

Table 2.4 Ships sailing to Asia from European countries

	16thC	17thC	18thC
Portugal	705	371	196
Netherlands	65	1,770	2,950
England		811	1,865
France		155	1,300
Other		54	350
Total	770	3,161	6,661
Netherlands' share	8%	56%	44%

Source: Data from Maddison (2007).

The VOC was profitable until the mid-18th century. Thereafter the company declined and was dissolved in 1800, shortly after the Netherlands was overrun by Napoleonic France. The demise of the VOC appears to have had several causes – increasing competition in the Asian trade from England, a high fixed cost structure, corruption on the part of VOC personnel and loss of drive in a monopoly organization more than 200 years old.

2.4.2 Economic performance

The growth record for the Netherlands and the other leading countries of western Europe is shown in Table 2.5.

Table 2.5 Growth rates for the Netherlands and Europe

Growth rates of GDP per capita

	1000 - 1500	1500 - 1600	1600 - 1700	1700 - 1820
Netherlands	0.1%	0.6%	0.4%	-0.1%
United Kingdom	0.1%	0.3%	0.3%	0.3%
Portugal	0.1%	0.2%	0.1%	0.1%
Spain	0.1%	0.3%	0.0%	0.1%
Italy	0.2%	0.0%	0.0%	0.0%
Europe (1)	0.1%	0.1%	0.1%	0.2%

Note (1) 12 northern and western European countries.
Source: Data from Maddison (2006b).

These countries were almost static until 1500 with per capita GDP growing at just 0.1% a year. Growth began to accelerate over the periods of the Renaissance and the Reformation. The Netherlands then grew more rapidly for more than 200 years. This growth was based on the development of trade, first within western Europe and then between Europe and Asia. By 1700 the Netherlands was the highest income country in Europe with GDP per capita of $2,130 (in 1990 dollars), more than twice the European average. Dutch growth slowed after 1700 and ceased around 1750 but its lead was so large that it was only late in the century that an industrializing England surpassed the Netherlands. Dutch population grew comparatively rapidly in the 16th and 17th centuries but growth then slowed so that the overall population growth over the three centuries was the same as the European average.

The Netherlands broke new ground in Europe. For the first time, with the possible exception of Venice, commercial activity played the central role in the life and aspirations of a nation. The result of this successful commercial activity was economic leadership with, for some 250 years, the highest incomes around.

The flourishing of Flemish art, especially in the first half of the 17th century, reflects Dutch economic success. The paintings of Rembrandt and others of the Flemish school are remarkable in a number of ways - these paintings reflect the substantial economic surplus that was being generated and used for conspicuous consumption while the subject matter of the paintings reflects the life of the Dutch people and celebrates their commercial activities and their material success. Particularly noteworthy is that commercial activity took the leading place in everyday life and was the subject of celebration, replacing the religious focus of the southern European countries.

Dutch economic success was based on one activity, well designed and well implemented, but only one activity at that. This was mercantile capitalism, facilitated by advances in shipbuilding and navigation and underpinned by new forms of business organization and finance. This activity propelled the Netherlands for more than 200 years but finally the growth stopped. Growth stopped for several reasons – the market became saturated, the VOC trading company fell victim to monopoly success (becoming fat, dumb and lazy) and competitors (mainly the English) increasingly encroached on its market. The Netherlands then stood still economically while leadership passed to other countries.

The economic leadership of the Netherlands was based on a brilliant set of innovations. However, there was nothing to succeed these innovations. There was nothing sustaining about the Dutch economic success. The Dutch had not discovered economic growth. The Netherlands was the first country to develop a commercial, capitalist culture and supporting institutions. But it was its neighbor across the English Channel which used the same conditions – stable government, personal security, rule of law, capitalist culture – to break into sustained economic growth. The crucial differences were first, that British growth was based on producing goods rather than trading goods and second, that Britain was able to develop a sequence of brilliant new commercially successful products.

2.5 Imperial China

2.5.1 Expansion

China encompasses large areas of fertile, well-watered land. China long ago developed effective technology to farm this land; the resulting production was able to sustain a large population. By the year 1000, China's population was 59 million, larger than all of western Europe (26 million) although smaller than India (75 million). China's agricultural technology in 1000 included iron implements, the horse collar harness, the cattle-drawn plow, the seed drill and crop rotation. Three centuries of stability under the Song dynasty (960 – 1279) saw agriculture continue to expand with irrigation and improved seeds. Later, in the Ming dynasty (1368 - 1644) and in parts of the Qing dynasty (1644 – 1912) geographic expansion, terracing and reclamation saw increases in the area of cultivated land which, together with improved seeds and a move to double cropping (two crops a year), allowed food production to keep increasing.

This millennium was characterized by periods of stability punctuated by decades of armed conflict and instability. There were invasions from the north and west, there were succession struggles and there were insurrections inside China. As a result, economic activity grew in an irregular way although around an upward trend. Climatic changes complicated the picture, in particular with a drastic contraction brought on by the "Little Ice Age" around the 17th century.

Chinese manufacturing advanced during the Song and Ming dynasties, particularly in the production and use of coal, iron, pottery and textiles. China invested in massive projects for irrigation and transportation. For example, the Grand Canal, more than 1,700 km long, linked Beijing to the food growing regions to the south. Chinese scientific knowledge also advanced. The famous voyages of Admiral Zheng He (from 1405 to 1433) demonstrated Chinese accomplishments to much of the World. Gavin Menzies (2008) argues that Zheng He presented the Venetians with an encyclopaedia of Chinese knowledge and technology, then far ahead of Europe's, and that this could well have been instrumental in beginning the Renaissance. In any event,

Chinese knowledge of mathematics, navigation and engineering was probably the most advanced in the world at that time.

However, Chinese government policies were less productive. Some governments opened China to international trade, others closed the borders. Some governments taxed and regulated, others were more laissez faire. The vaunted Chinese civil service was good at administration but resisted, if not prevented, change. The Confucian philosophy was useful in creating an orderly society but it too was resistant to change. Government policies, the conservatism of Confucianism and the periodic invasions and power struggles combined to produce an atmosphere that allowed incremental change, punctuated by periods of stability or even decline, in economic activity.

Nonetheless, more and better resources going into agriculture allowed food production to increase over the centuries. GDP increased, although along an irregular path, at an average rate of 0.2% a year from 1000 to 1913.

2.5.2 How was the expansion used?

China's production increased almost nine-fold over the millennium. How was this increase used? In particular, how was the rising income divided between higher per capita incomes and more people?

Population followed food production. Population rose during times of plenty and fell during times of scarcity. The result was that per capita incomes remained remarkably constant over the centuries. Table 2.6 tells the story.

Table 2.6 Income and population in China

	GDP per capita	Population	
	1990 dollars	Millions	Growth p.a.
1	450	60	
1000	466	59	0.0%
1400		73	0.1%
1500	600	103	0.4%
1600	600	160	0.4%
1700	600	138	-0.1%
1770		270	1.0%
1820	600	381	0.7%
1850	600	412	0.3%
1900	545	400	-0.1%
1913	552	437	0.7%
1950	448	547	0.6%

Sources: Data from Ho Ping-ti (1959), Perkins (1969) and Maddison (2006b).

For more than a thousand years China's per capita income was $600 or less. Total income grew at an average of 0.2% a year and population grew at this same rate; per capita income changed very little. Population increased to absorb the additional production. Population grew during the expansion of the Song dynasty, then more rapidly during the Ming dynasty and less rapidly during the Qing dynasty but declined during the unrest accompanying dynastic transitions. When production increased, population increased; when production declined, population declined.

China's expansion was taken up in population growth. Population, not per capita income, did the equilibrating. This was a Malthusian system in action.

China expanded enormously over the millennium after 1000 - its geographic extent increased, its population increased seven-fold. However, per capita incomes scarcely changed; the new production was absorbed in supporting an increasing population. This was not economic growth. The economy expanded, it did not develop. China's ancient history was a story of Malthusian development, not of economic development or economic growth.

2.6 Other countries

Several other countries, empires or civilizations were prominent in their times but did not achieve economic growth.

The Incas ruled vast areas of western South America through an effective governmental structure. However, their agricultural economy was static. Their empire then collapsed in the face of invasion by Spaniards with superior military technology and with novel diseases.

The empires of the Indian subcontinent were the most populous in the world for several centuries, until around 1500. However, Indian development paralleled that of China. The growth in production which did occur was reflected in a rising population rather than higher per capita incomes. Maddison's (2006b) numbers show that GDP increased at an average of 0.1% a year between 1000 and 1500; population also rose at 0.1% leaving just a minute increase in per capita incomes. The economy expanded but did not develop. The arrival of the British, initially to trade in spices and cotton but later to occupy and subjugate the many Indian states, converted India into a colony. Britain ran India for the benefit of Britain, not India. Indian GDP per capita barely changed. From 1820 until India's independence in 1947, per capita GDP increased at just 0.1% a year (comparable to growth in pre-industrial Europe) while average incomes in Britain increased at 1.1% a year.

The Ottoman Empire dominated the eastern Mediterranean and Middle East for more than 400 years until its collapse in the early 20th century in the face of military expansion by several European nations. The Ottoman Empire had many similarities to ancient Rome, even having its administrative capital in the same city, Constantinople (modern Istanbul). Like Rome, the Ottoman Empire grew geographically but not economically.

2.7 Why no growth?

We have looked at the Roman Empire, the Spanish Empire, the Netherlands, and ancient China, and we have touched on the Incas, India and the Ottoman Empire. Each of these civilizations or countries enjoyed considerable economic success in its time yet none moved onto a path of economic growth. Why did they not achieve economic growth?

Lack of growth in fact was the default situation. No country had ever achieved economic growth so unless these countries were doing something different, and the right things at that, they would not move onto a growth path. None of these countries changed so as to initiate growth. These countries kept doing the same old things and they achieved pre-eminence by doing them better than their neighbors. These countries exploited their advantage to expand in scale but there was nothing to replace the initial advantage and expansion ultimately stopped.

Rome exploited its superior management and engineering technologies to conquer its neighbors. Rome then grew wealthy by expropriating labor and the economic surpluses from its colonies. Roman citizens used their higher incomes to consume more of their traditional goods and to consume more leisure. Roman society itself essentially was static. There was no pressure to change and, as the state made the key economic decisions, no opportunity or incentive to change.

Spain extracted huge treasure from its territories in the New World. However, Spain confused treasure with wealth. As Adam Smith worked out in 1776, economic wealth arises from productive capability, not from holding treasure. The Spanish ruling elite and monarchy increased their spending but most was directed to religious and military purposes. From an economic point of view this was consumption; it did not create greater productive capability for the future. The military expansion ended in defeats, the religious thrust ended in the Inquisition and Spain ended up essentially where it had started. Not only was there no incentive for economic growth in the Spanish Empire, there was no opportunity for growth.

The Netherlands developed a highly successful trading industry. The Netherlands brought together all the components, such as shipbuilding, navigation, finance and public companies as well as strong commercial attitudes, to build an international trading empire. The Netherlands grew rich on the back of trading, particularly between Asia and Europe. However, the Netherlands had no repeat innovation industry. When its trading markets were saturated and as its trading institutions rigidified, there was nowhere new to go. The Netherlands could not repeat its first success. Like Rome, the Netherlands exploited its strategic advantage extremely well but there was no second act.

China had a different problem. Its agricultural production increased substantially over time but its people used this expansion to support a larger population, not to sustain higher per capita incomes. The larger population consumed more of the same, there was no market for innovative products. Government policies and the social structure tended to reinforce the status quo so there were no real opportunities or incentives for introducing new products. The result was a static economy, expanding but not developing. There was no scope for the forces generating economic growth even to get started.

The Old World did not contain the forces needed to start economic growth. Economic activity was tradition-bound; change was slow if it was permitted at all. Static economies were the norm; economic growth was not the norm, in fact sustained growth was unknown. The country which got the nearest to starting economic growth was the Netherlands. The Netherlands took the first step with its development of a commercial infrastructure and international trade. However, production not trade is the basis for growth and the Netherlands never got past trade.

These Old World countries were successful in their time but were unable to break through the constraint represented by their existing resources, existing attitudes, existing technologies and existing products. It was England which started on the path of economic growth by doing that one thing which previously had proved impossible – breaking through the status quo by developing a sequence of major new products and new technologies.

Chapter 3

The start of growth - Britain

3.1 A succession of changes

England entered an era of economic change early in the 18th century. These changes started with agriculture. Whereas in other countries expansion stopped when an initial advantage had been fully exploited, England moved through a succession of new products and new industries. This succession of changes created economic growth – the continuing increase in per capita incomes.

In this chapter we look at this sequence of changes in leading industries, from agriculture through textiles, the steam engine, coal, iron, railways and shipping and to steel. Then we bring these changes together to see what they reveal about the nature and processes of economic growth.

3.2 British agriculture

3.2.1 The Agricultural Revolution

The "Agricultural Revolution" is the name given to a period of around 200 years, from the mid-17th century to the mid-19th century, when British agricultural practices changed and output grew substantially. The causes of this agricultural advance are conventionally given as land enclosure, four-field crop rotation, improved equipment and selective breeding. The effects were to increase the food supply; at a time when more than half of the household budget went on food, this increased the purchasing power of incomes. This increase in agricultural production had far-reaching effects – it helped sustain a greater population, it created discretionary income (income that could be spent on other than basic goods), and it released labor from what otherwise would have been required for food production.

The Agricultural Revolution preceded the Industrial Revolution, the application of machines and mechanical power to the production of manufactured goods. We will argue that the Agricultural Revolution not only permitted the Industrial Revolution but also was one of the causes of the Industrial Revolution.

3.2.2 Climate

The northern hemisphere experienced a "Little Ice Age", a period of relatively low mean temperatures, which began in the 16th century and persisted into the 19th. This was the time when, for example, the Swedish army marched across the Baltic Sea to invade Copenhagen (1658). "Frost Fairs" were held on the frozen River Thames in London; the first such Fair was held in 1607, the last in 1814. Palaeoclimatic records show unusually low temperatures from around 1575 to around 1730 although there were episodes of low temperatures in the following century. The Maunder Minimum, a period of low sunspot activity which lasted from 1645 to 1715, was associated with lower than average global temperatures. These physical records suggest that Britain entered a warmer period somewhere between 1715 and 1730. There is a causal connection - warmer weather leads to higher yields of grasses and grains so that more food is available for livestock and for people. It appears, then, that climatic conditions had changed by 1730 to favor increased agricultural output.

3.2.3 Land

Some arable areas in England were traditionally "common" and used by the people of the village for grazing livestock and for the collection of firewood. Some other areas were organized as "open-field" farms, in which non-enclosed and often non-contiguous strips of land were owned by individual families. Many aspects of cultivation of these strips were carried out jointly, for example by sharing the use of scarce draught animals and plows.

In time, this open-field and commons tenure system was replaced by consolidated ownership. This was the "enclosure" movement, the process whereby single owners gained ownership of larger areas of land, enclosed this land by fences or hedges, and farmed the land as a single productive unit. Enclosure gave an owner control over his land and allowed him to gain the full rewards of managing the land. This increased the scale of farming and also, by changing the incentives associated with farming, encouraged sustainable management, investment and experimentation.

Enclosure appears to have started in the 15th century and accelerated in the 18th century. The years after 1760 saw a particularly rapid sequence of enclosures reflecting the use of private acts of Parliament to effect enclosure through legal force. B.R. Mitchell (1988) records that 6.8 million acres, or 21% of the total county land area, was brought into enclosure. Most of the land enclosed, around 75%, had previously been common or waste; the remaining 25% of the area was of open-field arable land.

The area of land available for modern farming was further increased by draining the fens. The fens were low lying, swampy lands in the east of England. The fens were drained and protected from rivers and the sea by earthen banks, converting them into arable land. This land was particularly well suited to wheat farming. This increased the area of productive land by around 4%.

The enclosures and land reclamation increased the area of land under modern agricultural tenure and management systems by as much as 25%. This must have had a considerable effect in allowing an increase in agricultural output.

3.2.4 Mechanization

The early 18th century saw the beginning of the widespread application of capital equipment to farming.

Jethro Tull was a leading figure in advancing the use of agricultural equipment. Tull's strategy was to use light implements which could be drawn by horses. This departed from tradition where oxen were used as draught animals. Horses are more costly, requiring more food, but are stronger and faster. In 1701 Tull developed a practical horse-drawn seed drill which sowed seeds in rows and at the correct depth. Tull did not invent the seed drill but he did develop a light drill which could be drawn by horses. He went on to develop other equipment, such as a horse-drawn hoe for clearing weeds, improvements to the plow, and horse-drawn rakes and harrows. His famous book *Horse-hoeing Husbandry* (1731) was part of his effort to promote his designs.

The basic design of the modern plow appears to have been Chinese. It was brought to the Netherlands in the 17th century by Dutch traders. In turn, Dutch engineers brought to England to drain the fens brought this design with them. Joseph Foljambe of Rotherham, a Yorkshire town noted for making high quality iron, improved on this Chinese-Dutch design and made the critical parts out of iron. While not the first iron plow, the 1730 Rotherham plow was the first to gain commercial success. The plow was progressively improved. James Small introduced the "Scots Plough" in 1763; this featured an improved shape and used a single piece of wrought iron for the cutting blade. Robert Ransome in 1785 introduced the self-sharpening plow. Ransome made a further significant step in the design of the plow - his design was modular and used standardized parts. Kristine Bruland (2004, p 127) describes the effect: "a plough-frame to which components were bolted – new parts could be easily substituted for damaged or worn-out parts, a development that significantly reduced the cost and time involved in plough repair."

Grain has to be threshed to separate the seed from the chaff. Traditionally, this was done manually using flails. Andrew Meikle, a Scottish engineer, is credited with inventing the threshing machine, first used in 1786. This machine was hand-fed and horse-powered. It vastly improved labor productivity in grain farming. This effect was so great that displaced agricultural laborers rioted against this, as well as other labor-saving agricultural changes. These, the "Captain Swing" protests of 1830, have similarities to the Luddite protests against mechanization in textiles. (The fact that the riots occurred more than 40 years after the introduction of the threshing machine indicates the slow spread of the new technology.)

The seed drill, hoe, rake, harrow, plow and thresher are the principal examples of the application of capital equipment to British farming beginning in the 18th century. These innovations had several features in common: they made use of horse power which is considerably more productive than human or cattle power, the critical parts were made of iron, they were suited to large scale farming rather than to the small peasant farms of earlier epochs, and they were capital-using and labor-saving.

3.2.5 Crop rotation

Crop rotation is the practice of growing a sequence of different crops on the same land. There are two main reasons for rotation. The first is to reduce the build-up of pathogens and pests that occurs when one species is cropped continuously. The second is to reduce the depletion of specific soil nutrients by cereals by means of alternating grains with plants, such as legumes and clover, which replenish the soil's nitrogen. Effective crop rotation enables crop yields to be maintained over time without reliance on fertilizers.

Two-field rotation, alternating between growing and fallow, was used in Europe as far back as Roman times. In the Middle Ages, Europe began to shift to the more effective three-field rotation system. This involved rotation of grain, legumes and fallow; legumes provided a food but their main purpose was to replenish soil nitrogen. A four-stage rotation system was pioneered by farmers in (what is now) Belgium. The English Ambassador to the Netherlands, Charles Townshend, learnt of this system. On retiring to his farm in Norfolk in 1730, he introduced the system and worked assiduously to publicize it. Townshend's promotion was so effective that he became known as "Turnip" Townshend (as turnips were part of the new rotation system).

Four-field rotation had wheat, barley, turnips and clover planted in successive years. The turnips helped keep the weeds down and also provided year-round food for ruminant animals such as sheep and cattle. Clover added nitrates to the soil, obviating the need for the fallow stage, and also provided good pasture. The inclusion of clover and turnips in the cycle allowed more animals to be kept which not only provided more products (meat, milk, cheese, wool and hides) but also provided organic fertilizer when the manure was plowed under. But the principal gain to productivity came from reducing the impact of fallow – holding land fallow for one year in three was replaced by growing something useful every year.

3.2.6 Selective breeding

Selective breeding of plants and animals had been used for centuries but it began to be systematized in 18th century England. The most famous proponent of systematic selective breeding of animals was Robert Bakewell. Bakewell began his efforts in 1760 when he inherited his father's farm and by the 1770s had begun producing superior strains of livestock. Bakewell worked over successive generations to select specific animals for mating in order to accentuate target characteristics. He applied selective breeding to horses and cattle but achieved his greatest success with sheep.

Bakewell developed the Lincoln Longwool breed of sheep for wool and the Leicester line for wool and meat. The Leicester was a fast-maturing sheep which did well on turnips (which were becoming plentiful as part of four-field crop rotation). Also, Bakewell was prominent in the development of cattle for meat. Previously, cattle were used primarily as draught animals but the new lines gave a high yield of beef. In 1700, the average weight of a bull sold for slaughter was 370 pounds; by 1786, the average weight had increased to 840 pounds. Horses were bred for draught purposes – large horses with pulling power and endurance. Bakewell and his followers led the development of the Shire breed which became one of the principal draught horse breeds in Britain through the 19th century.

3.2.7 Agricultural output

Agricultural output started increasing during the 17th century. Few numbers are available for the 17th century but Gregory Clark (2009) estimates that real wages started to increase around 1630. The birth rate started a long term increase around 1660 while the death rate started to decline around 1690. Improved tools, such as Tull's seed drill and horse-drawn implements, appeared on the scene early in the 1700s. All these suggest that agricultural expansion must have been well underway by 1715 - 1730 when the climate started to warm.

Agricultural growth accelerated after 1730. Climate, implements, land tenure, soil management and selective breeding all worked to increase inputs and productivity, and so output. The changes took decades, after all these were among the most radical changes ever seen (until that time), but they gradually and steadily increased agricultural output. Overall output grew at an average of 0.5% a year from 1730 until 1800. Figure 3.1 shows quantities of various agricultural products in England.

Figure 3.1 Indicators of agricultural output

Quantities, 1730 = 1

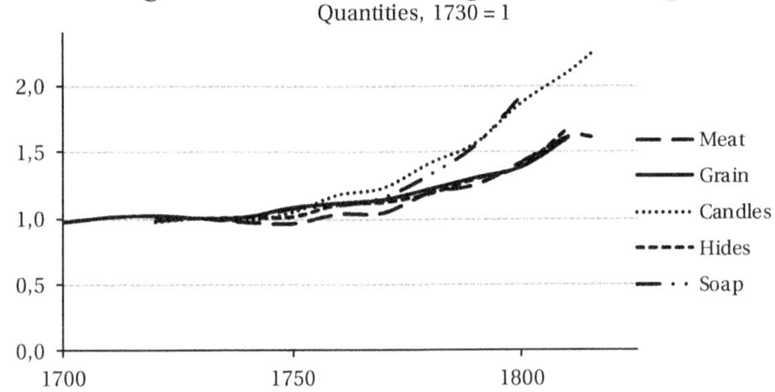

Source: Data from Deane and Cole (1969).

Grain, primarily wheat and oats, was the main food for most people while beer, from barley, was the principal beverage. Meat and cheese were important but secondary foods. Hides are a by-product of meat production. Another by-product, animal fat, was used as a spread, for tallow candles and as an input to soap. The growth in grain production started before 1750 while animal products increased more rapidly after 1750.

Agricultural output grew at an accelerating rate going into the 18th century, shown in Table 3.1. Input of capital increased substantially while more land and more labor also were used. Most of the growth in production though, 70% of the total, came from increasing productivity. Some of the changes in agricultural management and technology were incorporated in capital but it appears that most of the advances were in management and led directly to greater productivity.

Table 3.1 Growth in English and Welsh agriculture

Average growth rates, % per annum

	1700-1750	1750-1800	1800-1850
Land	0.0	0.1	0.1
Labor	0.0	-0.1	0.4
Capital	0.1	0.4	0.8
Factor inputs (1)	0.1	0.1	0.3
TFP (2)	0.2	0.5	0.7
Output	0.3	0.6	1.1

Note (1): Composite of the factors of production - land, labor and capital.

Note (2): Total Factor Productivity, output per unit of factor input.

Source: Data from Allen (2004).

The increase in agricultural output allowed incomes to increase and population to expand. After 1775 though, population increase started to outstrip the growth in food production. Food prices started to rise. Exports of wheat declined as supplies were diverted to the British market while imports began to increase. Agriculture continued to grow but now less rapidly than the economy as leadership passed to the new manufacturing industries.

3.2.8 Advances in technology

British agriculture by 1730 had entered an accelerating growth path. Part of the increasing output was due to more inputs, particularly of capital, but most was due to increasing productivity. Production grew by qualitative change rather than simply by quantitative expansion.

This productivity growth had many causes and we can point to several distinct innovations in management practices, seeds, livestock and equipment which would have contributed significantly. The more interesting questions, though, are not what happened but who made it happen and why.

Those who came up with the innovations were individuals already active in agriculture who looked deliberately and systematically to improve their businesses; the changes were decentralized, not centralized; and the changes were led by practical men, not by scientists or governments. The innovations involved tinkering, trial and error, or recognizing a new approach and transferring it to a different environment. There are two possible reasons motivating these innovations. The first is that they were supply driven - innovation took place for the sake of innovation, because someone had discovered a new process. The second is that they were demand driven - innovation resulted from the drive by farmers to expand their production and to increase their incomes. The evidence is entirely consistent with the demand-driven hypothesis. The nature and the timing of the innovations all is consistent with the idea that innovation was a response to a problem, the problem being to increase output and/or to reduce costs and so to increase incomes. Innovation was the response to business opportunities, not the cause.

Adoption of the new technologies took decades - productivity improvements continued for at least 150 years. The aggregate productivity gain reflects a sequence of innovations, some large and some incremental, stretching over decades. It is difficult to gauge the speed of adoption. However, it is clear that adoption was gradual. The innovations started in the early 18th century while productivity growth picked up in the later 18th and into the 19th centuries. There could well have been a 50 year lag between innovation and mainstream adoption. The mechanical thresher is a case in point – the riots against the labor-saving effects of the thresher occurred 44 years after its invention. Also, it is clear that the adoption process was commercially driven – farmers did not change their ways for the sake of change, they changed because they had seen friends and neighbors benefit from these new procedures.

3.2.9 Agriculture and growth

Agriculture formed the major part of the economy in the 17th century. Increases in agricultural output led to corresponding increases in incomes. Real wages grew between 1630 and 1730 at an average of 0.3% a year and national income per capita grew at this same rate. Population grew at 0.1% a year. The growth in total income of 0.4% a year was split 25:75 between sustaining more people and allowing higher incomes. Most income was spent on food. But, if people were already reasonably fed (reasonably in terms of what they were accustomed to) it is unlikely that all of the increase in their income would have been spent on food; it is more likely that a considerable part would be directed to other purchases, what today we call discretionary income or discretionary spending. By 1730, then, it is likely that discretionary purchasing power was emerging. These trends continued with the accelerating advances in agriculture. The population increased but total incomes grew even faster; average incomes continued to grow. The total amount of discretionary purchasing power continued to increase. This discretionary purchasing power almost certainly lay behind the growing demand for cotton goods and other manufactures that were the leading edge of (what turned out to be) the Industrial Revolution.

The role of agriculture changed as industrialization got under way. For most of the 18th century British farms had fed the nation and their increasing output had allowed population and incomes to rise. From around 1775, though, Britain entered a huge restructuring, moving from agriculture to manufacturing. Agriculture no longer fed the nation – food exports declined while food imports increased. Growth was now driven by the new manufacturing industries. Over the first half of the 19th century agricultural output increased at around 1.1% a year while population grew at 1.3% and GDP at 2.1%. Britain was now following its comparative advantage, exporting manufactures and importing food.

Agriculture played two vital roles in industrialization. First, increasing mechanization and productivity increased agricultural output and so incomes in general, allowing the emergence of the discretionary income and discretionary spending that created the growing markets for manufactured goods. Second, agriculture released labor. Many of the changes in agriculture, especially those involving new implements and equipment, were capital-using but labor-saving. In addition, the greater part of the increase in output came from increases in total factor productivity. Agriculture grew while releasing labor (18th century) or requiring only small increases in labor input (19th century). This left substantial numbers of people available for other work. This provided much of the labor for the new manufacturing industries. Whether it was in the growth of cottage industry, such as in weaving, or in the growth of the mills and factories, productivity change in agriculture provided the labor absorbed in the start of the Industrial Revolution.

3.3 The cotton industry

3.3.1 The starting point

The dominant industry in Britain before the start of economic growth was agriculture. The typical household spent more than half its budget on food. The next largest industry was textiles with clothing absorbing 12% of the household budget. Also, textiles dominated exports and imports – 69% of export value in 1700 was of woolens and 19% of imports, the largest single share, were of linens. Within textiles, production of woolen goods was far and away the principal activity. Production of cotton goods was extremely small although some cotton cloth was imported, mainly hand-made cloth from India. Cotton was so expensive that cotton goods represented only 0.2% of the typical household budget.

Production of woolens was a cottage industry – it took place in the homes of workers. Production was labor-intensive. The wool was prepared by hand, spun into thread on a treadle-powered spinning wheel, and woven into cloth on a hand-operated loom. This equipment was made of wood. The technology had been established for centuries.

For all intents and purposes, there was no cotton industry in Britain. This was not because of lack of interest as cotton goods - for clothing, curtains, sheets and towels - are far more comfortable and serviceable than woolens. Rather, the reason was that the high price of cotton cloth put cottons out of reach for all but the wealthiest.

3.3.2 Cotton production

Then, in the first half of the 18th century, cotton production started to increase. Production grew for more than 150 years and it was only with World War I in 1914 that growth ceased. Figure 3.2 shows this enormous growth in cotton processed in Britain. (The smooth curve is a logistic growth path fitted to the actual path for 1730 through 1913.) From 1 million pounds (lbs) weight of cotton processed in 1730, this new industry grew to processing 2,178 million lbs in 1913. This was a trend growth rate of 4.5% a year. Something happened – production of cottons entered a prolonged expansion the likes of which had never been seen before.

Figure 3.2 Cotton processed

Raw cotton consumption, million pounds weight

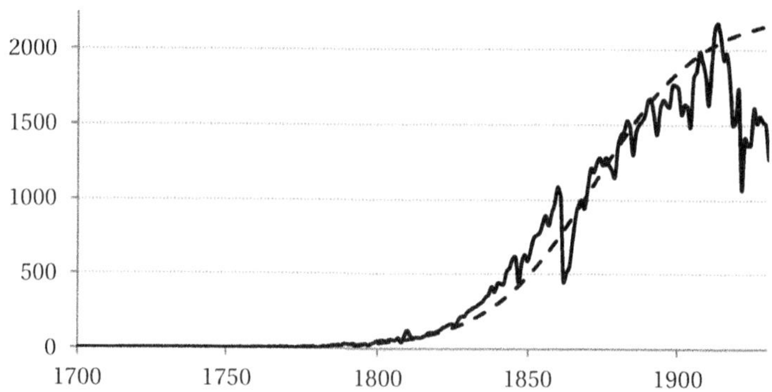

Source: Data from Mitchell (1988).

3.3.3 Market growth

Market conditions were ripe for the growth of the cotton industry. By the first part of the 18th century, increasing incomes in Britain were creating discretionary purchasing power and cotton goods were high on the list to receive this new spending. Cotton goods initially were expensive – hand-made goods were imported under a monopoly arrangement by the East India Company. The clear demand for cheaper cottons drove efforts to cut the cost of processing in Britain. It took decades for these efforts to bear fruit, to make available cotton goods at more affordable prices. Early improvements in processing started to lower prices but when spinning mills began to appear in the 1770s, prices really started to decline and domestic demand took off. British cottons soon became competitive in world markets and exports too took off.

The broad trends are shown in Table 3.2. Population growth and income growth underpinned the growing market in Britain. Declining prices then made cotton goods accessible to more and more people, at home and abroad. Prices declined so much that mass markets emerged for British cotton goods. The result was that demand and production increased rapidly for more than a century.

Table 3.2 Growth rates related to demand for cottons
Average growth rates

Population (1)	1.0%
Average wage, constant prices (1)	0.4%
Relative price of cotton goods (2)	-1.3%
British consumption of cottons, quantity (2)	5.6%
Exports of cottons, quantity (2)	6.2%

Note (1): Growth over the period 1730 - 1860.
Note (2): Growth over the period 1760 - 1860.
Sources: Data from Clark (2005) and Mitchell (1988).

The place of cottons within spending is shown in Table 3.3. Discretionary income is income per capita over and above the level of 1730 (which we take to indicate the start of income growth). Purchases of cottons started to increase as people spent some of this discretionary income on cottons, which at the time were luxury goods or at least aspirational goods. The price of cotton goods then started to decline rapidly in the 1770s. People responded by buying more cotton goods. We estimate that over the first two decades of declining prices, people spent fully 30% of their discretionary labor income on new cottons (that is, purchases over and above their per capita level in 1730). Even into the 19th century, people were still spending more than 10% of discretionary labor income on cotton goods. Cottons by that time had become a mass market.

Table 3.3 Cottons in discretionary income

Spending on cottons as a share of discretionary income

	Labor income	National Income
Before 1770	4%	1%
1770 - 1789	30%	16%
1790 and on	12%	7%

The first cotton mill, applying water-power to drive cleaning and spinning equipment, came into operation in the 1770s. The price of cotton goods began to fall. Spinning was improved steadily and, after around 1830, weaving began to be mechanized; the result was that the price of cotton goods kept declining for more than 100 years. Clark (2005, p7) says "The cost of manufacturing 1 lb of cotton yarn in 1784 was equivalent to one week's wage for an unskilled manual laborer. By 1832 it was equivalent to less than 3 hours wages." This was a reduction of around 95% in relative manufacturing costs. Product prices would not have fallen this rapidly but we calculate that the average price (in £/lb) itself declined by 95% but over a longer period, 1760 to 1900.

Demand for cotton goods in Britain was driven by rising incomes and declining prices. Income per capita started to increase in the 18th century and continued to increase through the 19th century. Prices of cotton goods declined with the mechanization of spinning beginning in the 1770s with a further reduction with the mechanization of weaving beginning in the 1830s. Together, these drove demand upwards. Ultimately, the British market became saturated - British demand for cotton goods was fully satisfied and additional spending was directed to other goods and services. But the growth in the British market had lasted for more than 100 years.

Exports, though, kept growing, driven by declining prices. Figure 3.3 shows this growth. Exports initially were dominated by yarn as yarn production (spinning) was the first to be mechanized and yarn prices were the first to fall. Weaving was mechanized later, after 1830, and when this happened and cloth prices further declined, the demand for finished goods took off. Exports of piece goods displaced exports of yarn and were still growing strongly when World War I brought an end to the established order.

Figure 3.3 British cotton exports

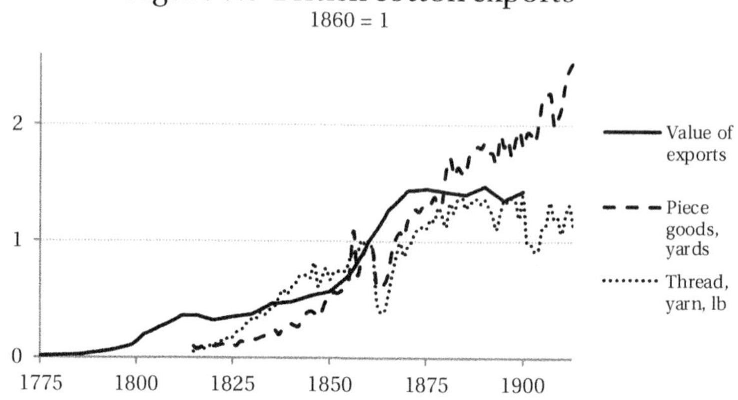

Source: Data from Deane and Cole (1969).

Both incomes and prices were driving forces behind the growth of cottons but which was more important? Income growth in Britain created a latent demand for cotton goods but it took falling prices to convert this into large scale, actual demand. Falling prices were the crucial force in increasing the demand for cotton. This is reflected in the timing of the increase in demand – demand started to take off in the 1770s, when the first spinning mills appeared, and continued to increase over the 19th century as weaving became mechanized and prices declined further. Demand in export markets was purely price driven as the new, factory-produced British cottons displaced hand-made cottons and also opened up new markets for cotton goods.

Similarly, both domestic and export demand grew rapidly but which was important? The demand for cottons in Britain was the crucial first step as this stimulated the development of machinery and factories for cleaning and spinning and later for weaving. The low cost factory-produced cottons then expanded the market in Britain and also allowed British produces to break into and then dominate markets in many other countries. The rest of the world represented larger markets than

Britain and exports soon exceeded domestic sales. Exports increased from 17% of the value of output in 1785 through 61% in 1850 and reached around 80% by the turn of the 20th century. In the fullness of time, exports to world markets were far more important than production for the British market.

Cotton processing was the first modern industry in Britain and indeed the world. Production technology shifted from human-powered, hand operated devices to large scale, mechanically powered, factory-based equipment. These production advances drove costs down. Competition forced prices to follow costs down. Rapidly diminishing prices created the first consumer good mass market in Britain. These low prices also allowed British producers to break into world markets and expand these markets. The British cotton industry really grew by exploiting its low costs to expand by means of international trade.

3.3.4 Technological change

Production of cotton goods in early 18th century Britain was minimal. This production started with women using spinning wheels in their homes (the origin of the word "spinster") to produce yarn with men, also working in cottages, then weaving yarn into cloth using hand looms. 150 years later, cotton goods were made in factories and cotton was the largest industry in Britain. These developments were due to changes in production processes which reduced costs and allowed prices to decline. In this section we look at the long process of change in the production of cotton goods.

Cotton does not grow in Britain; the British industry has always involved the processing of imported raw cotton. Processing involves four steps – cleaning and preparing the raw cotton, spinning the cotton into yarn, weaving the yarn into cloth, and finishing the cloth by bleaching, dyeing or printing.

Most cotton cloth in the early 18th century Britain was imported by the East India Company. This supply monopoly offered high priced cottons to the British market. The British industry, using home spinning and hand weaving, could not compete with Indian cloth produced, as it was, with low wage labor. The only way for British producers to compete effectively was to drive costs out of the production process. Accordingly, the commercial drive was to reduce costs. This pursuit of lower costs drove more than 100 years of innovations in production and management in the cotton industry.

The first equipment improvement was the "flying shuttle" patented by John Kay in 1733. This improved the effectiveness of the hand loom and also allowed cloths to be woven which were broader than arm length. The flying shuttle reduced the cost of weaving and so of finished cotton cloth. Robert Kay, son of John Kay, by 1760 had developed the "drop box" which enabled the hand loom to use multiple flying shuttles, allowing multicolor weaving. These developments improved the effectiveness of hand weaving. They had the effect of transferring the production constraint away from weaving and onto obtaining spun yarn at an affordable price.

Around 1765, James Hargreaves, a weaver and carpenter, devised a simple hand machine, called the "jenny", which enabled a woman (women generally did the spinning, men the weaving) to spin multiple threads at once. The jenny was small (it could be used in a cottage), cheap to construct (it could be purchased by individual spinners) and did not require strength to operate (it could be used by any woman). As such, the jenny was taken up in the existing system of home-based spinners. However, the jenny produced soft yarn which was suitable for the weft but not the warp of cloth. (Weaving combines two sets of threads – the framework is provided by the warp while the weft lies at 90 degrees to the warp and fills it.) Richard Arkwright, a barber and wig-maker, with assistance from a clock-maker named John Kay (not the John Kay who had invented the flying shuttle), solved the warp problem by developing a "frame". This used rollers to draw out the cotton before it passed to the spindle, producing a strong although coarse thread suitable for warps. Arkwright's frame was patented in 1769.

Arkwright's frame required more power than could be provided by a person or animal. This problem was solved by moving spinning to areas, such as Lancashire, with abundant rivers and powering the spinning frames by water wheels. A water wheel can produce considerable power so there quickly emerged a new way of organizing the spinning – in a factory, where one or more water wheels powered shafts that drove multiple spinning frames. The first factory was set up by Arkwright in the 1770s, the Cromford mill (named after its location). Its size is indicated by the fact that ultimately some 600 people were employed at Cromford.

As spinning could now be done in quantity, the preparation of the cotton became the binding constraint on production – the traditional manual methods of preparing the cotton (known as "carding") had trouble keeping up with the growing demand. Arkwright and his people turned their attention to carding. Integrating several ideas, they produced a carding machine, patenting this in 1775. This machine used rollers and spikes to draw out and clean the cotton. It needed considerable power, more than could be provided by muscles. As such, it fit naturally into the spinning mills which were already based on water power. The norm quickly became for carding and frame spinning to be organized into the same factory.

Meanwhile, attempts were being made to develop a spinning machine which could produce yarn suitable for warp and weft as well as produce either coarse or fine threads. The breakthrough was made by Samuel Crompton, a Lancashire weaver. After some seven years of experimentation and development, Crompton in the mid-1780s completed a machine which could produce a yarn that was strong, fine and even, suitable for making all types of cotton cloths. Because the machine had features of both the jenny and the frame it was viewed as a mixture and became known as the "mule".

Thomas Newcomen, a blacksmith in the tin mining districts of England, had developed a steam-powered engine for pumping water out of deep mines. Newcomen's first engine was in 1712. Newcomen engines were applied to the spinning mills by pumping river water back upstream so that it could flow again past the water wheel. Matthew Boulton and James Watt, by the 1780s, had improved on the Newcomen engine so that it could provide rotary power suitable to drive directly the shafts of a spinning mill. Steam power was given further impetus in the 1800s with the development of the high pressure boiler, pioneered by Richard Trevithick. The stage was set for further expansion of the industry as factories no longer needed to locate alongside fast flowing rivers for motive power. Use of steam engines allowed the center of spinning to move away from the rivers of Lancashire to the area around Manchester which had sufficient water for washing the cotton but was closer to Liverpool (the port of entry for cotton and port of loading for exports).

By the turn of the 19th century, production of yarn had been mechanized and, with growing demand for the new cotton goods, weaving became the constraint on production. Earnings of weavers rose. Traditional weaving capacity was increased with conversion of existing buildings and additions to cottages to form "loom houses". This increased weaving capacity but simply by replicating the old processes using hand looms. There was now a huge opportunity for mechanizing the weaving process.

Many people took up the challenge of devising a practicable power loom. An early example was Edmund Cartwright, a clergyman, who in the 1780s devised a loom which could be powered by horses, water-wheel or steam-engine. However, this loom proved unsuitable for factory use. Efforts continued but it took almost 40 years for the problem to be solved. The cast iron loom of Richard Roberts, patented in 1822, was the first power loom which was economically better than the hand loom. Roberts' company put his loom into production; demand was so great that, even producing 4,000 machines a year, it was not until the early 1830s that supply caught up with the order backlog. It then took another 20 years for loom design to approach maturity. William Kenworthy and James Bullough in 1841 introduced an automatic loom. In 1852 William Dickinson introduced what was the basis of the modern "overpick" loom. Finally, James Henry Northrop (a Yorkshire textile worker who had emigrated to the United States and was working in the cotton industry in Massachusetts) completed the development with a mechanism which could charge (replenish) the shuttle when it was empty. The Northrop loom was introduced in 1895.

The Roberts loom made machine weaving economic. There was rapid uptake of this design, creating new capacity as well as replacing hand looms. The number of handloom weavers peaked at 240,000 in 1831, the year in which production of the Roberts loom caught up with the backlog of demand. Weaving now switched to power and then automatic looms. By the 1860s there was no handloom weaving at all but 400,000 power looms were in operation. The adoption of power loom technology was rapid, going from introduction to complete penetration in 40 years.

With the introduction of power looms, the constraint on production shifted back to spinning. Roberts shifted his attention to this problem. In 1830 he patented his most famous invention, the self-acting or automatic spinning mule. Roberts' inventions transformed the nature of the cotton textile industry. Mechanization was now such that cloth production was no longer a skilled craft but a capital-intensive industrial process which could be operated by semi-skilled and unskilled workers.

The finishing segment of the cotton industry went through its own, parallel set of technical changes. Bleaching was traditionally done by exposing the cloth to sunlight or else by boiling it in a solution of ashes and then in sour milk. It was known that sulfuric acid could bleach fabric but its use depended on being able to produce the acid. The industrial production of sulfuric acid began with a plant constructed by John Roebuck (a physician interested in chemistry) and Samuel Garbett in 1749. Later in the century a method of bleaching using chlorine was brought in from France. However, these acid-based methods took several months to yield bleached cloth. Bleaching could not keep up with the growth of production. The breakthrough was produced by Charles Tennant. Tennant, a weaver, worked on the problem for some years until, in 1798, he perfected a bleaching powder, based on chlorine and lime, which provided rapid, effective and safe bleaching.

Printing the cloth was traditionally done by hand, by craftsmen using wooden blocks. In time, blocks were replaced by copper plates but printing was still a time consuming, manual process. Printing was mechanized beginning in 1783 when Thomas Bell developed a printing machine using revolving cylinders.

Natural dyes, mostly based on vegetable extracts, were used when cotton cloth was to be colored. A range of colors was available but these dyes were expensive. The most widely used color (other than plain bleached cloth) was black. Black dye was produced from a particular tree, native to central America, in combination with ferrous sulfate. It was not until the mid 19th century that synthetic dyes became available. The breakthrough came in 1856 with the discovery by William Perkin of "mauveine", a purple dye derived from coal tar. Perkin, an 18 year old chemistry student, was assisting his professor in searching for a way to synthesize quinine when he inadvertently extracted the dye. Perkin then established a company to produce mauveine commercially. (Perkin named his dye mauveine as a marketing device.) By 1880, low priced synthetic dyes had largely replaced natural dyes in the textile industry (although it was not until the 20th century that a wide range of colors in synthetic dyes became available).

3.3.5 Nature of the innovation process

We have gone into some detail on the changes in the cotton industry to indicate the scope and complexity of the changes – it took the efforts of many people and more than 150 years to perfect the many elements of industrializing the production of cotton cloth. In the present section, we look at the nature of this long sequence of changes which industrialized cotton.

The physical innovations involved materials and equipment. Two sets of innovations mainly involved materials - the development of industrial bleaches and of synthetic dyes. The remaining and more important physical innovations involved machinery. Equipment replaced labor in carding, spinning, weaving and printing. Engines, whether water-powered or steam-powered, replaced muscles in driving these machines. The result of these changes was that cotton production became mechanized, capital replaced labor. Machines took over the functions which formerly were performed by skilled labor, the traditional artisans. Labor was still needed to feed, operate and maintain the machines but the new workflow used essentially unskilled workers.

Managerial and organizational changes were just as important. Machinery needed power and power was best provided on a large scale, whether from a water wheel or a steam engine. One power source could run hundreds of machines. The mill (the modern factory) emerged. These mills were large and complex organizations. For example, the first cotton factory, the Cromford Mill employed 600 operatives. These mills required new employment practices, operational management, financial management, business management, logistics and marketing practices. These pioneering mills were the originators of the factory and, ultimately, the modern corporation.

The industry moved forward in a series of steps, overcoming a succession of constraints on production or business. In all cases the problem came first, the solution emerged from trial and error practical tinkering. Each major innovation dealt with the binding constraint of the day and the industry progressed as these constraints were successively overcome. (There was also a multitude of smaller changes which incrementally reduced costs and improved throughput of existing processes.) The flying shuttle improved the efficiency of weaving such that performance was then limited by spinning. A sequence of spinning machines was developed. The binding constraint was then preparing the cotton for spinning; this was relieved by the carding machine. Powering the new machines was a problem as the available fast-flowing rivers were fully exploited; this constraint was overcome by adapting the steam engine, first for pumping and then for direct rotary drive. Weaving now returned as the binding constraint. It took decades of effort but finally power looms and then automatic looms were developed. Finally, there was the market need for colored cottons; the development of synthetic dyes overcame this constraint.

There are three stages in this technological advance. The first is recognizing the existence and nature of the problem. The binding constraint in cotton processing went back and forth between the four steps in production. The pressing problems were identified rapidly. Identifying the problem is equivalent to identifying the opportunity to gain by overcoming the problem. The second stage is developing the procedure or technology which deals with the problem, which exploits the opportunity. This typically moved through several steps of increasingly effective technology, a process which took decades to complete. The final step is adoption of the improved technology. In most cases, the new technology was embodied in capital. New investment quickly switched to adopt the new technology but it took time for old equipment and old practices to be retired and replaced by the new. This adoption stage, of fully exploiting the opportunities for improvement, also took decades.

The next question concerns the sort of person who developed the innovations in process and equipment. Only one of the innovations, mauveine dye, could be called a discovery. And this discovery was serendipitous; it was not the result of a targeted search. The other innovations were all the result of targeted practical tinkering directed to solving practical problems. This was done by practical men working in or at least closely involved with the cotton business. These men knew the business, the processes used and the equipment used. The innovations came essentially from individuals within the industry.

What motivated the innovators? These men (and business was a male preserve in those days) were seeking to overcome problems, to relieve bottlenecks in processing cotton, to cut costs and increase throughput. The motivation was always the same - to create and/or grow a business, to acquire income and wealth. Today we might call this the capitalist motive but the application of capital was one way in which the cotton industry developed, it was the enabling rather than the motivating force. The motivating force was simple – income and wealth.

Here are two examples of this process in action. Richard Roberts, who developed the first viable power loom, went into business producing these looms. He achieved wealth from making the equipment, not from weaving cotton. Even the development of mauveine, the one breakthrough that did not come from inside the cotton industry, was economically driven. Although William Perkin chanced upon mauveine in his work related to quinine, he immediately recognized its practical potential. Perkin, working in secret, set up a laboratory in his garden shed, refined his discovery, worked out how to scale up production, raised capital, set up production and was active in marketing his product and managing his company. Even the name, mauveine, was made up by Perkin as a marketing tool. Perkin became a rich man from business, not chemistry.

Table 3.4 indicates the time scales involved in these changes. This shows the time taken for a technology to mature, to go from its initial operational form to its fully developed form. Although preparation of the cotton was mechanized quickly once the problem became apparent, it took much longer for spinning to be mechanized, longer still for coloring to be developed and much longer, around 160 years, for weaving to become fully developed.

Table 3.4 Time taken for innovation in cotton

	Preparing the cotton	Spinning	Weaving	Coloring
Start	Carding machine 1770s	The jenny 1760s	Flying shuttle 1730s	Printing machine 1780s
Completion		Automatic mule 1830s	Northrop loom 1890s	Synthetic dyes 1900s
Time taken	Little	70 years	160 years	120 years

3.3.6 Productivity in the cotton industry

Traditional production of cotton cloth was highly labor-intensive. Gradually, machines were introduced to help clean, spin and weave cotton. Ultimately, these machines were mechanically powered and largely automatic in operation. This industrialization of cotton replaced skilled with unskilled labor and replaced labor in general with capital. Gross labor productivity (output per unit of labor) soared over the course of industrialization.

Spinning provides an example. The spinning mule was considerably more effective than the spinning wheel. In turn, Roberts' automatic mule was much more effective than Crompton's mule. Operator hours needed to spin 100 lbs of cotton went from 2,000 down to 135. Labor productivity in the overall industry increased at an average rate of 2.8% a year between 1806 and 1907. This growth path, along with the smooth logistic curve fitted to the data, is shown in Figure 3.4. Labor productivity then levelled off towards the end of the 19th century as the processing technologies were fully developed and became fully adopted.

Figure 3.4 Cotton processed per worker

1860 = 1

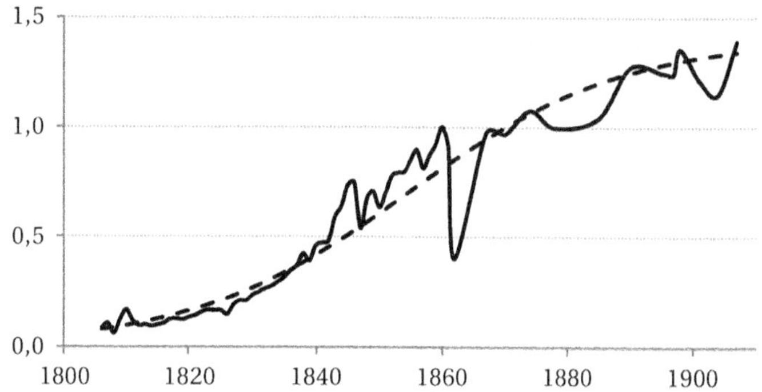

Source: Data from Mitchell (1988).

Productivity is better measured in terms of Total Factor Productivity (TFP), output per unit of factor input where factor input is a composite of labor and capital. Growth in TFP can be viewed as increasing output per unit of factor input or, equivalently, as decreasing relative prices of cotton goods. We have assembled information from both the quantity side and the price side to get the best practicable estimate of TFP growth in the British cotton industry.

Table 3.5 gives trends for the relative prices of cotton cloth. There is some uncertainty in using price trends to indicate TFP change as falling prices also reflect lower prices of raw cotton from the United States. Nonetheless, there clearly was a pervasive reduction in prices. The simple average is a declining trend of 2.3% a year.

Table 3.5 Trends in prices of cotton cloth

Trend in price of cloth relative to general price level, % p.a.

Time period	Prices	Based on
1780 - 1850	-2.4%	Clark (2009)
1780 - 1860	-2.6%	McCloskey (1981)
1760 - 1860	-2.0%	Mitchell (1988), Deane and Cole (1969)

We have found two estimates of TFP growth measured on the quantity side. C. Knick Harley (1999) estimates average growth over the period 1780 – 1860 as 1.9% per annum; Donald McCloskey (1981) estimates for this same time period average growth of 2.6%. The simple average is a growth rate of 2.3% a year.

Both quantity and price approaches suggest that TFP increased at around 2.3% a year. This is indeed rapid growth when sustained for decades. This growth implies that productivity over 150 years (such as from 1760 to 1910) increased by a factor of 30.

Output of cottons grew at 6.6% a year from 1780 to 1860. Table 3.6 shows how this growth was sustained by more inputs of labor and capital and by increasing Total Factor Productivity.

Table 3.6 Cottons, sources of growth

Average growth rates, 1780 - 1860, % per annum

	Contribution % per annum	Share
Labor	0.4%	7%
Capital	3.8%	57%
Inputs	4.2%	64%
TFP	2.3%	35%
Output	6.6%	100%

Source: Our calculations based on data from Mitchell (1988), Deane and Cole (1969), Clark (2009) and McCloskey (2004).

This Table tells several stories. First, labor played only a small part in the growth of the cotton industry. Second, more inputs (of labor and capital) accounted for almost two thirds of industry growth with TFP accounting for just one third. Although productivity improvement was important, the growth of the cotton industry relied mainly on using more and more inputs. Third, the role of capital was critical. More inputs of capital (or capital quantity) by itself accounted for more than half of all growth. But, much of the increase in productivity was embodied in better capital. Most of the technological advances – from steam engines through spinning machines to power looms and then automatic machines – were embodied in new equipment. Taking account of capital quantity and of capital quality, it must have been that almost all the growth of the industry was associated with capital.

Our conclusion is that the transformation of the British cotton industry (1) was driven by producers creating and responding to market opportunities for cotton goods, and (2) was enabled by innovation and investment. Demand increased partly through income growth but mainly as a result of the rapid decline in prices made possible by production process innovations. In turn, the key feature of these production innovations was their embodiment in capital. In all these dimensions – emergence of a mass market, technological change and use of capital – the cotton industry represented a complete break from the past. The British cotton industry was the first manufacturing industry to enter into sustained growth and established, through the interaction of demand, technological change and capital, the typical pattern for subsequent economic growth.

3.4 The woolen industry

3.4.1 Slow growth

The woolen industry had long been established in Britain. Before the rise of cotton, wool was one of the largest non-food industries, accounting for around 10% of the economy. But, the industry grew only slowly. The weight of wool processed increased, from 1775 to 1913, at an average rate of 1.4% a year. This growth was only slightly more rapid than population (with a 1.2% growth rate) and less rapid than the economy (which grew at a 2.4% rate). The woolen industry grew slowly and steadily, it did not experience the explosive growth of cotton.

3.4.2 Innovation in the woolen industry

Wool, just as cotton, needs to be prepared, spun, woven and colored. However, technical progress in the wool industry was less rapid than in cotton. Part of the reason involved legislation – the Wool Act of 1699, designed to protect the British industry, restricted and taxed trade in wool and wool products; this Act was not repealed until 1867. Protecting the market reduced the potential for competition and so the incentive to innovate. The other part of the reason lies in the difficulty of working with wool which is much coarser, heavier and oilier than cotton (the oil from fleece is lanolin). Preparation of wool for spinning is a specialized process which had to be developed from scratch. And, weaving wool is more difficult than weaving cotton. The first power loom for weaving worsted (woolen cloth) was produced by George Hattersley in 1834. The breakthrough to producing more appealing products was the Hattersley Dobby Loom, which allowed the weaving of intricate patterns, introduced in 1867. It may or may not be coincidental that this sophisticated loom was introduced at the same time that protection was repealed.

In any event, the 1860s saw, on the demand side, the emergence of strong competition and, on the supply side, the emergence of sophisticated new looms. The nature of production started to change as indicated in Figure 3.5. The quantity of wool processed continued on its upward trend but processing became much more capital-intensive (reflected in the rising use of mechanical power) and less labor-intensive (reflected in employment levelling off after the 1860s).

Figure 3.5 Inputs to the woolen industry

Quantities, 1850 = 1

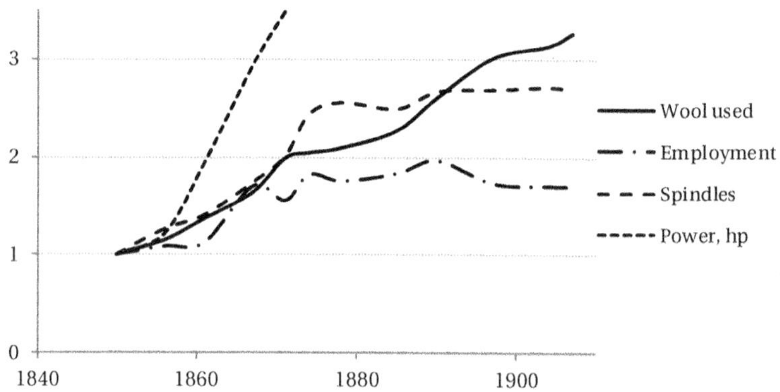

Source: Data from Mitchell (1988).

Gross labor productivity increased steadily as weaving was mechanized. It is not clear what happened to capital productivity as production was becoming steadily more capital-intensive. However, Total Factor Productivity was increasing. Harley (1999) estimates that TFP in the production of worsted was increasing at 1.3% a year and in knitted goods at 0.6% a year over the period 1780 – 1860. We estimate that TFP in the industry as a whole increased at a little over 1.0% a year over the period 1860-1907.

3.4.3 The nature of growth in the woolen industry

The quantity of wool processed increased steadily but slowly, more or less in line with population. Relative prices of wool products probably declined at 1% a year (the rate of growth in TFP) but demand per capita was hardly increasing, despite falling prices and despite rising incomes. Wool was pulled along by developments elsewhere, most likely just growth in population; wool certainly did not lead economic growth.

Woolens were fundamentally different from cottons – advances in cotton processing made cotton goods accessible to everyone, creating a new market whereas advances in wool processing slightly reduced the price of an already established product. This highlights the importance of demand in industrial growth. Cotton and woolens each experienced radical innovation in processing technology; each was transformed from a cottage industry to a mechanized, capital-intensive, factory production system. However, cotton grew rapidly while wool grew slowly. In fact, wool grew less rapidly than the economy despite this transformation of production. The reason for the difference lies in the nature of demand for the product. Wool was already a mature product, even though its production processes were about to be transformed. The production improvements simply made woolens a bit cheaper but the market was already saturated and so grew only slowly. Cottons, in contrast, were a new product in new markets. The production advances in cotton reduced costs and prices sufficiently to make cottons accessible to everyone. This was equivalent to creating new and potentially huge markets. Cottons then followed the classic S-shaped (logistic) market adoption pattern - slow adoption initially then rapid adoption and rapid growth before the market finally reached maturity (became saturated) with sales, and so production, levelling off.

3.5 The steam engine

3.5.1 Steam technology

Mining lead, tin, copper and coal had always been important in Britain. However, by the start of the 18th century many mines were so deep that water seeping into the mines was hampering activity. There was an emerging need for an effective pump. Animal-powered pumps were not sufficiently powerful; the need was for a pumping engine.

The first effective pump was an atmospheric engine built in 1712 by Thomas Newcomen, a blacksmith. Gravity acting on a pivoted beam pulled up a piston, drawing steam into a cylinder. Cold water then cooled the cylinder, condensing the steam, so that atmospheric pressure drove down the piston. This atmospheric engine produced irregular reciprocating motion of sufficient power to drive a pump. However, cooling the entire cylinder in order to condense the steam was thermally inefficient – the early Newcomen engines were less than 0.5% efficient. Operating costs, to purchase coal to raise steam, were high. Consequently, Newcomen engines were used only where coal was cheap, such as in coal mines, or where the mining product was particularly valuable, such as in Cornish tin mines.

Gradual improvements, such as those by John Smeaton, improved the efficiency and increased the power of the Newcomen engine. By the 1770s, Newcomen engines had reached 1.4% thermal efficiency and increased in size to as much as 75 horsepower. By this time the engines were widely used in collieries and tin mines, with around 500 installed.

Smeaton's work had pushed the basic Newcomen engine to its performance limits. Atmospheric engines continued in use, primarily in pumping, but further improvements in engine performance required a change in technology. The first technological change was achieved by James Watt. Watt, an instrument maker in Glasgow, had been asked to repair a model Newcomen engine used at the university to illustrate the latent heat of steam. Watt realised that the design had an inherent problem arising from the alternate heating and cooling of the cylinder. Watt determined through experimentation that around 80% of the energy in the steam was consumed in the repeated heating of the cylinder. Watt's solution conceptually was extremely simple - have a separate steam condenser which could be kept permanently cool while the cylinder was kept permanently hot.

Watt, in 1765, constructed a model of his new design but then ran out of money for development. John Roebuck, a founder of the Carron

Ironworks, injected new capital in return for an interest in Watt's patent. But, Roebuck's money ran out in 1774. Roebuck then sold his interest in the patent to Matthew Boulton who owned the Soho Manufactory, a leading producer of metal products in Birmingham. The Boulton-Watt partnership was established; Boulton provided finance and commercial drive, Watt provided technical direction. Boulton lobbied Parliament and succeeded in getting the patent renewed until 1800. The partnership then concentrated on commercializing the engine. A number of factors came together here. Boulton's craftsmen at the Soho ironworks had the skills needed to make the precision steam-proof valves required for the engine. Nearby was the Coalbrookdale iron works which had long experience in producing castings for the Newcomen engine and which was able to produce castings for the Watt engine. Also nearby was the iron maker John Wilkinson who, from his experience in boring cannon, had the expertise for the precision boring of cylinders.

The first Boulton-Watt engines were sold in 1776. These engines had a thermal efficiency of 2.7%, double the efficiency of the latest Newcomen engines. Of course, doubling the thermal efficiency of the engine halved the fuel cost, making the new design economically attractive. In addition, Boulton-Watt found a market in retrofitting condensers to existing Newcomen engines.

The Newcomen engine and the early Boulton-Watt engines produced erratic reciprocating motion and operated at low cycles per minute. This was acceptable for pumping but not for driving machinery. The search was on for the smooth, rotary power needed to drive machinery. James Pickard in 1780 obtained a patent for using a crank to connect the engine to a separate shaft, providing rotary power. However, Boulton-Watt used their patent protection on the basic engine to block the application of Pickard's technique. Boulton-Watt then circumvented Pickard's patent by developing the so called "sun and planet" system of gears to produce rotary power. Boulton-Watt continued to refine this engine over the 1780s. They introduced a flywheel to smooth the power delivery; they introduced the "double-acting" engine in which steam was applied alternately to each side of the piston, before being vented into the condenser, producing smoother power and improving the efficiency of the engine; they replaced the chain connecting the piston to the beam with rods, allowing the piston to push the beam as well as pull it; and finally came the "governor", a centrifugal device which automatically regulated the flow of steam so as to maintain engine speed within a pre-set range. These improvements raised the thermal efficiency of the Boulton-Watt engine to 4.5% and also made the engine suitable to drive machinery. The first use of a steam engine in a factory was in 1785 when George and John Robinson installed a Boulton-Watt engine in their cotton mill.

Boulton and Watt did not pursue further development of their engine, instead, they set about getting rich - protected by their patents, they exploited the demand for their engines. Leadership in engine development now passed to Richard Trevithick. An engineer with a mining background, Trevithick had started working on high pressure engines in order to dispense with the condenser and avoid Boulton-Watt's patents. In 1802 Trevithick obtained a patent for his high pressure engine and built a demonstration stationary engine at Coalbrookdale. This engine, with a boiler pressure of 10 atmospheres and operating at 40 strokes per minute, showed the way forward. Trevithick continued to develop his engines with advances in control systems, reorienting the boiler to the horizontal, running flues through the boiler for better heat extraction, and connecting the piston through a rod and crank directly to a rotating output shaft, eliminating the rocking beam. Eliminating the condenser and the rocking beam reduced the cost and weight of the engine while increasing the steam pressure and other innovations vastly increased engine power. The power-to-weight ratio of the engine was increased substantially, setting the stage for the later application of steam engines to mobile uses.

By the early 1800s, steam engines were being used for pumping and for providing rotary power to mills. These engines, though, were too heavy and bulky for mobile applications. There was now a clear demand for mobile power to take over from animal power in moving coal within collieries and from collieries to ports. This led to two decades of effort to develop mobile power. The technical breakthrough came with the high pressure boiler pioneered by Richard Trevithick but it fell to others to apply this engine to transport.

George Stephenson led the application of the high pressure engine to mobile use. Stephenson built his first locomotive in 1814 at the Killingworth colliery. The first public railway, the Stockton and Darlington, also engineered by Stephenson, opened in 1825. The first commercially successful railway, the Liverpool and Manchester, began operations in 1830 using locomotives, the *Rocket* and the *Planet*, built by George's son, Robert Stephenson.

Improvements in boiler design continued. By the late 1820s the thermal efficiency of the best engines reached 12% and by the 1830s as much as 17%. But adoption of high pressure engines in the largest industry of day, textile manufacturing, was slow. The hard coal found in the textile regions did not perform well in high pressure boilers so low pressure or atmospheric engines continued to be used for pumping (recycling river water over water wheels) and directly for factory power.

The need now was for more powerful and more economical stationary engines to power the mills. The breakthroughs came in the 1840s. Edward Green in 1845 patented the "economizer" which used hot exhaust gasses to pre-heat the water going into the boiler. William Fairburn in 1844 patented what became known as the "Lancashire boiler". The flue, firebox, grate and gas flow features allowed this design to burn hard coals; this permitted large scale, high pressure engines to use the hard coal of the textile regions. William McNaught in 1845 patented a high pressure compound steam arrangement which could be retrofitted to Boulton-Watt or even Trevithick engines. (Compound engines extract more power from the steam by using a sequence of cylinders at progressively lower pressures.) The Fairburn and McNaught advances transformed the economics of applying steam power to industry; they marked the start of the rapid adoption of steam power in manufacturing.

Steam engines were incrementally improved over the rest of the 19th century. There was, however, one more fundamental design step, the steam turbine. The first steam turbine was built by Charles Parsons in

1884. This turbine, which was used to generate electricity, had a capacity of 7.5 kilowatts (kW). Subsequent development of the steam turbine saw capacities increase to more than 1,000,000 kW with thermal efficiencies approaching 50%. High efficiency and high scalability made steam turbines the technology of choice in thermal generation of electricity. In fact, the steam turbine permitted the rapid expansion of electricity generation which took place in the 20th century.

3.5.2 The nature of innovation

The development of the steam engine was a gradual process. It was a sequence of small steps with a small number of major steps, each step building on what had gone before. The most important players were Newcomen, who built the first useful steam engine, Watt, who brought together the elements needed to produce rotary power, Trevithick, who built the first useful high pressure engine, the Stephensons, who built the first successful railway engine, Fairburn, who designed a boiler optimized for local coal, McNaught, who built the first successful compound engine, and Parsons, who built the first steam turbine. And, there were many others who improved the performance, reduced the fuel requirements and reduced the cost of the steam engine through a process of detailed technical improvements. James Watt is frequently credited with inventing the steam engine but Watt was just one of several who made major improvements to the existing technology. Watt's real fame is commercial, stemming from the success of the Boulton-Watt partnership in using patent protection to monopolize the market for (what were then) high performance engines. In fact, others made technical innovations which were at least as important as Watt's but these others were unable to achieve commercial renown to equal Watt's.

Newcomen, who started the process, was a blacksmith in the tin mining region of Britain; he worked with coal and iron and knew of the need for effective pumps in the mines. Newcomen was familiar with an engine built by Thomas Savery. Savery's engine was impractical but it provided the germ of the idea to Newcomen. The subsequent development of the steam engine was done by practical men who were trying to overcome problems in existing designs. Improvements in the steam engine required a combination of skills. Watt's efforts exemplify this – his engines ultimately were technically and commercially successful but this success required the efforts of financiers, iron-makers, iron-workers, tool-makers and others in the metals business. The Boulton-Watt partnership operated in Birmingham where this connection of complementary resources and skills was to be found.

The time scale in the evolution of the steam engine was measured in decades. Newcomen-type atmospheric engines, many with Watt-style condensers, were in use for around 150 years and for the first 100 years of this were the engines of choice for many applications. These atmospheric or low pressure engines were gradually improved over this life cycle – early engines used 35 pounds weight of coal per horsepower-hour but by 1780 fuel use had been reduced to 15 pounds and by the 1840s the best engines were using around 2 pounds. The first high pressure engine was built by Trevithick around 1800 but it was not until the 1830s that it was used successfully in railways and not until the late 1840s that its use in textiles and other factories and in steam ships really took off. The first Newcomen engine was built in 1712 and it was only around 1850 that reciprocating steam engines reached a degree of technical maturity. Compound engines continued to be improved for decades after this and the ultimate steam engine, the steam turbine, was introduced late in the 19th century and then began its own life cycle.

The steam engine has been developing for more than 250 years. Figure 3.6 shows the development of thermal efficiency of steam engines. Improvement in the technical performance of steam engines has closely followed the S shape of the logistic curve.

Figure 3.6 Thermal efficiency of steam engines

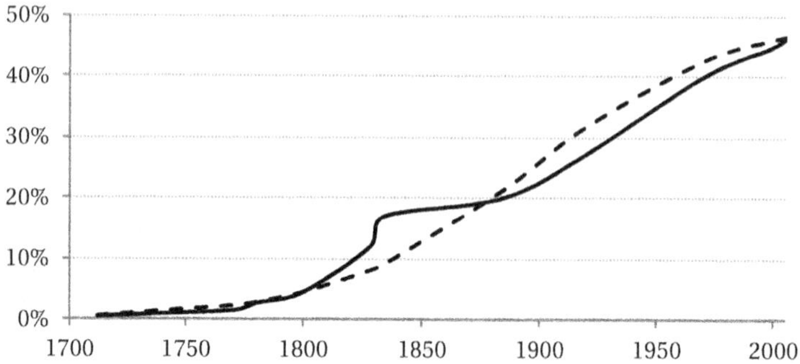

Sources: Data from Clark (2005); Wikipedia, *Steam engine* and *Engine efficiency*, viewed 20 August 2014; Parsons (1934).

The emergence of the steam engine and its entire subsequent development was driven by market needs. The original need was to pump water out of mines. A blacksmith in the mining industry, Newcomen, worked out how to do this. It happened that Britain had the key ingredients that Newcomen used – a sizable coal industry, an iron industry and ample capital. Newcomen's engine was intensive in use of coal and capital. These cost features limited the use of the Newcomen engine to two markets – collieries (which had access to low cost coal) and tin mines (which were sufficiently profitable to be able to sustain the high costs). Improvements in pumping engines were directed to reducing fuel costs. The opportunity to apply steam to powering factories motivated Boulton-Watt to extend the atmospheric engine to provide controllable, rotary power. In the 19th century, Trevithick's development of the high pressure engine and subsequent improvements in boiler technology brought down both fuel and capital costs for rotary power, allowing steam to meet the demands of the burgeoning cotton industry. Parallel development of the high pressure engine increased its power-to-weight ratio sufficiently that steam was able to power mobile applications – railways and steamships. Later, the steam turbine was applied to sustain one of the growth industries of the

20th century – electricity. In all cases, technology was developed to meet market needs or exploit market opportunities; technology did not lead, it followed, market opportunities.

3.5.3 Steam power and economic growth

The new cotton industry was based on mechanization. These machines needed power, more power than could be provided by humans or horses. Water power was effective and, where it was available, was economic but availability was limited. The textile industries grew initially in Lancashire precisely because of the presence of rivers which could turn the wheels of the mills. But there was only a limited number of suitable rivers. Water and wind power could not keep pace with the power needs of industrial growth. Initially, steam engines were used in the mills to pump water back upstream, enhancing the power available to the mill. With further improvement, steam engines began to be used directly to run factories. And, steam engines could be produced without limit; mills could now be built to meet whatever was the demand for textiles.

By 1800, 1,454 Newcomen engines and 496 Boulton-Watt engines had been installed. Of these Boulton-Watt engines, 33% drove reciprocating pumps, 5% served iron works and 62% served mills. 21% of all stationary horsepower came from steam engines. The use of steam power in factories then increased steadily, at around 5% a year. In the 1830s, steam overtook water and wind as the leading source of stationary power. In the 1840s, the performance of stationary steam engines accelerated and with it the use of steam. By 1870, steam was providing 90% of stationary power and, by 1907, 98%. Figure 3.7 shows the power of stationary engine installations in Britain. Steam power goes off this graph, reaching 9.7 million horsepower in 1907. The great factory expansion in Britain was powered by steam.

Figure 3.7 Stationary power
Millions of horsepower installed

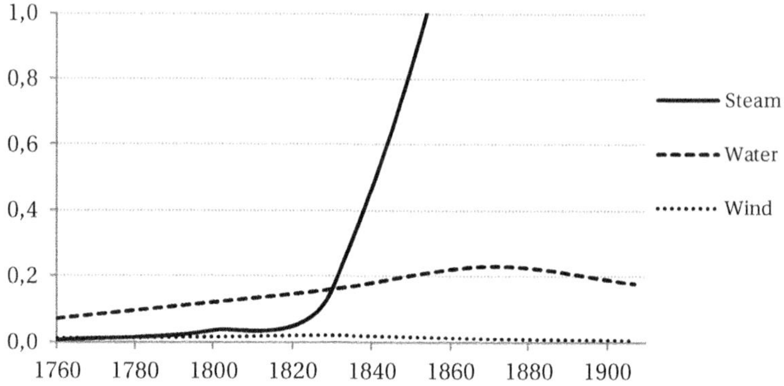

Source: Data from Allen (2009).

The steam engine was just as important in transport. The growth in economic activity that started in the 18th century required increasing input of motive power to transport food, materials and products. Marine transport at the time relied on sailing ships (wind power); inland transport relied on horses whether for canal or road carriage. The use of draught horses increased enormously. However, by the start of the 19th century the supply of animal power became a real constraint on economic activity. The demand for horses and fodder from the army in fighting the Napoleonic Wars was superimposed on a rising demand for horse power to service agriculture and transport. The result was a scarcity in supply and rising prices. Expansion of animal power had in effect reached its limit. The search was on for a viable mobile steam engine. The breakthrough came in 1830 with Robert Stephenson's *Rocket* and *Planet* locomotives. Then, steam powered the growth in land transport for the rest of the 19th century. Similarly, steam began to take over from wind power in marine transport in the 1840s until steam had virtually all the market by the end of the century. Over time, steam power met the transportation needs of the Industrial Revolution.

G.N. Von Tunzelman (1978) has estimated the reduction in incomes in 1800 if Watt had not existed. This is the counterfactual of the condensing engine and other improvements made by Watt not having occurred so that all steam engines then in use would have been Newcomen engines. His conclusion is that the drop in income would have been less than 1%. This is not surprising as the effect of Watt's innovation essentially was to reduce the coal use of atmospheric engines. Had all Watt engines in fact had been Newcomen engines, the same work could have been done but more coal input would have been required. The difference is essentially one of coal use and coal in Britain was plentiful.

Von Tunzelman's conclusion is plausible concerning Watt but it should not be taken as denying the importance of the steam engine. For a start, the Newcomen engine still dominated even during Watt's time. Second, the performance and efficiency of the steam engine increased steadily after 1800 with the development of high pressure boilers and other advances. The rapid rise of the factory over the course of the century required far better performance and efficiency than Newcomen engines could deliver; this rise depended on the steam engine. At the same time, the rise of railways and steamships depended entirely on higher performance steam engines. Von Tunzelman's conclusion is plausible for 1800 but is not for 1850 or beyond.

Steam engines were essential to the industrial growth of Britain. Steam power released constraints on production which were becoming ever tighter – these constraints were the need to power the machines which produced the goods of the Industrial Revolution and which transported these goods and their materials. The steam engine, being most efficient in powering large scale, centralized production, was central to the growth of the factories that characterized the Industrial Revolution. The steam engine equally was essential to the growth in international trade that allowed Britain to grow, exporting manufactures and importing food. The steam engine did not cause industrial growth but it was one of the features which permitted industrial growth; it was necessary although not sufficient for growth. But we must recognize the steam engine as central to Britain's growth.

3.6 Coal

3.6.1 Growth of the coal industry

Coal mining is a long established industry in Britain. Large coal reserves in northeast England, Lancashire, south Yorkshire and in Wales have been mined for centuries. In 1770, for example, coal production was equivalent to 0.9 tons per person and the value added in the coal industry accounted for around 1.3% of GNP.

Production of coal increased at an average of 2.6% a year from 1750 to 1913; this was more rapid than the economy which grew at 2.1%. Production, shown in Figure 3.8, did not grow at a steady rate, though; rather it followed the S shape of the logistic curve, increasing rapidly from late in the 18th century until growth was halted by World War I and its aftermath.

Figure 3.8 Coal production in Britain
1700 - 1939. Million tons a year

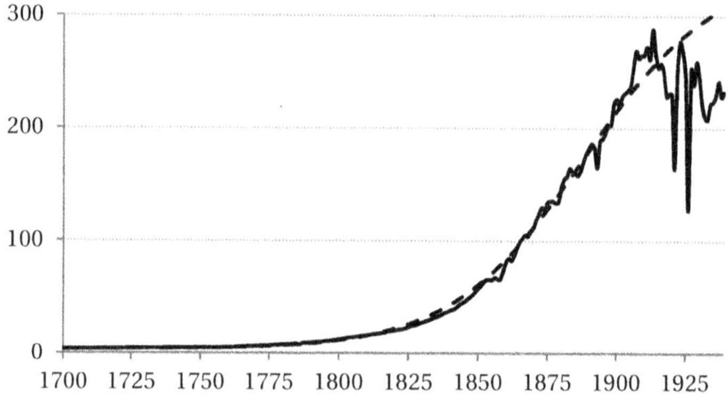

Source: Data from Mitchell (1988).

3.6.2 Markets for coal

Coal played an increasing role in the British economy. Figure 3.9 shows the rise in the coal intensity of the economy. Something started to happen early in the 18th century, accelerated in the 1760s and kept going for another 100 plus years. However, the move to coal had been largely completed out by early in the 20th century with production then increasing more or less in line with the economy. These changes followed a logistic path over a life cycle of more than 150 years.

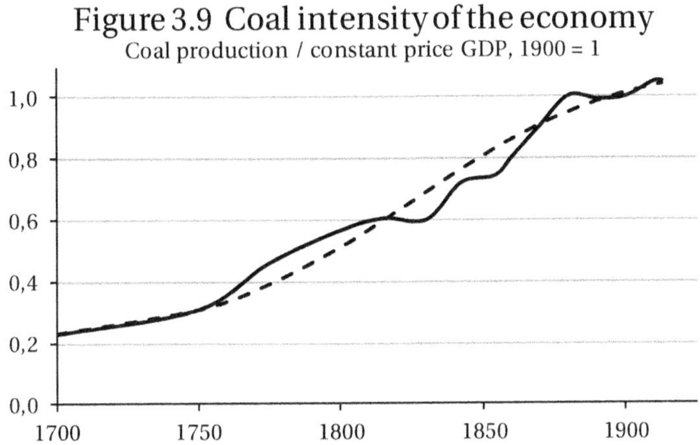

Sources: Data from Maddison (2006b), Clark (2005) and Mitchell (1988).

Initially the main use of coal was for household heating and cooking. Even in the early 19th century more than half of coal production was consumed in households. Household demand continued to increase, mainly due to the increasing number of households. Table 3.7 shows the trends in household demand. These trends are consistent with a population elasticity of demand of 1.0, an income elasticity of 0.15 and a price elasticity of 0.2. This suggests that there was nothing special about coal as far as households were concerned, it was just another consumer good.

Table 3.7 Household demand for coal, 1811 - 1913

Growth trends, percent per annum. Britain

Coal consumed by households	1.4%
Population	1.2%
Consumption per capita	0.1%
Income per capita	1.3%
Real price of coal	-0.3%

Sources: Mitchell (1988), Mitchell and Deane (1969) and Clark (2009).

The growth in coal use came from the new industries. Demand growth is shown in Figure 3.10.

Figure 3.10 Coal use in Britain

Millions of tons per annum

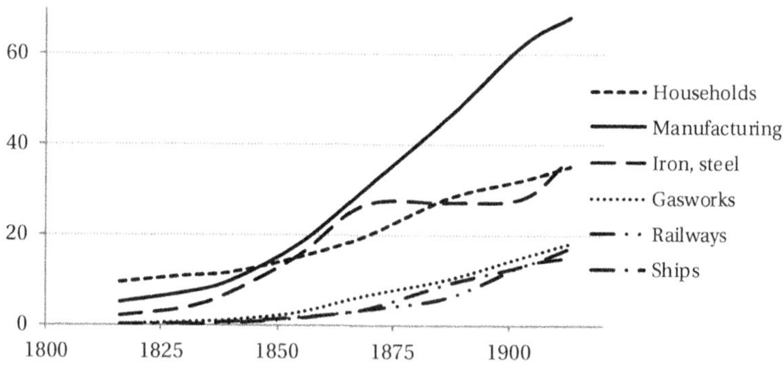

Source: Data from Mitchell (1988).

The largest demand was to run stationary engines - coal was the fuel of the steam engine. More than 60% of coal use was in the new factories of industrial Britain. Use of steam engines in the cotton industry grew particularly rapidly after weaving began to be mechanized after 1830. These developments went hand in hand with the use of iron, and later steel, in the new equipment as production of these metals used coal in large quantities. (Indeed, it was the discovery of how to use coal in producing pig iron, instead of using wood-based charcoal, that allowed the production of iron and steel to rise to meet the growing demand.)

The new transportation industries of railways and steamships were based on the mobile steam engine, fuelled by coal. Coal for transportation increased rapidly after the first railways of the 1830s and the first steamships of the 1840s. Town gas was a new product. As Britain at that time had no natural gas, an industry developed producing synthetic gas from coal and piping this to urban users.

The growth in demand for coal was driven by manufacturing industries and transportation where coal was an essential input. Indeed, the growth industries depended on coal either as a fuel for steam engines or as an input to iron and steel production. Coal played an essential part in the industrialization of Britain. And because coal was so closely tied to industry, its growth followed the logistic path of cotton and the other new industries.

3.6.3 Productivity in coal production

The increasing use of coal might have been caused by declining prices (caused by productivity improvements within coal) or might simply have reflected increasing levels of activity in the coal-using industries.

Productivity appears not to have improved. Clark (2005, p24) shows real extraction costs and resource rents for the period 1745 to 1869. Initially, these costs were flat at around 9 shillings per ton. After 1815, costs fluctuated around an upward trend, reaching around 12 shillings per ton. This suggests that productivity actually declined by around 0.3% a year. However, transportation improvements, with the introduction of the railway, reduced the cost of coal to the user. We estimate that this was equivalent to an overall productivity gain of around 0.2% a year. However, this reduction in the delivered price of coal is not sufficient to explain the huge increase in demand.

The growth in coal use came from the new industries. This demand reflects new processes – the steam engine and metallurgical demand – not a reduction in coal prices. The rise of coal was due to the rise of the coal-using manufacturing and transportation industries.

3.6.4 The role of coal in Britain's growth

The 19th century saw a fundamental change in the role of coal – whereas initially more than half of coal was used by households, by 1913 more than 60% was used in steam engines and more than 80% was used in factories and transportation.

Coal use increased rapidly but British economic growth was not an age of coal, it was an age of machines. Coal was the fuel for mechanizing production and transport. New products created new industries, industries such as cotton, steel, railways, town gas, electricity, piped water and sewerage systems. New machines lowered costs and were then adopted in existing industries, industries such as shipping and woolens. Coal provided the energy to drive the new machines.

The new processes and products of the Industrial Revolution needed motive power, whether stationary or mobile, and coal provided this power. Coal also provided a crucial raw material input which allowed the expansion of iron and steel production. The technical changes that allowed these developments were capital using and energy using. Britain was well endowed with capital and with coal. This permitted the process of industrialization. It is difficult to see that any other source of power was available. Britain had fully used its wood resources, and water and wind power were insufficient for the emerging needs. Coal was essential to Britain's economic growth but it was necessary, not sufficient. Abundant coal was an enabling factor in Britain's industrialization.

3.7 Iron and steel

3.7.1 Forms of iron

Iron ore has been smelted into usable iron for centuries. The production sequence has not changed although production processes have changed enormously over time. Iron is smelted using a high carbon fuel (such as charcoal or coke) and with a material such as limestone as a cleaning agent. The emerging iron has a high (around 5%) carbon content and often other impurities and has only limited direct use. This iron was conventionally poured into molds with a central channel and billets running off of this channel; the arrangement resembles a sow suckling piglets which gave rise to the name, "pig iron".

Pig iron was then processed to make more useful forms of iron which are cast iron, wrought iron and steel. The crucial feature is the carbon content of the metal. Cast iron is made by reducing the carbon content of pig iron, to between 2.1% and 4%, and then casting the molten metal into its final form. Cast iron is strong, machinable and resistant to oxidation (rusting) but its usefulness is limited by its brittleness. Wrought iron has a low carbon content, less than 0.25%, and is strong and malleable; wrought iron, being malleable, is not subject to the brittleness problem of cast iron. Steel is an iron alloy with a carbon content between 0.25% and 2%. The composition of steel can be varied to control for hardness, malleability and tensile strength. Steel is the most useful alloy of iron but has two main problems - it is challenging to make (as the carbon content must be controlled fairly precisely) and it oxidizes with water (it rusts). The rust problem can be overcome by adding chromium (to make stainless steel) or, in applications, by coating with a barrier such as paint.

3.7.2 Production technologies

Iron traditionally was smelted in a blast furnace. A blast furnace is a vessel in which ore, a carbon fuel and limestone are introduced through the top while air is blown in at the bottom; high carbon iron is tapped from the bottom, typically by pouring into pigs. Charcoal (partially burnt wood) was the traditional fuel and source of carbon. However, by the beginning of the 18th century scarcity of wood for charcoal had made iron scarce and expensive. Abraham Darby in 1709 began to fuel his blast furnace, at the famous Coalbrookdale iron works, with coke (partially burnt coal). Darby used this iron to make cast utensils such as pots but his process was not economic for making pig iron. His son, Abraham Darby II, kept experimenting with coke and, by around 1760, succeeded in producing pig iron which was cheaper than charcoal pig. Freed from the constraint of wood supply, the production of pig and cast iron increased to meet a growing demand. Cast iron was used for utensils, machinery (such as steam engines and textile machines), ordnance (such as cannon) and structures (such as bridges and building frames). The next large advance in cast iron production was the "hot blast", patented by James Neilson in 1828. This process used the waste gasses from the blast furnace to preheat the air blown into the furnace; by reducing fuel requirements; this significantly reduced the cost of making pig iron.

Wrought iron was used where malleability or sharpness was important, in uses such as nails, fasteners, boiler plate and rails. As the Darby technology could not produce iron suitable for hammering into wrought iron the hunt was on for a coal-based way of making wrought iron bars. Henry Cort succeeded. Cort had set up a rolling mill to shape barrel hoops. In 1784 Cort combined a reverberatory furnace (a type of furnace that plays the combustion gasses onto the molten pig iron but keeps the fuel itself out of contact from the iron) with his rolling process. These techniques had been developed by others but Cort was the first to combine them. Cort's combination allowed the large scale production of wrought iron bars using coal as fuel. The cost of this wrought iron was so low that it soon replaced charcoal wrought iron in everything except making steel.

Steel was still being produced by traditional processes using charcoal iron. As a consequence, steel was so expensive that it was used only in a few high value applications. The rise of industrial Britain used iron, cast or wrought, rather than steel. It was not until the 1860s that steel became competitive with iron.

The engineer Henry Bessemer in 1848 patented a method for making plate glass. Bessemer then directed his expertise in furnaces to the challenge of making cheap steel for the purpose of ordnance production. He patented his new method, embodied in the "Bessemer converter", in 1856. Bessemer's insight was that the heat generated by burning the impurities in molten pig iron would create a self-sustaining process which would ultimately get rid of all the impurities. His process removed the impurities, including carbon, by oxidation with air blown through the iron. The Bessemer process then added appropriate amounts of carbon and other elements in order to obtain the desired quality of steel. Other people refined the Bessemer process. In particular, Robert Forester Mushet achieved control over malleability by adding precisely controlled amounts of carbon and manganese to the molten iron. Mushet went on the develop "Mushet steel", an alloy later known as tungsten steel, which was especially hard, allowing the development of cutting edges for metal-working equipment.

The Bessemer process was the first process which allowed the volume production of steel from pig iron. It reduced the cost of steel by as much as 85% compared to earlier technologies. Low priced steel was now widely substituted for cast iron. Steel was also competitive with wrought iron and gradually replaced wrought iron in virtually all applications.

Carl Wilhelm Siemens, a German-born engineer working in Britain, developed a regenerative furnace which used waste gasses to preheat the fuel and air, allowing the furnace to operate at temperatures high enough to burn the impurities out of pig iron. The regenerative furnace was first applied to steel-making by French engineer Pierre-Emile Martin in 1865. The process is now known as the Siemens-Martin process and the furnace as an "open hearth furnace". Initially, steel-making was dominated by the Bessemer process but new investment tended towards the Siemens-Martin process which came to dominate steel-making for the first half of the 20th century.

These steel technologies continued until the 1950s when the "basic oxygen furnace" was introduced. The basic oxygen process was invented by Swiss engineer Robert Durrer in 1948. The principle of the basic oxygen process is similar to that of the Bessemer process; the key difference is that the Bessemer process used air whereas the basic oxygen furnace used pressurized oxygen as the oxidizing agent. The basic oxygen process slashed the capital cost and the labor cost of steel-making, compared to the open hearth method, and so has come to dominate primary steel making.

Finally, electricity-based processes, electric arc and electric induction furnaces, have come into use. These processes began to be adopted in the post World War II reconstruction in Europe due to their low capital costs - as little as 15% of the cost of an integrated mill. Electric processes typically use scrap steel, in contrast to integrated steel mills which make steel starting from either iron ore or pig iron. Electricity-based mills, often called mini mills, typically produce "long" products, such as structural steel, rod and bar, while integrated mills can produce all products including sheet and plate. In this way, mini mills are somewhat complementary to integrated mills.

The use of the different steel making technologies in Britain is shown in Figure 3.11. The modern industry started with the Bessemer converter. The Bessemer process was gradually superseded by the open hearth process which dominated production from the late 19th century until around 1960. The demise of the open hearth process was much more rapid with the industry now bifurcating into integrated steel mills, using the basic oxygen process, and mini mills, using electric furnaces.

Figure 3.11 Steel technologies in Britain
Share of production, percent

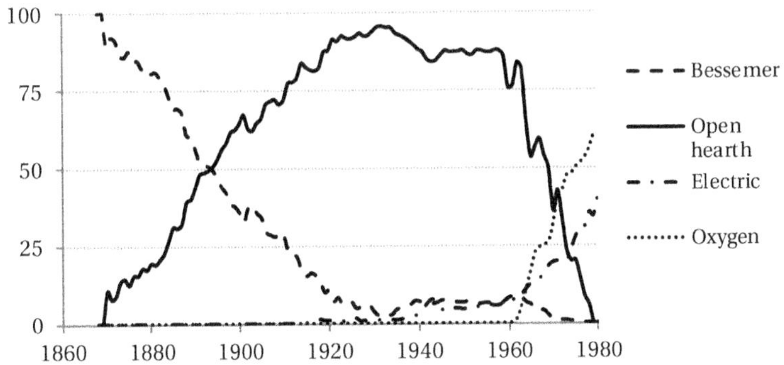

Source: Data from Mitchell (1988).

The adoption of each of these steel-making technologies followed a logistic pattern – there was slow adoption initially, followed by rapid growth and then by saturation. Over time, new (and cheaper) technologies took over from the established technology. The time pattern for open hearth steel is shown in Figure 3.12. Use of the open hearth process started in the late 19th century, growing rapidly over the next 50 years until it dominated the industry. This would have continued had more economical processes not come on the scene. The basic oxygen and electric process were so much cheaper than the open hearth process that they completely took over from open hearth in only 20 years.

Figure 3.12 Steel production by open hearth
U.K. production, million tons

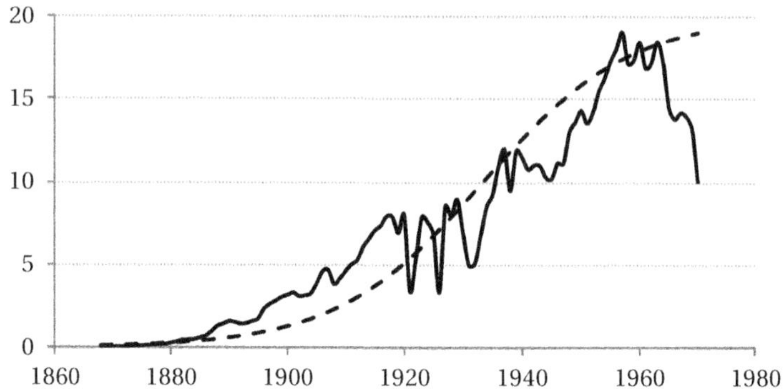

Source: Data from Mitchell (1988).

3.7.3 Nature of technical change in iron and steel

One theme runs through the history of innovation in iron and steel – the drive to cut costs. Iron and steel had been made in Britain for centuries but production was based on wood-derived charcoal. Shortages of wood limited production and forced up prices. The breakthroughs in producing low cost iron and steel came from replacing wood with abundant and cheap coal, and in new furnace designs. Many iterations of new technology, primarily in the nature of the furnace, would be required before first iron and later steel became available in large volumes and at low prices. The development of iron is replete with instances of a newer, cheaper technology supplanting the established technology. When low cost steel became available it gradually supplanted iron in virtually all uses. Finally, steel itself has been replete with a succession of cheaper technologies replacing the established processes.

The people who achieved these technological advances all were involved in iron and steel or related industries. Abraham Darby, who made the first big step to using coal, was in the business of making cast iron utensils; Abraham Darby II, who made the first economic coal-fired smelter, was in his father's business. Cort was in the rolling business and applied rollers to make the first coal-based wrought iron. Bessemer, who made the breakthrough in steel production, was an expert in furnaces (for his glass-making) who turned his mind to the steel problem. Siemens and Martin improved on Bessemer's furnace design. And, Durrer refined the Bessemer process. All these pioneers were practical men already in industry. Their motivation was the same – business success. And their route to business success was also the same – break through the existing barriers in making low cost iron or steel.

The time required for the modern iron and steel industry to develop was prolonged. Abraham Darby started using coal in 1709 but it took until 1760 before his son worked out the process. Henry Cort extended the coal-based process to produce wrought iron in 1784. The next big step was Henry Bessemer's converter, developed in the 1850s. It then took around 50 years for steel to displace iron. Steel production then went through a sequence of technologies – Bessemer, open hearth, basic oxygen and finally electric – taking another century. Iron ruled for around 150 years while the development of steel-making has taken another 150 years. In total, it has taken almost 300 years for the modern iron and steel industry to emerge.

3.7.4 Growth in iron and steel production

Iron and steel made by the traditional technologies were so expensive that these materials were not widely used. New technology for smelting iron, introduced around 1760, made available large quantities of low cost iron; use of iron started to rise quickly. Production of pig iron grew at an average of 4.9% a year between 1760 and 1860. Low cost technologies for making steel began to be introduced after 1860. Steel use then started to grow rapidly, peaking only around 1970. The average growth in Britain of steel from 1868 to 1913 was 9.9% a year while the growth rate until to final peak in 1970 was 5.6% a year. These growth rates for iron and for steel considerably exceeded the growth of the economy as a whole.

Iron and steel were not new in a physical sense but were new in an economic sense - the development of new technologies slashed costs and so prices, making iron and steel accessible to massive new markets. As a result, the growth of iron and steel was like the growth of a new product – slow initial uptake followed by rapid and widespread adoption and finally by market saturation. The logistic model describes this process of new product adoption. The growth paths are shown in Figure 3.13.

Figure 3.13 Production of iron and steel

Million tons

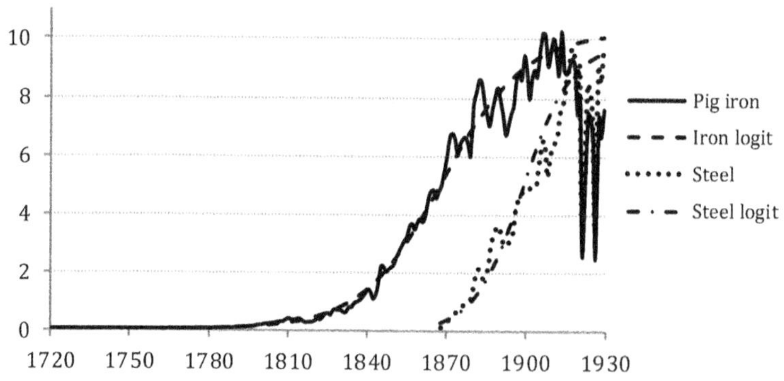

Source: Data from Mitchell (1988).

3.7.5 Iron and steel and economic growth

There was ongoing technical change in iron and steel production. The key changes involved furnace design and were embodied in capital. These advances caused costs to fall. Total Factor Productivity growth in the iron industry 1780 - 1860 has been estimated by both Harley (1999) and McCloskey (1981) at 0.9% a year. Productivity in steel production after 1860 was even more rapid – we estimate that it increased at more than 2% a year. Even with this growth in productivity, more and more resources went into the production of iron and steel to support output growing at 5% a year or more; the industry was using resources, not contributing directly to economic growth.

The real benefits of the advances in iron and steel were felt in other industries, not in the iron and steel industries themselves. Competition ensured that the cost reductions flowing from new technologies were passed on to customers in the form of lower prices. These lower prices stimulated the use of iron and steel in other industries. By contributing to the growth in these other industries making consumer goods and investment goods, iron and steel contributed to economic growth in Britain.

Industrialization in Britain was led by the cotton industry and at the heart of this industrialization was the use of machinery. Iron was an essential part of this machinery and of the steam engines that powered most of it. Iron was also an essential part of the early railways and steamships that transported people, raw materials and finished goods. The availability of low-priced steel from the 1860s sustained the further growth of factories, steam engines, railways and steamships. In short, the capital which was central to the development of the British economy depended on iron and steel.

Low priced iron and steel made its contribution to economic growth by enabling the development of capital goods and the growth of the manufacturing and transportation industries. Advances in iron and steel were necessary to the industrial growth of Britain. They were not sufficient but British growth could not have taken place without them.

3.8 Railways

3.8.1 Development of railways

Collieries in the north of England had long used tramways to move coal. These early tramways had horse-drawn wagons running on wooden rails. In 1769 the Coalbrookdale iron works began to produce cast iron rails for collieries but motive power was still provided by horses. Animal power worked but was becoming increasingly expensive, especially with the rising price of fodder resulting from the demands of the army in the Napoleonic Wars (1803 to 1815). Existing sources of mechanical power, typified by the Boulton-Watt steam engine, were too heavy for mobile use; a new design was needed for a mobile engine to be feasible.

Trevithick's high pressure boiler provided the breakthrough technology. With steam pressures of 10 atmospheres (compared to slightly over one atmosphere in Boulton-Watt engines) and with no condenser, Trevithick's design had a much higher power-to-weight ratio. Trevithick in 1804 mounted his engine on a wagon on the tramway at the Pen-y-Darren ironworks, creating the first locomotive. This could pull five loaded wagons along the 9.75 mile track at an average speed of 2.4 miles per hour. However, the engine was too heavy for the cast iron rails of the tramway, breaking the rails. Trevithick returned the engine to stationary application.

Experimenting with mobile engines continued. The first successful locomotive was the *Puffing Billy* built in 1813 by Christopher Blackett and William Hedley for the Wylam colliery. George Stephenson, an engineer at the Killingworth colliery, created a better design with his 1814 locomotive called *Blucher*, after the Prussian general at Waterloo. It was the first to use flanged wheels and could pull 16 tons at 4 mph. The Stephenson locomotives also were too heavy for their cast iron tracks. Stephenson turned his attention to the track problem, experimenting with suspensions and wheel arrangements before finally overcoming the problem by using wrought iron rails.

Coal mine owners around the northeast England town of Darlington were endeavoring to improve the transportation of their coal to the port of Stockton. A group of owners in 1820 established the Stockton and Darlington Railway with the intention of constructing a horse-drawn tramway. George Stephenson persuaded the Company to use steam rather than animal power. An Act of Parliament was secured, approving Stephenson's proposed route and allowing the use of "locomotive or moveable engines". The resulting Stockton and Darlington Railway Company (S&DR) commenced operations in 1825. This 26 mile railway used a combination of steam locomotives, horse-drawn wagons and stationary engines pulling trains by means of cables. S&DR's track was designed to accommodate the horse-drawn wagons used in the older tramways serving the mines; this accounted for its 4 feet 8½ inch gauge. (This gauge became the industry standard and is today used in around 60% of the world's railways.)

In the 1820s, a group of cotton manufacturers and merchants in the new textile towns around Manchester wanted a faster and cheaper way, than the canals then in use, to move their materials and products from and to the port of Liverpool. They formed the Liverpool and Manchester Railway (L&MR) in 1823, raised finance by taking up shares and appointed George Stephenson to design and build the railway. Stephenson's main accomplishment was the track which included tunnels, cuttings, viaducts and a bog crossing, all designed to minimize grades over the 35 mile distance. The locomotive was chosen by competitive playoff at the famous Rainhill trials. The *Rocket*, designed and built by a company headed by Robert Stephenson, George's son, won the contract. The L&MR commenced operations in 1830.

The *Rocket* brought together a large number of innovations which were refined in the successor engine, the *Planet*, built later in 1830. The *Planet* was so successful that it provided the template for steam locomotives for the rest of the century. The main innovations were (1) the multi-tubed boiler with 25 copper tubes running the length of the boiler for more effective heat transfer from the flue gasses to the water; (2) the blastpipe which directed exhaust steam to the chimney/smokestack to create a partial vacuum and so increase gas flow through the boiler; (3) the firebox was separated from the boiler and was double walled to contain a blanket of water, thereby pre-heating the water fed to the boiler; (4) the wheel configuration with large diameter driving wheels plus a set of non-driven but load carrying wheels under the firebox; and (5) the cylinder alignment with horizontal cylinders at the front of the engine giving smoother transmission of power.

George Stephenson also set the standard in his track design. His efforts to minimize track gradients led him to substitute higher construction costs for lower locomotive capital and operating costs. In addition, he was the first to use a double track design with two adjacent sets of tracks. And, the L&MR pioneered the use of color signals for traffic management - the L&MR system was red for stop, green for caution and white for clear.

The L&MR had been intended for carrying cotton but it achieved immediate, although unexpected, success in carrying passengers. Rail passenger service was considerably faster, more comfortable and cheaper than the previous technology of road travel by horse-drawn coach. The company decided to emphasize the passenger business, providing timetabled inter-city service. The passenger business grew rapidly with the freight business also increasing. The L&MR was a commercial success.

Railways then developed rapidly. By 1837 London was linked to the L&MR. The 1840s saw a period of easy money and a fall in lending rates to as low as 3.25%. This caused a flow of money into railway shares, leading to a run-up in share prices and a speculative bubble in the years 1844 – 46, the so called "Railway Mania". The process reached a peak in 1846 when 272 Acts of Parliament setting up new railway companies were passed. The bubble then burst, share prices collapsed. But the bubble led to a construction boom that ran until 1851. There were 6,266 miles of track by 1851, more than four times the 1,498 miles of 1840.

There was a contest for the track standard, the so called "battle of the gauges". The early railways, under the leadership of George Stephenson, used a track width of 4 feet 8 1/2 inches. However, the Great Western Railway, engineered by Isambard Kingdom Brunel, opened in 1841 with a gauge of 7 feet and 1/4 inch. Much of the wide gauge network added a third rail so that rolling stock of either gauge could be used. On a practical level, this dealt with half of the problem but it was clear that the narrower gauge, already the de facto standard, would prevail. Despite this, the government got involved. The Gauge of Railways Act of 1846 required the use of the more common narrow gauge. Even so, some wide gauge track remained in use until 1892.

Railway construction continued, the rail network continued to increase and serve more and more towns and factories. These railways were built and operated by separate companies. Some cities were served by several competing railways. London, for example, had 12 mainline terminal stations. Amalgamations began in the 1840s with George Hudson creating the Midland Railway. By 1845 he controlled 33% of all track. Ownership gradually was consolidated until by 1923 there were just four major railway companies.

Locomotive technology advanced within the general framework established by Robert Stephenson's *Planet*. There were improvements in boiler design, firebox design, exhaust design and steam control. Locomotive design began to specialize into functional segments. Passenger locomotives were built for speed with large diameter driving wheels and several sets of non-driven wheels for weight carrying. Freight locomotives were built for traction with their greater power transferred to the tracks through several sets of medium diameter driven wheels. In addition, there were ranges of power and size as locomotives were targeted to the weights they were to pull. Similarly, wagons were developed into a range of specialized passenger carriage designs and a range of different freight wagon designs. Passenger facilities were improved. Signalling and traffic control systems were improved. Train management evolved with marshalling yards and locomotives optimized for this work.

3.8.2 The market for railway services

A network of canals had evolved in England. The network was expanded until in 1805 a link was completed from the industrial midlands to London. This network provided an intercity transport capability but it did not serve many of the coal mining areas nor did it go to the doors of the new factories. In addition, barge traffic was slow, moving at the pace of a draught horse, and was expensive as operators exploited their market power. Meanwhile, people (passenger traffic) moved by horse or in horse-drawn carriages on dirt roads. Given this situation, there was a considerable potential demand for cheaper, faster and more extensive transport. The most pressing demand was to move coal from the mining areas followed by the demand to move materials to and products from the new textile mills.

These needs stimulated the development of railways. The first three decades of development were in the coal mining areas as collieries sought better ways of getting their coal to market. Then, as cotton processing expanded around Manchester, the definitive step took place with local industrialists organizing the L&MR, the world's first public railway. Although the L&MR was intended for freight, passenger demand immediately became apparent and the railway responded by developing passenger services. By the 1830s, railways had established the three main transport markets – moving coal, moving cotton and textiles, and moving people – and were rapidly expanding to cover these markets over the whole country.

Growth rates are shown in Table 3.8.

Table 3.8 Railway growth rates

		Number	Revenue	Price
Track, miles	1840 - 1913	3.6%		
Passengers	1843 - 1913	6.3%	4.2%	-2.0%
Freight, tons	1856 - 1913	3.9%	3.1%	-0.8%

Source: Data from Mitchell (1988).

These growth rates, continued over several decades, lead to large changes. Miles of track increased by a factor of 14 between 1840 and 1913 while the number of passengers carried increased by a factor of 130. The average price per passenger journey declined by more than 75% over this time.

Figure 3.14 shows the growth paths for passengers and freight in Britain and how each closely followed a logistic path. This is not unexpected as new products typically follow a S-shaped adoption path with a slow adoption early in the process followed by rapid growth and then levelling off as the market becomes saturated. The adoption process took around 80 years, from the introduction of rail service in the 1830s until World War I brought an end to the established order in 1914.

Figure 3.14 Railway traffic
Million passengers, million tons of freight

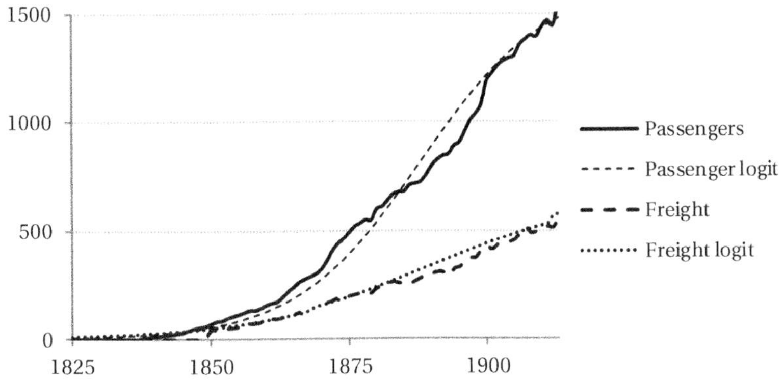

Source: Data from Mitchell (1988).

3.8.3 Isambard Kingdom Brunel

Isambard Kingdom Brunel was an English engineer. His early work, on tunnels and bridges, established a reputation for boldness and flair. He was then retained by the Great Western Railway (GWR), a company established by merchants in Bristol to build a railway between London and Bristol. By the 1830s, Bristol's leading position as a trans-Atlantic port was being challenged by the cotton port of Liverpool; the merchants of Bristol wanted to strengthen their competitive position. GWR's strategy was to appeal to customers by the speed and comfort of its service. Brunel was charged with executing this strategy.

Brunel's design decisions were driven by this business objective. First, he selected a route from London which had minimal gradients and no sharp curves even though this involved high engineering costs for the tunnelling, bridges and extra distance involved. Second, he selected a wide track, of 7 feet and 1/4 inch, rather than Stephenson's standard narrower track, to allow stability at high speed and also to allow greater room and comfort for passengers. Third, Brunel chose a powerful locomotive to provide high speed travel. Fourth, Brunel constructed expansive terminals at London and Bristol which provided the best possible convenience and aesthetics. The line came into operation in 1841. GWR later expanded its operations by building new lines and by buying adjacent lines. Ultimately, GWR provided the railway service for the entire south-western part of England.

The GWR was a commercial success, growing to be one of the largest railways in Britain. Its strong growth over a half century is summarized in Table 3.9.

Table 3.9 Growth of the Great Western Railway

Average annual growth rates, 1850 - 1900

Passengers	7.2%
Average fare per passenger	-2.8%
Freight tons	9.8%
Average price per ton	-2.6%

Source: Data from Wikipedia, *Great Western Railway*. Viewed 14 April 2011.

Although the GWR was not a large part of the economy (representing only 0.5% of GDP) it does illustrate the economic growth process. GWR was part of a growth industry – an industry supplying a new market and growing at up to 8% a year, for decade after decade. This growth was driven by new demand, as people adopted the new service and as population and incomes grew; demand growth was further stimulated by declining prices. Supply responded to sustain this demand. Increasing productivity (reflected in prices declining at 2.7% a year) helped sustain the expansion but even so the railway drew in resources (increasing at a 5.5% rate) from the rest of the economy. Investment, labor and materials poured into the GWR to allow it to keep up with demand.

Brunel and his backers identified a related market opportunity - the London / New York shipping service. They formed the Great Western Steamship Company (GWS) to enter this market. GWS placed Brunel in charge of designing its ships. As with the railway, speed and service formed the core of its strategy. Brunel saw that steamships would be much faster than the sailing ships then in use. He also saw the potential in large ships, reasoning that revenue potential increased with the cube of size while cost increased with the square of size. These objectives led Brunel to pioneer a new generation of faster, larger ships.

The first GWS ship was the *Great Western* which began operations in 1838. This was at the time the largest passenger ship in service with a registered tonnage of 1,340. It was constructed mainly from wood but was strengthened with iron bracing. It had steam-powered paddle wheels together with four masts for sails. The *Great Western* completed her maiden voyage from Bristol to New York in the record time of 15 days and five hours. The *Great Western* proved the commercial viability of trans-Atlantic steamship service.

Brunel then moved on to a larger ship, the *Great Britain.* At 3,675 tons the *Great Britain* was more than 1,000 tons heavier than any other ship of the time. Brunel constructed the hull from iron, designed the most powerful mobile engines then existing, and used the marine screw for propulsion. This was the first time that all these technologies had been combined in one ship. The ship was a technical success although its high cost led GWS into financial difficulties. When the ship ran aground in 1846 the company ceased operations. The *Great Britain,* though, was salvaged and re-entered commercial use. Brunel designed one more ship, the *Great Eastern,* launched in 1858. The *Great Eastern* had a gross weight of 18,915 tons, could carry 4,000 passengers and had the range to circumnavigate the world. However, the ship was expensive and directed to a market which did not exist – there was little demand to travel around the world non-stop. The *Great Eastern* was a commercial failure.

The history of Brunel, the Great Western Railway and the Great Western Steamship Company illustrates the nature of technical progress. The commercial need comes first with the effort to exploit new market opportunities drawing forth new technologies and/or new designs. Brunel did not invent anything but drew imaginatively on existing technologies, extending, combining and applying them in new ways to exploit new market opportunities. New technology is useful if it satisfies an unmet need in the market, as the GWR and the *Great Britain* demonstrate. In contrast, technology developed for its own sake is likely to fail commercially. The *Great Eastern* typifies this – the most sophisticated passenger ship in the world could not attract passengers and ended up being used to lay submarine telegraph cables.

3.8.4 Railways and economic growth

Output from railways, from 1830 to 1913, increased at around 5% a year. This was considerably faster than the growth of the economy which was 2.5% a year over this period. Railways were one of the growth industries of Britain. Total Factor Productivity growth was a little over 1% so the resources put into railways would have been increasing at around 4% a year. The growth contribution of railways must therefore have been in terms of the services it provided to its users.

Railways created a new type of personal mobility as inter-city travel became accessible to millions of people. The population of the new industrial and commercial towns gained the ability for leisure travel, such as to the resort areas in the south and west of England. In the latter part of the 19th century urban railways were developed, providing the capability for rapid intra-city travel. All these types of consumption grew rapidly. Spending on passenger rail travel rose from nothing in 1829 to 0.9% of GNP in 1845 to 2.4% in 1871 and 2.5% in 1913. Not all of this would have been final consumption but it could well be that personal consumption of railways services accounted for 2% of GNP. Capital expenditure by railways from 1856 to 1913 averaged 1.1% of GNP. Together, consumption of railway services and investment by railways would have amounted to around 3% of final demand in the economy. Mitchell (1988, p545) has calculated the receipts of the railways. Net receipts correspond to value added, the contribution to GDP on the income side. This contribution amounted to 2.8% of GDP in 1890. Spending and income estimates each suggest that railways contributed directly around 3% of the economy.

In addition, railways contributed to the growth of other industries. Moving coal was vital to the growth of the textile, iron and steel industries; moving cotton input and finished goods similarly was vital to the textile industries. Railways provided much of this transport of goods in the industries that led economic growth in Britain. Railways might not have been essential as other industries probably could have grown on the basis of horse, canal and costal shipping transport; railways lowered the cost of freight transport rather than provided transport which would not otherwise have been available. However, since much of the growth in cottons and other industries was due to lower prices, anything that reduced transport costs would have contributed to the growth of these other industries.

Clark (2005, p24) has examined the components of the cost of coal delivered to London. There was a large reduction in the real price after the emergence of railways. For example, from 1825 to 1865, the real price went down by 30%; almost 80% of this reduction was due to lower transport costs. This would have left more purchasing power in the hands of consumers, who would have spent it on other consumption goods, and in the hands of London producers, where it might have gone to higher profits. These kinds of indirect effects of the spread of railways would have increased GDP. The 2004 Input-Output tables for the U.K. (Office for National Statistics (2006a)) show that transport contributed around 3% of GDP. If the price reduction observed for coal applied to this figure then the corresponding benefit to GDP would have been around 2%.

The direct effect of the growth of railways was to increase GNP by around 3%. The indirect effect, by reducing costs and so increasing spending and incomes elsewhere, contributed another 2%. Together, railways might have represented 5% of the economy, rising from nothing in earlier times.

Robert Fogel (1964) has considered for the United States the question of the contribution of railroads to economic growth. He concluded that railroads in America did improve economic efficiency in other industries but that the extent of the gain was limited. Fogel estimated that the use of railroads, compared to a hypothetical equivalent transport system using horse-drawn wagons, canals and ships, would have increased GDP in 1890 by around 2.7%. Fogel's estimate corresponds to our estimate of the indirect contribution of railways in Britain; however, our estimate of the total contribution of railways to the British economy is larger than Fogel's estimate.

3.9 Shipping

3.9.1 Technical change in shipping

Shipbuilding exploited two of the major new technologies developed in 19th century Britain – the steam engine and low cost iron and steel. Ships at the start of the century were wooden hulled and wind powered, ships by the end of the century were steel hulled and steam powered.

There are several key dates in the development of steam propulsion. The high pressure steam engine was pioneered by Trevithick around 1800. By 1812 the first steamship was in operation - the paddle steamer *Comet* which began a passenger service on the River Clyde at Glasgow. This was an isolated case, however. It was only in the 1830s, following Robert Stephenson's successful locomotive (the *Planet*), that high pressure steam engines were developed sufficiently to be viable for marine use. The marine screw (propeller) was patented by Francis Pettit Smith in 1836. Isambard Kingdom Brunel at the Great Western Steamship Company brought these innovations together. Brunel's first ship, the *Great Western* of 1838, used both steam and wind propulsion and both wood and iron in the hull. His second ship, the *Great Britain* of 1845, was built of iron and powered by a steam engine driving a marine screw. The *Great Britain* established the design principles for ships for the rest of the century.

The British Navy was reluctant to adopt the new technology. The Navy decided to test the competing propulsion systems. The climax in 1845 was a tug-of-war in which the screw-driven ship *Rattler* pulled the paddle steamer *Alecto* backwards. The Navy then adopted as its standard Brunel's design of iron (later steel) hull, steam engine and screw propulsion.

An important subsequent improvement to steam engines involved compounding - using a sequence of cylinders at progressively lower steam pressures in order to extract the most energy from the steam. William McNaught introduced compounding to stationary engines in the 1840s and John Elder in the 1850s successfully applied compounding to marine engines. Compound engines then became standard in shipping.

The adoption of steam power in British ships is shown in Figure 3.15. The proportion of ships powered by steam went from zero in the early 1800s to almost 100% in the early 20th century. The shift to steam was a long process, it took 100 years for steam power to saturate the market but ultimately all transport ships were steam powered. The adoption of steam followed a standard logistic process – there is a close fit between the actual and logistic lines.

Figure 3.15 Market share of steam ships

Steam ships as % of total registered tons

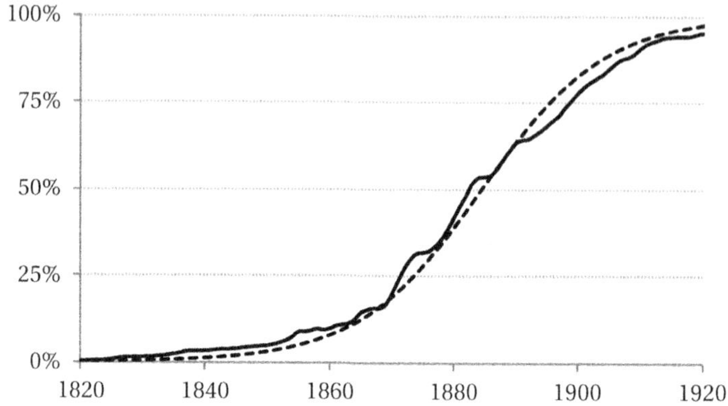

Source: Data from Mitchell and Deane (1971).

In the 20th century, diesel engines emerged as a more economical alternative for most types of ships. High performance ships, such as heavy naval vessels, continue to use steam engines, although nowadays steam turbines, while commercial shipping has largely changed to diesel power.

The other key change was the use of metal for the hull and other components. Historically, ships were built entirely of wood. Wood was available and was functional but it had an inherent size limitation – as wooden hulls did not have the rigidity required for large vessels, wooden ships were limited in size and hence carrying capacity. The advent of cheap metal not only reduced the cost of construction but also allowed larger ships to be used, with the associated reduction in transport costs. These benefits were sufficiently compelling that metal was bound to replace wood in ship building; the shift to metal depended only on the availability of low-priced iron and steel.

The use of metal, either iron or steel, in new British ships is shown in Figure 3.16. There is only one observation in the early 19th century which complicates the fit. However, the adoption pattern is clear – it is closely described by a logistic curve.

Figure 3.16 Adoption of metal hulls

% of new ships with metal hulls

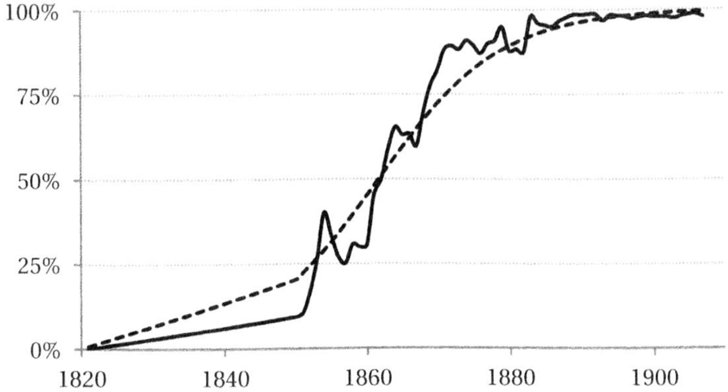

Source: Data from Mitchell and Deane (1971).

Although low cost iron had been available since the start of the 19th century it was only around 1850 that metal hulls began to be adopted. The reason is that the real advantages of metal hulls, particularly in size, depended on greater power being available so had to wait for the development of powerful mobile steam engines. Brunel's *Great Britain* in the 1840s showed the way to commercially viable steam ships.

There was also technological change going on in the metal industry. Steel is superior to iron in most applications, including shipbuilding, and when low cost steel became available it was inevitable that steel would take over from iron. However, the large scale shift from iron to steel took a decade to begin. There was a noticeable lag between the availability of steel in the late 1860s and its adoption in shipbuilding, which began in the late 1870s. When the shift began though it proceeded rapidly – it took essentially just five years in the 1880s - and followed a standard logistic process, see Figure 3.17.

Figure 3.17 Adoption of steel in ships

% of new metal hull ships that were steel

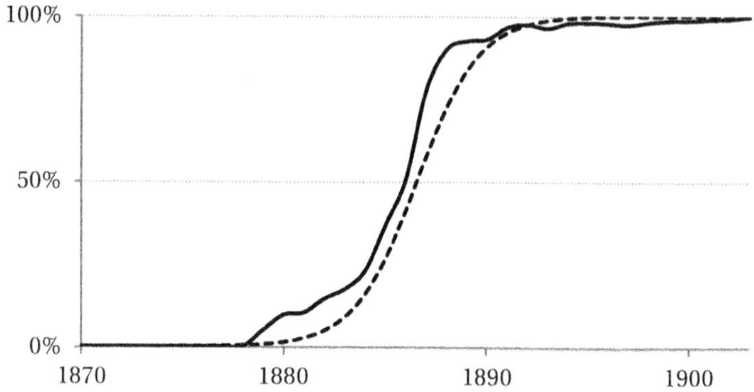

Source: Data from Mitchell and Deane (1971).

3.9.2 The market for shipping

The number of ships registered in the U.K. grew at an average of 0.4% a year over the period 1790 to 1910. However, ships got larger with the average weight increasing at 1.4% a year over this period. The carrying capacity of the fleet therefore would have increased at 2.5% a year. The increasing speed of ships, with the move to steam propulsion, would have further increased the service capacity of shipping. The economy over this period increased at an average of 2.5% a year. Shipping capacity increased more rapidly than this. This means that the growth industries of the economy were using ships to transport the increasing volumes of materials and products associated with industrial Britain.

Shipping growth over the 19th century shows a distinctive pattern. Figure 3.18 shows this growth in British shipping with the acceleration around mid century and then the slowing of growth in the 20th century.

Figure 3.18 Ships registered

Registered weight of all ships, million tons

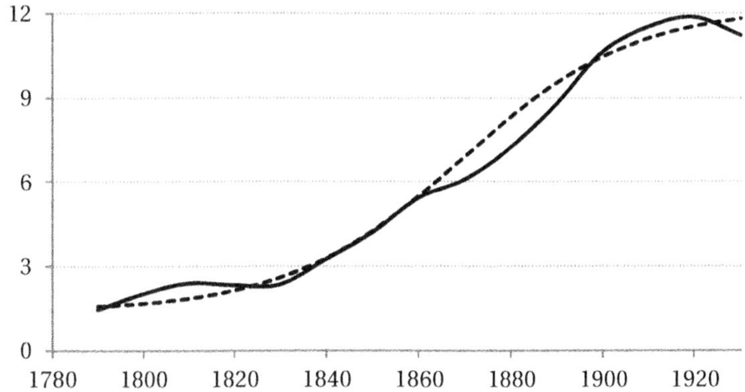

Source: Data from Mitchell and Deane (1971).

The cotton industry imported all of its raw cotton and exported more than half its output. The use of shipping would have reflected the growth of cotton. Reduced transport costs would have had a significant effect in reducing the delivered cost of cotton goods, further stimulating the growth of the cotton industry. In addition, coal was a large user of coastal shipping so this segment of shipping would have followed the growth of factories and cities throughout Britain. Imports of food, as Britain switched from an agricultural to an industrial economy, came by ship. And the growing export of British machinery and other goods went by ship. The acceleration in shipping capacity over the 19th century coincided with the acceleration of growth of industrial Britain. Shipping helped sustain the growth of British industry.

3.9.3 Shipping and the economy

The output of shipping services, allowing for the number of ships, their increased carrying capacity and their increased speed, grew rapidly, probably at more than 3% a year. Productivity in shipping also increased rapidly. McCloskey (1981) estimates that Total Factor

Productivity increased at 2.3% a year between 1780 and 1860; growth after 1860 would probably have been even more rapid in view of the switch to steel, to more efficient compound steam engines and to larger ships. It is likely, therefore, that shipping productivity was advancing so fast that a declining share of resources was needed to sustain the increase in shipping output. In this case, shipping helped sustain economic growth over the 19th century while also releasing resources for use elsewhere.

Improvements in the efficiency of shipping benefited the economy by reducing costs to those industries using shipping either to acquire their raw materials or to deliver their products to market. In particular, shipping was vital to cotton, the leading growth industry, and to food, the most important element in the consumer budget. The steamship was not essential to British growth – trade would have grown even with the old technology of wooden ships and wind power. However, by reducing the cost of transport, the steamship greatly assisted in the growth of a Britain that came to be based on international trade.

3.10 Economic growth in Britain

3.10.1 Sustained growth

The world had never seen sustained economic growth before the emergence of industrial Britain. Madison's (2006b) numbers tell the story in Table 3.10. These growth trends are for the leading countries of the past and then for Britain.

Table 3.10 Growth rates in GDP per capita

	1 - 1000	1000 - 1500	1500 - 1600	1600 - 1700	1700 - 1820	1820 - 1870
World	0.0%	0.0%	0.1%	0.0%	0.1%	0.5%
China	0.0%	0.1%	0.0%	0.0%	0.0%	-0.2%
Italy	-0.1%	0.2%	0.0%	0.0%	0.0%	0.6%
Spain	0.0%	0.1%	0.3%	0.0%	0.1%	0.4%
Netherlands	0.0%	0.1%	0.6%	0.4%	-0.1%	0.8%
Britain	0.0%	0.1%	0.3%	0.3%	0.3%	1.3%

Source: Data from Maddison (2006b).

No country had achieved growth sustained over the long term. China had expanded but its growth had been absorbed in higher population, not incomes. The northern Italian states, by the time of the European Renaissance, had the highest income in the world but did not continue to grow. Spain had a burst of growth in the 16th century. The Netherlands then emerged as the leading country, growing on the basis of trade for the best part of two centuries, but could not sustain this growth in the 18th century.

This was the background, the starting point as it were. Britain had been growing slowly, in line with the rest of Europe, for hundreds of years. Britain's growth accelerated in the 18th century. Then, for the first time, this growth continued. In fact, growth not only continued but it accelerated. Table 3.11 shows this acceleration.

Table 3.11 Growth rates in British GDP per capita

1700 - 1820	1820 - 1860	1860 - 1913	1913 - 1939	1939 - 1975	1975 - 2003
0.3%	1.3%	1.0%	0.9%	1.8%	2.1%

Source: Data from Maddison (2006b).

Something happened in Britain that created the phenomenon of sustained growth. This was unprecedented in world history. Other countries have since taken over the economic leadership but Britain is where it began, where the process of sustained growth first took hold.

Sustained growth even at 1% a year changes lives. An increase at 1% a year for 100 years increases average incomes by a factor of 2.7. Growth at 1% a year for 300 years, the approximate time since the process started, increases average incomes by a factor of 20. Per capita income in the U.K. in 1700 is estimated by Madison to have been $1,250 in constant dollars of 1990. By 2003, the average income had risen to $21,310.

3.10.2 When did growth start?

Britain was growing steadily although slowly after 1000. The process was stopped by the "Black Death", a bubonic plague pandemic which spread through Europe in the 14th century. The plague peaked around 1350 but was widespread for another 100 years and reappeared sporadically until the 17th century. The plague killed more than 50% of the population. Of course, the economy contracted but average incomes increased as each (surviving) person now had more land and capital to work with. It was only in the 16th century that (slow) growth in GDP resumed and it took until 1650 for the English population to pass its pre-plague levels. Figure 3.19 shows these trends.

Figure 3.19 Growth in England, 1200 - 1860
Indices, 1600 = 1

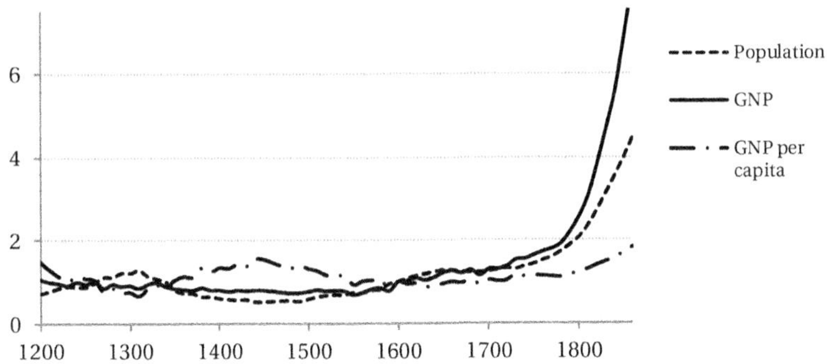

Source: Data from Clark (2009).

The key indicator is average income, GNP per capita. Average incomes increased after the Black Death but it was only in the 17th century that total income and the population grew past their previous peaks. Then, during the first few decades of the 18th century, something happened, growth began to accelerate. 1725-1730 saw the beginning of an unprecedented acceleration in average incomes.

Figure 3.20 shows that birth rates had been increasing since the mid-17th century but that a fundamental change took place around 1730 – birth rates moved ahead and stayed ahead of death rates. These changes were likely to have reflected changes in food supply. As agricultural output represented half or more of total production the implication is that real incomes started to accelerate at this time.

Figure 3.20 Birth and death rates for England

Rates per 1,000 population

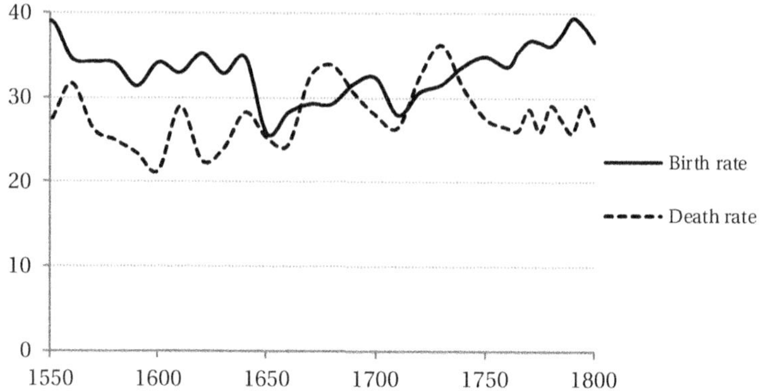

Source: Data from Mitchell (1988).

3.10.3 Getting ready

Output from English agriculture had been growing steadily, reflecting new farming techniques and improved equipment, over the 17th and into the 18th centuries. Figure 3.21 shows the movement of real wages. Wages increased following the Black Death but then declined as the economy returned to a more balanced structure. Wages then started to increase in the mid-17th century before accelerating around 1720.

Figure 3.21 Real wages in England
Index, 1860 = 100

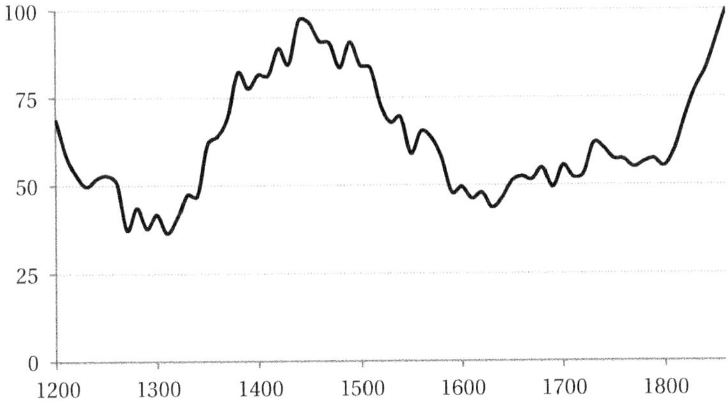

Source: Data from Clark (2009).

With incomes and population rising, spending accelerated. As the basic needs (of the time) were being met, the rise in incomes left some money over for new or luxury goods. This was the emergence of discretionary spending. People began to look towards purchases of previously inaccessible goods, such as cottons.

The rising demand, including for non-basic goods, began to put pressure on supply. Agricultural output was increasing but supply of other goods was constrained. Underground mining, for example of tin and coal, was being hampered by flooding of the deeper mines. A shortage of wood to make charcoal was hindering the growth of iron production. Supply of cotton goods was restricted by the monopoly of the East India Company in importing hand-made cloth from India. These problems stimulated efforts to alleviate the constraints. Thomas Newcomen in 1712 introduced a rudimentary steam engine which could pump water from underground mines. Abraham Darby in 1709 developed a rudimentary process to produce cast iron using coke (from coal) rather than using charcoal. John Kay in 1733 invented the flying shuttle which improved the productivity of weaving cotton. Change was now afoot in several leading industries – agriculture, mining, iron and textiles.

Operators and engineers made incremental changes to the steam engine which improved the operating efficiency of Newcomen's engine but it took 50 years for the thermal efficiency of this design to be doubled. These improved engines were introduced to power pumps for mines and bellows for iron works. It took a similar time for new techniques in land management, animal breeding and equipment design to spread through the farming sector. By the 1760s, Abraham Darby II had developed an economic method for producing pig iron using coke and James Hargreaves invented the spinning jenny. In the 1770s, the first cotton mill came into operation, using water-powered machines to produce thread. This was a sequence of change – new methods and new machines were developed to push back supply constraints. The process of change had well and truly started.

3.10.4 The breakthrough

The breakthrough to rapid growth came in a new industry – cotton cloth. Cotton goods previously were imported under a monopoly arrangement and were expensive. British consumption of cotton goods was so small in the first decades of the 18th century that cotton cloth does not even show up in Clark's (2009) itemization of the household budget. People instead used wool. However, cotton is much more desirable for many uses. And now, with rising incomes, people could begin looking at cottons. Spending on food, fuel and other necessities continued as before but people were beginning to have some discretionary income; cotton goods were a target for this new spending. There was a large potential market for affordably priced cottons.

The race was on to cut the cost of producing cotton cloth in England. Processing cotton from the raw material involves four steps – cleaning, spinning, weaving and coloring. The first production breakthrough came in weaving. John Kay in 1733 invented the flying shuttle, which improved the effectiveness of hand weaving. Next came spinning and cleaning where a series of innovations such as the jenny, the frame and the mule allowed processing to be done by machine. These machines required considerable motive power so were organized in factories (cotton mills) based on water and later steam power. Spinning had been mechanized by the end of the 18th century, slashing the price of thread. It took decades for weaving to be mechanized but this too was accomplished, in turn slashing the price of cloth. Finally, later in the 19th century, synthetic bleaches and dyes were developed, reducing costs as well as introducing new patterns and colors to cotton goods.

Local demand increased as incomes increased and prices of British cottons declined. Exports took off as British cottons became the cheapest in the world. Britain became the center of the world cotton processing industry. During its peak growth phase, from 1770 to 1860, the weight of cotton processed increased at an average of 6.7% a year. The British market became saturated but exports continued to increase so the industry continued to grow, right up to World War I.

The rise of cotton in turn stimulated the development of the iron industry and of the steam engine. Cotton processing equipment increasingly used iron. The development of smelting using coke reduced the cost of cast iron sufficiently that cast iron was available for the rise of cotton mills. The early mills were water-powered but Newcomen-style steam engines were applied as pumps to recycle the river water used to drive mills. Then, the Boulton-Watt partnership not only improved the efficiency of steam engines but also converted their output to the rotary power needed to run factories. Finally, the coal industry expanded to meet the growing demand for coal for home heating, for iron-making and for steam engines. Steam engines improved the efficiency of the coal industry by draining mines as well as by transporting coal.

Figure 3.22 shows production growth until 1820. Consumption of the basic goods, such as grain and candles, increased at a moderate rate, broadly in line with population and incomes. The rapid growth was in the new industry of cottons. Production of iron increased rapidly but with a lag as demand rose with the machinery going into cotton and other new industries. Coal grew at an intermediate rate as demand responded to rising population and then to the increases in production of manufactures. There was a happy interaction – cotton drew forth the other industries whose growth, in turn, increased incomes and population, leading to further growth in the cotton industry.

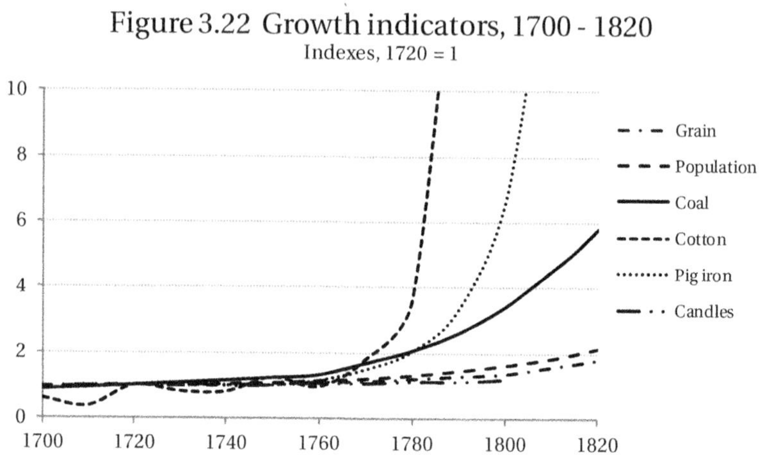

Sources: Data from Deane and Cole (1969) and Mitchell (1971).

A new dynamic was well under way by the late 18th century. Agricultural production was increasing, raising incomes. Discretionary income was directed towards purchases of manufactures. An industrial sector had been created and was powering ahead. The early cotton industry had been a cottage industry. However, the development of spinning machines required the input of more power than muscles could provide; the factory emerged. The early factories were water powered but, with improvement of the steam engine, factories turned increasingly to steam power. Technical breakthroughs provided low cost iron for the cotton equipment and the steam engine. Coal production followed the upward path of consumer spending, iron production and use of steam engines. Agriculture, cottons, iron, machinery and coal were moving forward in a mutually reinforcing way.

By the early 19th century, Britain had been changing and growing for almost a century. Other countries had experienced income growth for this length of time but Britain was different – its economy was changing, not just getting bigger. The growth came from doing things differently – agriculture became more productive, the cotton industry emerged and grew, iron production moved to a sustainable basis and, in the steam engine, a new source of power was developed. These changes worked together and supported each other. Britain had started on the path of economic growth.

3.10.5 Growth consolidates

The British economy by 1800 was being driven forward by cotton production with iron, supporting the machinery and engines being used in cotton mills, following close behind. This growth was still relatively narrow. But then growth broadened with the development of new markets served by new products, stimulated by the new products that had already emerged – cotton, iron and the steam engine. The initial burst of industrialization gave rise to a new and wider round of products and markets which were previously unimagined. The sequence of new products moved through stationary steam engines, mobile steam engines, railways, steamships, woolen goods, steel and chemicals. Some of these were new products, others fed back to reduce costs in existing industries and to reinforce the growth of these industries.

The mechanization initially of cotton processing and then of transportation and goods production in general was based on machinery, initially of iron but later of steel. This gave rise to a whole new industry devoted to making machines – these were the capital goods, machine tools and specialty metals industries.

Getting these new products to their customers drove the growth of service industries – transportation (railways and shipping), wholesale trade, retail trade, insurance, advertising and finance were created and/or grew on the back of the manufacturing industries. These service activities followed general economic growth. For example, GNP increased by a factor of 3.0 from 1855 to 1913 while the output of distribution and other services also increased by a factor of 3.0.

This new manufacturing was based on factories and characterized by interaction between different industries. The factories concentrated around common resources or transportation links. In turn, workers lived nearby. Cities were created. These were new types of cities, based on the factories which produced the new goods and the people who worked in the factories. These people needed to be housed; new industries emerged to construct and own this housing.

The emergence of cities led to the demand for urban infrastructure. Piped water supply, disposal of storm water, disposal of sewage, urban public transport, piped supply of coal gas, paved streets and streetlights were constructed. On the production side, these used the iron, steel, steam engines, pumps and bricks produced by the new industries; on the spending side, they used some of the surplus, the discretionary income, generated by the trend of rising incomes.

Part of rising incomes was directed to the public sector. Some of this covered the provision of urban infrastructure. But, a new area of production emerged – public services. These started with education and public health and, in the fullness of time, went on to provide a safety net of health services and income support. This signalled the beginnings of the final British growth industry – government. These government services required a new administrative structure, giving rise to the rapid growth of public employment; in the decades after the 1881 census "public administration" was the most rapidly growing of all employment categories.

Incomes were now well above the basic levels of the distant past. People had income left over, after buying the basics of food, shelter and clothing, for spending on the new goods and services now available. Expectations were increasing. People were able to and interested in buying these new goods. Producers of course were interested in encouraging them to spend. A new attitude had been created, the consumer society started to emerge.

British growth in the 19th century was self-sustaining. This growth was similar to 18th century growth in being led by a few industries but it was more widespread and more rapid. Britain had completed two centuries of something the world had never before seen – economic growth based on self-reinforcing and self-sustaining change. There had previously, such as in Rome and the Netherlands, been growth over one or two centuries but this earlier growth was based on the exploitation of a single innovation. Britain had achieved growth based on a succession of changes.

The politicians of Europe then ruined things by taking the continent, and much of the world, into a half century of war and instability. Britain lost its leading place, the mantle passed to the United States. But Britain had achieved the breakthrough into economic growth which the United States and other leading countries built upon.

3.10.6 Innovation

The move to growth was all about change. There were two sorts of changes. First, process innovations reduced costs and so prices of key products, opening up large new markets for these products. Second, product innovation created new products for which large markets developed. And, these combined so that new products saw their own process innovations, improving the products and reducing their prices so that market growth continued for decades. The critical feature was innovation, whether in product or process, which created/improved products for which there were large potential markets. Demand (new products with large potential markets) and supply (process and product innovation) combined to move Britain onto a path of sustained growth.

Innovation in agriculture set the scene for the subsequent growth by allowing population to increase and by allowing incomes to increase so as to permit discretionary spending. This provided the basis for the growing markets for manufactures.

The initial steps to manufacturing growth occupied the 18th century. These steps were based on process innovation. The motivation for these innovations was the same - demand was pressing against supply and people tried to break through the supply constraints in the pursuit of commercial gain. Demand built up gradually, stimulating people to work on improved methods of production. Demand was growing only by a couple of percent a year which is important as rapid demand growth probably would have spilled over into a price response and inflation rather than stimulating just a quantity response. The motive was economic – to profit from being able, as a result of lower costs, to undercut the prices of established producers and take custom from these producers. Many people tried but only a few succeeded in creating these advances. However, once an advance was demonstrated it was adopted widely, allowing whole industries to emerge and grow. These advances were developed to exploit strong demand conditions. Market opportunities came first, innovation followed.

Change in the 18th century was process innovation led by agriculture, cotton, iron and the atmospheric steam engine. Change in the 19th century became more complex with both process and product innovation gaining speed. Rapid innovation in cotton, especially in weaving, continued until mid century. The high pressure steam engine led to the development of railways and steamships. By hugely reducing transport costs, railways and steamships expanded two existing markets – for moving passengers and for moving freight. Production of woolens was transformed by the application of machinery based on cotton production. The introduction of low cost steel permitted further growth in cottons, railways, steamships and machinery. Innovation in chemicals led both to cheaper ways of performing traditional tasks, such as bleaching, and to entirely new products, such as synthetic dyes. Perhaps the main entirely new products were for municipal services – water, sewerage, public health, public education, town gas, paved streets, garbage disposal, street-lighting and police. These services were partly a matter of applying new materials, such as steel and pumps, but mainly were a result of higher incomes – people, through collective channels, decided to allocate part of their new discretionary income to public goods.

Figure 3.23 shows the actual sequence of adoption of new products (apart from public goods). Most of these graphs are of logistic curves fitted to each product; these curves retain the nature and timing of the growth process but smooth out the short term fluctuations in the growth path. The graph for steam ships is the percentage of new ships which were steam powered. The graph for chemicals is for employment (an input, not an output) growth over the level shown in the first census in 1841. These are products for which data is available; they cover the main growth drivers. Coal is not shown as it was not a new good but rather an existing good whose production expanded to meet the growing demands of its users. Each series has been scaled so that it is 100 in 1907; this scaling preserves the timing and shape but not the relative magnitude of the different growth paths.

Figure 3.23 Adoption of new products
Scaled, 1907=100

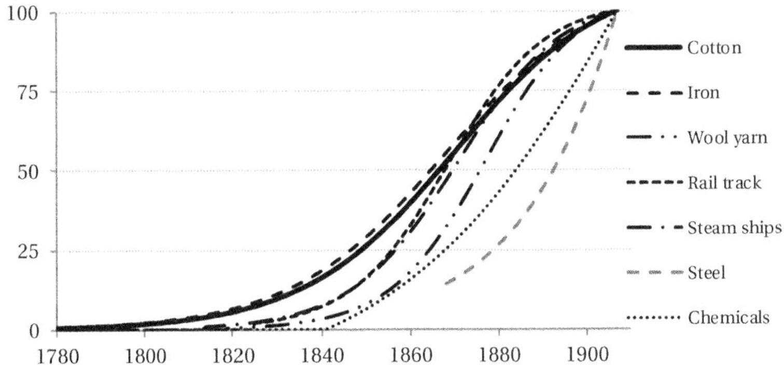

Sources: Data from Deane and Cole (1969) and Mitchell (1988).

One important message is the sequence. Cotton and iron were the first to move into rapid growth. These were followed 50 or so years later by mechanical transportation – railways and shipping. Production of woolen goods started its rapid growth a further 10 years on. Finally, steel and chemicals were the last to move, beginning their rapid growth in the 1870s.

The time pattern of adoption of new processes or of the industries created from new processes is shown in Table 3.12.

Table 3.12 Time pattern of adoption of new technologies

Product	Key innovation What	When	Year of 90% penetration	Years to 90%	Nature of the innovation
Iron	Coke blast furnace	1760	1907	147	Cost reduction
Cotton	Arkwright's Cromford Mill	1776	1908	132	New industry
Railway, passenger	Stephensons, L&MR	1830	1926	96	New industry
Railway,	Stephensons,	1830	1919	89	New industry
Woolen textiles	Hattersley loom	1834	1939	105	Cost reduction
Shipping	Metal hull, steam engine	1845	1897	52	Cost reduction
Steel	Bessemer converter	1860	1969	109	Cost reduction

Some industries had several key innovations; in these cases the earliest or the most important innovation is used. The two key innovations for iron were Abraham Darby II's coke blast furnace, cutting the cost of cast iron, in 1760 and Henry Cort's mill, cutting the cost of wrought iron, in 1784; we use the coke blast furnace in the Table as this opened the way to the widespread use of iron. The time taken for iron to achieve full market penetration is extended by the production of pig iron as a step in steel production with steel ultimately superseding iron in machinery and other applications. Cotton processing had several key innovations but Arkwright's Cromford Mill by 1776 brought together three of the most important – the spinning frame, the carding engine and the factory concept. The railway is treated as two industries as it created two different markets, one moving people and the other moving freight. Modern shipping was created by three innovations – metal hulls and steam engines with screw propulsion; we use the propulsion time pattern in the Table. The penetration dates refer to the maximum market achieved by the product in its life cycle.

The first feature of these patterns is the long time taken for the new process or the new product to be adopted or to achieve its full market potential. The average time required for the new process or product to achieve 90% of its final market was 104 years. Even excluding iron (which complicates the timing as pig iron is counted in the production of steel, a later product) the average time to reach 90% of the final market was 97 years.

Later innovations were adopted more rapidly than earlier ones. The early leaders - cotton, iron and wool - required an average of 128 years to move from key innovation to 90% adoption. The later developments – in railways, shipping and steel – took an average of 87 years, only two-thirds as long. This is probably not surprising as the early innovations had to change attitudes which had been in place for centuries whereas the later innovations were introduced into an economy which was getting used to change.

There was no difference in the pace of adoption of cost cutting innovations and new product innovations - each required an average of just over 100 years to reach 90% adoption. This similarity probably reflects the consumer adoption process. Even process innovation works through consumer adoption as lower costs and prices open up an expanded market, similar to a new product creating a new market, and the process of adoption and market penetration then begins.

There is finally the question as to whether the Industrial Revolution was due to just one core innovation. This question follows in particular from the notion of "General Purpose Technologies" (GPTs) which has gained some currency in recent years. [Prominent works on GPTs include T.F. Bresnahan and M. Trajtenberg (1996), Boyan Jovanovic and Peter L. Rousseau (2005), and Richard G. Lipsey, Kenneth I. Carlaw and Clifford T. Bekar (2005).]

A GPT is seen as an epoch-defining technology which spreads through many industries, allowing costs to fall and, equivalently, productivity to increase. Bresnahan and Trajtenberg argue that a GPT is characterized by (1) pervasiveness – it spreads to most industries, (2) improvement – its performance is progressively improved over time, and (3) it is innovation spawning – it stimulates the invention of new products or processes. The most commonly discussed GPTs are the steam engine, electricity and computers; obviously, the steam engine is seen as defining Britain's Industrial Revolution.

N.F.R. Crafts (2004) has addressed directly the question of the steam engine as the GPT. Crafts uses growth accounting to estimate the contribution of steam power to British economic growth. He finds that steam did make an important contribution but as just one among several major contributors. Craft concludes that: "At no time is its impact large enough to dominate." Similarly, Table 3.12, above, indicates the principal new technologies and shows that steam power was just one among several. In addition, the speed and nature of the adoption of these innovations can be explained by the standard S-shaped (logistic) process without having to appeal to GPTs.

Our review suggests that the most important technological change was the application of capital to manufacturing with this capital embodying new and more productive technologies. Table 3.16, above, shows that 93% of overall TFP advance occurred in textiles, transport and agriculture. The advances in textiles were all about replacing traditional labor-based production by capital-based techniques. The advances in transport drew on new designs and low cost metals as well as steam power. And, the steam engine played little direct role in the agricultural advances which underpinned the Industrial Revolution. It happened that much of the capital in the new manufacturing industries was powered by steam engines but steam was just one among several key input technologies.

The central feature of the Industrial Revolution was innovation in products and processes. Most of these innovations were embodied in capital. However, many new technologies were involved; no one technology – steam power or anything else - was dominant. Innovation took place on a broad front in the agricultural, metals, textiles and transportation industries.

3.10.7 Accounting for growth

Growth in final output can be allocated to growth in factor inputs (in this case capital, labor and land) and improvements in the efficiency with which these inputs are converted into outputs, Total Factor Productivity. This is the standard growth accounting procedure. A growth accounting for Britain is shown in Table 3.13.

Table 3.13 Contributions to growth, 1760 - 1860

	Growth rate	Contribution	Share of growth
Capital	1.5	0.5	31%
Labor	1.2	0.6	34%
Land	0.4	0.1	3%
Factor inputs		1.2	69%
TFP		0.5	32%
Output	1.7	1.7	100%

Source: Data from Harley (1998).

Growth in factor inputs contributed 1.2% of the 1.7% rate of growth in output. This corresponds to 69% of output growth. The remaining 32% of output growth came from productivity increases. Capital, labor and productivity each contributed about one third of the overall growth in of the British economy.

This same growth accounting expressed in terms of output per worker is shown in Table 3.14:

Table 3.14 Growth in Output per Worker, 1760 - 1860

	Growth rate	Contribution	Share of growth
Capital per worker	0.4	0.1	23%
Land per worker	-0.8	-0.1	-22%
TFP	0.5	0.5	99%
Output per worker	0.5	0.5	100%

Source: Data from Harley (1998).

This growth accounting implies that, at the macroeconomic level, most of the growth in output per worker was due to productivity advance. Capital contributed to income growth as the capital/labor ratio was increasing. However, the capital contribution was negated by the effects of using less land per worker. This reflects the growth of manufacturing and associated service industries relative to the previously dominant industry of agriculture.

But this cannot be the end of the story concerning capital. Our analysis at the industry level strongly suggests that capital was crucial to the growth of the leading industries and to productivity advance in these industries. The quality of capital unquestionably increased in the leading industries. Although the capital/output ratio was declining by 0.2% a year the capital/labor ratio was increasing by 0.4% a year. Each worker had more capital and that capital must have been sufficiently productive that output per worker increased even more rapidly. Also, it seems likely that the heavy investment in the growth sectors (agriculture, iron, textiles, railways and shipping) was offset by light investment in the larger part of the economy which was not leading the growth. The implication is that the quality of capital, with innovations embodied in new investment, was the driving force behind the increase in productivity.

Industry productivity growth patterns are summarized in Table 3.15.

Table 3.15 Sources of productivity growth, 1780 - 1860

Sources of growth in National Income

	Share of Income	Industry TFP growth rate	Macro TFP growth rate
Cotton	5.0%	1.9%	0.13%
Worsteds	2.5%	1.3%	0.05%
Woolens	2.5%	0.6%	0.02%
Iron	1.4%	0.9%	0.02%
Canals and railways	5.0%	1.3%	0.09%
Shipping	4.3%	0.5%	0.03%
Agriculture	20.6%	0.7%	0.19%
Sum of growth industries	40%		0.53%
All other industries	60%	0.02%	0.02%
Total	100%		0.55%

Source: Data from Harley (1998).

Seven growth industries account for virtually all of the TFP growth in Britain up to 1860. These leading industries, accounting for some 40% of the economy, created all the productivity growth experienced in Britain; the other 60% of the economy exhibited no productivity growth. In effect, British economic growth was due to advances in these seven industries.

The concentrated nature of productivity growth becomes even more apparent at the sectoral level. Table 3.16 shows the contribution of four sectors to Britain's TFP growth. Overall productivity growth was concentrated in just three sectors – textiles, transport and agriculture.

Table 3.16 Productivity growth by sector

	Macro TFP growth rate	Share of Macro TFP growth
Textiles	0.20%	36%
Transport	0.12%	22%
Agriculture	0.19%	34%
Sum of growth sectors	0.51%	93%
Macro TFP growth	0.55%	100%

Source: Data from Harley (1998).

These are striking conclusions – virtually the entire improvement in output per worker in Britain in the first century of the Industrial Revolution was due to improvement in productivity. It is likely that most of this productivity advance was embodied in capital. In turn, virtually all the improvement in TFP came in just three sectors – agriculture, textiles and transport. Innovation and investment in just these three sectors launched to world into the modern era of economic growth.

3.10.8 Creating the conditions for growth

The island of Britain evolved into a single nation dominated by the English. England had conquered Wales in the 13th century. The struggle for power between England and Scotland went on for longer until formal unification of the two countries, with England the dominant partner, saw the creation of the Kingdom of Great Britain by the Treaty of Union in 1707.

Britain was invaded from abroad a number of times in the first millennium but the last invasion was by the Normans (French) in 1066. Thereafter, England successfully repelled invasion attempts, most notably by the Spanish in 1588. Britain continued to be involved in armed conflict in Europe with the power struggle with France continuing intermittently for centuries. However, these conflicts were fought out in continental Europe. The cost to England and Britain of these struggles was in money and men, not in risks to the territorial and social safety of the country.

The Charter of Liberties of the year 1100 bound the King to certain laws in his treatment of the church and aristocracy. This was the start of a long process which introduced the rule of law in place of the arbitrary power the monarch. The Magna Carta of 1215 introduced further restrictions on the King's power including the provision that any "freeman" could be punished only through the law of the land. There followed centuries of struggle, sometimes peaceful, sometimes violent, to transform England into a constitutional monarchy. The Civil War of 1642 – 1651 led to the more formal transfer of power to the Parliament. The so called "Glorious Revolution" of 1688 strengthened the rule of law with the passage of the Bill of Rights. In addition, Parliament was to be the representative of (some of) the people, introducing the beginnings of democratic government.

The church, so long a brake on progress in other European countries, no longer controlled the economic life of the country. Henry VIII, monarch from 1509 until his death in 1547, had set in train a process which was drastically to curtail the power of the church. The Catholic Church had owned as much as 33% of the land of England; Henry confiscated this land, selling most to the aristocracy. The economic power of the church was destroyed. The legal power of the Catholic Church similarly was terminated. Henry established a protestant church, the Church of England, which became the leading religion. The monarch remained head of the Church of England but Parliament was separate legally from the Church. The Civil War and the Glorious Revolution were in part about religion; the constitutional outcome to these events included the separation of church and state.

By the late 17th century Britain had arrived at a beneficent juncture. The country had been unified politically. A strong central government had been created in London. There was no risk of invasion from abroad. There was peace within the nation. The church had been removed from the economic stage. The state was disciplined by a somewhat rudimentary but nonetheless effective form of democracy. Social and economic activity operated within a well-defined legal framework. Individuals or partnerships or companies could now pursue their own interests, enter into enforceable contracts and, in the absence of income tax or most forms of sales tax, keep the financial rewards of their efforts. Within this stable and secure environment people had the ability and the incentive to pursue their own economic interests.

Britain had a productive base of natural resources. Its rainfall was sufficient to create rivers in most of England, rivers which could be exploited for power and for navigation. The rainfall, with the temperate climate, was sufficient to make Britain self-sufficient in the basic foodstuffs. Agricultural productivity had been slowly increasing for centuries, starting apparently in the 14th century. Britain had ample mineral resources, in particular coal, iron and tin, which had been known and exploited since time immemorial.

Being an island helped Britain in several ways. One was the ability to use coastal shipping to transport goods and even people around most areas of the country. Another was the emergence of a maritime tradition which allowed the emergence of the British Navy as the most powerful naval force in the world. This went hand in hand with the growth of Britain as a trading nation and, later on, with the creation of the British Empire. In later centuries, international trade was of great importance to Britain as a source of food and materials, as a market for British goods, and as a source of income to those involved in trade, shipping, finance and insurance. International trade created a commercial base involving the skills and services of a complex market economy, skills not found in a domestic economy based on rural production.

Britain in the 17th century was producing an economic surplus. The surplus was not being used by the church or the state. The largest element in government spending was on the military but this was around 3% of GDP in most years (although in times of foreign wars it increased to over 10%, the increase being debt financed). General government spending was less than 1% of GDP. This left most of the surplus in private hands. In 1700, for example, labor income was approximately 60% of National Income with land income accounting for 20% and capital income for another 20%. The 40% of income that went to land and capital means that there was a substantial surplus; undoubtedly part of this was used for personal consumption but there must also have been substantial capacity for investment.

Incomes and population had been increasing slowly since, at least, the mid-17th century. This appears to have been based on slowly increasing agricultural output. Then, the pace of agricultural advance accelerated. A sequence of important innovations began around 1700, such as new iron implements, the shift from oxen towards horses for draught power, the shift to four crop rotation, changes in land tenure to allow larger farms, and selective breeding to improve livestock and seeds. These agricultural advances were fundamentally important as agricultural output represented the major part of the typical budget (food accounted for over 50% of spending with fuel, light and clothing, mainly wool, absorbing a further 20%). By the early 18th century incomes appear to have increased to the extent that there emerged a degree of discretionary income – income in excess of that needed to purchase the traditional basics and so available for the purchase of different, non-basic goods.

Rising spending was pressing on the supply capacity for several important goods. Agricultural output was increasing and agriculture could meet growing demands. However, some minerals and some manufactures were running up against supply constraints. The minerals constraint involved water entering underground mines; the supply of iron was limited by the dwindling availability of forests to yield the charcoal used in smelting; and the supply of cotton was limited by the practices of the East India Company and by import restrictions which limited the availability and raised the prices of imported cotton goods. These supply constraints created opportunities for commercial gain, stimulating efforts to develop new processes and ways of meeting the growing demand for these goods. The innovations that resulted, primarily in cotton processing, iron production and mechanical power, did indeed allow supply to expand. These innovations transformed the cotton and iron industries.

Once production and income growth started, the rising demand for these core products created continuing opportunities for production improvement. The result was a growth process, a feedback loop wherein growth in spending leads to improvements in production capacity (through investment or through process innovations) then to more production, more income, more spending and so on. One production bottleneck after another was relieved by the introduction of new processes or new forms of organization in a process that occupied almost two centuries - from the early 18th century until 1913. This was the Industrial Revolution; this was the emergence of self-sustaining economic growth.

The emergence of economic growth was the result of many conditions. All of these conditions were necessary, none was sufficient. However, once the core conditions were in place, it took just one spark to light the fire of self-sustaining growth.

By the early 18th century Britain had a stable and secure economic environment with the rule of law, property rights, low taxation, and accountable government. People had the ability and incentive to pursue their own economic opportunities. Britain had ample resources to produce food and materials. There was a significant surplus available for investment. British agricultural productivity had been expanding slowly but steadily, generating a slow but steady increase in real incomes which was now creating the opportunity for new, discretionary spending. The core conditions were in place for growth. The spark that ignited the growth process was the emergence of profit opportunities arising from growing demand hitting against the limits of current supply capacity. Enterprising people set about and succeeded in finding new methods of production which overcame the supply constraints. Production and incomes then moved onto a path of self-sustaining growth.

Total spending or demand did not expand rapidly. It was important that excess demand conditions were modest – there was sufficient demand to create clear financial incentives to innovate but not so much as to spill over into inflation and the associated misallocation of resources. This contrasts to Spain where rapid spending growth resulted in inflation. Also, the supply constraints were concentrated in goods, such as cotton and iron, which permitted a change in production processes. This contrasts again with Spain where increased spending was directed to religious and military purposes which did not lead to productivity improvements.

The fulfilment of these necessary conditions together was sufficient to launch Britain onto the path of economic growth.

3.10.9 Analytical features

In this section we look at some of the analytical features of British growth. These might be helpful in identifying the general processes of economic growth.

The key processes involved in growth operate at the industry level, not the level of the economy as a whole. Six industries created growth in Britain – agriculture, cotton, woolens, iron and steel, railways and shipping. Agricultural growth created the discretionary incomes that stimulated the growth of cottons. Developments in iron interacted with this growth and, with the steam engine, led to the emergence of industrial growth. Application of the steam engine to mobile use created new transportation industries which accelerated the growth of the core industries. Later, the introduction of low cost steel gave a further boost to all these industries. The rest of the economy was pulled along through the rising incomes and through the supply chains associated with the growth industries.

These industries grew because of innovation in products and processes. What mattered was not simply innovation, it was innovation in creating products for which there were large potential markets and in improving efficiency in making these products. Market opportunities stimulated these innovations. The motivating factor was economic, the desire for personal wealth.

There doubtless were thousands of innovators whose work has passed into oblivion either because their product didn't work or, if it did work, no one wanted it. The few innovators who made the ground-breaking changes which launched growth industries had two things in common

– their products worked and there was a large potential demand for their product. Probably the best way of knowing that there is likely to be a large demand is to create something that relieves a bottleneck in existing supply arrangements. Many of the key innovations were of this type – Newcomen's engine, Watt's engine, Trevithick's engine, all the innovations in textiles, Darby's blast furnace, Cort's reverberatory furnace and rolling mill, Bessemer's converter, Brunel's ships. Even Stephenson's' railway was designed to reduce the burden of transporting freight. Some major products though were entirely new. A small number, such as Stephenson's railway passenger services, were unexpected successes – a new product appeared for which there was a large but previously unrecognized demand. Other major new products though catered to an obvious unmet demand; examples include municipal services such as water and sewerage services, urban mass transport and even education.

Something that all of these growth products have in common is the nature of their adoption. Whereas established products might grow at 1 or 2% a year, in line with population and/or incomes, successful new products grow along a S-shaped curve – slow initial uptake then rapid growth then declining growth rates as the market approaches saturation. The analytical form which best fits this industry growth is the logistic model. Our examination of British growth showed that the logistic model fit the data time and again.

Application of capital was central to all the industrial advances. Capital embodied the new production technologies. Typically, this capital reduced the need for labor. But, the effect on labor was complex. The demand for unskilled labor surged. This was for low skilled labor to operate the new machines. The previous artisan class of skilled labor in manufacturing was replaced by machines and their unskilled minders. A new class of skilled labor emerged – people with engineering and similar skills to design, build and maintain the new machines. At the same time a completely new type of labor emerged – people with the skills to manage and operate complex organizations.

Growth in the leading industries brought forth organizational changes – the cotton mill employing hundreds of operatives, railway companies involving hundreds of employees, large industrial plants encompassing a multitude of activities and people. These changes depended on the development of management systems, administrative systems and support systems, and also support industries, to sustain large and complex organizations.

Finally, there was the growth of government activity. This initially took the form of providing public goods – products such as water and sewerage systems, public health and police. Then, governments started providing products for which there was a clear demand but which, possibly because of lack of profitability, were not provided privately, products such as urban mass transport, education and hospitals.

The driving force behind the emergence of economic growth in Britain was individual initiative – individuals taking advantage of opportunities, including making their own opportunities, motivated by the desire for economic success (and probably also social standing). The market provided the coordination needed to move the whole system forward; this was Adam Smith's "invisible hand" in action.

Chapter 4

The leader – United States

4.1 The new leader

Economic growth began in England early in the 18th century. The United States at that time was in the early stages of settlement. Development proceeded slowly with the establishment of a new nation and with expansion westwards. The Civil War, 1861 – 1865, hastened development in the Union although at great cost, human and economic, to both sides. After the War, energies were redirected to reconstruction and to continued expansion to the west. Immigration hastened the pace of expansion. The new technologies of Europe, in particular of Britain, were copied and further developed. By the 1890s, the United States was forging ahead and beginning to challenge Britain for economic leadership. Early in the new century, America was asserting its leadership in new industries such as automobiles and electricity. Since that time, America has led the world in continuing economic growth.

As with Britain, growth in the United States started with agriculture. Then, steel, railroads, automobiles, electricity, consumer appliances, telecommunications and chemicals were among the new industries that pulled America forwards. Later in the 20th century, entertainment, electronics and new service industries continued the growth. Immigration and financial expansion helped sustain the growth. At the same time there has been continuing improvements in production efficiencies. The result has been a succession of changes – new industries and increasing productivity – which have driven ongoing growth in spending, production and incomes.

In this chapter we look at this sequence of changes, starting with agriculture then moving through manufacturing and on to services, which have resulted in economic growth. We examine the leading industries and then bring these changes together to investigate the nature and mechanisms of economic growth.

4.2 Agriculture

4.2.1 Importance

Agriculture has always been of huge importance to the United States economy. In early times, some 80% of the people worked on the land or in directly related occupations. Tobacco and cotton were the largest export industries. Production increased in the 19th and 20th centuries to feed the rapidly growing population and to keep exports growing. Rapid productivity improvements, particularly in the 20th century, allowed production to increase even while labor input declined. Productivity increased so rapidly that farms now account for only 1% of workers and 2% of GDP.

Farming now takes place in all states across a wide range of products. The leading products in 2009 are shown in Table 4.1.

Table 4.1 10 highest value farm products, 2009

Value of farm receipts, $ billion

Cattle	44
Corn	42
Soybeans	30
Dairy products	24
Chickens, broilers	22
Vegetables	21
Fruits, nuts	19
Hogs	14
Wheat	11
Chickens, eggs	6
Subtotal	233
Total farm receipts	283
Relative to GDP	2.0%

Source: Data from U.S. Department of Agriculture (2011a).

4.2.2 Development of agriculture

Early America was largely agricultural. Agriculture was concentrated on the east coast with arable crops and livestock in New England and the mid-Atlantic states, tobacco in the Carolinas and long staple cotton in Georgia.

Two forces changed this picture. Eli Whitney's invention of the cotton gin ("gin" being an abbreviation of engine) in 1793 (allowing the mechanical removal of seeds from the bols) made practicable the production of thread from short staple cotton. Unlike the long staple variety, short staple cotton could be grown in the inland areas of Georgia across to Mississippi and, ultimately, in Louisiana and Texas. Cotton became the largest industry and largest export product. Cotton production increased at an average rate of 10% a year from 1793 to 1859. Meanwhile, the increasing population, looking for more land and better farming conditions than those in New England, pushed into the Midwest. Transportation links, such as the opening of the Erie Canal in 1825, stimulated the settlement of the Midwest. It is estimated that farm output increased by a factor of six between 1800 and 1860 (see Sidney Ratner et al (1979)). There was only limited growth in productivity; more than 85% of the increase in came from increasing inputs – applying more land, more labor and more capital, essentially scaling up the production configuration which existed in 1800.

Agricultural expansion entered a different phase after the Civil War. This was associated with opening up for farming the vast areas of productive land between the Alleghenies and the Rockies. Farming pushed westwards. The "wheat frontier" steadily moved west with high value farming filling in behind the frontier and low density farming, such as ranching, moving ahead of the frontier. The driving force was population growth and an important enabling force was the spread of railroads. A notable date was the completion of the first trans-continental railroads in 1869 but railroad construction continued apace until the length of track reached a peak in 1925. From 1865 to 1925 the length of track increased at an average rate of 4.2% a year.

Transportation advance went hand in hand with immigration and land policy. Federal land and homesteading policies together with railroads selling land cheaply, made farming accessible virtually to anyone who wished. Many of those who wished were immigrants to America. Large scale immigration continued until World War I. From 1860 to 1913, the area farmed rose from 0.4 to 0.9 billion acres; the area then increased more slowly, reaching 1.1 billion acres in 1936.

Agricultural production and population grew steadily until the 1930s. Productivity started to increase more rapidly in the 20th century but still most of the increase in output was due to more inputs. Use of capital was increasing; mechanization had started in the late 19th century and this gathered pace following the introduction of the Fordson tractor in 1917. However, growth until the 1930s was by expansion rather than restructuring.

The 1930s marked a transition in agriculture. The Great Depression had cut demand for agricultural goods and had slashed farm incomes. The Dust Bowl, particularly severe in 1934 and 1936, further cut incomes in Oklahoma and neighboring states. Many farmers left their land. Some went to agricultural work in California, others went to the cities. In any event, there was a basic change in the nature of agriculture. Farmers started producing in a different way – farm management improved, farms became fewer and larger, the trend to mechanization, which already was underway, accelerated and there was a steady increase in use of capital, soil management improved with changes in crop selection, use of fertilizer and irrigation, and there was considerable development of seeds and pesticides. Agriculture moved into the modern era.

Figure 4.1 indicates these changes. Agriculture expanded until the 1930s mainly due to the application of more inputs. Productivity then took off, providing most of the subsequent growth in output. Input of capital increased slowly until the 1980s but has since declined. Labor input has decreased dramatically. Meanwhile, farm output increased at 1.7% a year, exceeding population growth of 1.2%. Agriculture has not only fed the growing population but also has continued to export and has become an important source of materials for industrial processing.

Figure 4.1 Growth of U.S. agriculture
Year 1929 = 100

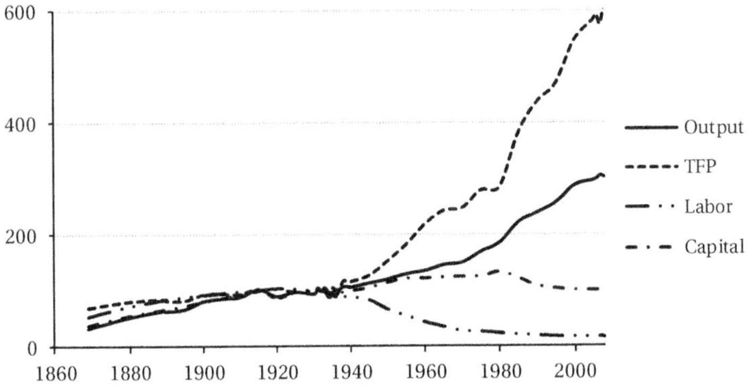

Sources: Data from Kendrick (1961) and (1973). U.S. Department of Agriculture (2011b).

The changing productivity of agriculture is shown in Table 4.2. Output grew by 1.7% a year but productivity growth allowed inputs, particularly of labor, to decline. The growing number of tractors suggests that the equipment component of capital increased rapidly. Use of chemicals, mainly fertilizers, herbicides and pesticides, also grew rapidly and doubtless the productive effectiveness of these inputs also has continually been improved.

Table 4.2 Growth rates for agriculture, 1936 - 2008

Output	1.7%
Farm land	-0.2%
Labor input	-2.3%
Number of tractors	3.7%
Agricultural chemicals	3.0%
Total inputs	-0.8%
Total Factor Productivity	2.5%

Sources: Data from Kendrick (1961) and (1973). U.S. Department of Agriculture (2011b). U.S. Census Bureau, Historical Statistics of the United States and annual Statistical Abstracts.

The mechanization of farms and the continuing increase in productivity has released labor. There has been massive movement of people off of farms. The farm population in 1936 was 31.7 million; the number of farm operators in 2007 was just 3.3 million. Farm people moving to the cities, internal migration, was an important feature of mid-20th century America.

4.2.3 Capital

The application of capital, partly to replace human and animal effort and partly to carry out new functions, has been central in the development of agriculture. This has been a story of structures, equipment and the internal combustion engine. We mention the highlights of this process.

Eli Whitney's cotton gin permitted the farming of short staple cotton across broad reaches of the southern states. Whitney's gin was inexpensive to build, easy to copy and did not have effective patent protection so its use spread widely and rapidly. Production of cotton, already substantial, expanded massively.

John Deere, a blacksmith, developed a cast steel plow in 1836. This smooth sided plow was well suited to turning the Midwestern soils as it avoided the need for frequent cleaning. Deere's company moved to Illinois, for access to transport links, and began supplying implements throughout the Midwest. John Deere began a network of independent dealers in 1869. The company later moved into the manufacture of tractors and other farm machinery.

Cyrus McCormick and his family developed a mechanical reaper which was introduced in the 1850s. Like John Deere, the McCormicks moved to Illinois because of its transport links to materials and to markets. The McCormick Harvesting Machine Company developed new marketing techniques, in particular a network of trained salesmen able to demonstrate products in the field and sell directly to farmers.

The combine harvester has become central to grain operations. The combine does reaping, threshing and winnowing so that the seed is delivered from the machine to an accompanying truck. The combine was invented in 1834 by Hiram Moore but it took until the 1880s for commercially viable combines to be developed (in Australia). These combines were pulled by horse or mule teams. A steam-driven self-propelled combine was produced by the Holt Manufacturing Company in California in 1911. The Curtis brothers in Kansas introduced a gasoline-powered combine, using a Fordson tractor engine, in the 1920s. Gasoline powered and more recently diesel powered combines have become the norm. Improvements in the cutting head, in power (with the move to diesel engines) and size, in threshing and, more recently, in instrumentation and control systems have continued to improve the effectiveness of combine harvesters. John Deere and International Harvester (the successor to the McCormick Company) are among the leaders in combine production.

Grain elevators use elevators, conveyers and bins for the storage and handling of grain. Grain elevators mechanize movement of grain from one transport mode, such as wagons or trucks, to another, such as railroads or even ships. The first grain elevator was steam powered, built in Buffalo, New York at the meeting of the Erie Canal and the Great Lakes shipping routes. Subsequently, grain elevators have spread throughout the grain areas of the Midwest and central United States.

Irrigation is used to allow crops to be farmed in the west, particularly California, and to increase crop production in states west of the Mississippi River. Western irrigation mainly uses surface water, transported by pipeline and aqueduct, while irrigation in states such as Nebraska, Texas and Arkansas uses aquifer water. Around 5% of the total farmed area is irrigated.

Probably the central player in farm mechanization has been the tractor. Tractors initially replaced horses and mules in providing tractive power – pulling plows and other farm implements. The first tractors were steam powered, the so called "traction engines". Gasoline powered tractors emerged in the early 20th century. The breakthrough came in 1917 when Henry Ford introduced the Fordson tractor. This had an innovative design, using the engine block as the backbone of the vehicle, and established the standard design for subsequent tractors. Reflecting its simple design and Ford's manufacturing efficiencies, the Fordson was affordable, priced as low as $750, and created a mass market in tractors. More than 500,000 Fordsons were built at Ford's Dearborn factory.

There has been enormous development of the tractor since the basic design was established by the Fordson. Important advances include:

- Power shifted from gasoline engines to diesel engines from the 1950s and 1960s;
- Tractors came in a variety of power and sizes, with modern tractors ranging from under 20 to more than 550 horsepower;
- Transmissions were extended to cover multispeed and multirange, manual and automatic gearboxes;

- Drive was extended to cover 2 and 4 wheel drive and even caterpillar tracks;
- Enclosed cabs with climate control improved safety and operator comfort;
- The three point hitch allowed easy management of towed equipment;
- Power delivery through mechanical, hydraulic and electrical linkages enabled many types of attachments to be operated;
- A wide range of implements attaching to or pulled by tractors mechanized all sorts of farm operations in plowing, planting, cutting, lifting, digging etc. etc.;
- Electronics have improved navigation, control and performance.

The tractor has become the ubiquitous farm tool. However, adoption of the tractor and its application to farm tasks took many years. Figure 4.2 shows the average number of tractors per farm as well as a logistic model of these numbers. The model suggests that the market has probably now reached saturation at around 2.1 tractors per farm and that it has taken around 70 years to reach this point.

Figure 4.2 Tractors per farm, 1910 - 1985

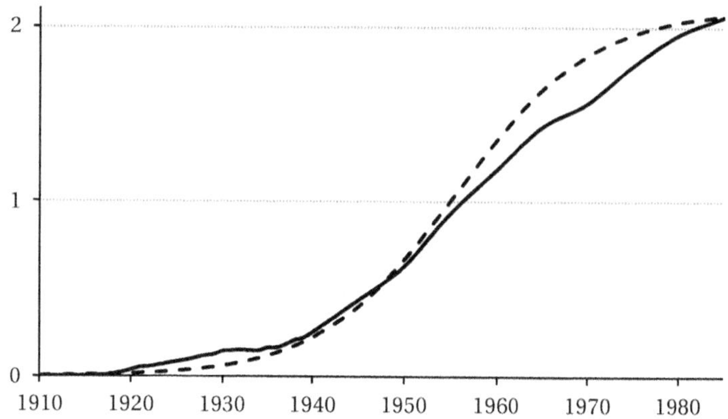

Sources: Data from U.S. Census Bureau, Historical Statistics of the United States and annual Statistical Abstracts.

The structure of capital in the growth of agriculture is shown in Figure 4.3. This graph goes only through 1955 but it clearly shows the mechanization of farming. Land and structures have increased modestly. The big change has involved equipment – the replacement of animal power by machines and the use of equipment. The use of work animals grew strongly over the 19th century, as equipment such as plows, threshers and harvesters was introduced, but peaked in the 1910s; since then tractors have taken over the provision of motive power. Tractors have provided a capable and flexible power source which has allowed the mechanization of agriculture.

Figure 4.3 Growth of capital in agriculture

Capital stock in constant dollars. 1937 = 100

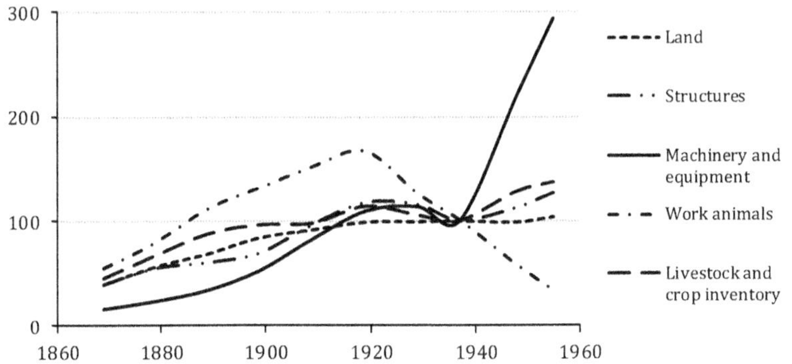

Source: Data from Kendrick (1961).

4.2.4 Biology

The application of biology has greatly increased the productivity of agriculture. Selective breeding of seeds and livestock has been going on for centuries but the pace picked up in the 1920s, leading to higher crop yields from the 1930s. This was followed by mutational breeding and the development of hybrid varieties; this allowed yields to continue to increase for many decades. Development is now focused on genetic modification using biological engineering.

Corn gives a good example of these changes. Yields, in bushels per acre, increased at an average of 1.6% a year over the 20th century. It is estimated that genetic improvements accounted for 59% of the increase in yields between 1940 and 1980 (see V.B. Cardwell (1982)). The remaining 41% of the increase was mainly due to increased use of synthetic fertilizers. After the introduction of genetically engineered seeds in the 1990s, the increase has been due entirely to genetic improvements.

The adoption of genetically engineered seeds after their introduction in 1996 provides an interesting example of technical change. Genetic engineering has incorporated desirable characteristics in seeds, the main characteristics being herbicide tolerance (HT seeds) and insect resistance (Bt for seeds which contain a gene from the soil bacterium Bacillus thuringienis). The U.S. Department of Agriculture has surveyed farmers as to their reasons for adopting genetically modified seeds. The findings, summarized in Table 4.3, show that the principal motivation was to obtain higher yields. Secondary reasons were to reduce pesticide and herbicide costs and to reduce the time spent on operations and management. About two thirds of the motivation was to increase revenue, the rest was to reduce costs.

Table 4.3 Farmers' reasons for adopting GM crops

	HT soybeans	Bt corn	Bt cotton	HT cotton
Increase yields	63	79	59	60
Decrease pesticide costs	17	9	15	11
Save time	17	6	23	26
Other	3	6	3	3
Total	100	100	100	100

Source: Data from Fernandez-Cornejo, Jorge and Margriet Caswell (2006).

Adoption of genetically modified crops has been rapid. Figure 4.4 shows that adoption reached more than 90% in just 15 years. Adoption has followed a logistic pattern (although the smooth logistic curves are not shown in the Figure). The speed of adoption is not entirely unexpected as the change involved switching seed purchases while the rest of farm operations and management remained essentially the same; no new consumer products or markets were involved.

Figure 4.4 Adoption of genetically modified crops

Percent of acres using gm seeds

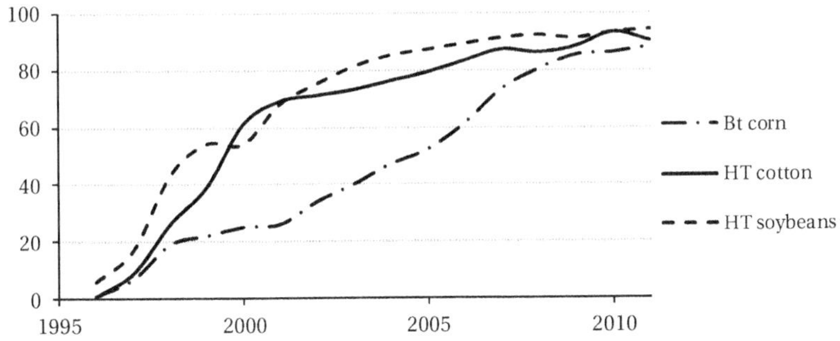

Source: Data from Fernandez-Cornejo, Jorge and Margriet Caswell (2006).

4.2.5 Chemicals

All plants need carbon, hydrogen and oxygen; these are supplied by water and air (for carbon dioxide). Plants also need macronutrients (elements needed in relatively large quantities) and micronutrients (elements needed in trace quantities). The three main macronutrients are nitrogen (N), phosphorus (P) and potassium (K); these form the so called "NPK" mixture. Fertilizers to provide the main macronutrients have been in use for centuries. Today, synthetic fertilizers, which are manufactured rather than directly mined, provide the required macro and micronutrients.

The use of synthetic fertilizers began with nitrogen fertilizers using technologies developed in Europe in the 19th and early 20th centuries. There are many forms of nitrogen fertilizer, providing nitrogen either in ammonium or nitrate form. A common manufacturing method is the Haber-Bosch process, invented in the 1910s, which uses natural gas for the hydrogen and air for the nitrogen to make ammonia which then serves as the basis for fertilizers such as urea. Phosphate fertilizers are produced by treating rock phosphate with acid – either sulfuric acid to make P fertilizer or nitric acid to make a P and N fertilizer. Potassium fertilizers are made from mined potash.

The use of commercial fertilizers began to increase early in the 20th century then accelerated after World War II. Figure 4.5 shows this growth. The adoption of fertilizer has closely followed a logistic path. It took almost 100 years for the process to work through, from introduction of commercial fertilizers to market saturation.

Figure 4.5 Use of commercial fertilizers

Tons, year 2000 = 100

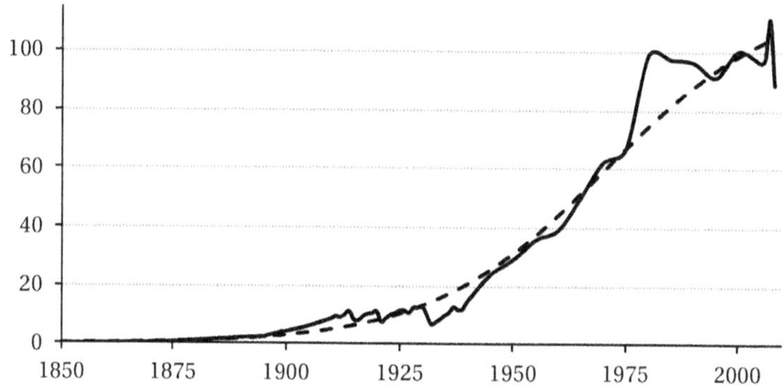

Sources: Data from U.S. Census Bureau, Historical Statistics of the United States and and annual Statistical Abstracts.

These fertilizers allow the continuous farming of land, obviating the need for the previous practice of crop rotation and/or fallow cycles. Obviously, continuous farming of single crops improves the productivity of land. In addition, the application of fertilizer allows the more intensive farming of land. This is particularly important today as fertilizers are essential in obtaining the high yields associated with modern hybrid and genetically engineered seeds. It has been estimated that 30 to 50% of the increase in yields since 1940 has been due to the increased use of commercial fertilizers (see L.B. Nelson (1990)).

Chemical herbicides have become widely used since World War II. The first widely used herbicide was 2,4-D, effective against broad leaf plants, and developed by a paint company in the late 1940s. Atrazine, used against broadleaf plants and grassy weeds was introduced in the 1950s. Glyphosate, often used under the brand name Roundup, was introduced in the 1970s and is widely used for non-selective weed control. Glyphosate-tolerant strains of several crops have been developed; these allow glyphosate to be used for weed control, reducing costs compared to the use of mechanical weeding.

A wide range of other pesticides have been developed to target specific pests. Examples are insecticides, fungicides and rodenticides. These are used to reduce losses of crops, to improve the health of livestock and to improve the lifetime of horticultural products.

4.2.6 Chickens

A prime example of agricultural change is in chicken farming. Chickens produce two separate outputs - eggs and meat. In early days, chickens were kept on farms as an adjunct to other activities. Eggs were the main product with old females and surplus males used for meat. Then, a series of technical and management changes transformed chicken farming into an industrial operation.

The first change came in the 1920s with the discovery of vitamin D. Adding vitamin D to the feed allowed the birds to do without sunlight so they could be kept inside. Chickens now began to be farmed. By the 1950s, the norm was a family farm with up to 1,000 birds. A move to large scale farming began in the 1960s. The family chicken farm gave way to corporate businesses. Scale increased so that today there might well be more than 100,000 birds on one farm. Buildings and equipment were optimized for particular tasks with mechanized handling systems, climate control, artificial lighting cycles and artificial incubators. Feed was optimized, particularly to give rapid weight gain for meat birds, and came to include grain products, vitamins and antibiotics.

By the 1930s, scientific breeding had developed two different lines of birds, one for eggs and a different one for meat, or what became known as broilers. These specialized lines became much more productive. In

1900, average egg production was 83 eggs per hen per year; by 2000 this figure was over 300. For broilers, the aim was to get the bird to target weight as quickly as possible. With specially bred species and carefully designed feeding, a bird today reaches the target weight in as little as five weeks.

The combination of management change, scale, application of science and application of specialized capital has vastly increased productivity. Labor requirement per unit of output declined at 6.2% a year over the period 1930 to 1985. We estimate that input-to-output productivity has increased at 2.2% a year over the period 1965 to 2005. This productivity growth has allowed prices to decline. For broilers, the price decline has been so great that it has created a new market in chicken meat. In 1930 virtually the whole market for chicken products was for eggs; the market for meat was extremely small. With the development of the broiler and the rapid reduction in broiler prices, the consumption of broilers has grown rapidly (at an average of 8.4% a year from 1936 to 2008) and chicken has now passed beef as the principal meat consumed in the United States.

4.2.7 How did agriculture grow?

The development of American agriculture is a long story of growth. It is instructive to look at how it happened.

A necessary reason for the growth was that there was demand for agricultural products. The markets initially were to sustain the population and, with tobacco and cotton, to export to European markets. Natural increase and massive immigration then led to rapid and continuing growth in demand to feed and clothe the domestic population. Export demand for new products, such as wheat, soybeans and corn, added to growth. Finally, declining prices allowed new markets to be developed, such as chicken broilers for meat and corn for animal feed and industrial feedstock.

Although there were important steps to mechanization, such as Eli Whitney's cotton gin, John Deere's plow and Cyrus McCormick's reaper, most of the growth right into the 20th century came from bringing more land and other resources into agricultural production.

This growth in output, more or less in line with population, came from expansion rather than change. The Great Depression and the Dust Bowl of the 1930s brought this expansion to an end, forcing farmers to do things differently and better just to survive. Modern agriculture began at this time. Agricultural growth since the 1930s has come predominantly from productivity advance, not from increasing inputs. These large productivity gains have been the result of (1) mechanization, in particular based on the internal combustion engine, (2) chemicals, in particular the development of synthetic fertilizers and pesticides, (3) biological science, in particular the selective breeding of seeds and livestock, and the genetic modification of seeds, and (4) better management as farming became a market-driven, capital-intensive and technologically advancing business.

The early productivity advances were the result of individuals looking for ways of easing production bottlenecks. These were individuals such as Eli Whitney, John Deere and Cyrus McCormick. Over the 20th century though, sources of innovation were more the work of companies, whether the Fordson tractor or Monsanto with seeds and herbicides or Tyson Foods and other large producers of broilers. Applied science has become an important source of innovation, particularly in seeds and agricultural chemicals. The thread running through all these advances has been profit-oriented farmers looking for and adopting new methods of production either to ease production bottlenecks or to exploit market opportunities.

4.2.8 Agriculture in economic growth

Agriculture has fed the growing population but has not grown as rapidly as the rest of the economy; agriculture has been important in enabling growth but it did not lead economic growth. Table 4.4 shows the trends.

Table 4.4 Agriculture in economic growth

Average annual growth rates

	1860-1931	1937-2008
Farm output	1.9%	1.7%
Population	1.9%	1.2%
Real GDP	3.4%	3.7%

Sources: Data from Kendrick (1961) and (1973). U.S. Department of Agriculture (2011b). U.S. Census Bureau, Historical Statistics of the United States and annual Statistical Abstracts. U.S. Bureau of Economic Analysis, National Economic Accounts.

In fact, agriculture has declined from being the dominant industry almost to insignificance. In colonial times, agriculture and related activities absorbed 80% of the population; after the Civil War approximately half of the population was on farms but today this figure is down to 1%. Figure 4.6 shows the decline of agriculture in terms of labor and in terms of production.

Figure 4.6 Agriculture in the economy

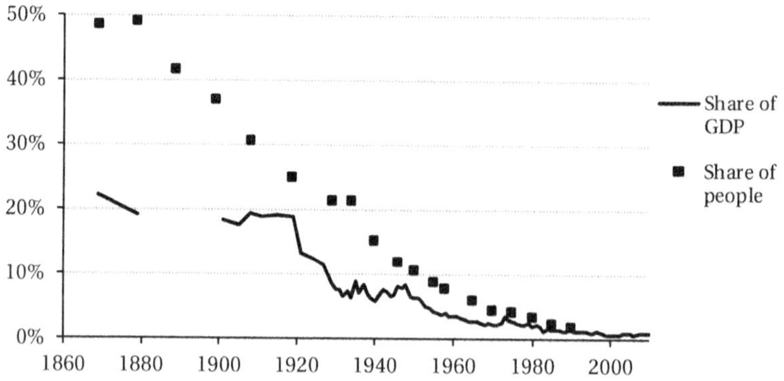

Sources: Data from U.S. Census Bureau, Historical Statistics of the United States and annual Statistical Abstracts.

Agriculture clearly did not lead U.S. economic growth but it nonetheless was essential to growth – agriculture fed and clothed the growing population and also generated income from exports but the main contribution was to do this while releasing enormous volumes of resources to the rest of the economy. The dual effect was, through declining prices, to release enormous purchasing power into the hands (or wallets) of consumers for the purchase of new goods and services.

As farming today employs 1% of the labor force, agriculture has released around 79% of the labor force (compared to 1776) or 47% of the labor force (compared to 1869) for use elsewhere in the economy. If this labor had not been released, the nonfarm economy, today 99% of the economy, would have been smaller. If the size reduction is the same as the labor reduction then the economic growth rate from 1870 to 2010 would have been 3.0% instead of the actual 3.5% a year. The growth in real GDP per capita would have been reduced from 2.0% a year to 1.5%. The economy would still have increased if there had been no increase in farm productivity but the growth rates would have been significantly less. Agricultural advance contributed up to 0.5% a year to growth or one fourth of all growth in average incomes.

Increasing agricultural productivity had a similar effect when looked at in terms of spending. Increasing productivity allowed the relative prices of agricultural products to decline. This meant that demand for agricultural goods could be met with a reduced expenditure, releasing income for spending on other goods and services. This effect was large as agriculture was such a large part of the economy - in 1869 it represented around 22% of GDP. Agricultural productivity over the next 140 years increased at an average of 1.6% a year. The income released by these productivity gains would have allowed other spending to increase more rapidly. This effect added around 0.4% a year to the growth of the economy and of average incomes. (This is a different way of looking at the growth effects examined in the previous paragraph.)

4.3 Electricity

4.3.1 Electricity supply

Michael Faraday in Britain constructed an electrical generator, a machine which produced electricity from motion within a magnetic field; that was in 1831. James Clerk Maxwell later expressed Faraday's many discoveries in electro-magnetism in systematic, mathematical form. Faraday and Maxwell laid the intellectual basis of electric generation and electric drive. However, it would be many years before these insights were converted into useful form.

It was 50 years later, in 1882, when Thomas Edison put electricity to commercial use. Edison's famous Pearl Street generating plant in New York City, powered by steam engines, supplied a number of Wall Street offices; the electricity was used for lighting. Although Edison's name is closely associated with electricity his contribution in fact was relatively limited. Edison developed an effective and durable light bulb and a system to provide customer and public lighting and this initially was the principal market for electricity. However, Edison used direct current (DC) which was difficult to distribute as the voltage could not be changed (transformed). Alternating current (AC) proved to be much more useful. It was Nicola Tesla who pioneered AC, obtaining his key patents in 1887. AC can be transformed, allowing high voltage to minimize resistive losses in transmission and low voltages for safe use in the customer's premises. And, Edison's steam engines were not well suited to electricity generation. The generation breakthrough was made by Charles Parsons in Britain with his steam turbine generator (turbogenerator) being introduced commercially in 1889.

George Westinghouse made electricity accessible for practical use. Westinghouse had been working on distribution systems, including AC transformers and also a meter to record power use. He then obtained patent rights to Tesla's AC electric motor. The elements were now in place. Westinghouse in 1895 constructed the breakthrough system – a generating plant at Niagara Falls with three 3.7 megawatt (MW) Tesla-style generators supplying an aluminum smelter at Niagara and also transmitting electricity by tower line 25 miles to supply the city of

Buffalo. This system defined the core features of the entire industry that followed – three phase alternating current at 60 hertz (cycles per second) with high voltage transmission and with most residential application at 120 volts.

The principal supply developments since 1895 have been in generation. Hydro generation – using flowing water to turn generators – was the initial preference but the shortage of suitable sites limited its expansion. The steam turbine was more flexible. The Parsons steam-powered turbogenerator was progressively improved in efficiency and increased in size. Fuel choice has always reflected the economics at the time of design. Coal has generally been competitive and has accounted for around 50% of generation. Oil was used in the early days but became too expensive after the 1973 price shock. Nuclear generation, using fission to raise steam to drive a conventional turbogenerator, came into use in the 1960s and 1970s but regulatory uncertainty and high capital costs have limited its subsequent growth. In recent decades, gas turbines were introduced for peaking generation and then as fuel-efficient combined cycle generators (a gas turbine with the waste heat used to drive a steam turbine). Large scale generators, such as units of 1,000 megawatts each, have provided economies of scale and have been integrated into the supply system by means of extensive high voltage transmission networks.

The final feature in the development of the electricity industry has been the growth of specialist producers – electric utilities. In the early days, most electricity was generated by industrial customers for their own use. In 1902, only 42% of generation was by specialist producers. Since then, however, it has proved more economic for generation to be done by specialist utilities rather than in-house. Today, more than 95% of all generation is by electric utilities.

4.3.2 Generation productivity

John Kendrick's (1961) numbers imply that total factor productivity in the electric utility industry from 1899 to 1953 increased at a trend rate of 5.1%. Our calculations give a trend increase from 1907 to 1970 of 3.1% a year. Both approaches suggest that there was rapid productivity advance for the first 75 years of the industry. This allowed declining prices which added to the growth of electricity consumption.

After the early 1970s, though, productivity growth appears to have slowed or even stopped. There were several reasons for this slowdown. The thermal efficiency of generation from fossil fuels, which had been rising at more than 3% a year, was largely over by the 1960s. Related to this, the adoption of large central station generators, which are relatively efficient, had been completed by the 1970s. The growth of nuclear generation, rapid after 1970, was bad for productivity as the capital cost of nuclear plants turned out to be extremely high. The rise in oil prices after 1973 led to the phasing out of generation using petroleum, previously a low cost option. Finally, the introduction of environmental regulations beginning in the early 1970s increased the capital and operating costs of coal generation.

4.3.3 Demand for electricity

Electricity was initially used mostly for lighting where incandescent light bulbs provided far better service than previous, combustion lighting. After Westinghouse's creation of an AC system, the market for electricity in residences, manufacturing and offices took off. In manufacturing, electric drive was far more convenient and economical for most factory applications than steam engines and internal combustion engines. The adoption of electric drive in manufacturing is shown in Figure 4.7. This adoption, which followed a standard logistic pattern, was relatively rapid, taking only around 40 years.

Figure 4.7 Electricity share of drive in manufacturing

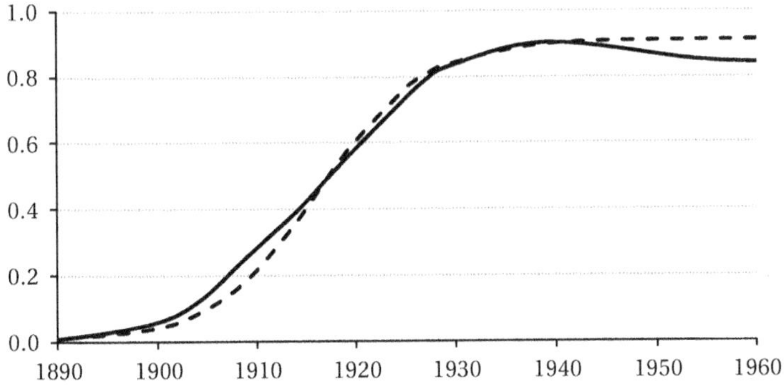

Sources: Data from U.S. Census Bureau, Historical Statistics of the United States and annual Statistical Abstracts.

Meanwhile, work was proceeding apace on building distributed generation plants and connecting residences, as well as businesses, to the electricity system. Figure 4.8 shows the time path of residential connections, along with a fitted logistic curve. The Great Depression and World War II slowed the adoption of electricity, delaying saturation by at least 10 years, but by the mid-1950s virtually all of America was connected to electric utilities.

Figure 4.8 Share of residences with electricity

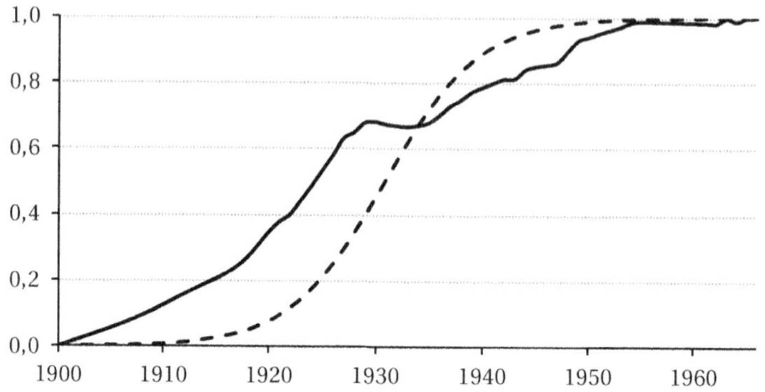

Sources: Data from U.S. Census Bureau, Historical Statistics of the United States and annual Statistical Abstracts.

Electric drive provided an effective way of mechanizing many household tasks. A wave of labor-saving home appliances appeared. The clothes washing machine became available by 1910, the electric vacuum cleaner in the 1910s, the refrigerator in the 1920s, the automatic washing machine in the 1930s. The 1950s saw a plethora of new electric appliances, from major appliances such as dishwashers, clothes driers and room air conditions to dozens of small appliances and tools for kitchen, home and workshop use.

Electricity allowed the creation of a whole new set of goods and services – those such as entertainment and information processing – based on electronics. Radio was introduced in the 1920s and television in the 1940s. Electronic entertainment and information devices - such as televisions, audio systems, video systems, games and computers – followed in the 1970s and beyond.

Figure 4.9 shows the electrification of the home, with actual electricity use along with its fitted logistic curve.

Figure 4.9 Average electricity use per residence

Thousand kilowatt hours per annum

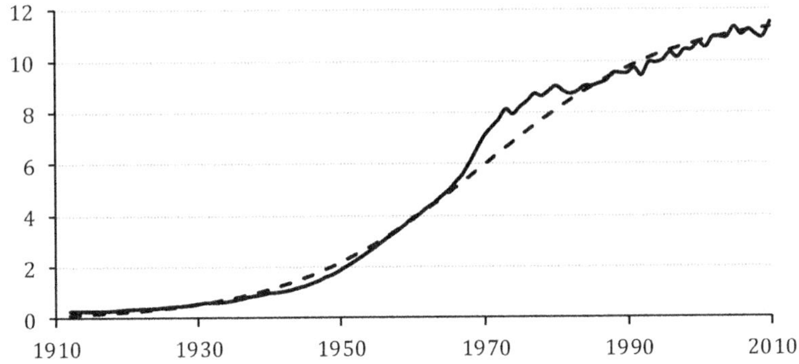

Sources: Data from U.S. Census Bureau, Historical Statistics of the United States and annual Statistical Abstracts.

The residential market for electricity is now saturated. The process has taken around 100 years. This is similar to the time taken to reach saturation in manufacturing. Although the market for electric drive in manufacturing reached saturation in only 40 years, the market for electricity in manufacturing in general became saturated only around 2000, some 100 years after its introduction. The reason for the different speeds of adoption is that the key industrial using devices, the light bulb and the electric motor, involved replacing existing, less efficient equipment (so there was no new market to be created) whereas the great growth in household demand, apart from lighting, came from appliances and devices which were invented only after electricity had become established (so whole new markets had to be created).

Electricity has become essential to virtually all aspects of the modern economy, the modern home and the modern office. In households it provides light, powers appliances and entertainment devices; in manufacturing it provides drive; in business and government it provides lighting, ventilation and cooling, and powers elevators, office equipment and communications systems. And, electricity is essential to every motor vehicle, every telephone and every piece of electronic equipment.

4.3.4 Electricity and economic growth

Electricity has become one of the most widely used goods in the modern economy. Demand has been increasing ever since its introduction in the 1890s. However, growth has decelerated, as expected in the adoption of any new product. Table 4.5 shows the changes in trend in 1929 and 1973. 1929 saw the onset of the Great Depression, bringing an end to the initial stage of rapid expansion. 1973 saw both the saturation of some use markets and also the end of the declining price of electricity. After 1973, electricity use continued to increase but now less rapidly than the economy.

Table 4.5 Growth of electricity and the economy

Average annual growth rates

	Generation	GDP
1902 - 1929	11.7%	3.2%
1929 - 1973	6.5%	3.7%
1973 - 2010	2.2%	2.7%
1902 - 2010	6.3%	3.2%

Sources: Data from Maddison (2006b). U.S. Census Bureau. Historical Statistics of the United States and annual Statistical Abstracts. U.S. Bureau of Economic Analysis, National Economic Accounts.

Figure 4.10 shows the electricity intensity of the economy. Electricity production and use increased much more rapidly than the economy until 1973. Since then, the electricity intensity has declined. Even electricity use per person, which continued to increase after 1973, appears now to have peaked.

Figure 4.10 Electricity intensity of the economy

Index of intensity, 2005 = 1

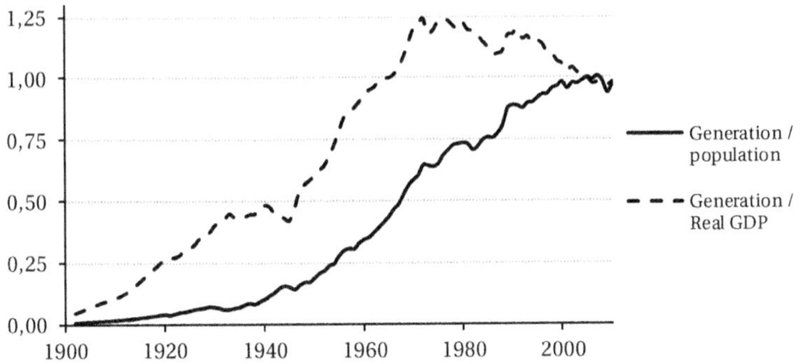

Sources: Data from Maddison (2006b). U.S. Census Bureau. Historical Statistics of the United States and annual Statistical Abstracts. U.S. Bureau of Economic Analysis, National Economic Accounts.

For around 80 years electricity was a growth industry. Generation grew twice as rapidly as the economy. Electricity has now saturated its markets and it is growing in line with the economy or, more recently, only in line with population. But, for many decades, electricity was one of the drivers of economic growth.

The electricity industry itself is only a small part of the economy. Even in 2010, electric utilities accounted for only 0.5% of GDP. The direct contribution of electricity to economic growth has been small. However, the indirect contribution has been enormous. Most of the growth drivers of the economy – appliances and consumer durables, automobiles and transportation equipment, financial activity, communications, entertainment, health care and government – depend on electricity for their production and operation. The actual figure is not knowable but arguably most of the modern economy would not have developed in the way and to the extent that it has without electricity. Electricity is a necessary input to the production of virtually all goods and services. In this sense, electricity has played a central role in U.S. economic growth.

4.4 Telecommunications

4.4.1 Development

The telegraph was the first form of telecommunication. Samuel Morse and Alfred Vail in the 1830s developed a system which could transmit code over wire over long distances. Western Union was established in 1855 by the merger of several telegraph companies. Western Union grew by its own expansion and by buying small companies until it completed the first transcontinental link in 1861. The Civil War greatly accelerated use of the telegraph. Telegraph was the only form of rapid long distance communication and even after the arrival of the telephone Western Union continued to grow rapidly. Figure 4.11 shows that the number of telegraph messages increased right up to the 1940s; the average growth rate from 1867 to 1945 was 4.8% a year. Telegraph growth followed a logistic curve, typical of the adoption of new products, until its peak in 1945; thereafter, the use of telegraph declined precipitously as customers switched to telephones. The life cycle of the telegraph took 90 years.

Figure 4.11 Telegraph messages

Million messages handled

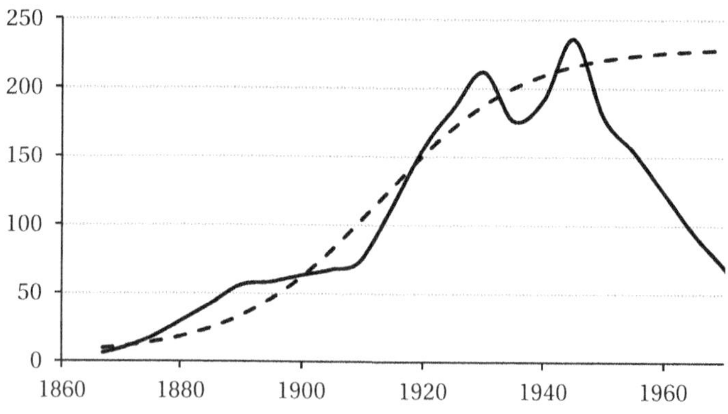

Sources: Data from U.S. Census Bureau. Historical Statistics of the United States and annual Statistical Abstracts.

The telephone grew out of efforts to transmit voice, avoiding the coding involved with telegraph. Several people claimed credit for the invention but the key people were Alexander Graham Bell, who was awarded the first patent in 1876, and Thomas Edison, who invented (and, after a long delay due to litigation, was awarded the patent on) the carbon microphone needed to generate a strong signal for transmission. Bell offered to sell to Western Union his telephone patents but Western Union, not seeing the customer appeal of the telephone, declined the offer and even sold Bell its interest in Edison's microphone patents.

The telephone system allowed voice to be carried all the way to the recipient, avoiding telegraph's need for encoding and decoding messages and avoiding the need to carry a printed message the "last mile". Telephone offered a better service than telegraph but first a telephone system had to be built. Bell's company, which became American Telephone and Telegraph (AT&T), grew rapidly by internal expansion and acquisition and became the dominant network provider. The key player in this growth was Theodore Vail, president of AT&T from 1885 to 1889 and again from 1907 to 1919. (Theodore Vail was the cousin of Alfred Vail, cofounder of the telegraph.) Vail created the telephone system, setting standards, organizing networks and organizing a single, consistent numbering plan. Vail called his approach "one system, one policy, universal service". The extensive coverage achieved by AT&T brought the company to the attention of the anti-trust authorities. AT&T reached a settlement with the U.S. government in 1913, becoming the sanctioned long distance monopoly. AT&T came under government regulation (by the Federal Communications Commission, FCC) in 1934 then continued as a regulated monopoly until breaking into separate regional telephone companies in 1984 as settlement of another government anti-trust challenge.

Technical advances in all aspects of the telephone system led to improving service and declining prices. The initial service used manual switchboard exchanges so that a caller needed to deal with one operator, for a neighbourhood call, all the way to many operators, for a long distance call. Connection gradually became automatic with the development of rotary dial telephones and automatic exchanges. The key invention was the "stepping switch" of Almon Brown Strowger, patented in 1891. Descendants of these electro-mechanical switches were in use for many decades until, beginning in the 1970s, electronic digital switches began to be introduced. Transmission was initially over wire but longer distance transmission in time moved to cable, in some cases to microwave radio, and then to glass fiber. Introduced around 1980, glass fiber provides high quality and high capacity transmission over short distances and, with repeaters, over long distances. Modern networks typically use (legacy) copper wire for the domestic connection, fiber optics for business connections and fiber optics for trunk transmission. Exchanges and trunk transmission have moved from analog to digital form. Digital transmission provides better quality and, particularly with fiber optics, huge increases in capacity and so much lower costs.

Cellphones, or mobile phones, use a radio connection between the customer and the network, forming a radio "cell", with fiber optics linking cells to form the network backbone. The telephone is switched between radio cells as the person moves, allowing continuous contact. As a result, cellphones are specific to a person whereas the traditional telephone is specific to a location. Cellphones were introduced by Motorola in 1983. Cellphones are now digital and have many features of computers, including allowing access to the internet and transmission of data.

The internet brings together computers, telecommunications and software to allow the virtually instantaneous transfer of information. The main elements of the internet are computers (to generate and store content), telecommunications networks (to carry the information), standard protocols (Transmission Control Program/Internet Protocol, TCP/IP, to allow communications to be processed), the world wide web (protocols to make content accessible) and browsers (to access content). The internet systems and protocols resulted from development managed by the Defense Advanced Research Projects Agency (DARPA) in the late 1960s and early 1970s. DARPA's objective was to create a robust (and therefore decentralized) information communications system. Key players in the growth of the internet include Vint Cerf, for work on interconnection protocols, Tim Berners-Lee who in 1990 created the world wide web, Marc Andreesen who in 1993 created the Mosaic (later Netscape) browser and Microsoft with email software.

4.4.2 The market for telecommunications

The adoption of telephones by households within the Bell system is shown in Figure 4.12. This adoption followed a standard logistic path. Landline telephones took 90 years to reach saturation. (This is the same time that the telegraph took to reach market saturation, many decades earlier.)

Figure 4.12 Share of households with landline telephone service

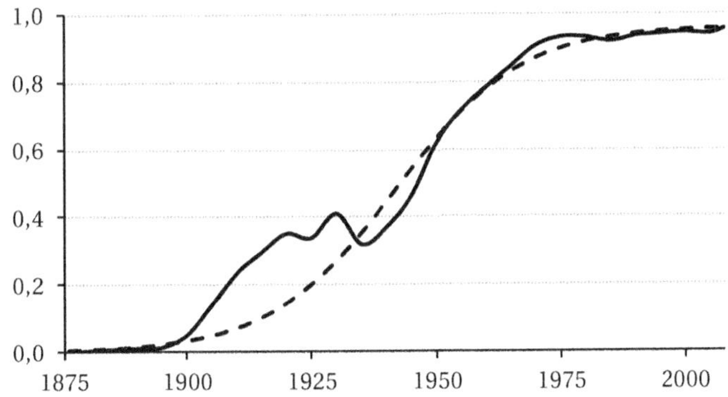

Sources: Data from U.S. Census Bureau. Historical Statistics of the United States and annual Statistical Abstracts.

Cellphones allow person-specific rather than location-specific communications. And, cellphones have taken on many features from computers, providing audio, video and internet capabilities. This convenience and continuing increase in service quality led to the rapid adoption of cellphones, despite the higher price of cellphone service. The adoption of cellphones is shown in Figure 4.13. Adoption has followed the standard logistic path and has been extremely rapid, going from introduction to more than 95% penetration in 25 years. (The logistic path suggests that saturation will be reached at more than 100% penetration – on average more than one phone per person.)

Figure 4.13 Cellphones per person

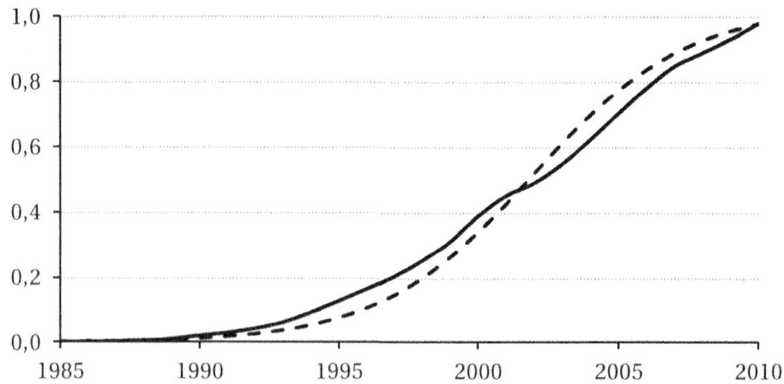

Sources: Data from Federal Communications Commission (2013) and U.S. Census Bureau, annual Statistical Abstracts.

The telephone system since the 1990s has adapted to providing carriage for a new service – data communication. The internet has provided the framework for this growth. The internet provides rapid sending in electronic form of messages (emails), documents, video content and audio content, in fact anything which can be expressed in digital form. The internet has made personal communications, business communication and control, and data access hugely easier and cheaper, leading to new ways of communication, entertainment, management and research.

The growth of internet traffic in the U.S. is shown in Figure 4.14.

Figure 4.14 U.S. internet traffic

Petabytes per month

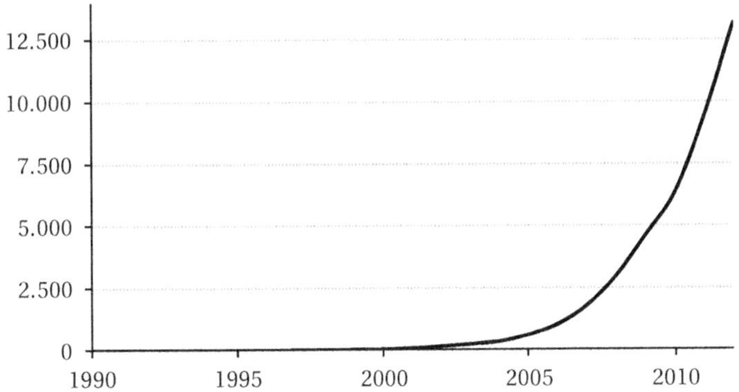

Source: Data from U.S. Telecom Association (2013).

The shape of this usage graph corresponds to a new product just getting established in the marketplace. There is gradual initial adoption followed by a move to rapid and widespread adoption. Growth rates through 2002 were particularly rapid, averaging 109% a year. Growth since 2002 has slowed somewhat, to 46% a year. If the internet is anything like a typical good the likelihood is that rapid growth will continue for years if not decades. Growth might not continue at 46% a year but rapid growth looks set to continue.

The extent of the market for telecommunications equipment and services is shown in Table 4.6. Telecommunications accounts directly for 2.4% of the economy.

Table 4.6 Final demand spending on telecommunications in 2010

Covers personal consumption, business investment and government purchases

	Spending $ billions	Spending as % GDP
Personal spending on telephone equipment	14.0	0.1%
Business investment in communications equipment	83.8	0.6%
Personal spending on internet access	53.8	0.4%
Personal spending on telecommunications services	161.1	1.1%
Government sector purchases	36.9	0.3%
Sum	349.6	2.4%

Source: Data from U.S. Bureau of Economic Analysis. National Economic Accounts.

4.4.3 Telecommunications and economic growth

Use of telecommunication services has grown rapidly since the industry began in the mid-19th century with the introduction of the telegraph. The growth trend in the quantity of personal consumption of telecommunications from 1929 to 2010 has been 6.6% a year. This is almost twice the growth trend of real GDP (3.6% a year). Clearly, purchases of telecommunications have been a leader in economic growth. However, telecommunications is a relatively small part of the economy. Even in 2010, final demand spending on telecommunications services and equipment accounted for just 2.4% of the economy. Despite its rapid growth, the direct effect of telecommunications on economic growth has been moderate, it has been just one among several leading growth industries.

There has been continuing productivity advance in telecommunications. Kendrick's (1961 and 1973) numbers imply an average productivity growth from 1879 to 1966 of 2.2% a year. We estimate that total factor productivity increased at a trend of 1.9% a year over the period 1929-2010. These rates of productivity advance are well above average. However, with output increasing at a 6.6% rate and productivity at 1.9%, the industry required 4.6% more resources each year. Telecommunications were absorbing resources from the rest of the economy. In return, a small part of the economy increased rapidly over many decades. The direct effect on economic growth, though, was relatively small.

Telecommunications are important to business, governments and households. Households arguably derive great benefit from telecommunications, whether for social or entertainment purposes, over and above the amounts that they pay for these services; this excess does not show up in GDP. Business and government probably also get considerable benefit over and above the amounts included in GDP. The contribution is partly a saving of people's time and travel costs by using telecommunications rather than face-to-face meetings but it also is likely that telecommunications allow businesses to be run more efficiently. Easy communication is essential to running a complex organization. It is plausible that telecommunications have contributed to the development of the modern corporation in which far-flung divisions operate independently but report to and, at a high level, are controlled by the center. But, how much of the growth of modern business is due to telecommunications is difficult to estimate. Robert Fogel (1964) constructed a counterfactual for America without the railroad and used this to infer that the growth contribution of railroads was relatively small. However, railroads provided a distinct and visible service. Telecommunications, in contrast, enter in a complex and non-obvious way into leisure, production, sales and management; it is difficult to see how a realistic counterfactual could be constructed for American business without telecommunications.

The development of telecommunications undoubtedly has had a beneficial indirect effect on the economy. Better quality, more accessible and cheaper telecommunications would have assisted business productivity by reducing costs, allowing better management and increasing the potential market. These indirect effects would have contributed to economic growth even though we cannot quantify these effects. All we can argue is that telecommunications have played an essential role in growth, that they have been a necessary element in U.S. economic growth.

4.5 Motor vehicles

4.5.1 The producers

The Columbia Automobile Company of Hartford, Connecticut began producing gasoline-powered cars in 1899. Columbia was the leading producer of its day, producing around 1,500 cars in 1899 and 1900. The lead was then taken by the Locomobile Company of America, making steam powered cars. Several manufacturers, including the Studebaker brothers, produced electric-powered cars. But steam and electricity proved unable to compete with the gasoline-powered internal combustion engine. Ransom E. Olds invented the assembly line for automobile production at his Olds Motor Vehicle Company in Detroit, Michigan. The efficiency of the assembly line allowed Olds to cut his prices and he soon emerged as the volume leader; by 1905 Olds was turning out around 20 cars a day.

The nascent industry had many, possibly dozens, of manufacturers, each producing relatively small numbers of cars. This changed with Henry Ford and his Model T. Ford was eased out of his first automobile company (which was later renamed Cadillac and ultimately purchased by General Motors). The Ford Motor Company was formed in 1903 in Detroit and grew rapidly. By 1906 Ford was the largest automobile producer, selling around 8,700 cars in that year. The Ford team designed a series of prototypes and models until the 19th design (given the letter T) provided what they were looking for. The Model T, which went into production in 1908, established the automobile design that was to last for 100 years – completely standardized (interchangeable) parts, steering wheel on the left, the engine cast as one block with a separate head, engine and transmission enclosed in a hood at the front of the car and, later on, an enclosed body. Ford's production leader, Charles Sorenson, developed foundry techniques, such as the use of metal patterns, which allowed production of the large number of standardized castings needed for mass production. Sorenson also introduced the first moving assembly line, in 1913, greatly speeding production.

The Model T was simple and, for its time, reliable. But most of all the Model T was cheap. The 1909 version was priced at (the then low price of) $850. Increasingly efficient production drove costs down and Ford reduced prices correspondingly. The base price had fallen to $360 by 1916 and to as little as $240 by 1925. Sales of the Model T soared. The price strategy was so successful that Ford ceased using advertising. In its first six years, sales increased at an average of 75% a year, passing 500,000 units in 1915. Sales peaked at 1.8 million in 1923. In total, more than 15,000,000 Model Ts were produced.

Ford developed two fundamental marketing techniques. First, Ford strove for production efficiencies and passed on the cost reductions in the form of lower prices. Second, Ford established a new distribution system - a network of independent, franchised dealers to retail and service its cars. Low price, accessibility and reliability created the mass market for automobiles. This was the first mass market for a consumer durable.

The Model T dominated the market for almost 20 years. Figure 4.15 shows the production of Fords and of the emerging challenger, Chevrolet from General Motors, for the first four decades of the industry. As incomes rose in the 1920s and as Chevrolet began offering a car with more features, new car customers switched to the more appealing car. The decline of the Model T was then precipitous. Ford ceased production of the Model T in 1928. Ford plants sat idle while Henry Ford led a team to design a new car, the Model A. The Model A competed effectively with Chevrolet but now as an equal; Ford never again dominated the market. In fact, the market had entered a new stage in which features were more important than simply price and it was General Motors which grew to dominate this market. In time, General Motors grew to become the largest industrial company in the world.

Figure 4.15 Automobile production, 1900 - 1940
Production of the top brands, millions

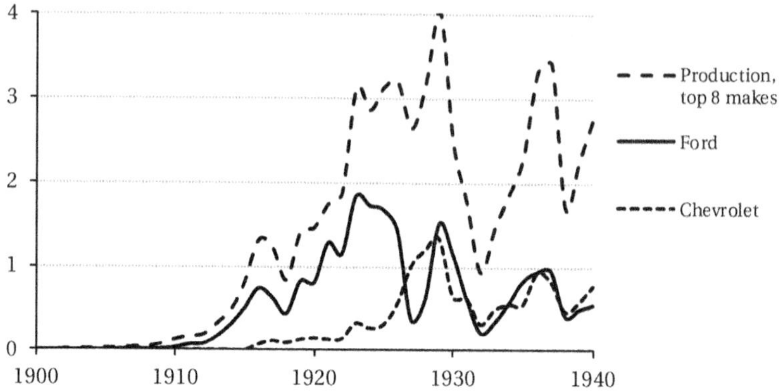

Source: Data from *U.S. Automobile Production Figures*, Wikipedia. Viewed 22 August 2012.

General Motors (GM) was established in 1908 by William C. Durant to produce Buick automobiles. By 1919 Durant had acquired Oakland (later known as Pontiac), Oldsmobile, Cadillac, Chevrolet and a truck producer. General Motors in 1919 established General Motors Acceptance Corporation (GMAC) to finance customers wishing to buy its vehicles on credit. The elements of a successful business were now in place but it took a new leader to exploit the potential. This was Alfred P. Sloan Jr who became President of GM in 1923 (and remained in charge until the 1950s). Sloan took over a company which produced a range of automobiles and which had a novel feature, a financing arm. But GM was a distant second to Ford in the marketplace. Sloan developed Chevrolet until it had a product that was clearly better – offering features that the customer wanted – than Ford's Model T. The appeal of a better product, heavily advertised and with credit purchase available, was so powerful that within four years Chevrolet had consigned the Model T to history.

Sloan then fine-tuned the complex organization that was GM. In doing this, Sloan created the modern business corporation. This development was based on two foundations – organizational design and marketing. The organization was the divisional corporation. This is a decentralized organization based on operating divisions which are essentially business units in themselves. Head office provides strategic but not operational coordination and controls the divisions through the allocation of financial capital and through monitoring and feedback against financial and market targets.

GM developed many of the techniques of modern marketing. Sloan (1963) characterized his approach as: "instalment selling, the used-car trade-in, the closed body, and the annual model". In fact, Sloan's contribution covered styling, market segmentation, model changes, advertising, consumer finance and market research. Styling involved product design to appeal to the customer rather than being purely functional. Market segmentation, based on GM's five automobile brands, allowed GM to extend its appeal and to reap the benefit in increased sales, for the lower priced brands, and, for the premium brands, higher prices. In Sloan's words, GM had "a car for every purse and purpose". Annual model changes, what came to be known as "planned obsolescence", stimulated customer demand and turnover of a durable good. The technique of trade-ins and used car sales by GM dealers facilitated the process of keeping up with new models. And, customer finance was crucial, allowing customers to pay for their automobile as they enjoyed it, not before. GM competed on design, features, marketing and finance but not solely price. Unlike Ford with the Model T, GM did not pass on efficiency gains in the form of lower retail prices. GM chose to retain these as profits which it used either for new investment or for dividends to shareholders.

General Motors lost its spark only a decade or so after Sloan's departure. GM began to lose touch with its customers in the 1960s and this accelerated with the increase in oil prices in the 1970s when customers sought more efficient and reliable automobiles. Cars from Japanese and European producers did to GM in the 1970s what GM had done to Ford in the 1920s – gave customers what they wanted. GM's market share went from over 50% in the 1960s to, in recent times, less than 20%. Inept management and acceding to the compensation and security demands of organized labor destroyed GM's profitability and led to the bankruptcy of the company in 2009.

Beginning in the 1960s and then with the oil price shocks of the 1970s, competition in the automobile market intensified with European and Japanese producers competing on economy, quality and price. Protectionist barriers intended to restrict imports led to foreign manufacturers setting up production inside the United States. Competition fragmented the market as producers sought to expand sales by catering to ever more specific market niches. The best-selling vehicle in recent times, a Ford light truck, has a market share of just 4%. Six producers (GM, Ford, Chrysler, Toyota, Honda and Nissan) have market shares over 5%, totalling 80% of the vehicle market, while a large number of smaller producers made up the remaining 20% of the market.

4.5.2 Development of the market

Sales of new motor vehicles over the past century are shown in Figure 4.16. The smooth line is a logistic curve fitted to actual purchases. There are a number of short term departures from the trend, in particular with the Great Depression of the 1930s, World War II and the financial crisis after 2007, but the overall pattern is clear. The market, after growing for a century, has now levelled off; automobiles (or personal motor vehicles) are now a mature market with little growth.

Figure 4.16 Sales of new motor vehicles
Millions of vehicles a year

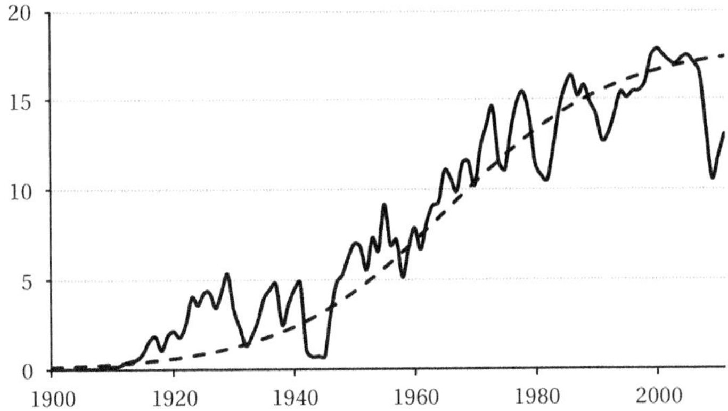

Source: Data from U.S. Department of Transportation, National Transportation Statistics.

The market is driven by consumer demand. Figure 4.17 shows the evolution of motor vehicle ownership. Demand picked up with the Model T then grew rapidly until ownership became saturated in the 1980s at around 850 vehicles per 1,000 people. Allowing for people, such as the young and very old, who do not drive the ownership rate is more than one vehicle per driver (these include commercial as well as personal vehicles). It took around 100 years for the market to grow from a new product to saturation. With ownership rates now at saturation, total ownership is likely now to increase just with population growth.

Figure 4.17 Motor vehicle ownership
Vehicles per 1,000 people

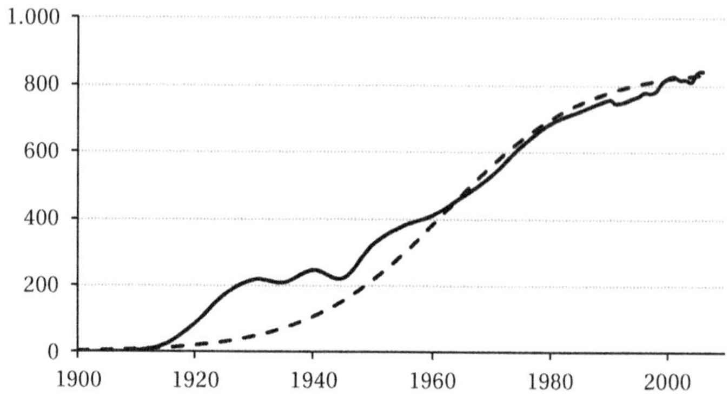

Source: Data from U.S. Department of Transportation, National Transportation Statistics.

4.5.3 Productivity growth in automobiles

The automobile industry has seen enormous gains in productivity over the past century. These gains resulted from major production improvements, such as the moving assembly line and the use of standardized parts, design improvements, such as the switch from body-on-chassis to unitized body, as well as steady, detailed improvements in design and production. The increase in scale must have created considerable economies in management, marketing, design and component manufacture. The emergence of strong competition from Japanese companies is likely also to have stimulated cost reductions and quality improvement.

Our estimates of productivity growth are shown in Table 4.7. Productivity growth was particularly rapid until the 1920s as Henry Ford and his team developed modern manufacturing techniques. Subsequently, productivity growth has continued, although less rapidly, with the gains showing up in both declining relative prices and increased product quality. The price-based productivity gains in the Table are based on National Economic Accounts data which take account of quality improvements.

Table 4.7 Productivity trends in vehicle production

Time period	Based on	Growth trend
1909 - 1929	TFP	7.7%
1929 - 1953	TFP	1.1%
1953 - 1969	Price index	1.4%
1969 - 2010	Price index	1.1%
1909 - 2010	Composite	2.2%

TFP is Total Factor Productivity, based on Kendrick (1961).
Price index is based on the National Economic Accounts.
Sources: Kendrick (1961) and U.S. Bureau of Economic Analysis, National Economic Accounts.

The rapid productivity growth of the first 20 years of the industry was not sustained but the industry has shown continuing gains. The average increase of 2.2% a year for more than 100 years means that the quality-adjusted price of an automobile today is only 10% the price in 1909.

The quality of automobiles, in terms of the services they provide their owners, has increased dramatically. Power, economy, safety, reliability, comfort and convenience have vastly improved. Some indicators of the improvement are: power per liter of engine capacity of the basic Ford increased by 2.5% a year (from 1909 to 2010), fuel efficiency per automobile has increased by 0.3% a year and fatalities per mile driven have declined at a rate of 3.3% a year (since 1925). Comfort has improved with heating and cooling control, seating has improved and audio entertainment is now standard. Ease of use has improved with most functions, other than steering and speed control, now automated. And safety has improved with better body designs, protections such as seat belts and air bags, and all manner of computerized controls on handling and braking.

4.5.4 Motor vehicles and the economy

Motor vehicles for many years led the growth of the U.S. economy. Motor vehicles may or may not have been the most rapidly growing industry but motor vehicles grew more rapidly than the economy, were massive in size and consequently pulled much of the economy along after them. Figure 4.18 shows growth rates for the number of new motor vehicles sold and real GDP. (This looks at the number of vehicles produced; in view of the improvement in quality of motor vehicles this would underestimate the growth in effective output.)

Figure 4.18 Growth of vehicle sales and GDP

Growth rates of 10 year moving averages

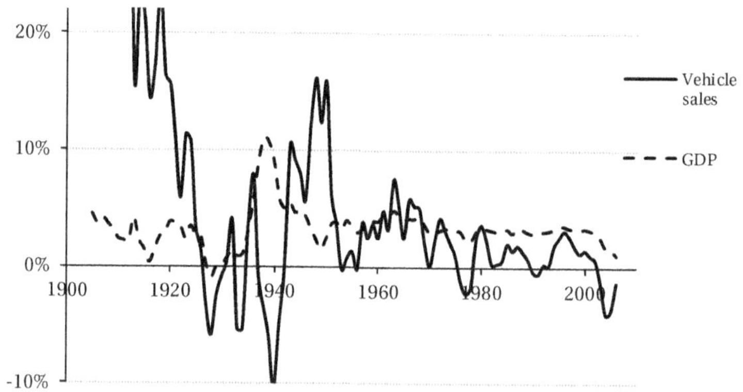

Sources: Data from Maddison (2006b). U.S. Department of Transportation, National Transportation Statistics. U.S. Bureau of Economic Analysis, National Economic Accounts.

Motor vehicle production and sales have been so volatile that it is difficult to pinpoint a year in which vehicle and GDP growth rates crossed. It appears that the crossover occurred in the 1970s. The logistic model of vehicle sales, which gives a smooth growth path, shows that 1969 was the year in which vehicle sales first fell below the trend growth of real GDP. This means that for 70 years the motor vehicle industry was a growth engine for the U.S. economy; rapid growth in motor vehicle production was pulling the economy along behind it. After 1969, motor vehicles have been an important source of production and generator of incomes but they have no longer been leading the economy forwards. Motor vehicles in recent decades have been moving with or even behind the economy, not ahead of it.

Producing and selling motor vehicles uses directly steel, components, paints, tires, electrical equipment, electronics and textiles as well as advertising, transportation, wholesaling, retailing, financial services and advisory services. In addition, vehicle production pays workers, generates income to capital and pays taxes. The direct purchases per $100 of output of motor vehicles in 2009 are shown in Table 4.8.

Table 4.8 Direct purchases for $100 of output

Inputs of more than $1, inter-industry accounts 2009

Utilities	1.0
Primary metals	6.9
Fabricated metal products	8.9
Machinery	3.4
Electronic products	2.6
Motor vehicles and parts	29.3
Chemical products	1.5
Plastics and rubber products	3.4
Wholesale trade	5.0
Truck transportation	1.1
Technical services	1.6
Management services	3.4
Imports	1.0
Gross compensation of employees	14.7
Gross income to capital	6.7
Other inputs (each less than $1)	9.5
Total purchases or inputs	100.0

Source: Data from U.S. Bureau of Economic Analysis, Input-Output Accounts.

A little over 20% of inputs is value added - income to labor and capital. The rest is purchases mainly of goods, such as vehicle parts, but also of services, such as wholesale trade. Direct inputs of intermediate goods and services in turn need to be produced using more basic inputs such as iron ore, coal, petroleum, financial services and management services as well as further labor and capital. Given all these connections with other industries, the growing motor vehicle industry pulled along many other industries on their own growth paths. In addition, all these industries generated growing income to labor and capital.

Motor vehicles represent a relatively large part of the U.S. economy. We have looked at the way in which production of motor vehicles affects other industries as well as capital and labor. This corresponds just to the investment aspect of motor vehicles, when owners make their initial purchase. Owners then have to operate their vehicles over the lifetime, typically 15 or more years, of their vehicle; this involves purchasing fuel, maintenance, repairs, insurance and other services. Vehicles operate on roads which need to be constructed (government investment) and maintained (government current expenditure). Table 4.9 adds up all these investment and current purchases related to motor vehicles.

Table 4.9 Expenditure on motor vehicles within GDP

Average share across all years with data available

Personal, purchase of new motor vehicles	2.3%
Private investment, purchase of new motor vehicles	1.2%
Defense, purchase of new motor vehicles	0.05%
Other government purchases of new motor vehicles	n.a.
Government, investment spending on roads	0.9%
Personal, operation of motor vehicles	4.0%
Government maintenance spending on roads	0.9%
Total spending	9.3%

Source: Data from U.S. Bureau of Economic Analysis, National Economic Statistics.

On average 9% and in the peak years of the 1950s and 1960s more than 10% of the economy is directly related to motor vehicles. This makes motor vehicles one of the largest parts of the economy. As such, the rapid growth of the vehicle industry over the first 70 years of last century would have had a huge effect in driving the growth of the entire economy.

4.6 Aircraft

4.6.1 Development of the technology

Orville and Wilbur Wright of Dayton, Ohio made the first verified controlled flight on 17 December 1903. Airplane performance then improved slowly. By the end of World War I, airplanes had been developed sufficiently in power and control that they were used in aerial reconnaissance and fighting. The U.S. Government in the 1920s stimulated aircraft development by awarding contracts for carrying the mail. Commercial aviation came a step closer with the introduction in 1926 of the Ford Tri-motor, an all-metal monoplane produced by Henry Ford's companies. The Boeing model 247, introduced in 1934, was the first modern airliner in a technical sense but it was uneconomically small and was not widely used.

The commercial breakthrough came with the Douglas DC3, introduced in 1936 as a development of the earlier DC1 and DC2 (which were too small to be economic). The DC3 had a highly researched wing and the most modern, of the time, engines - two Wright Cyclone radial engines of 1,100 plus horsepower (hp) each. With a cruise speed of 150 miles per hour (mph), range of 1,000 miles and payload of 21 passengers the DC3 made possible rapid passenger travel throughout the United States. Airlines rushed to purchase the DC3 and, during World War II, the U.S. Government bought large numbers of the military version, the C47. A total of 16,079 DC3s and C47s were produced from 1936 to 1942. With continued engine development and the shift to four engines, airliners got greater payload and longer range. The ultimate piston engine transport was the Douglas DC7C, introduced in 1956 and able to fly London to New York nonstop.

However, this was the last of the large piston engine airliners. At 3,400 hp each, the Wright radials had pushed piston engine capability to its limit.

The next stage in aircraft design was based on the gas turbine or jet engine, initially developed in Britain and Germany during World War II. The swept wing, also developed in Germany, provided the airframe design able to exploit the higher power of jet engines. The Boeing B47 bomber, which combined the jet engine with the swept-back wing to achieve cruising speeds of 550 mph, was the breakthrough heavy aircraft. Developments of this technology led to the B52 bomber and, applied to civil use, the Boeing 707 airliner which entered service in 1958. Engine technology progressed from the turbojet to the turbofan with successive engines becoming more powerful, less noisy and more fuel-efficient. The Boeing 707 technology was applied to smaller aircraft, such as the B727 and the B737, which brought jet travel to regional markets. The first "wide bodied" commercial transport was the Boeing 747, introduced in 1970. The airliner market has now segmented with many capacity and range combinations, ranging from short range 19 seat turbo-props to the long range, 550 seat Airbus 380. This has been made possible by continuing advances in materials, airframe technology and, in particular, engine technology. The most powerful engine currently in use, a General Electric turbofan used on one variant of the Boeing 777, has been run at more than 125,000 lb thrust, 100 times as powerful as the turbojet engines on the first operational jets of the 1940s.

Military aircraft have developed in parallel to civil transports. Military aircraft were produced in large numbers during the 1940s and 1950s but the subsequent market has not been large. Military sponsorship however has made a significant contribution to the development of aircraft engines and airframes with spill-over benefits to civil aviation. Similarly, military sponsorship led the development of helicopters. The breakthrough design was the Bell UH1 which saw widespread military use in the 1960s. Subsequent development has seen a small but ongoing market for military and civilian helicopters.

4.6.2 Aircraft productivity

The performance of civil aircraft has steadily increased as shown in Table 4.10.

Table 4.10 Performance trends for civil aircraft

Average growth rates, % per annum

Power: piston engines, 1916 - 1954	8.4%
Power: gas turbine (jet) engines, 1946 - 2010	4.7%
Fuel efficiency: revenue passenger miles/gallon, 1960 - 2009	2.6%
Size: passenger seats/aircraft, 1935 - 1990	5.1%
Speed: average speed, domestic flights, 1945 - 1990	2.4%
Ticket price: real cents/passenger mile, 1937 - 2009	-2.6%

Sources: Data from U.S. Bureau of the Census, Historical Statistics of the United States and annual Statistical Abstracts. U.S. Department of Transportation, National Transportation Statistics.

Engine improvements led the gains. Better engines have led to better performance – faster speeds, better fuel efficiency, larger aircraft; these indicators have increased by 2.5% or more a year. Overall productivity has increased at least by the reduction in ticket prices, 2.6% a year. In fact, productivity in terms of providing service to customers has increased by more than this as average speeds have also increased considerably.

4.6.3 Aircraft and the economy

Aircraft were produced in large numbers during World War II; for example, more than 46,000 were made in 1945. Since, then production has fallen back. Shipments of general aviation aircraft, small aircraft for personal and business use, rose until around 1980 but these numbers too have since fallen. Figure 4.19 shows the trends. It is clear from this Figure that there has been little growth in terms of numbers of aircraft produced. Airliners (civil transports) are perhaps the best known product but production of airliners has increased only slowly – the trend growth rate over the past 50 years has been just 1.0%.

Figure 4.19 Aircraft produced

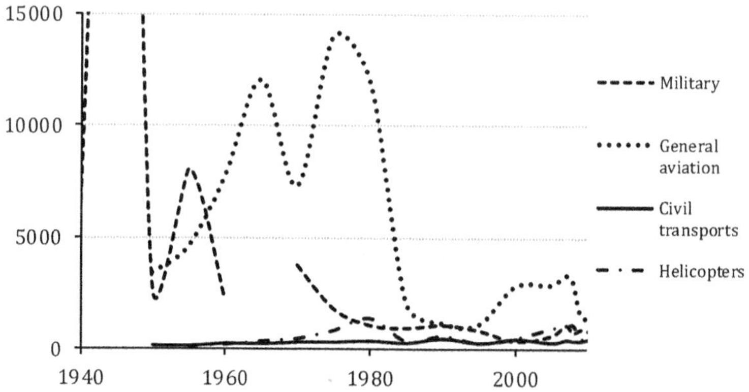

Sources: Data from U.S. Census Bureau, Historical Statistics of the United States and annual Statistical Abstracts.

Not only is the aircraft industry slow growing but also it is relatively small. Aerospace sales are equivalent to around 1.5% of GDP but less than 0.5% of GDP (value added) originates in the industry. Although prominent during World War II, the aircraft industry has not made a large direct contribution to ongoing U.S. economic growth.

However, aerospace has contributed to the growth of the transportation industry, particularly for passenger travel. Airline service has become steadily more widespread and prices have fallen. Inflation-adjusted prices have fallen relatively steadily, at an average rate of 2.6% a year, ever since the introduction of the DC3. This is the real contribution of the aircraft industry to the economy. Better aircraft and better management in the airline industry have created a mass market in distance travel, allowing rapid travel within the United States as well as making the world accessible to people for personal, pleasure and business purposes.

4.7 Transportation

4.7.1 Waterborne freight

Early transportation of freight used sailing ships for coastal trade and horse-drawn wagons for interior trade. The expense of this movement, particularly in the interior and between the eastern ports and the Midwest, generated a demand for new modes of transport. Canal technology had already been developed in England and was applied in several parts of the eastern United States. The most important was the Erie Canal, opened in 1825, which allowed waterborne traffic to move between the port of New York and Lake Erie. Tons shipped on the Erie Canal rose from 1.2 million in 1837 to a peak of 6.5 million in 1880. However, the new technology of railroads began to compete with canals. It took several decades for a workable railroad network to be developed but by 1869 the first transcontinental link was completed. By the 1880s, the railroads provided carriage from the east to the Midwest that was faster and cheaper than canals. Waterborne transport subsequently focused on its areas of advantage – moving bulk cargo on the Great Lakes, moving bulk cargo on the Mississippi and Ohio River systems, and moving coastal cargo.

Table 4.11 shows the growth patterns in tons of freight moved by water within the United States.

Table 4.11 Growth of waterborne freight and GDP

Average annual growth rates

	Freight	Real GDP	
New York state canals, 1837 - 1880	3.7%	4.4%	(1)
New York state canals, 1880 - 1970	-0.3%	3.6%	
Great Lakes, 1900 - 1925	4.5%	3.4%	
Great Lakes, 1925 - 1970	0.7%	3.6%	
All domestic waterborne freight, 1924 - 2009	1.2%	3.3%	

Note (1): GDP growth is for 1830 to 1880.

Sources: Data from U.S. Census Bureau, Historical Statistics of the United States and annual Statistical Abstracts.

All the growth rates in this Table are less than economic growth rates except for one instance – tonnage moved on the Great Lakes in the early part of the 20th century. The reason for this growth was the growth of the motor vehicle and steel industries in Michigan and the Midwest. This growth created a demand for massive movements of iron ore and coal on the Great Lakes. In these and other examples, waterborne transport helped sustain economic growth but did not drive economic growth; it was a permissive rather than a causal force.

Ocean shipping played a similar role. The trend growth in net tonnage of vessels entering U.S. seaports from 1890 through 1995 was 3.5% a year. This is the same as the growth trend in GDP. Ocean shipping grew with the economy. The composition of sea-borne imports and exports, shown in Table 4.12, indicates why:

Table 4.12 Composition of waterborne international trade

Trade in 2005, million short tons

	Imports	Exports
Coal	40	49
Petroleum and products	685	76
Chemicals	48	59
Crude materials, inedible	113	55
Foods and farm produce	37	155
Primary manufactures (1)	123	19
Manufactured equipment, machinery and produ(	79	19

Note (1): Mainly lime/cement/glass and primary iron/steel products.

Source: Data from U.S. Bureau of the Census, Statistical Abstract of the United States, 2008.

Waterborne imports are dominated by energy, materials and semi-processed goods. All these enter into further processing before being sold to domestic customers. These goods all help sustain activity in the U.S., they are supportive of growth rather than leading growth.

Efficiency improvements have massively reduced the cost of ocean transportation. These have been the increasing scale of ships and the introduction of containerization. Bulk goods, such as oil or iron ore or grain, are moved in specialized carriers. Increasing the size of these carriers reduces unit costs (although the effect is restrained by the size of ship that can pass through the Suez Canal or the Panama Canal). Roughly speaking, doubling the size of a carrier will halve the unit cost of shipping. The largest crude oil carriers, for example, have increased from 47,500 deadweight ton capacity in 1955 to around 440,000 in recent times, an annual rate of increase of 4.6%. In addition, costs have been reduced by the shift from steam to diesel propulsion. Containerization, introduced by Malcolm McLean in the late 1950s, uses standard sized, sealed steel boxes to move goods, whether by ship, truck or rail. Containerization has reduced freight costs by as much as 90% compared to earlier break-bulk handling. In addition, containerization has reduced time taken in transport and reduced costs due to damage and theft.

These efficiency gains have been vast. They have released resources from moving materials and freight. And, by reducing the cost of movement, they have accelerated the growth in international trade. The reduction in freight costs has accelerated the shift of the U.S. economy from producing low value manufactures (many of which are now imported) to producing high value added foodstuffs, manufactures and services.

4.7.2 Growth of railroads

The Baltimore and Ohio Railroad (B&O) was established by merchants in Baltimore concerned about loss of business to competitors using the newly opened Erie Canal. These merchants wanted a cheaper and faster route between the Midwest and markets and ports on the east coast. The first section of the B&O opened in 1830; the line steadily pushed west, reaching the Ohio River at Wheeling, West Virginia in 1853. Construction of railroads proceeded apace with a transcontinental link established in 1869 and with an extensive network through the Midwest in place by 1880. The network was steadily extended, reaching a peak in the 1920s. Figure 4.20 shows the growth of the track system (along with a fitted logistic curve).

Figure 4.20 Railroad track in use

Thousands of miles

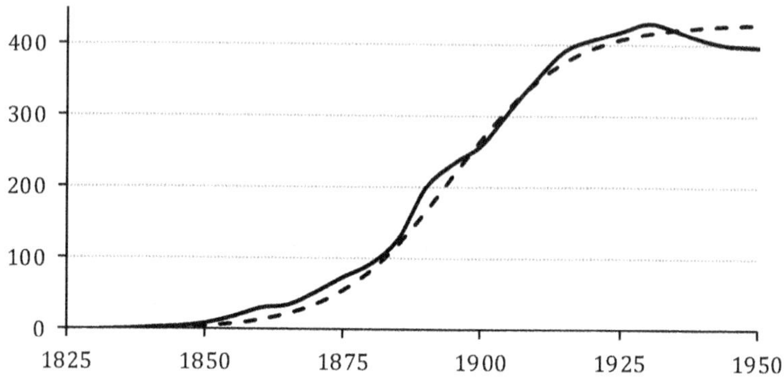

Sources: Data from U.S. Census Bureau, Historical Statistics of the United States and annual Statistical Abstracts.

There was continuing advance in railroad equipment. Steam locomotives became specialized, for example into freight, passenger and switching engines. Steam locomotives became more powerful with average tractive effort increasing at 1.6% a year. George Pullman introduced sleeping cars and luxury passenger cars, starting in 1865. George Westinghouse introduced the air brake system in the 1870s. Compressed air brakes greatly improved safety and also allowed heavier trains. Then came the switch to diesel. The first diesel-electric locomotives were 300 horsepower General Electric units in 1925. Larger engines were developed in the 1930s with General Motors demonstrating a 1,350 hp freight locomotive in 1939. Diesel-electric locomotives have become larger and, especially with the switch from direct current to alternating current systems, more efficient. The average horsepower of diesel-electric locomotives has increased at 1.6% a year (which happens to be the same rate as that of steam locomotives in their day).

Diesel engine, electric drive locomotives had substantially lower operating costs than steam locomotives, were more flexible in use and, through volume production of standardized units, had lower capital costs. Figure 4.21 shows the rapid adoption of diesel-electric technology. The diesel-electric locomotive went from proof of concept in 1925 to initial adoption in 15 years and then to complete adoption in a further 25 years, by 1965. The adoption process, which followed the typical logistic path, was particularly rapid as the new product did not have to establish a new market; it was simply replacing an existing way of carrying out work.

Figure 4.21 Locomotive technology in use

Share of total number of locomotives

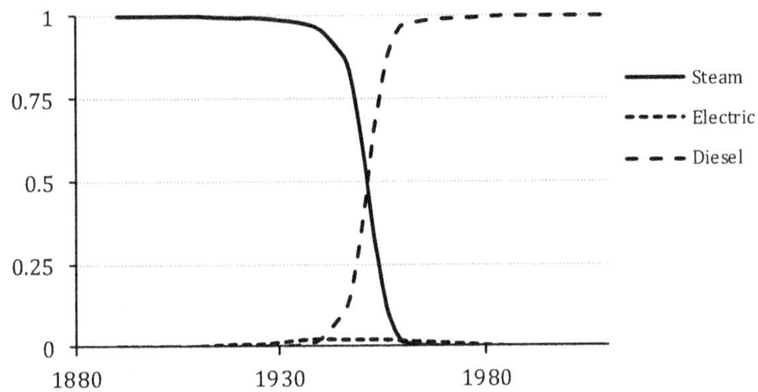

Sources: Data from U.S. Census Bureau, Historical Statistics of the United States and annual Statistical Abstracts.

The market for railroad services grew rapidly over the 19th century. This was partly a matter of railroads taking freight away from water-borne transport and from horse-drawn wagons, and partly a matter of railroads sharing in the growth of that time, including the settlement of the Midwest. Railroads had passed water-borne transport by the 1880s to become the principal mode of freight transport. Railroads continued to grow rapidly until the 1920s when road transport began its rapid growth. Railroad transport of freight has continued to increase, but now more slowly than the economy, while passenger travel by rail began a slow decline. Table 4.13 shows these growth trends with the shift from rapid to slow growth around 1920.

Table 4.13 Growth rates in railroad traffic

	1890 - 1920	1920 - 2000
Tons	3.9%	0.5%
Ton-miles	4.9%	1.7%
Passenger-miles	4.9%	-1.7%
Real GDP	3.7%	3.6%

Sources: Data from U.S. Census Bureau, Historical Statistics of the United States and annual Statistical Abstracts. Maddison (2006b). U.S. Bureau of Economic Analysis, National Economic Accounts.

4.7.3 Railroads and the economy

Robert Fogel (1964) has argued that railroads contributed relatively little to U.S. economic growth. His analysis looks at 1890, when an extensive rail network had been constructed, and asks what would have been the reduction in GDP if the rail network did not exist. Without a rail network, freight would have gone by canals and horse-drawn wagons. Fogel argues that a relatively small share of the agricultural land then in use would have been unserviceable with this alternative transport and that the reduction in GDP would have been only around 2.7%. Fogel goes on to argue that the opportunity to service unused lands in the Midwest would have stimulated improvements in rural roads and also accelerated the development of the internal combustion engine, cars and trucks so that the longer term effect would have been even smaller.

We approach the question from a different point of view but our conclusion is consistent with Fogel's. Railroad passenger revenue in 1890 was 2.1% of GDP while freight revenue was 5.6%. The contribution to GDP is the value added component of revenue. The 1987 Input-

Output Accounts from the U.S. Bureau of Economic Analysis give value added as 62% of railroad output. If the same traffic had gone by other means the value added by railroads would have been less. We use the share for water transport where value added is 32% of output. The difference in value added, which might indicate the additional contribution of railroads, is 2.3% of GDP. This figure is not dissimilar to Fogel's.

However, railroads helped sustain other industries which were leading economic growth. An important part of this was the role of railroads in opening up the Midwest and the Great Plains which underlay much of the agricultural and population growth of the years until World War I. Here too, railroad service helped allow growth even if it did not cause growth.

We estimate that railroad productivity increased at an average rate of 1.9% a year from 1890 to 2000. Output of railroad freight services over this time increased at a trend rate of 2.3% a year. This means that most of the increase in output was sustained by higher productivity with only a small increase in factor inputs, around 0.4% a year, being required. Kendrick's (1961 and 1973) numbers imply that the overall growth in factor inputs between 1899 and 1966 averaged 1.8% a year. This means that inputs into railroads claimed a diminishing share of all inputs. Railroads were able to service other industries while releasing, in a relative sense, resources for the other industries which were driving growth.

4.7.4 Trucking

Trucking has provided local transport of freight ever since motor vehicles became established in the 1910s. Most long distance transport though was provided by railroads. However, as trucks became more powerful and as the highway system improved, trucks began to penetrate the intercity freight market. The use of increasingly powerful six cylinder then V8 gasoline engines, the introduction of the semi-trailer, and the introduction of diesel engines made trucks more capable and more economical. The construction of the interstate highway system reduced the time required for truck transport. Trucking grew rapidly. From 1945 to 2007, intercity ton-miles by truck increased at an average rate of 5.0%, well in excess of the GDP growth rate of 3.1%. Trucking growth has slowed in recent years and from the 1980s, trucking ton-miles have increased less rapidly than GDP.

The growth in intercity trucking relative to GDP is shown in Figure 4.22. Trucking rapidly penetrated the intercity freight market in the 1950s and 1960s as trucks and highways improved. The logistic curve, which closely fits the actual growth, suggests that trucks had reached saturation in their markets by the end of the 1970s. It is likely that the steady shift of the economy from goods to services and the resurgence of railroads ended the rapid growth of trucking. It had taken trucks around 60 years (from the 1910s to the 1970s) to achieve saturation.

Figure 4.22 Truck intercity ton-miles / GDP

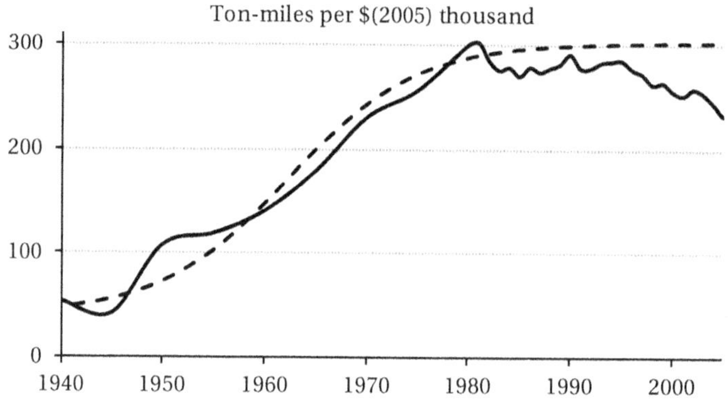

Sources: Data from U.S. Census Bureau, Historical Statistics of the United States and annual Statistical Abstracts.

Trucking helped sustain economic growth but did not lead growth. The rapid growth in trucking was a case of adoption of a less expensive product as the development of trucks and highways made trucking progressively cheaper than sending freight by rail or water. Trucks increasingly did the job previously done by other modes, helping to sustain the growth of the leading goods industries.

4.7.5 Passenger transportation

Personal transport initially was by horse. The railroads took over in providing longer distance transport in the second half of the 19th century. The coming of the automobile then transformed the scene. The automobile rapidly became dominant in all but long distance and dense inner-city movement. By the end of the 20th century there was approximately one motor vehicle for every adult in America. Inter-city travel distances could be so long, however, that the automobile was at a disadvantage. The railroads filled this gap for many decades until airlines, when they could offer seats at affordable prices, took over. Today, long distance passenger travel is dominated by the airlines, movement in high density urban areas is by bus and subway, and everything else is by automobiles.

The development of inter-city passenger travel is shown in Figure 4.23. Rail and bus have largely disappeared from inter-city travel while airlines have been increasing rapidly. Today, around 20% of inter-city travel is by air and just under 80% by automobile. People have chosen travel modes to minimize cost in terms partly of money but mainly of time.

Figure 4.23 Shares of inter-city passenger transport

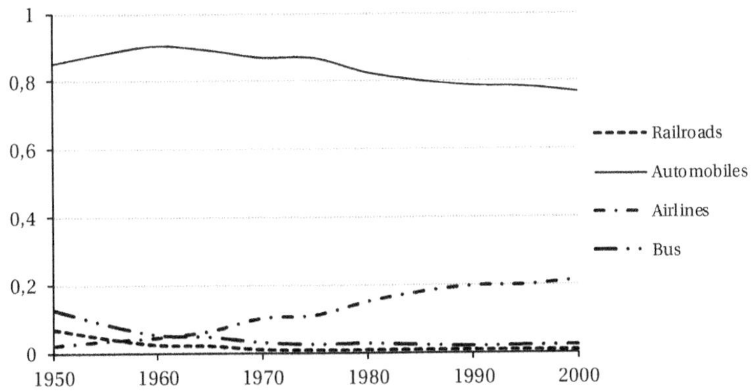

Sources: Data from U.S. Census Bureau, Historical Statistics of the United States and annual Statistical Abstracts.

4.7.6 Airlines

The main feature of inter-city passenger travel in recent decades has been the rise in air travel. Air travel is far quicker on long trips than any form of road or rail transport but this time advantage became accessible only as the price of air travel fell. The airline ticket price per passenger-mile since 1937 has declined at an average of 2.6% a year. The price relative to household income has declined by around 5.0% a year. The result is that domestic revenue passenger-miles have increased rapidly, at an average of 7.3% a year between 1950 and 2010, more than twice as fast as the GDP growth of 3.2%. The growth in domestic air travel is shown in Figure 4.24. The logistic model fitted to the data suggests that the market is approaching saturation although it has taken around 75 years to get to this point.

Figure 4.24 Domestic air travel

Billion revenue passenger miles

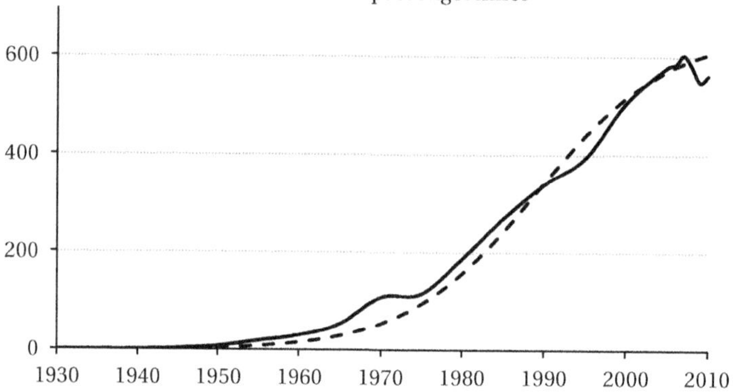

Sources: Data from Airlines for America, *Annual Results U.S. Airlines*. U.S. Census Bureau, Historical Statistics of the United States.

Airlines similarly have vastly expanded the market for international travel. Most travel outside of North America previously was by ocean liner. The introduction of long range piston aircraft after World War II began to establish an airline market and this market took off with the introduction of jets. Jets slashed travel time from days to hours while also cutting fares. International traffic of U.S. airlines increased at an average 7.2% a year from 1950 to 2010 while the economy increased at an average rate of 3.2%. Figure 4.25 shows these changes. A new market has been established. The logistic curve in the graph suggests that this market, after 60 or so years, is still growing although now less rapidly.

Figure 4.25 U.S. airlines, international travel

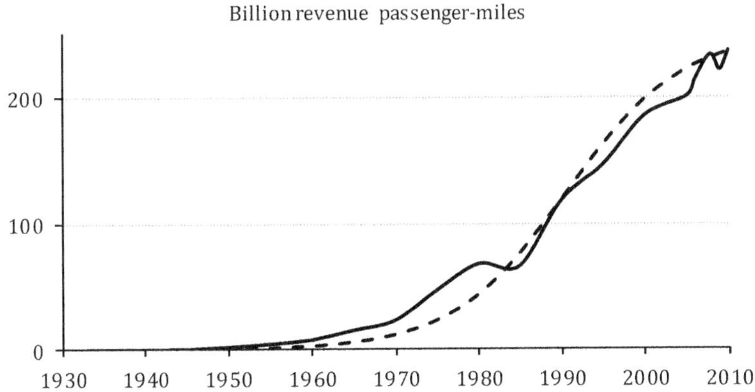

Sources: Data from Airlines for America, *Annual Results U.S. Airlines*. U.S. Census Bureau, Historical Statistics of the United States.

4.7.7 Transportation and the economy

Advances in transportation technology, such as the automobile, have vastly increased personal mobility. These gains are not fully reflected in GDP. But for-hire transportation is included in GDP. In this section we look at the effects on the economy of the growth in for-hire transportation.

Use of transportation grew rapidly in the 19th and early 20th centuries, in fact it grew about twice as rapidly as the economy. Table 4.14 shows the trends. This growth may have been overstated by measurement issues as purchased railroad services replaced self transport using horses. Despite this, there is no question that transportation was growing rapidly. This almost certainly was due to the opening up of the Midwest and then the west where railroads played a central role. It would also have reflected the growth in agricultural and steel production where waterborne traffic was so important. Since 1919, however, for-hire transportation has increased less rapidly than the economy. Transportation served the agricultural and manufacturing industries which now grew less rapidly and private motor vehicles took over some of the market from for-hire transport.

Table 4.14 For-hire transport in the economy

Average annual growth rates

	Transport output	GDP	Transport/GDP
1869 - 1919 (1)	6.2%	3.9%	2.2%
1919 - 1948	3.3%	3.4%	-0.1%
1948 - 1966	2.4%	4.1%	-1.7%
1966 - 2010	2.7%	2.8%	-0.1%

Note (1): The growth of constant dollar GDP is for 1874 to 1919.
Sources: Data from Kendrick (1961). Maddison (2006b). U.S, Bureau of Economic Analysis, National Economic Accounts.

The ongoing productivity improvement in transportation has made its own contribution to economic growth. Table 4.15 shows that early growth in transportation drew roughly 50:50 from greater productivity and more inputs. Over the middle part of the 20th century, though, productivity growth has been so rapid that resources were released from transportation, despite ongoing increases in output. Over the past half century, the situation has returned to productivity growth and inputs contributing roughly 50:50 to output growth. Transportation has grown roughly in line with the overall economy while using a steadily declining share of the nation's resources.

Table 4.15 Growth of for-hire transport

Average annual growth rates

	Output	TFP	Inputs (1)
1869 - 1919	6.2%	2.9%	3.3%
1919 - 1948	3.3%	4.0%	-0.6%
1948 - 1966	2.4%	3.4%	-1.0%
1966 - 2010 (2)	2.7%	1.2%	1.5%

Note (1): Input of capital and labor.
Note (2) Total Factor Productivity growth is for 1960 - 2007.
Sources: Data from Kendrick (1961) and (1973). Jorgenson, Mun Ho and Samuels (2010).

The growth in most surface transport took the form of new technologies, such as railroads and trucks, being cheaper than the old modes and so taking their markets away. This assisted economic growth by releasing resources from the transportation industries. But, one form of transportation was so different that it created an entirely new market. This was air travel.

Airlines have changed existing markets so radically that they in effect have created two new markets, one for long distance travel within the United States, the other for international travel. Much of this travel is personal in nature so is part of personal consumption and contributes to GDP directly. Business air travel would have reduced costs in other industries and so contributed to productivity elsewhere. These effects are relatively small, amounting to around 0.5% of GDP, but nonetheless have added to the benefits from transportation.

Transportation has contributed to economic growth in three ways. Directly, it helped sustain the growth of the agricultural and manufacturing industries which drove growth in the economy. Indirectly, transportation has supported these industries while using a declining share of the economy's resources - transportation in effect has been releasing resources. And separately, airlines have created entirely new markets and added directly to personal consumption.

4.8 Consumer appliances

4.8.1 Major appliances

Every household has cooking and heating equipment. These have become more efficient and sophisticated over time but their numbers have grown more or less with the population. However, there has been enormous growth in new types of household equipment – this has come from the development and adoption of electrical appliances. We look at major appliances in this section and smaller appliances in the next.

Hand laundering of clothes, sheets etc. is a time consuming chore which traditionally took hours out of the day of every housewife. As a result, efforts to mechanize washing began centuries ago. The 19th century saw hand-powered machines which assisted with washing. The first big advance, though, came around 1910 when electric washers began to appear. These machines were accompanied by a separate wringer to squeeze water out of the clothes. Adoption of these machines was slow as few houses were connected to the electricity network. As electricity reticulation was extended, so washing machine sales began to rise. Machine design was then improved by powering the wringer. The Great Depression slowed sales and then home washers were not produced during World War II. Post-war, the automatic washing machine became widely available; this combined washing with a spin function (using centrifugal force to remove most of the water from the clothes) in a single machine, reducing cost and increasing convenience. Adoption of washing machines then increased rapidly.

The portable electric vacuum cleaner was invented in 1907 and the patent was bought by William Henry Hoover. Hoover developed a practical cleaner and then successfully commercialized it in the United States and in many other countries. Vacuum cleaners have been improved over the years including, in recent times, using centrifugal force in addition to filtering to remove dust from the airflow.

Electric refrigerators were introduced in the 1910s although it was not until 1923 that the first self-contained refrigerator was introduced (by

Frigidaire, then part of General Motors). Freezers, either as part of the refrigerator or as separate units, were introduced after World War II.

Adoption of these major appliances was rapid, as shown in Figure 4.26. Refrigerators reached saturation first, in the 1960s, vacuum cleaners next, in the 1970s, and washers last, by the end of the 1970s. For the 50 years or so it took to reach market saturation, major appliances were purchased in large numbers by American households.

Figure 4.26 Adoption of major appliances

Share of wired households with the appliance

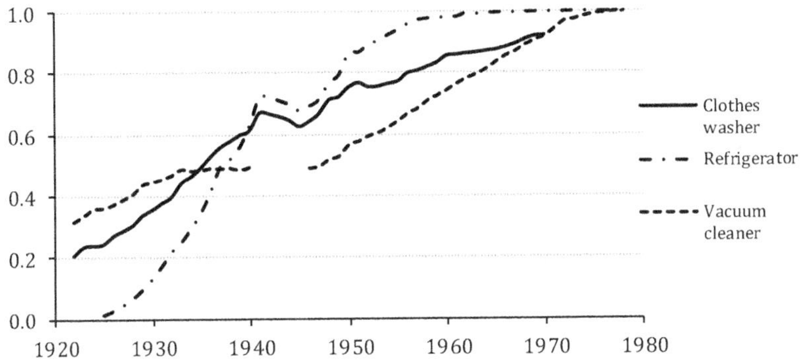

Sources: Data from U.S. Census Bureau, Historical Statistics of the United States and annual Statistical Abstracts.

After the core appliances had become accepted, consumers started to purchase further appliances to reduce work or add to comfort. Newer appliances such as dishwashers, clothes dryers and air conditioners entered the picture. By 1980, 47% of households had a clothes dryer, 37% had a dishwasher and 57% had air conditioning. Adoption has since increased but not to the levels of the core appliances. The greatest penetration has been of air conditioning which reached 89% adoption in 2009.

4.8.2 Smaller appliances

After these major appliances had become established, the focus of development shifted to smaller electrical appliances. The 1960s saw the rapid spread of kitchen and household electrics. Here is a list of smaller appliances with more than 1 million shipped in 1970: food waste disposers, blenders, broilers, coffeemakers, food processors, frypans/skillets, irons, mixers, slow cookers, toasters, waffle irons/sandwich grills, floor polishers, fans, portable electric heaters, hair dryers, hair setters, heating pads and oral hygiene devices. Many electrical appliances for the workshop, garage and garden also have been introduced. The result was that, by the 1970s, consumers had filled their residences with all sorts of electrical appliances to assist in carrying out most household tasks.

4.8.3 Appliances and the economy

Spending on appliances grew more rapidly than current dollar GDP until 1973, despite falling relative prices of appliances. Since then, spending on appliances has grown less rapidly than total spending. Production of appliances continues to grow more rapidly than total production. From 1929 to 1973, production of appliances grew at a trend of 6.2% a year, compared to 4.3% for constant dollar GDP. Even since the slowdown in the 1970s, the growth trend for appliances after 1973, at 3.8% a year, is still slightly more rapid than the 3.0% growth trend for the economy as a whole.

Appliances have contributed to growth even though they account directly for only 1% of the economy. For a start, purchases of consumer appliances have been a growth driver for the economy. Also, their indirect effect has been expansionary. The production of appliances is unusually intensive in its use of metals (accounting, in 1987, for 15% of its costs) and other mineral products (plastics, rubber, paint etc., a further 9%). Appliances were one of the drivers of industrial growth in the steel, chemicals and other materials industries. This is their second contribution to growth – to help spread growth through the rest of the economic system.

4.9 Steel

4.9.1 The market for steel

Demand for steel started to rise rapidly in the 1870s with the expansion of the railroads. Demand further increased with the rise of the automobile and general manufacturing in the first part of the 20th century. Rapid growth continued until around 1925. The trend growth rate until this time was 10% a year – the industry doubled in size every seven years. Production dipped in the Great Depression but rapid growth resumed in World War II and the growth era of the 1950s. Growth began to slow in the 1970s with use of steel peaking around 2000.

The growth of apparent consumption (U.S. production less exports plus imports) is shown in Figure 4.27. The market has followed a logistic path, the smooth line on the graph, with a gradual start followed by rapid growth which slowed as the market matured. Although considerable amounts of steel continue to be used, there is little further growth. It took a long time for the steel market to reach maturity - more than 100 years.

Figure 4.27 Consumption of steel mill products
Million short tons

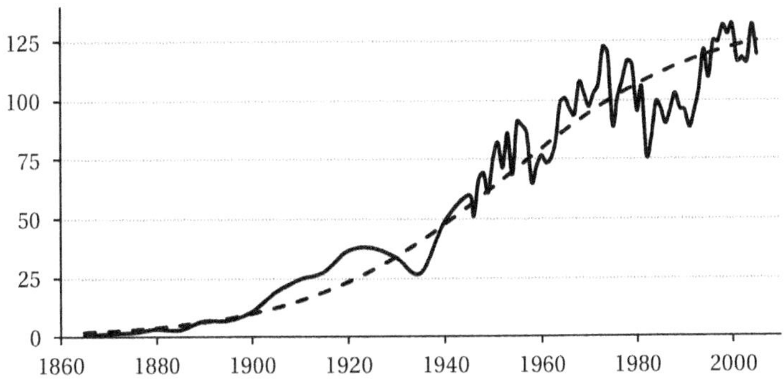

Sources: Data from U.S. Census Bureau, Historical Statistics of the United States and annual Statistical Abstracts.

The main uses of steel are shown in Table 4.16. Steel is an intermediate product – it is not a final demand item but is used in making products for consumers and for plant and equipment investment. More than half the current market for steel is for motor vehicles and for construction. Rail transportation, which formed most of the market in the early days, is still there but today accounts for only 2% of the market.

Table 4.16 Purchases of steel, 2002

	Shipments (1)	Share
Automotive	14.0	22%
Construction	20.5	33%
Containers	3.2	5%
Oil and gas industries	2.1	3%
Appliances, utensils	1.7	3%
Machinery	1.4	2%
Electrical equipment	1.3	2%
Rail transportation	1.0	2%
Other (2)	17.5	28%
Total (3)	62.8	100%

Note (1): Net shipments, million short tons.
Note (2): Industries each purchasing less than 1 million short tons.
Note (3): Total excluding steel service centers, steel distributors and steel for further processing.
Source: Data from U.S. Census Bureau, Statistical Abstract of the United States, 2008.

U.S. production supplied the market during its rapid growth years but imports began to displace local production after 1973. Figure 4.28 shows what happened. The logistic curve in the graph reflects the fact that the market was still growing but that something happened abruptly in 1973 to drive customers away from local production.

Customers began to switch to imported steel as imports became cheaper for many types of steel. The change in relative prices might have been influenced by U.S. environmental regulations which came into effect around this time but the main changes probably were the decline in the exchange rate of the U.S. dollar and the rise in oil prices which increased the cost structure of U.S. industry in general.

Figure 4.28 Production of raw steel

Million short tons

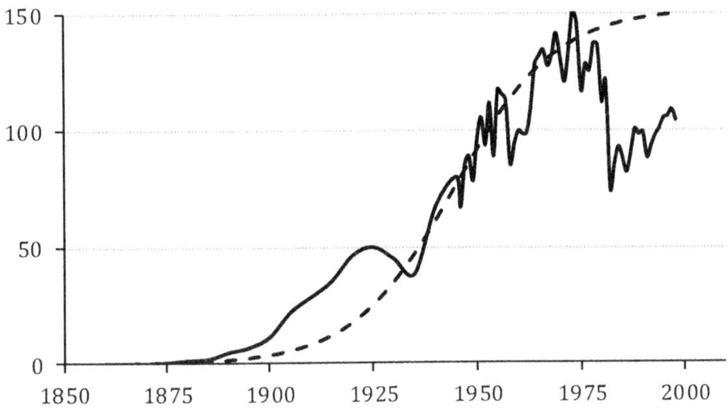

Sources: U.S. Census Bureau, Historical Statistics of the United States and annual Statistical Abstracts.

4.9.2 Steel-making technology

The first integrated ironworks in America was at Saugus, Massachusetts and dates from the mid-17th century. Over the 18th century iron technology changed by replacing charcoal (from wood) with coke (from coal) as the fuel and agent for oxidation. Since then the great changes occurred in steel-making rather than iron-making. Early steel-making started with wrought iron (low carbon iron) and added carbon to make steel in heated clay pots (crucibles). Although this produced high quality steel it was limited in scale and was expensive.

The breakthrough to making low cost steel was the Bessemer converter, developed in England by Henry Bessemer in the 1850s and refined in the 1860s. The Bessemer process was observed by Andrew Carnegie while in England in 1872. Carnegie recognized its potential and returned to build a plant in Pittsburgh (which was well placed in terms of access to the essential materials - coking coal and iron ore). Carnegie, over the next 30 years, proceeded to develop the modern American steel industry. Carnegie implemented a complex set of technical and commercial strategies; he (1) introduced the Bessemer process allowing large scale and cheap production, (2) targeted a large market – steel rails for the burgeoning railroads – and rapidly gained volume, (3) kept at the technological forefront, for example being an early investor in the open hearth method, (4) bought out rival producers to create large scale in production and marketing, and (5) pursued vertical integration, from mining the ore to making pig iron, making coke then making and marketing steel. Carnegie ultimately sold his company to J.P. Morgan who merged it with others to form U.S. Steel in 1901. In its early years U.S. Steel dominated the industry, supplying two-thirds of the steel market.

The steel industry grew rapidly in Pennsylvania, in Alabama and, in particular, in the Midwest. The Midwest offered access to iron ore (via Great Lakes shipping from the vast deposits in Minnesota), coking coal (from Pennsylvania) and to markets, supplying the rapidly expanding railroad, automobile and construction industries.

The Bessemer process gave way to open hearth steelmaking which was cheaper and easier to control. In turn, open hearth in the 1950s gave way to lower cost basic oxygen steelmaking (BOS). BOS is a refined version of the Bessemer process with oxygen rather than air being blown through the molten iron mixture. The most recent development has been the growth of electric furnaces. So called "mini mills", using electric arc furnaces and typically using scrap steel rather than pig iron, cut the cost of producing several types of steel products, particularly bar products. Today, integrated BOS mills and mini mills each account for around half of U.S. production.

The evolution of steelmaking technology is shown in Figure 4.29. This history is of one technology crowding out its more costly predecessor until it too is crowded out by a new and cheaper process. The most rapid adoption was of the Bessemer process where the traditional crucible process all but disappeared within a decade (reflecting the fact that the Bessemer process was more than 80% cheaper than the crucible process). Subsequent cost differences have been smaller and adoption times corresponding longer - the rise of the open hearth process then took more than 50 years and then the demise of open hearth, to be replaced by BOS and electric furnaces, also took around 50 years.

Figure 4.29 Adoption of steelmaking technologies
Shares of U.S. raw steel production

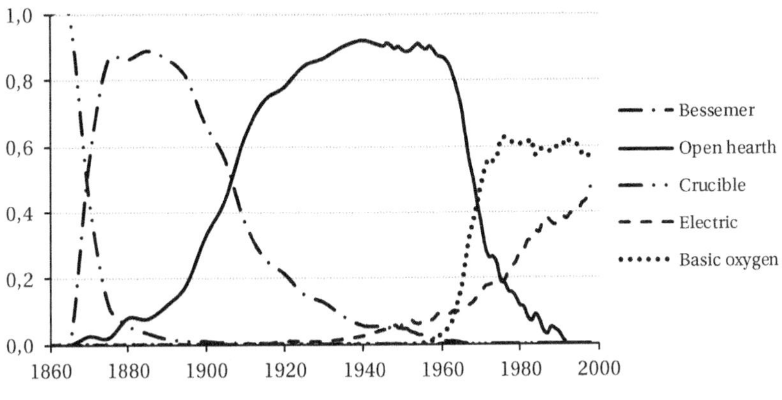

Sources: Data from U.S. Census Bureau, Historical Statistics of the United States and annual Statistical Abstracts.

4.9.3 Contribution to economic growth

Iron and steel have been a relatively small part of the economy, accounting at their peak (in the 1920s) for only 2 – 3% of GDP and just 0.3% today. Nonetheless, the iron and steel industry has been important to U.S. economic growth. Steel has been the visible heart of industrialization. But, steel has been a sustaining, not a driving force in economic growth. Steel is used to make things that people want, it is not used in its own right. Iron and steel provided a key input that helped sustain the growth in agriculture, transportation, construction and consumer durables which has driven the economy forward over the past 125 years. The availability of cheap steel underpinned the emerging industries which mechanized American production, movement and the American home.

Kendrick's estimates of growth in the primary metals industries and of the economy are shown in Table 4.17. These estimates go through 1966 so cover the rapid growth years of iron and steel, not the slow growth after 1973.

Table 4.17 Primary metals and the economy

Growth trends, 1899 - 1966

GDP	3.4%
Total factor input	1.8%
Metals output	3.3%
Labor input	1.2%
Capital input	2.2%
Factor inputs	1.6%
Total Factor Productivity	1.7%

Sources: Data from Kendrick (1961) and (1973).

The growth in steel output, at 3.3% a year, was pretty much the same as the growth of the economy, at 3.4%. Productivity growth in primary metals, at a 1.7% annual trend, was sufficiently rapid that it sustained slightly more than half of the increase in metals output so that factor inputs, labor and capital, needed to increase at just 1.6% a year. Factor inputs in the economy as a whole were growing at 1.8% a year. Metals were claiming a slightly decreasing share of overall inputs while helping sustain industrial growth and the general growth of the United States.

4.10 Petroleum

4.10.1 A visible industry

Petroleum is a highly visible industry. It is however, a relatively small part of the economy. For example, consumer expenditure on motor fuels and lubricants in 2009 absorbed 2.8% of personal consumption expenditures and accounted for 2.0% of GDP.

4.10.2 Growth of the industry

The petroleum industry grew rapidly for around 70 years. From 1907, the year before the Model T was introduced, until 1977, the year of peak oil intensity of the economy, the apparent consumption of crude oil grew at an average rate of 5.1% whereas constant dollar GDP grew at just 3.4%.

Figure 4.30 shows the oil intensity of the economy – crude oil consumption relative to population and to constant dollar GDP. There was rapid growth until the 1970s. The oil price increases of the 1970s led to a switch from energy-intensive goods to new goods, such as electronic equipment, and to services. In addition, the markets for energy-intensive goods such as automobiles reached saturation. But, for many decades, petroleum was a real growth industry.

Figure 4.30 Intensity of use of petroleum
Indexes, 1945 = 1

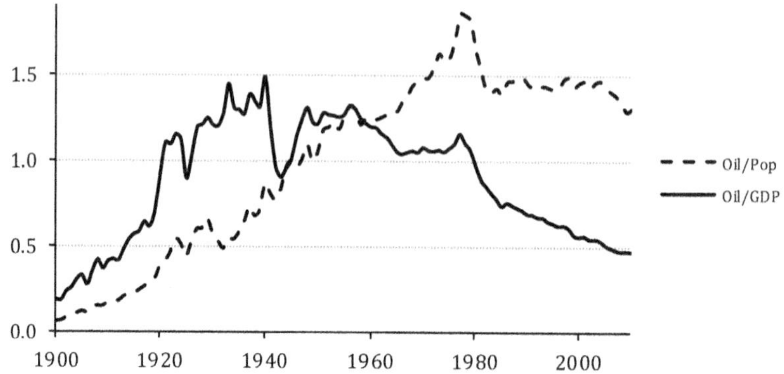

Sources: Data from Maddison (2006b). U.S. Energy Information Administration (2011). U.S. Bureau of Economic Analysis, National Economic Accounts. U.S. Census Bureau, Historical Statistics of the United States and annual Statistical Abstracts.

4.10.3 Petroleum and economic growth

Petroleum products are used to power transportation equipment - motor vehicles, aircraft and ships – as well as construction equipment and many stationary engines; petroleum products are also used for heating, as a basis for asphalts and as a feedstock for many plastics and chemicals. The years until the 1970s saw rapid growth in these products. Petroleum was carried along by this growth.

Petroleum was essential to growth but it was an enabler, not a driver. Petroleum was an essential input to many of the growth drivers of the 20th century. Consumers purchased petroleum products to run their automobiles; producers purchased petroleum products to fuel their equipment and as a feedstock.

Table 4.18 shows the most petroleum-intensive forms of production – the 10 most intensive industries in the Input-Output Accounts for 1987.

These are the direct requirements – purchases of petroleum products per dollar of output of the industries shown. Air transport, for example, in 1987 purchased 11 cents of petroleum products for every dollar of its own sales.

Table 4.18 10 most intensive petroleum using industries. 1987
Purchases of petroleum products per dollar of output. 1987 input-output structure.

Air transportation	0.11
Petroleum refining and related products	0.07
State and local government enterprises	0.06
Motor freight transportation and warehousing	0.05
Railroads and related services; passenger ground transportati(	0.05
Forestry and fishery products	0.04
Water transportation	0.03
Automotive repair and services	0.03
Electric services (utilities)	0.02
Water and sanitary services	0.02

Source: Data from U.S. Bureau of Economic Analysis, Industry Economic Accounts.

Petroleum is typical of many industries which have grown rapidly but as a result of helping to sustain the growth drivers rather than being growth drivers in their own right. In particular, motor vehicles were one of the main growth drivers in the years until the 1970s and petroleum was an essential input to producing and operating motor vehicles.

4.11 Chemicals

4.11.1 Development

Natural rubber, from trees grown in tropical climates, must be treated to make it suitable for practical use. One of the main treatments is vulcanization in which rubber is heated with sulfur to produce an elastic and durable compound. Vulcanization was developed by Charles Goodyear working in Springfield, Massachusetts and patented in 1844. Rubber was first synthesized by the Russian inventor Sergei

Lebedev in 1910 although it took Lebedev until 1928 to develop a method for the industrial manufacture of synthetic rubber.

Basic chemicals are those used in producing other goods. For example, sodium hydroxide (caustic soda) is used in the manufacture of pulp and paper, textiles, soaps, detergents and cleaners; ammonia is used as a precursor to fertilizers, pharmaceuticals, explosives, cleaners, antiseptics and as a refrigerant; and sulfuric acid is used in making fertilizers and also is used industrially in making products such as detergents, synthetic resins, dyestuffs, pharmaceuticals, catalysts, insecticides and antifreeze. The principal processes for producing basic chemicals were developed in Europe in the 19th and early 20th centuries. For example, the electrolytic chloralkali process, developed in the 1890s, is used to produce caustic soda starting from brine; ammonia is produced from hydrocarbons using the Haber-Bosch process, developed in the early 20th century in Germany; and sulfuric acid is produced using a development of the method pioneered by Peregrine Phillips in Britain in the 1830s.

The development of specialty chemicals - such as adhesives, sealants, coatings, industrial cleaning chemicals and catalysts – was led by the United States and took place in the mid-20th century. Chemicals associated with the life sciences – such as pharmaceuticals, diagnostics, animal health products, vitamins and pesticides – have been developed more recently, led by Britain and the United States.

Plastics are organic (carbon-based) chemicals which can be formed into useful shapes. Most plastics are made from petrochemicals but they can also be made from other hydrocarbons such as coal or from natural compounds such as cellulose and starch. Early plastics such as rayon, which was introduced in 1910 and acetate, introduced in 1924, were made from cellulose. The first synthetic plastic was invented in 1907, by Leo Hendrik Baekeland working in New York state. With the trade name Bakelite, it was originally used for electrical and mechanical parts, coming into widespread use in consumer goods in the 1920s. Modern plastics began in the 1920s. Although polyvinyl chloride (PVC) had been discovered in the 19th century, it was not until 1926, when the B.F. Goodrich Company developed a way of making it formable, that it came into practical use. Polystyrene was brought into practical use by the German company I. G. Farben in 1931. The basic production method for polyethylene (now widely use in bags, films and membranes) was discovered in Britain in the 1930s. Polypropylene was discovered by Giulio Natta in Italy in the 1950s.

The first synthetic fiber was polyamide, now known by its trade name, nylon. Nylon was developed by the Du Pont Company. Development was led by chemist Wallace Carothers; from its discovery in 1927 development of a commercial product and manufacturing processes took until 1939. Subsequent synthetic fibers include acrylic (introduced in 1950), polyester (in 1953) and carbon fiber (1968).

Several features stand out in the development of the chemicals and plastics industries. First is the distinction between the science and the engineering. Particularly for plastics, it took many years, often decades, for practical ways to be developed for producing and applying the compounds which had been discovered in the laboratory. Second is the geographical mobility of technology. Discoveries have been made and production technologies developed in many countries but the knowledge has been transferred widely. The United States, with its large market, has attracted much of the subsequent production as well as refinement in production technologies. Third, the industry has grown into products and applications which were never even thought of in the early days. The range of applications of chemicals as inputs to productive processes and as final goods has continued to increase. Finally, there is the time element. The development of new products continues and the range of applications widens to this day, more than 150 years after Charles Goodyear started the industrial chemical industry. The industry suffered a shock in the 1970s as increases in the prices of oil and gas, its principal raw materials, caused prices to rise, which slowed the growth in demand. However, some growth continues, especially in newer chemicals supplying growing final markets such as health care.

4.11.2 Demand for chemicals

Some chemicals, including soaps, some plastics and pharmaceuticals, cater directly to personal consumption and other final demand. Demand for these chemicals tends to grow rapidly when the products are new and then, when the market is saturated, to grow just with population. Most chemicals though are used as inputs to other products. For example, a major use is for fertilizers, an input to agriculture. This demand grew rapidly when the chemicals became available in large volume but the market is now saturated and demand grows only in line with agricultural production. The principal demand for rubber comes from motor vehicles and the rubber industry grew in line with automobile production – rapidly until the 1970s and then slowly. Chemicals used in the manufacture of other goods similarly grew rapidly during the industrial expansion of the United States through to the 1970s. Plastics really only became established after World War II and their growth has been more recent. Most chemicals, and in particular plastics, use oil or gas as feedstock. As a result, their costs, and so their prices, have risen after oil and gas prices started to rise in the 1970s; this greatly slowed their demand growth. Finally, pharmaceuticals began to increase after World War II and their growth is continuing.

The growth in the chemical, excluding rubber and plastics, intensity of the economy is shown in Figure 4.31. Demand followed a logistic growth path until two things - the oil and gas price increases of the 1970s and the shift of new spending from manufacturing to services - led to a shift away from chemicals.

Figure 4.31 Chemicals production / GDP

Quantities. 2005 = 100

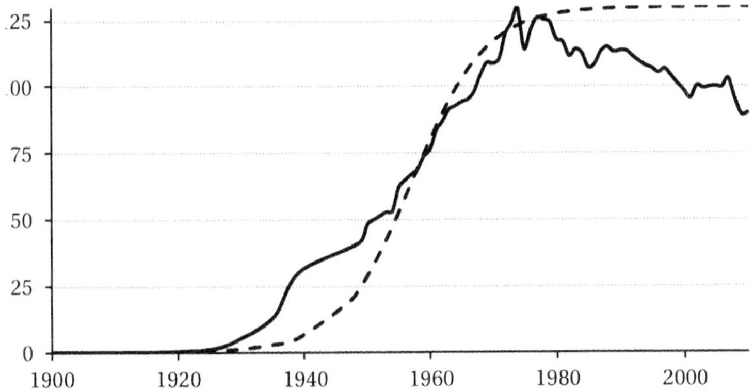

Sources: Data from U.S. Census Bureau, Historical Statistics of the United States and annual Statistical Abstracts.

The use of rubber grew rapidly with the rise of motor vehicles through the 1960s; the production of plastics grew rapidly when a wide range of useful plastics became available after World War II. Figure 4.32 shows that the intensity of use of rubber and plastics declined after the 1970s. The logistic curve suggests that the growth of demand was brought to an early end by the price rises of the 1970s.

Figure 4.32 Rubber and plastics/GDP
Quantities. 2005 = 100

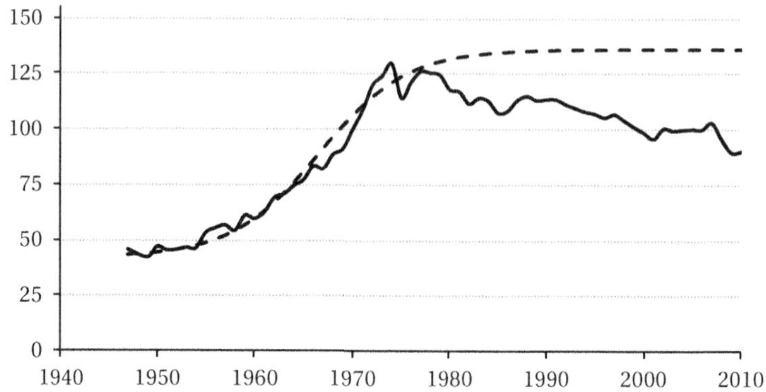

Sources: Data from U.S. Census Bureau, Historical Statistics of the United States and annual Statistical Abstracts.

4.11.3 Chemicals and economic growth

Chemicals, plastics and rubber products, grew more rapidly than GDP until 1974. The first data on their contribution to GDP is for 1977 when they accounted for 2.8% of GDP. Their slower growth since then has brought their share of GDP down to 1.9% in 2009. But, for the first six decades of the 20th century chemicals were a leading industry. Table 4.19 shows growth patterns for the years through 1966.

Table 4.19 Growth in chemicals, rubber and plastics

Growth trends in percent per annum

	Chemicals	Rubber and plastics
Time period	1899 - 1966	1948 - 1966
Growth trends in		
Output	6.4%	6.5%
Inputs	2.7%	2.8%
TFP	3.7%	3.7%
Gross Domestic Product	3.4%	3.7%

Sources: Data from Kendrick (1961) and (1973). U.S. Census Bureau, Historical Statistics of the United States and annual Statistical Abstracts.

Output quantities grew rapidly – at more than 6% a year compared to the overall economy which grew in the 3% range. Productivity growth in chemicals was sufficiently rapid that output growth was sustained by inputs growing slightly less rapidly than the economy. Chemicals also contributed to economic growth indirectly by contributing to productivity growth in using industries such as agriculture, motor vehicles and consumer durables.

4.12 Retailing

4.12.1 The development of retailing

Retailing has seen a succession of innovations; here are some of the highlights. Alexander Turney Stewart established (what appears to be) the first department store, this was in New York City in 1848. He opened a larger store in 1862 – in a six story building occupying most of a city block, employing 2,000 staff and ultimately comprising 31 departments of different types of merchandise. Rowland Hussey Macy was another early developer of the department store. The McCormick Harvesting Machine Company in the 1850s established a network of trained salesmen to demonstrate and sell its agricultural equipment. Richard Sears in 1888 established a catalog and mail order business which made accessible to farmers and small town America (which at that time was most of America) the manufactured goods which were beginning to appear in such diversity. Sears Roebuck grew rapidly just as a mail order business and continued to grow after it established its first store in 1925. Sears Roebuck for many years was America's largest retailer (until surpassed in the 1980s by Walmart). The Cleveland Arcade, opened in 1890, was a prominent, early enclosed mall. The concept of the self-service grocery store was established by Clarence Saunders in Tennessee in the 1910s. The concept was popularized by the Great Atlantic and Pacific Tea Company (A&P), already a large grocery chain, which moved to self-service in 1936, creating the supermarket. The Ford Motor Company in the 1910s, with the Model T, led the development of the franchised dealer system for retailing and servicing goods. General Motors extended the use of the franchised dealer system, along with offering consumer credit, attractive features, styling and advertising, and with these led the later growth of the automobile industry.

The automobile changed the shape of retailing. The first "automobile friendly" stores were the strip malls –collections of shops located on roads and with parking on the premises - which started to appear in the 1920s. The first shopping center with parking integrated into the design was opened in Columbus, Ohio in 1928. The fully enclosed mall, with integrated parking, was pioneered by architect Victor Gruen with the Southdale Mall in Minneapolis, opening in 1956.

Discount stores were pioneered by the F.W. Woolworth Company. Woolworth established what became known as "five and dimes" in Pennsylvania in the 1880s. Modern versions emerged much later. Wal-Mart Stores was founded in 1962 by Sam Walton in Arkansas with Kmart and Target opening in the same year. Walmart grew to become the largest retailer in the United States. More recently, retailing has extended to the internet. Jeff Bezos established Amazon.com in 1995; Amazon.com started as a bookstore but has diversified into retailing many kinds of consumer goods. eBay is a large producer-to-consumer and consumer-to-consumer marketplace, started as an internet auction system by Pierre Omidyar in 1995.

The development of retailing has shown a number of core trends: (1) continuing change as new retailing formats compete for the consumer's dollar in what is an enormous market, (2) the drive for scale in order to cut costs and prices, (3) the drive to reduce information and search costs by retailers establishing reputations for known quality, taking the quality risk out of buying, (4) the drive to reduce search and transaction costs by making purchasing accessible, first by mail order then by department stores, then by malls and most recently by the internet.

4.12.2 Contribution of retailing to economic growth

Retailing is a huge industry. Retailing today accounts for more than 6% of GDP and for more than 10% of employment.

Retailing is essential in selling most types of consumer goods. But, spending has been moving from goods towards services. In 1929 consumption of goods accounted for 42% of GDP but that share has steadily declined, today it is down to 23%. As a result, retailing has been growing less rapidly than the economy. Retailing current dollar GDP has grown at 5.9% a year from 1948 to 2010 compared to 6.6% for GDP.

Retailing, then, is a large industry but not a growth-leading industry. Its growth is related to growth of consumer spending on goods, not to the growth of the overall economy. Nor has retail been to the fore in releasing resources for other uses. Retail productivity has been increasing but we estimate that productivity growth has averaged around 0.3% a year which is less than average and certainly not enough to release large volumes of resources.

However, in a quite different sense, retailing has played a vital role in economic growth. Economic growth has been led by new consumer goods such as automobiles, appliances and electronic goods. Retailing helped create and sustain the growth of demand for these goods. More generally, retailing has been part of the development of marketing which has created the consumer society and the consumer society has been central to economic growth.

4.13 Advertising

Advertising originally was a matter of providing information. Merchants used the media of the time, essentially signs, newspapers and magazines, to inform the public of the goods available and their prices. The emphasis was on the goods and their features. However, over the course of the 19th century, the rise in discretionary income and the increase in the range of goods available led to greater competition for the consumer dollar. Advertising became a central feature in this competition. Advertising began to change in two ways. First, the nature of advertising gradually changed from information to persuasion and second, advertising gradually changed to a business service.

While information advertising continues to this day, the rapid growth took place in persuasion advertising. The essence of persuasion is to associate desirable features or desirable outcomes with the consumption of the product. The implication is that the consumer will be happier as a result of consuming the particular product. These features might be accomplishment and success as a homemaker, recognition and success socially, in personal appeal and in matters of sex, excitement, entertainment, power and so on.

Among the most famous persuasion advertisements were those using the Marlboro Man, created by Leo Burnett Company to promote Marlboro cigarettes. These advertisements, which ran from 1954 to 1999, featured a rugged outdoorsman, generally in a cattle ranching setting. The persuasion element was the association of smoking Marlboro cigarettes with masculinity, toughness, self-reliance and so on. The association of the rugged outdoorsman with Marlboro became so well established that some later advertisements showed neither a cigarette nor the Marlboro packet nor even the word Marlboro.

The rise and efficacy of persuasion in advertising was so pronounced that it stimulated two of the classic management books of the 1950s – Vance Packard's *The Hidden Persuaders*, which lamented the manipulation of consumers for commercial purposes, and J. K. Galbraith's *The Affluent Society*, which lamented the ascendency of personal consumption over public goods and society-wide objectives.

The introduction of broadcast radio and then television gave rise to another form of advertising to complement information and persuasion – sponsorship. Here, an advertiser would gain attention by sponsoring a program. This is typified by the "soap opera" which got its name from Proctor & Gamble's sponsorship of episodic programs in order to promote Ivory soap and other household products.

Advertising gradually emerged as its own industry. Advertising agencies specialized in creating advertisements and in placing these in media and other display channels. The first agency was N.W. Ayer & Son, established in Philadelphia in 1869. James Walter Thompson bought an existing placement agency in 1877 and proceeded to turn it into the forerunner of the modern agency. Thompson focused on creating the advertisement rather than just placing it. He developed the role of the creative department and later the role of the account executive.

John Wanamaker, a merchant who, among other things, started the well-known department store in Philadelphia, was an early proponent of advertising. Concerning his considerable spending on advertising he said "Half the money I spend on advertising is wasted; the trouble is, I don't know which half." It was many years later that advertising people began to grapple with this problem. The Young & Rubicam agency led the move into consumer and media research in the 1930s. Young & Rubicam, with the assistance of George Gallup, pioneered market research using surveys, questionnaires, audience measurement, panels, focus groups and similar methods to try to work out which advertisements worked, to what extent and how. The objective, naturally, was to use consumer information to improve the efficacy of advertising and also of other marketing tactics. In recent times, the internet has generated new ways of finding consumer interests and delivering targeted advertising.

Comprehensive data on advertising go back to 1935, much of it compiled by Robert J. Coen of McCann-Erickson. This historical data, used in Table 4.20, shows the changing structure of advertising as new delivery channels have become available. Delivery has shifted from print towards electronic broadcast media while internet advertising is now emerging. The main point from this Table, though, is that importance of advertising has not changed – it has continued to absorb 3% of consumer expenditure. The form of advertising has changed to take advantage of new channels but the broad role of advertising has not changed.

Table 4.20 Spending on advertising

	1935	2007
Newspapers	44%	15%
Magazines	8%	5%
Miscellaneous	20%	13%
Direct Mail	16%	22%
Farm Publications	1%	
Business Papers	3%	1%
Billboards, out-of-home	2%	3%
Yellow Pages		5%
Radio	7%	7%
Broadcast TV		16%
Cable TV		9%
Internet		4%
Total	100%	100%
Total advertising spending, $ bn	1.7	280
Advertising as % of Personal Consumption Spending	3%	3%

Sources: Data from U.S. Census Bureau, Historical Statistics of the United States and annual Statistical Abstracts. U.S. Bureau of Economic Analysis, National Economic Accounts.

4.14 Marketing

Marketing is the name given to the set of business measures directed to increasing the revenue from the sale of a product. Advertising, considered in the previous section, is just one element of marketing. These elements all relate to consumer behavior and aim to increase demand for the good. These measures might be expressed as (1) product, encompassing features such as functionality, ease of use, appearance, reliability, durability, warrantees and servicing; (2) selling, encompassing features such as retail outlets, distribution channels, sales practices and price; and (3) promotion which encompasses features such as advertising, publicity, promotions and branding.

Customer-focused marketing used to be presented in terms of the "four Ps", shown in Table 4.21. Modern views of marketing use similar concepts but express them in terms more related to the customer as SIVA, again as shown in the Table.

Table 4.21 Components of marketing

Four Ps	SIVA
Product	Solution
Promotion	Information
Price	Value
Place (Distribution)	Access

The rise of marketing has been central to the growth of American business. Virtually all large businesses have a marketing section of similar importance to the production and financial sections. And, marketing has become a central component of business education in American colleges and universities.

Two examples illustrate the importance of marketing in modern business. These are the growth of Coca-Cola and the growth of General Motors.

Coca-Cola is one of the biggest success stories in marketing. Coca-Cola initially retailed its product via soda fountains. Asa Griggs Candler gained control of the company around 1892 and set about improving sales. Candler did this by what we know today as marketing. Candler established a decentralized system of bottlers to produce the product (from syrup supplied by Coca-Cola) and sell to their market regions. Candler then created the image of a unique and desirable product by means of packaging (in the distinctive shaped bottle) and, most importantly, by massive and sophisticated advertising that persuaded consumers of the desirability of the product. Over time, Coca-Cola established a distinctive brand which gained recognition and attracted custom worldwide. Coca-Cola then continued its growth by creating different beverages and leveraging the core brand to gain sales in these new market segments.

Whereas Coca-Cola sold a product which could be bought with the change in your pocket, General Motors was selling a capital good which cost the equivalent of your annual income. GM developed new marketing techniques to sell these big ticket items. Whereas the established leader, Ford, aimed to maximize units sold and based its sales strategy on low prices, GM was more interested in maximizing revenues and developed its marketing with this in mind. GM did not compete on price with the early market leader, Ford's Model T. Instead, GM competed on product quality, offering features and comfort which the Model T lacked. GM offered credit to make its cars accessible. GM developed the idea of the annual model with styling and performance changes to make the new models more desirable and, to make it easy for existing owners to buy, started a trade-in scheme. GM developed an extensive dealer network to sell and service its automobiles and to take trade-ins on new purchases. And, GM was a pioneer in segmenting the market. GM had, in the words of its President, Alfred P. Sloan Jr, "a car for every purse and purpose". The payoff was that GM could increase volume of its entry-level cars while charging higher prices for its up-market brands, all working to increase its earnings. GM pioneered a wide range of marketing techniques which led to the company becoming one of the largest in the world.

4.14.1 Marketing and economic growth

Economic growth has been led by new consumer goods such as automobiles, appliances and electronic goods. Consumers do not truly need these goods - they are not essential; after all, consumers got along without them for centuries. But these goods make lives easier, more interesting or otherwise more enjoyable. Consumers want these goods and the task that marketing has accomplished has been to turn these wants into needs. Marketing helped create the mass consumption society, the consumer society. The consumer society has driven the growth in consumption spending which has fuelled economic growth for the past century. Without consumers buying the new goods and services which have been developed, it is not unrealistic to argue that per capita spending, production and incomes would still be around their levels of 1900, or only a small fraction of their levels today.

Marketing and the consumer society have been at the very least permissive of economic growth but we consider them causal factors, essential parts of the process that has created new goods and services, created markets for these new products, and thereby kept driving the economy forwards. Marketing has been essential to economic growth in the United States.

4.15 Entertainment

4.15.1 Growth of entertainment

Entertainment has grown to account in 2010 for more than 8% of personal consumption expenditure and around 6% of GDP. Entertainment in the National Economic Accounts is called recreation. The growth of recreation within GDP over the past century is shown in Figure 4.33.

Figure 4.33 Recreation spending in GDP

Share of current dollar expenditure

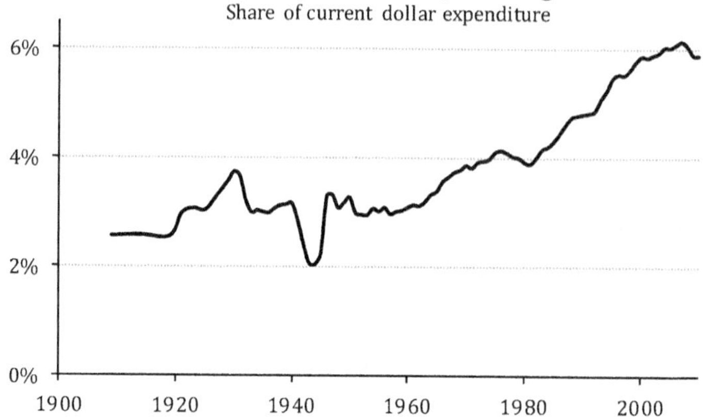

Sources: Data from U.S. Census Bureau, Historical Statistics of the United States. U.S. Bureau of Economic Analysis, National Economic Accounts.

These accounts measure as recreation the purchase of goods and services used in the enjoyment of leisure activities. They cover most but not all of leisure-related goods and services; for example, they do not include magazines, newspapers, internet access, personal travel, tourism or social and religious activities. Clearly, entertainment measured in the accounts underestimates total spending on entertainment, recreational and leisure activities.

Entertainment has grown rapidly for a number of powerful reasons: (1) people's incomes have risen, creating much more purchasing power; (2) leisure time, or time not spent in paid work or in household chores, has risen substantially; (3) new types of entertainment goods and services have become available; and (4) the relative prices of entertainment goods and services have declined. Simply put, people have more free time and they have the purchasing power to buy goods and services to help them use this time enjoyably.

The evolution of consumer spending within entertainment or recreation is shown in Table 4.22.

Table 4.22 Changing composition of entertainment expenditures
Share of recreation spending in constant dollars of 2005

	1929	2010
Video, audio, photographic and information processing equipment and media	1%	37%
Sporting equipment, supplies, guns, and ammunition	1%	6%
Sports and recreational vehicles	2%	3%
Recreational books	8%	3%
Musical instruments	0%	1%
Recreational items, nondurable goods	9%	15%
Membership clubs, sports centers, parks, theaters, and museums	73%	13%
Audio-video, photographic, and information processing equipment services	3%	10%
Gambling	0%	9%
Other recreational services	4%	4%
Total consumer spending on recreation and entertainment	100%	100%

Source: Data from U.S. Bureau of Economic Analysis, National Economic Accounts.

Entertainment purchases in 1929 were primarily of admissions to and memberships of theatres, museums, clubs and sports activities. The situation in 2010 was vastly different as entertainment purchases were dominated by electronic equipment and services, goods and services which did not even exist in 1929. And (legal) gambling had risen to become a significant part of entertainment activity. Much of entertainment has moved from group to individual activities while providing entertainment services has become less labor-intensive and more capital-intensive.

The main growth in entertainment has come through the advance in electrical and electronic equipment. The first equipment was the phonograph, invented by Thomas Edison in the 1870s. In the 1920s, electronic amplification was introduced, giving rise to the record player. Also in the 1920s, the amplifying vacuum tube was introduced into radio, allowing sound to be transmitted and received. A new industry emerged, broadcasting. Growth of the radio industry was made possible by the development of a new business model – "free-to-air" broadcasting paid for by advertising. Being free assisted the extremely rapid adoption of radio, especially in the Great Depression when family budgets were so stretched.

Radio was joined in the 1940s by television broadcasting. Intensive research had begun in the 1920s into recording, transmitting and displaying moving pictures. Philo Farnsworth and RCA (founded as the Radio Corporation of America) emerged as the leaders in developing a practical television system. By the late 1930s a number of companies were broadcasting television, using different technologies. The breakthrough to developing the television industry came in 1941 when, led by RCA, the various parties agreed on a set of technical and broadcast standards, the National Television System Committee (NTSC) standards. These standards, with later modification to allow for color, remained in force for the lifetime of analog television (until 2009). Television used the same business model as radio – broadcast of programs free-to-air with costs covered by advertising interspersed in the broadcast material. All the consumer had to do was purchase a standard television receiver. The entertainment value of television was so great that adoption of (black and white) TV in the home was one of the most rapid ever recorded – it took only 15 years to go from 1% to 90% market penetration. A similar response awaited color television. Introduced in the 1960s, color television also went from 1% to 90% penetration in 15 years.

The rise of gambling reflected a change in laws – what had not been legal in the early days later became legal, allowing the growth of casinos and lotteries. An early law change in Nevada coupled with cheap electricity from the Hoover Dam and lots of cheap land allowed Las Vegas to take the lead in legal gambling. The real development of Las Vegas began after World War II with the first modern resort, the Flamingo, opening in 1946. There followed the growth of a new type of entertainment – the resort complex offering gambling, accommodation, dining, entertainment and shopping. Gaming complexes also developed elsewhere in Nevada and, when laws were changed to allow casinos, in other locations such as Atlantic City and on riverboats on the Mississippi River. States have found that lotteries are a convenient source of revenue as well as being a popular consumer product. Most states, beginning with New Hampshire in 1964, now run lotteries.

Cinema began with developments in cameras, film and projection made by Thomas Edison's companies in the 1890s. The initial development of the movie industry featured silent movies shown in cinemas. The breakthrough sound movie was Warner Brothers' *The Jazz Singer*, released in 1927. By this time the movie industry was centered in Hollywood and was organized around studios with marketing based on the star system. Animated movies began to appear in the 1930s, led by *Snow White and the Seven Dwarfs* from Walt Disney Productions in 1937. Color film became the norm in the 1950s and movie sound reproduction also progressed, for example with four channel stereo sound used by *Star Wars* in 1977.

Electronics advanced rapidly from the 1950s. The transistor, developed in the early 1950s, gradually replaced the amplifying vacuum tube. The first successful consumer application was a portable radio introduced by the Japanese company Sony in 1957. The integrated circuit, combining many transistors onto a single piece of material, was developed in the late 1950s and greatly reduced the cost per transistor. By the late 1960s, integrated circuits were being used in consumer products such as television receivers. Integrated circuits were later extended into central processing units. These microprocessors made possible a wide range of information and entertainment products such as personal computers and game machines. Path-breaking video games included *Pong* by Atari Inc., introduced in 1972 and *Pac-Man* introduced in 1980. The first widely adopted personal computers were the Apple II, introduced in 1977, and the IBM PC, introduced in 1981. In more recent times, the performance-cost level of personal electronic equipment has been increased by the shift from analog to digital information formats. Also, integration with the internet has further increased the ability of many types of personal electronic equipment to provide information and entertainment.

The most rapid growth in entertainment has been in video, audio and information processing goods and services. The growth trend for constant dollar spending on these goods and services, for 1949 to 2010, has been 7.8% a year. Growth at this rate for 60 years took an industry which accounted for only 0.2% of the economy in 1949 up to 3.5% in 2010. This growth has been enabled by repeated rounds of new technologies permitting new, better and cheaper products. Television created new industries in content and hardware. Television then went through successive rounds of quality improvements and price reductions, from black and white to color, from cathode ray tube to flat panel display, from analog to digital, and from terrestrial broadcast to satellite, cable and internet narrowcast. Audio went through similar cycles. Computers and video games created entirely new industries in hardware, software and content. The electronic technology which became available in the early 1970s allowed the creation of new products and markets whereas before there was nothing. These better and new products have met a large customer need so that spending grew rapidly.

4.15.2 Entertainment and economic growth

Spending on entertainment or recreation has increased rapidly – the growth trend from 1909 to 2010 has been 7.7% per annum compared to 6.8% for total spending (current dollar GDP). Recreation spending went from 2.5% of the economy in 1909 to around 6% today. The rise in recreation or entertainment spending has been particularly rapid since 1962. Whether coincidentally or not, this rapid growth began with the arrival of the baby boom generation into its earning and spending years.

Relative prices of recreation have been declining so the growth in production has been even more rapid than the growth in spending. Measured in constant dollars of 2005, recreation went from 2.9% of GDP in 1929 to 7.4% today – the share of recreation or entertainment in total production has more than doubled over this period.

Entertainment spending and production have helped pull the economy forward over the past 80 or so years. The growth effect has accelerated since the early 1960s. This happened to be the time when some of the old growth drivers, such as automobiles, were decelerating, ceasing to lead the economy. Entertainment is one of the industries which have taken over from the old durable goods industries in driving U.S. economic growth.

We estimate that total factor productivity in the entertainment sector increased by around 1.8% a year between 1949 and 2010. Output from entertainment increased at 5.3% so factor inputs grew at 3.4%. The industry was absorbing an increasing share of the economy's resources so entertainment was not leading growth from the supply side. However, entertainment has been one of the leading industries on the demand side, helping to lead economic growth for many decades. And, it appears likely that entertainment will continue to pull the economy forward.

4.16 Finance

4.16.1 Size

Finance - covering banks, lending, financial securities and insurance – is a significant part of the U.S. economy; its average share in GDP between 1977 and 2009 was 4.3%. The volume, value added in constant dollars, of financial services and insurance has been increasing – the trend growth rate from 1929 to 2010 was 4.0% compared to the growth trend in GDP of 3.6%.

As financial services are increasing more rapidly than the economy they are contributing to growth. But, a more important contribution comes from the role of financial services in allowing spending and investment to grow. A considerable amount of investment, whether by households spending on residences, automobiles and other durable goods, or by business capital spending, is financed by borrowing. This investment creates growth in demand as well as productive capacity.

4.16.2 Residential investment

Every household needs a place to live and, whether owning or renting, accommodation typically is the largest single component of household spending. Most accommodation is in existing structures but the stock of residential units is added to each year by what is called residential investment. Residential investment is an important part of economic activity, accounting for an average of 4.1% of GDP from 1929 to 2010.

Buying a house or apartment, whether to live in oneself (owner occupying) or for renting out, is so costly that the purchase typically is financed by mortgage. Indeed, the cost is so great that few people would be able to purchase a residence were mortgages or similar credit not available. In this sense, residential investment is dependent on credit. The link from credit to residential investment is close - the change in mortgage debt outstanding explains statistically 91% of residential investment over the period 1946 to 2005.

The importance of mortgages has been increasing over time - from 1896 to 2010, the value of household mortgages has increased at an average of 8.1% a year while the economy, measured by current dollar GDP, has increased at only 6.3%. The importance of mortgages also shows up in the debt status of housing. In 1890, 28% of non-farm owner-occupied housing units were mortgaged with an average debt to value ratio of 40%. In 1971, 61% were mortgaged with an average debt ratio of 52%. In 2009, 68% were mortgaged. It is likely that the 32% of residences not mortgaged are owned by people who have paid off their mortgage, not that these residences were originally purchased without a mortgage. It is clear, then, that most residences have been purchased using mortgages and that the role of mortgages has been increasing over time.

4.16.3 Consumer durables

Consumer durables are goods which continue to provide useful services over a lifetime of at least three years. The principal consumer durable is the motor vehicle used for personal transport. In addition, many consumer durables are used for household work or for entertainment – refrigerators, washing machines, ovens, televisions, computers and so on. People use so many consumer durables that production of these goods is one of the largest components of the economy. On average from 1929 and 2010 spending on consumer durables amounted to 8% of (current dollar) GDP.

Many durables are bought using credit. New automobiles are typically bought either on credit or leased, many major appliances are purchased along with the purchase of a residence and many appliances and entertainment durable goods are purchased using credit secured over the item. A model fitted over the years 1946 through 2005 shows that the change in household credit explains statistically 89% of personal spending on durable goods. This does not mean that credit causes the purchase of these goods but it does suggest that credit enables their purchase. Finance is a critical factor underlying purchases of consumer durables which drive a significant part of the economy.

4.16.4 Business investment

The remaining forms of investment are investment in non-residential structures, purchases of equipment and software, and inventory change. Business investment is funded partly from business cash flow and partly from new funds, whether debt or equity, brought into the business. In the past 50 years, new credit has corresponded to 43% of business capital expenditure. Not all credit goes on capital expenditure and not all capital expenditure is funded by credit but the relationship between investment and credit is reasonably close. In numerical terms, the correlation coefficient between the increase in business credit and business investment, over the period 1947 through 2007, is 0.86. The correlation coefficient for those years in which capital expenditure has increased more rapidly than average is higher, at 0.94. This suggests that credit has been an important enabling factor underlying business investment, particularly when business investment has been increasing.

4.16.5 Investment and economic growth

Investment helps drive economic growth from both demand and supply sides. An increase in investment spending leads to higher GDP through the spending multiplier, an established Keynesian process. At the same time, an increase in investment leads to higher productive capacity and an increase in the future supply potential of the economy.

The spending side of this process can be represented using a standard Keynesian model. Here, spending on GDP is given by:

$$Y = C + I + G + X - IM$$

Where Y is current dollar GDP, C is personal current consumption, I is private gross investment including personal or household investment, G is government purchases, X is exports and IM is imports. We consider a simple form of this model in which consumption is a constant fraction of disposable income, taxes and government purchases each are a constant fraction of total income, the government budget is balanced and foreign trade is balanced. In this model, the growth rate of Y is the same as the rate of growth of I.

Table 4.23 shows the growth in investment spending and the economy for the years 1929 to 2008. (1929 is the first year of the data series; 2008 is taken as the finishing point as it avoids the severe downturn in residential investment in the recession after the 2007-2008 financial crisis.)

Table 4.23 Investment and the economy, 1929 - 2008

Average growth rates of current dollar spending

Consumer durables	6.2%
Residential investment	6.2%
Private nonresidential fixed investment	6.6%
Total private fixed investment	6.4%
Consumption of nondurables and services	6.4%
GDP	6.4%

Source: Data from U.S. Bureau of Economic Analysis, National Economic Accounts.

Personal consumption and the overall economy, in terms of spending, each has increased at 6.4% a year. The components of investment have increased at slightly different rates but total investment has increased at this same rate of 6.4%. These trends are precisely in line with the simple spending model. This is consistent with investment spending driving total spending along its growth trajectory.

And, central to the increase in investment spending is credit, a product of the finance industry. Each type of investment spending is closely related to the finance that flows into the households and businesses doing the investment spending. This spending could not take place without this flow of finance. Spending growth has been enabled by the financial system and growth in credit.

Spending growth has driven economic growth. Production also needs to grow but this is in response to spending, not the cause of spending – spending comes first as higher production could not persist without demand. Increasing spending relies on credit and credit is the product of the financial system. In this way, the financial industry has been central to U.S. economic growth.

4.17 Information technology

4.17.1 Development

Guiglielmo Marconi is credited with establishing the first long distance radio service, in England in the 1890s. But it was not until the invention of the triode vacuum tube by Lee De Forest in 1906 that radio became a practical tool. The triode tube, allowing rectification, amplification and switching, or similar processing or creation of electrical signals, was the foundation of modern electronics. Commercial radio and then television spurred the development and use of electronic goods and services.

Vacuum tubes, used for switching, made possible electronic computers. The first general purpose computer was the ENIAC (Electronic Numerical Integrator and Computer), designed and built by a team at the University of Pennsylvania led by John Mauchly and J. Presper Eckert. ENIAC, commissioned in 1946, was built for the U.S. Army to calculate artillery firing tables. The ENIAC was subsequently modified to a “stored program” computer whereby instructions were entered as software rather than being hard-wired by electrical circuits.

The vacuum tube was superseded by the transistor, invented and refined at Bell Labs in the 1940s and early 1950s. The leading players were John Bardeen, Walter Brattain and William Shockley. The first use of transistors was in telephone exchanges in the mid-1950s. An early consumer use was in portable radio receivers. Integrated circuits, putting multiple transistors onto a single semiconductor chip, were invented by Jack Kilby at Texas Instruments and Robert Noyce at Fairchild Semiconductor in 1959. Integrated circuits perform better than discrete component circuits and, as they are produced on a large scale by automated machines, are vastly cheaper. Integrated circuits provided the cost-performance breakthrough which made electronics viable in a wide range of practical applications.

Modern commercial information processing began with the IBM System/360, introduced in 1964. This was a family of computers, of varying capacities, using a uniform operating system, the instructions or software that controlled the computer, and available with a range of standard peripherals for input, output and storage. The operating system supported "high level" languages, such as COBOL (Common Business-Oriented Language). High level languages, which are concerned with the manipulation of data rather than the detailed control of the electronic components of the computer, facilitated the use of computers in a wide range of business, academic and government applications. And, the availability of these high level languages allowed users and other vendors to develop their own programs, giving rise to the applications software industry.

Computers need memory for storing programs and data, and also for storing the ongoing calculations. Data storage on paper or punched cards gave way to the magnetic hard disk (introduced by IBM in 1956), then to various forms of solid state memory and recently to optical memory. Processing memory typically is provided by DRAM, dynamic random access memory, invented by Robert Dennard at IBM in1966.

The Intel 4004, introduced in 1971, placed a central processor on a single silicon chip. The 4004 was one of the first microprocessors, the forerunners of all modern computers and information processing equipment. Microprocessors soon found application in calculators, video game machines, industrial control devices and, probably most importantly, computers. Personal computers brought together processing, memory, display, operating systems and application software making computers accessible, economically and in terms of ease of use, to vast numbers of people. The first commercially successful personal computer was the Apple II, created by Steve Jobs and Steve Wozniak and introduced in 1977. The application to the personal computer to business was led by the IBM PC, introduced in 1981. The PC XT, the first personal computer with standard hard disk memory, was introduced in 1983. The IBM PC included an operating system which led ultimately to Microsoft Windows, the most widely used modern operating system.

Application programs, programs which make computing operations accessible to the user through simple commands, have made computing power accessible to almost anybody. The first popular application programs were word processors, introduced in the 1970s. The spreadsheet started with Visicalc, developed by Dan Bricklin and Bob Frankston and introduced in 1979. The most widely used application programs today are database management systems, such as Oracle, and the Microsoft Office suite of software products.

Electronics and information technology have become widespread in controlling machinery and equipment. An example is the role played by computers in the modern automobile where microprocessors manage entertainment, climate control, fuel injection, ignition, emission controls, engine diagnostics, automatic transmission control, traction control, anti-lock brakes, stability control, airbags and other functions. The modern automobile might have anywhere from 40 to 100 microprocessors.

Electronics and information technology have also become central to the development of telecommunications. Modern telephone exchanges are massive digital switches while handsets, in particular cellphone handsets, today incorporate considerable amounts of information processing power.

4.17.2 Demand for computers

The commercial use of computers started in the 1950s but it was only after IBM introduced the System/360 family in the 1960s that use began to become widespread. With capability increasing and relative prices decreasing, commercial use of computers has grown rapidly. From 1963 (when the U.S. National Economic Accounts data series starts) to 2010 the growth trend for the quantity of private investment in computer equipment has been 27% a year and for software 15%.

The growth in business investment in computers is shown in Figure 4.34. The trend growth rate since 1963 has been 28% a year. The graph also shows a logistic curve fitted to purchases. Both lines suggest that the rapid growth in computer investment has not finished although the growth rate might be starting to slow. (This Figure refers to investment; the private capital stock of computers and peripherals has also increased at a 28% annual rate.)

Figure 4.34 Private investment in computers

Billions of 2005 dollars

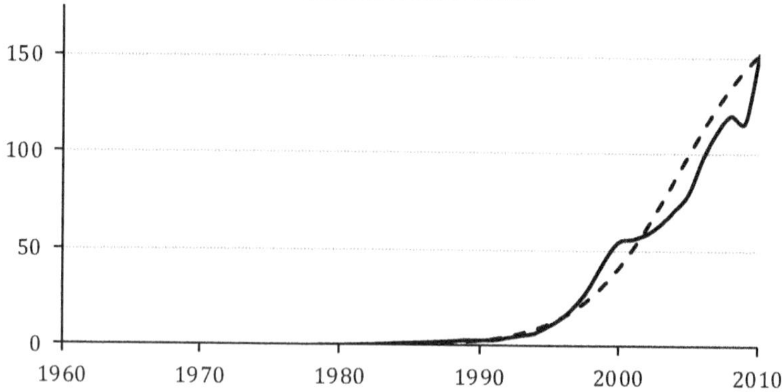

Note: Investment for production activities, consumer purchases are excluded.
Source: Data from U.S. Bureau of Economic Analysis, National Economic Accounts.

Investment in computer equipment and software has come to play a large part in business investment. Investment in information processing, averaged over the years 2000 through 2010, has absorbed 50% of private non-residential equipment investment and 36% of all private non-residential investment (which covers purchases of land, structures and equipment). Computers have accounted for more investment than any other good or service.

Consumption purchases of computer equipment started to take off after 1980. The trend growth rate in constant dollar purchases 1980-2010 has been 35% a year. Figure 4.35 shows this growth as well as how closely it has followed a logistic path.

Figure 4.35 Computer purchases by consumers

In 2005 dollars, 2005=100

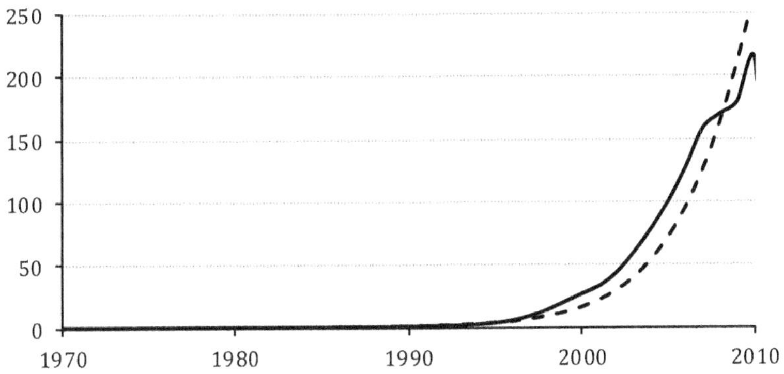

Source: Data from U.S. Bureau of Economic Analysis, National Economic Accounts.

4.17.3 Productivity

Electronic hardware technology has been developing rapidly for a century. The vacuum tube was replaced by the transistor which, in turn, was replaced by the integrated circuit. Costs were slashed with each step forward. The development of the microprocessor allowed the same sequence of cost reductions for computing engines. Increasing numbers of transistors were placed on each chip, continuing the downward path of computing cost. The move from analog to digital processing in communications, audio and video brought similar gains in processing and control to these applications.

These trends are summarized by Moore's Law. This trend was identified in 1965 by Gordon Moore in an article in *Electronics* magazine. Moore's law is that the number of transistors which can be placed inexpensively on an integrated circuit doubles every two years (or less). Moore's Law has proved to be remarkably accurate. Figure 4.36 shows the trend in the transistor count of microprocessors up to 2011. The Figure uses a logarithmic scale so the straight line trend corresponds to a constant rate of growth. (The logarithmic trend line shows an annual growth rate of 37%.)

Figure 4.36 Illustration of Moore's Law

Transistors per microprocessor, log scale

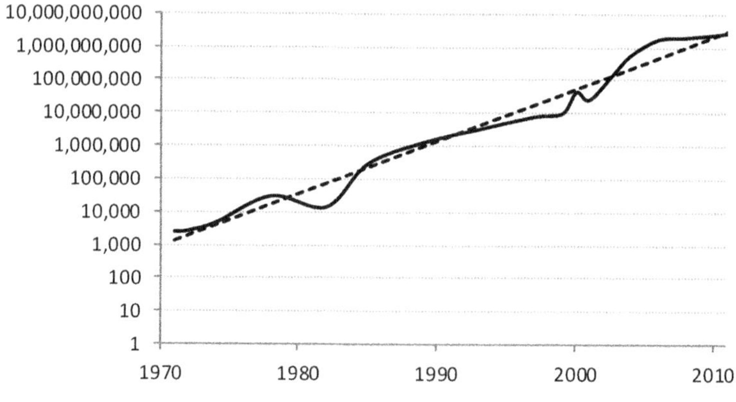

Sources: Intel Corporation press releases and industry public information.

The implication of Moore's Law is that the cost per unit of computing power has approximately halved every two years. This type of advance has also characterized the development of semiconductor memory and several other information processing components. The cost of hard disk storage per unit of information has declined similarly (sometimes called Kryder's Law). Butter's Law of Photonics (after Gerald Butters of Bell Labs) says that the amount of data which can be transmitted through an optical fiber doubles every nine months while advances in optical transmission technology have been such that the bandwidth available to users doubles each year (Nielsen's Law). These mean that the cost of transmitting information over a network has been declining even more rapidly than the cost of computing power.

The cost of information processing hardware and of information transmission has declined rapidly. Other components of costs, such as software, have not declined similarly although the productivity of software has continued to increase. Our estimate is that productivity in information processing equipment (covering computers and software but not communications) has increased at an average of 20% a year over the period 1959 – 2010 and that productivity of information technology as a whole has increased at a rate of 9% a year. This rapid growth in productivity means, for example, that each unit of information processing output produced in 2010 needs only 2% of the resource inputs needed in 1959.

4.17.4 Extent of information technology

Electronics and computers play an important role in the modern economy. Table 4.24 shows final demand spending on electronic-related goods and services in 2010. This spending accounted for 5.0% of GDP.

Table 4.24 Final demand for electronics and computers, 2010
Covers personal consumption, business investment and government purchases

	Spending $ billions	Spending as % GDP
Personal spending on audio and video equipment	113.3	0.8%
Personal spending on information processing equipment	91.3	0.6%
Business investment spending on computer equipment	93.8	0.6%
Business investment spending on software	257.9	1.8%
Government spending on computers	38.2	0.3%
Government spending on information processing	45.2	0.3%
Personal spending on services related to electronic goods	93.2	0.6%
Sum	733.0	5.0%

Source: Data from U.S. Bureau of Economic Analysis, National Economic Accounts.

And this does not cover all purchases of information technology. Purchases of telecommunications products and services accounted for a further 2.4% of final demand. Electronics incorporated in other equipment, such as automobiles or appliances or machinery, are yet another use of information technology which is not included. It is likely that spending on information technology represents between 5 and 10% of the economy.

4.17.5 Computers and economic growth

The information processing industry, not including communications, grew at a trend of 20% per annum from 1959 through 2010. This refers to its direct contribution to constant dollar GDP. This makes information processing the fastest growing component of the economy in the past half century. However, the computer industry started from a small base and even with this rapid growth represented only 4% of the economy by 2010. The direct effect of information processing on growth has been significant but not overwhelming. But, if other electronics and related services are included, such as from entertainment and industrial and automotive control, the size becomes large, accounting possibly for up to 10% of the economy.

In addition, the indirect effect of information technology on enhancing growth has been considerable. Computers have allowed more precise control of manufacturing; computers have allowed gains in productivity in most service industries; and, computers have improved management effectiveness in all industries. The resulting increases in Total Factor Productivity are indicated in Table 4.25.

Table 4.25 Contributions to growth in Total Factor Productivity
Growth rates, average percent per annum

	1948-73	1973-89	1989-95	1995-2002
Gross Domestic Product	3.99	2.97	2.43	3.59
Total Factor Productivity	1.00	0.29	0.26	0.71
TFP from Information technology	0.05	0.20	0.23	0.47
Computers	0.02	0.13	0.13	0.33
Software	0.00	0.03	0.06	0.06
Communications equipment	0.03	0.05	0.04	0.08
TFP other than information technology	0.95	0.09	0.03	0.24

Source: Data from Jorgenson (2005).

Growth in Total Factor Productivity in these accounts excludes the effects of improvements in the quality of labor and capital inputs. TFP growth since 1973 has been dominated by information technology – around 70% of TFP growth has been due to information technology. In the most recent years, the productivity effects of information technology contributed around 0.5% to the annual growth rate of the economy. For the whole period since 1973, the contribution of information technology to economic growth has averaged 0.27% a year.

Combining the direct and indirect growth effects of information technology, its contribution to economic growth over the past 40 years has been 0.3% a year. This is the largest growth contribution from any industry. Information technology has increased the rate of economic growth from 2.8 to 3.1% a year.

4.17.6 Computers in the growth process

The development of computers and information technology sheds light on the nature of the innovation process.

The development of information technology has taken place through a sequence of innovations, one building on another. Most of these innovations did not occur through "blue sky" research, they occurred as people were searching for ways to break through a constraint in existing ways of doing things. The innovations were demand-driven – they provided solutions to pressing practical problems. The innovations tended to be made in institutions, rather than by lone researchers, as the facilities and technical support needed for physics and electronic research are so substantial. The institutions leading the development, such as IBM, Intel, Microsoft and Apple, have been commercial organizations. The closest to a research organization was Bell Labs with the invention of the transistor but this research was motivated by the commercial interests of the parent company, AT&T. Government and university research has not been prominent in information technology advances. The one area in which government leadership was extremely important was in the early development of the internet but here again the nature of the leadership was not research but the need for to solve a practical problem - in this case the need for a robust system for data communication.

It is striking that important innovations in electronics have almost always had applications in many areas in addition to the original use. For example, the transistor has been ubiquitous in application even though it was first developed for telephone exchanges and the microprocessor similarly has found a vast number of uses quite apart from its motivating application of a hand-held calculator. Information technology in general has been applied to more and more uses as people realize its power to record, analyze, communicate and control. These uses were not the target of the original development and probably were not even considered at the time of the original development. The widespread application of information technology has been a case of availability leading to more and new and diverse uses.

Adoption of information technology in computer equipment, software and personal consumption has followed a logistic pattern. Adoption of information processing has been proceeding now for 50 years and is still growing strongly. The logistic models suggest that purchases of information technology have a further 20 years or more until they approach saturation. This would mean that information technology would have taken around 70 years to work its way through the consumption and production features of the economy. This is similar to the time taken for the adoption of the automobile and of electricity, the growth engines of the first two thirds of the 20th century.

4.18 Health care

4.18.1 Demand for health care

Spending on health care has always been significant. In 1909, personal spending on health care amounted to 2.3% of GDP; by 1929, when detailed statistics commenced, this had increased to 2.9% with Government provision of health care adding a further 0.5%. Personal spending on health care began to accelerate after World War II. By 2010, this spending accounted for 20% of total Personal Consumption Expenditure and 14% of GDP. Health care is now the second largest component of the economy, after the government sector.

The growth in spending has covered all categories of health care. Table 4.26 shows that current dollar health spending increased much more rapidly than GDP with spending on inpatient services growing particularly rapidly.

Table 4.26 Increase in personal spending on health care

	Share of GDP		Growth trend
	1947	2010	1947 - 2010
Medical products, appliances, equipment	0.7%	2.7%	9.2%
Outpatient services	1.4%	5.3%	9.5%
Hospital and nursing home services	0.7%	6.2%	10.6%
All personal spending on health	2.7%	14.1%	9.9%
GDP			7.1%

Source: Data from U.S. Bureau of Economic Analysis, National Economic Accounts.

Figure 4.37 shows the growth in health spending per capita. A logistic curve fits this spending path closely. The logistic model suggests that, if present policy conditions continue, spending will continue to increase rapidly although the rate of growth is starting to diminish.

Figure 4.37 Health spending per capita
Personal consumer expenditure, current dollars

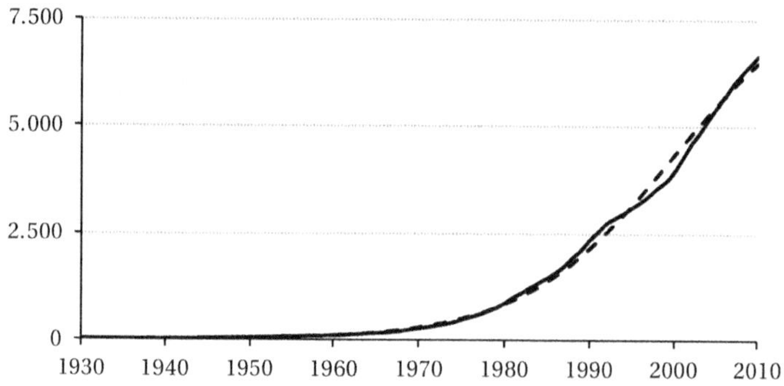

Source: Data from U.S. Bureau of Economic Analysis, National Economic Accounts.

There are several likely reasons for the rapid increase in purchases. Fundamentally, people attach considerable importance to their health and, as incomes rise, they devote much of their additional spending to health-related services. Then, there are all the effects of accessing health care by means of insurance. Health care insurance has become available to increasing numbers of people and this has sustained a rapid increase in the use of health-related goods and services. The tax deductibility of employer-provided health insurance has accentuated the take-up of health insurance. The marginal cost to consumers of using health-related services under insurance often is low or even zero; this often prevents the price system from working to limit the use of health services. And, as there is only limited consumer resistance to higher prices, prices have been rising rapidly.

Once rising prices are taken out of the equation, as in Figure 4.38, it emerges that per capita health purchases are increasing but at a decelerating rate. In fact, the quantity of health services purchased per capita shows signs of beginning to level off.

Figure 4.38 Health spending in constant dollars

Spending per person in constant dollars of 2005

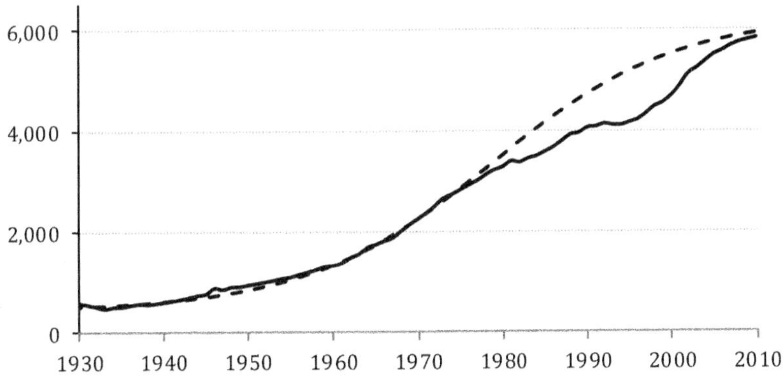

Sources: Data from U.S. Bureau of Economic Analysis, National Economic Accounts. U.S. Census Bureau, Historical Statistics of the United States and annual Statistical Abstracts.

4.18.2 Productivity in health care

Price trends for health care goods and services are shown in Table 4.27. The relative price of health care goods has declined but the relative prices of services, particularly of inpatient services, have increased rapidly. Overall, prices for health care have been increasing rapidly. (The relative price column in the Table gives the price trend relative to the price level of all goods and services in GDP.)

Table 4.27 Trends in health care prices, 1947 - 2010

	Price trend	Relative prices
Medical products, appliances, equipment	3.6%	-0.2%
Outpatient services	5.4%	1.5%
Hospital and nursing home services	6.3%	2.4%
All personal spending on health	5.5%	1.7%
GDP	3.8%	0.0%

Source: Data from U.S. Bureau of Economic Analysis, National Economic Accounts.

The likely explanation of this distinctive price behavior involves the nature of the market for health care. The market for goods, such as pharmaceuticals and appliances, is competitive. It appears that this competition has been sufficiently strong to restrain prices for health care goods despite the strong demand for these goods and despite the considerable advances in the quality of these goods. In contrast, market forces for health care services are not as strong. The consumption of health care services takes place to a considerable extent under the umbrella of medical insurance. Under many insurance arrangements, the decision-maker (the consumer) does not carry the (full) cost of his/her decision and does not necessarily take cost into account in making his/her decision. The results are first, a tendency to use more rather than less medical services, and second, a tendency for costs and prices to increase, unrestrained by competitive market forces. A further reason for the rapid increase may be the growth of "defensive medicine". The tort features of the American legal system encourage medical providers to make use of extensive tests and extensive backup in order to minimize personal exposure to legal action; the result is further upward pressure on costs.

The implication of these features of the market for health care is that the economic productivity of the health care industry has not been increasing and probably has been declining. A long term trend rate of increase in relative prices of 1.7% suggests an underlying decline in productivity.

Looking at trends in health outcomes similarly raises questions about productivity. Life expectancy at birth increased from 38 years in 1850 to 78 years in 2010. Most of this increase had taken place by the mid-1950s as nutrition, clean water, public health measures, vaccinations and antibiotics had virtually eliminated mortality from infectious diseases. Life expectancy increased at 0.75% a year over this period. After the 1950s the leading causes of death became heart diseases, cancers and strokes, often known as "lifestyle diseases". These have proved more difficult to counteract. Life expectancy has increased at only 0.23% a year since 1955 despite the large and increasing amount of resources being put into health care.

The overall mortality rate has been declining at 1.2% a year since 1940. This period of time has corresponded, approximately, to the rapid rise in personal spending on health care. We have built a model of this decline in the age adjusted mortality rate. The model gives the (statistical) explanation given in Table 4.28.

Table 4.28 Expected change in the mortality rate

Annual change in the age-adjusted mortality rate, 1940 - 2008

Due to increased personal spending	-0.2%
Constant annual reduction	-1.0%
Total reduction	-1.2%

Personal spending on health care has been increasing at almost 10% a year but has contributed a relatively small part of the reduction in mortality. Most of the increase in mortality rates has come from other factors such as public health and lifestyle changes. The model implies that the cost of delaying mortality by one year, by means of more spending on health services, in 2005 was $383,000. This high cost raises questions about the benefit-cost ratio of much health care spending. These considerations raise further doubts about the productivity of the massive increase in personal expenditure on health care.

4.18.3 Health care and economic growth

Personal spending on health care declined during the Great Depression and remained low during World War II. Then, however, this spending started to grow rapidly. The average growth rate from 1948 to 2010 was 9.5% a year, far in excess of the growth rate of the economy at 6.7% (for spending in current dollars). Health care spending absorbed 2.8% of GDP in 1948, rising to 6.3% in 1975 and 14.0% in 2010. Health care spending has provided a substantial and continuing boost to spending growth in the economy.

However, the poor productivity record of health care has meant that this growth has been achieved by devoting an ever greater share of resources to the health care industries. The growth in health care has been sustained by transferring massive amounts of resources from other, slower growing industries. This side of the rise in health care has been bad for economic growth – resources have been taken away from industries with more rapid productivity growth. On balance, the rise in health care has boosted growth from the demand side but the boost would have been still greater if the productivity record in health care had been better. Even if there had been zero productivity growth in health care, the rise in overall productivity would have enabled the economy to increase at an additional 0.2% a year, taking the post World War II trend rate from 3.3% to 3.5% a year.

4.19 Economic growth in the United States

4.19.1 Economic growth

The United States has enjoyed economic growth for more than two centuries. Figure 4.39 shows the actual growth path since 1820 as well as the smoothed exponential path for average income (GDP per capita in constant dollars). The trend growth rate has been 2.0% a year.

Figure 4.39 GDP per capita, 1820 - 2010
Thousands of 2005 dollars

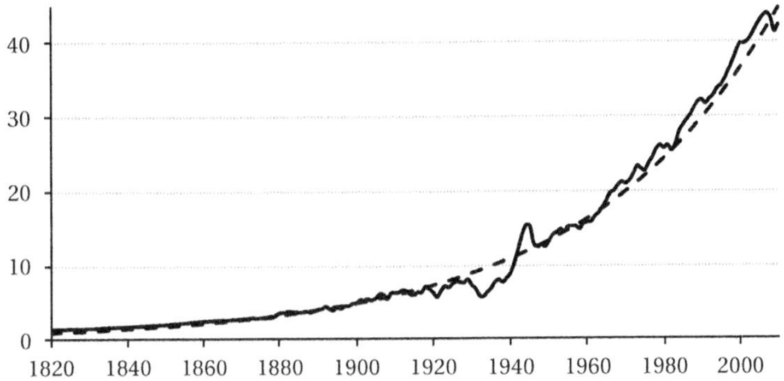

Sources: Data from Maddison (2006b). U.S. Bureau of Economic Analysis, National Economic Accounts.

The growth has been relatively steady as seen from the close fit of the exponential to the actual growth path. There have been, though, periods of slow growth or even decline as a result of huge policy mistakes - Europe's politicians taking the world to war in 1914 then mishandling the subsequent peace while America's economic policy mistakes led to the Great Depression of the 1930s. After 1945, growth returned to a relatively steady pace until a further series of policy mistakes led to a downturn after 2007. Broadly speaking, though, the United States has experienced sustained economic growth.

Population has been growing rapidly also. Over the years 1870 – 2007, population grew at a 1.5% average rate so, with GDP per capita growing at 2.0%, GDP has increased at an average of 3.6% a year. Growth in spending and production has been spread between more people (around 40% of the GDP growth) and higher incomes (around 60% of the growth).

The pace of U.S. economic growth has been striking. Britain led the world into economic growth but its average growth in per capita incomes over its heyday of 1775 – 1913 was only 1.0% a year. The U.S., over a period of similar length, 1870 – 2007, has averaged 2.0%, twice as fast. Britain pioneered economic growth before the U.S. took over leadership; the U.S. has then grown on a sustained path twice as fast as Britain's pioneering rate.

Sustained growth at 2% a year changes lives. An increase at 2% a year for 150 years increases average incomes by a factor of 16. Per capita income in the U.S. in 1870 is estimated to have been $3,040 in constant dollars of 2010; by 2010 the average had risen to $46,960.

4.19.2 The start of growth

The U.S. economy, and average incomes, have been growing for as far back as the statistics go. Table 4.29 above shows that per capita income was growing, although slowly, over the 18th century. Growth accelerated going into the 19th century but the shift into rapid growth occurred around 1870. The modern period of economic growth started around 1870.

Table 4.29 Growth rates in GDP per capita

Period	Growth rate
1700-1820	0.7%
1820-1870	1.4%
1870-1913	2.0%
1913-1947	1.9%
1947-1973	2.5%
1973-2007	1.9%

Sources: Data from Maddison (2006b). U.S. Bureau of Economic Analysis, National Economic Accounts.

The reasons for this shift to rapid, sustained growth after 1870 are not entirely clear but it seems that the main reasons must include the following.

The Civil War, 1861 – 1865, brought about profound changes. The industrialization of the North was accelerated by the Civil War, partly in the sense of doing things differently but mainly in the sense of increasing the size of manufacturing activity. Much of the economy of the South was destroyed by the War; reconstruction of infrastructure and industry then accelerated growth of demand as well as creating new productive capacity. The old Southern agricultural production and processing economy was eliminated by the War and, with reconstruction, Southern agriculture had to enter the modern, market economy.

At the same time, settlement of the Midwest, then the mountain regions and the Pacific regions was proceeding apace. The farming frontier rapidly moved westwards. Transportation links, water-borne and railroad, began to tie the country into a single market. The original Erie Canal opened in 1825 with the enlarged Canal opening in 1862. Railroads were expanding rapidly and the first transcontinental railroad link was completed in 1869. By the 1870s, an effective transportation network was in place. The abundant physical resources of the Midwest and west began to be exploited; with massive immigration, the labor became available to drive a rapid expansion of production.

As well as the scale of production increasing, there were the beginnings of changes in the methods of production. In agriculture, which was particularly important as it generated half of all production, mechanization and improved implements began to accelerate productivity. The movement to more capital-intensive production began.

Low cost steel became available after Andrew Carnegie introduced the Bessemer process from Britain, opening his first mill in 1875. Carnegie's mills kept improving production techniques and reducing the price of steel. Industrialization, which previously was centered on processing cotton and wool, now accelerated. The growth in steel was joined late in the 19th century by the introduction of electricity and electrical equipment. Then, early in the 20th century, the introduction of the automobile and the internal combustion engine firmly established the economy on a path of rapid growth.

How the United States moved into rapid growth is clear – industrialization in conjunction with development of new products and new processes. Why the U.S. moved onto a rapid growth path is not so obvious. It appears that the driving force was the rapid growth in demand associated with population growth (natural and through immigration) and income growth as the Midwest was developed and as agricultural production increased. This growth in people, incomes and spending created opportunities for profit by providing new products and by increasing efficiencies in production. Entrepreneurial people responded to these opportunities. Undoubtedly, most of these innovators did not succeed but sufficiently many did succeed in creating and bringing to market new products which met an unsatisfied demand that the economy moved forward rapidly. The growth in manufacturing, communications and services which began in the late 19th century was all about doing things differently, primarily to take advantage of unmet market opportunities. At the same time, a steady improvement in production efficiency allowed incomes to continue to increase.

4.19.3 Accounting for growth

GDP growth can be attributed to its sources of more inputs and greater productivity. This is an accounting allocation measuring what happened rather than why it happened. Nonetheless, it is important as it helps to show how growth took place. Kendrick (1961 and 1973) has constructed growth accounts for the years 1899 through 1966. We have summarized Kendrick's aggregate results in Table 4.30. Average GDP growth of 3.5% a year resulted in almost equal measure from more inputs (of labor and capital) and productivity growth, or using labor and capital in more productive ways. Some people have equated productivity growth to technical progress but this is incorrect as productivity growth might result from technical progress but it might also result from better management, better education or from more experience and better training of the labor force. Capital input grew much more rapidly than labor but, because capital input was starting from such a low base, the contribution to growth of labor was greater than the contribution of capital.

Table 4.30 Sources of growth, 1899-1966

	Average growth rates	Contribution to growth
Labor input	1.5%	32%
Capital input	2.6%	19%
Factor input	1.8%	51%
Total Factor Productivity	1.7%	49%
Output	3.5%	100%

Sources: Data from Kendrick (1961) and (1973).

For recent decades we use the results of Jorgenson (2005). Our summary of these results is shown in Table 4.31. More than 60% of growth since 1973 has originated from greater input quantities and less than 40% from higher productivity. The role of productivity growth has been important but has been relatively smaller than earlier in the century. Most productivity growth in recent decades has come from advances in the quality of capital, next came the contribution of total factor productivity followed by improvements in labor quality.

Table 4.31 Sources of growth, 1973 - 2002

	Average growth rate	Contribution to growth
Labor hours	1.4%	27%
Capital stock	2.6%	35%
Factor quantity	1.9%	62%
Labor quality	0.4%	8%
Capital quality	1.2%	17%
Total Factor Productivity	0.4%	13%
Total productivity	1.1%	38%
Output	3.0%	100%

Source: Data from Jorgenson (2005)

These numbers can be recast to answer the question – what was the (accounting) source of economic growth in the sense of increasing income per worker. Table 4.32 shows the sources of growth in GDP per labor hour. The numbers for the early years are from Kendrick, for the later years from Jorgenson. The answer is clear – although more capital per worker contributed to growth in average incomes, most of the contribution came from productivity improvement. Around 80% of the growth in average incomes over the 20th century came from higher productivity.

Table 4.32 Sources of growth in GDP per person hour

	Growth rate	Contribution to growth	Share of growth
1899 - 1966			
Capital stock per person hour	1.1%	0.3%	14%
Total Factor Productivity	1.7%	1.7%	86%
GDP per person hour	1.9%	1.9%	100%
1973 - 2002			
Capital stock per person hour	1.2%	0.5%	29%
Total Factor Productivity	1.1%	1.1%	71%
GDP per person hour	1.6%	1.6%	100%

Sources: Data from Kendrick (1961) and (1973). Jorgenson (2005)

4.19.4 Industry growth

Table 4.33 shows industry growth rates for the years 1899 – 1966, based on Kendrick's data. The industries are ranked in descending order of growth rate; the line across the middle of the Table indicates the economy-wide growth rate of 3.5% so marks the transition from industries growing more rapidly to less rapidly than the economy.

Table 4.33 Industry growth, 1899 - 1966

Average annual growth rates. Industries in descending order of growth.

	Output	Labor input	Capital input	Factor input	TFP
Electric machinery	7.6%	4.9%	6.3%	5.1%	2.4%
Rubber products	7.5%	3.0%	5.0%	3.3%	4.1%
Communications and public utilities	7.4%	3.1%	4.6%	3.7%	3.6%
Chemicals and allied products	6.5%	2.4%	4.3%	3.1%	3.3%
Transportation equipment	6.4%	2.8%	4.3%	3.0%	3.3%
Petroleum and coal products	5.9%	1.6%	4.7%	3.4%	2.4%
Paper and allied products	5.0%	2.2%	3.8%	2.5%	2.4%
Fabricated metal products	4.8%	2.2%	3.5%	2.3%	2.4%
Instruments	4.8%	2.2%	3.7%	2.4%	2.3%
Printing and publishing	4.4%	1.6%	2.1%	1.7%	2.6%
Machinery, nonelectric	4.3%	2.4%	3.1%	2.5%	1.8%
Stone, clay, glass products	3.8%	1.0%	2.7%	1.2%	2.5%
Primary metal industries	3.7%	1.4%	3.3%	1.8%	1.9%
Transportation	3.4%	-0.1%	0.9%	0.1%	3.4%
Furniture and fixtures	3.4%	1.6%	1.9%	1.6%	1.8%
Apparel and related products	3.4%	1.3%	3.4%	1.5%	1.8%
Tobacco products	3.3%	-1.5%	3.5%	0.3%	3.0%
Food and kindred products	3.3%	1.1%	1.9%	1.2%	2.0%
Trade (1)	3.3%	0.9%	2.3%	1.1%	2.1%
Contract construction	3.1%	1.1%	7.2%	1.6%	1.5%
Beverages	3.0%	1.1%	1.2%	1.1%	1.9%
Textile mill products	2.8%	-0.1%	0.8%	0.1%	2.7%
Mining	2.6%	-0.3%	0.9%	0.0%	2.5%
Leather and products	1.2%	-0.2%	0.3%	-0.2%	1.3%
Farm segment	0.9%	-1.5%	0.7%	-0.7%	1.6%
Lumber and products	0.8%	-1.1%	1.0%	-0.6%	1.4%

Factor input covers the input of labor and capital. TFP is Total Factor Productivity.

The economy increased at 3.5%, indicated by the line across the Table.

Note (1): Trade includes retail and wholesale trade, automobile servicing, eating and drinking places.

Sources: Data from Kendrick (1961) and (1973).

26 industries have both output and input data. Economic growth was reasonably broadly based – fully half of all industries (half by number, not size) were leading the economy in growth. Of course, the weighted average of industry growth rates is equal to the overall economy growth rate. But it is clear that, unlike the preceding economic growth in Britain, growth in the United States was fairly broadly based.

The years covered by the previous Table corresponded, approximately, to the industrialization of the United States. This is evidenced in the type of industries which were growing rapidly. Only two of the 13 industries – Printing and publishing, and Communications and public utilities – are not manufacturing or resource processing industries.

11 of the 13 more rapidly growing industries had factor inputs growing more rapidly than average. This means that almost all the growth industries were claiming relatively more economic resources - these industries were using relatively more labor as well as more capital. Where was this labor and capital coming from? Seven of the 13 slow growth industries released labor but none released capital. For inputs as a whole, only three industries actually released resources, the remaining 10 slow growth industries used more inputs but their use was growing less rapidly than average.

Most of the slower growth industries released resources in a relative sense, not in an absolute sense. This suggests that, at the industry level, there was a little Schumpeterian "creative destruction" (see Joseph A. Schumpeter (1942)) going on but that the real story was that resources were being released by differences in positive growth rates with some industries using a declining share of the economy's resources. The release of resources from slower growth industries was a process of "benign stagnation" rather than "creative destruction".

All 13 of the rapidly growing industries had TFP growing more rapidly than the economy-wide TFP rate. The growth industries, then, were characterized by rapid productivity growth. But these industries also had rapid growth of labor and capital inputs. Approximately half of the growth of these industries came from more inputs and half from greater productivity so both input growth and productivity growth were vital in sustaining the growth industries.

Did productivity growth drive industry growth or did it just help sustain this growth? Table 4.34 shows the key correlations.

Table 4.34 Industry correlations, 1899 - 1966

The correlations refer to the industries in Table 4.33

	Growth industries	All industries
Correlation coefficient between		
Output growth and growth in factor input	0.88	0.94
Output growth and growth in TFP	0.73	0.70
Factor input growth and growth in TFP	0.33	0.41

Industry growth is more closely related to inputs, not TFP. There is a direct relationship between growth and TFP but it is not as strong as the link between industry growth and inputs. This implies that industry growth is more closely related to demand growth than to productivity growth. The most plausible explanation is that demand growth leads to production growth with inputs then growing to match production growth less TFP growth.

Demand rather than supply drives industry growth. Supply responds to demand growth. Productivity growth does not of itself drive industry growth. The effect of productivity is first, to reduce the need for more factor inputs, and second, to reduce relative prices and so stimulate demand growth. Productivity growth allows the economy to grow more rapidly than factor inputs but productivity growth enables economic growth, it is not the driving cause. Demand or spending leads, production, based on labor and capital and TFP responds. Productivity growth however is vital both to help sustain increasing production and to allow increasing incomes.

4.19.5 The growth sequence

The industries of the United States have grown in a particular sequence; this is shown in Figure 4.40. Industries above the line grew more rapidly than the economy during the decades indicated by the shaded bars. Their growth rates, over and above the average economy-wide growth rate of 3.5%, are shown by the percentages on the vertical axis. Similarly, slower growth industries are arranged below the line. The purpose of this Figure is to show which industries were leading the economy and over which decades. (This Figure covers a longer time period than Table 4.33 and the set of industries covered differs from Table 4.33 so the two exhibits are partially but not fully comparable.)

Figure 4.40 Growth in production of final goods and services

Average annual growth rates shown as deviations from the average growth rate of constant dollar GDP

1890s 1900s 1910s 1920s 1930s 1940s 1950s 1960s 1970s 1980s 1990s 2000s

42%	Defense
14%	Computers
8.0%	Vehicles
4.9%	Electricity generated
4.2%	Telecommunications
3.6%	Electrical equipment & appliances
2.1%	Entertainment
2.0%	Health
1.7%	Petroleum products
1.7%	Railroad services
1.6%	Education
0.8%	Personal care
0.7%	Finance
0.3%	Publishing
0.2%	Health
-0.01%	Household fuels
-0.1%	Entertainment
-0.3%	Furnishings
-0.5%	Clothing
-0.6%	Dining & accommodations
-0.6%	Electricity generated
-0.7%	Health
-0.8%	Construction
-1.2%	Education
-1.3%	Food
-1.6%	Education
-1.7%	Household fuels
-1.9%	Publishing
-1.9%	Personal care
-2.0%	Vehicles
-2.2%	Petroleum products
-2.3%	Defense
-2.3%	Electrical equipment & appliances
-2.5%	Finance
-4.0%	Railroad services

Sources: Data from U.S. Bureau of Economic Analysis, National Economic Accounts. U.S. Census Bureau, Historical Statistics of the United States. Kendrick (1961).

Economic growth was generated by a sequence of leading industries. Only one industry, telecommunications, grew rapidly over the entire 140 years shown. No other industry grew rapidly over the whole time. Instead, there was a sequence in which an industry grew rapidly for some decades then slowed, to be replaced by new growth industries.

It has been this succession of growth products and growth industries which has generated sustained growth for the economy as a whole. Sustained growth is the result of a succession of individual growth products. Each individual product follows its life cycle of introduction, rapid adoption then maturity. Individual products generate rapid growth for only a few decades. Only by having back-to-back growth products did the economy continue to grow.

Railroads grew rapidly for a short time in the late 19th century. Then there emerged the two products and industries which led economic growth for the next 70 years – first, electricity and electrical equipment, and second, the internal combustion engine and automobiles. These two sets of products found huge markets which grew rapidly for decades. Their expansion pulled along other, supplying industries as their influence spread throughout the economy. Electricity and motor vehicles had reached maturity, had saturated their markets, by the 1970s. Thereafter, they continued to grow but only slowly. Growth leadership was taken over by new industries – entertainment, computers, health care, personal care and finance. The separation point of the 1970s, with old industries fading and new industries rising, was precipitated by the oil price increases which started in 1973 but the change would have happened anyway. The old industries had reached the peak of their life cycles and were bound to fade back to slow growth, growing now in line with the population as market penetration was complete. It so happened that this change in the 1970s was from goods to services. Industrial goods led growth until the 1970s, services and electronic goods have led growth since then. This has been the change from an industrial to a post-industrial economy.

4.19.6 The keys to economic growth

Economic growth is the continuing increase in per capita incomes, spending and production. The United States has experienced sustained growth since 1820 and rapid, sustained growth since 1870. The sequence of growth industries set out in the previous section shows why and how this happened.

Why did growth happen? Because people kept spending, buying more and more goods and services, with a particular fondness for new types of goods and services. How did growth happen? Because there was a succession of industries which provided what consumers wanted. These new industries grew rapidly until their markets became saturated; these industries then faded to slow growth and were replaced by new growth industries. This succession of growth industries pulled the rest of the economy along. Purchases of inputs by the growth industries created demand and income through the whole economic system. Spending from this rising income led to growth, although at more modest rates, across the whole range of goods and services which consumers wanted and producers needed.

Each growth industry is based on a new product or possibly, although this is less likely, on an existing product which becomes vastly cheaper and/or better, thereby opening up a large new market. The key is a large, unsatisfied market so that demand and production expands rapidly as that potential market comes to be satisfied. Demand is the key to this growth.

This process of rapid growth to satisfy a new market suggests that the S-shaped curve of the logistic model of adoption might provide a good summary of actual demand and production growth. The logistic model picks up the typical life cycle of a new product which becomes successful – introduction, a few sales followed by broadening customer recognition, then rapid growth until finally the market is saturated and there is no growth potential left. This process of introduction, adoption then saturation has been seen time and again in the sequence of growth industries.

These driving products have been in final demand for goods and services - consumption, business investment, government purchases or exports. Business investment is driven ultimately by other demand so growth comes down to consumption or government or exports. U.S. growth was led by defense purchases in the 1940s but otherwise government purchases have not been a leader. Nor have exports been the main driving force. It has come back to consumers - household and individual spending - to drive economic growth.

Why have consumers kept spending (with the unintended but fortunate result of driving the economy ever upwards)? Because, the United States has seen the creation of the consumer society. The United Sates was not the first consumer society – the consumer society first emerged in Britain as rising incomes and new goods during the 19th century led consumers to keep buying and buying. But, the United States has seen the consumer society developed and refined. Advertising and marketing have been extensively developed in America. Consumers have been reassured by decades of prosperity. After economic stabilization was demonstrated (Franklin Delano Roosevelt's New Deal) and the theory developed (Keynesian economics) in the 1930s, governments have broadly succeeded in reducing economic fluctuations. One result has been that consumers are less risk averse and more willing to spend and even to borrow and spend. Finally, the United States has pioneered the growth of consumer credit. The widespread availability of credit for major purchases, such as residences or automobiles, or for current spending, through personal loans and credit cards, has let consumers follow through on their spending desires, even if it means spending in excess of current income. Credit-based spending has provided a vital link in the chain of economic growth as it has allowed final demand to keep growing.

At the same time, growth in production capability has been essential in sustaining the growth in spending and in allowing incomes to increase. Production capability per person has increased as a result of more capital per person and increases in productivity. Spending drives the value of production but this production is enabled by more inputs and increasing productivity. In turn, rising incomes are the value added component of the increasing value of production; more capital per worker and higher productivity allow income per person to increase.

There is a circular flow from income and credit to spending to production to income. Spending is based on income and new credit, spending drives production, production creates income and so on. Both demand and supply aspects have been essential components to the story of American growth. It boils down to this - there have been two keys to economic growth in America: (1) the continuing sequence of new products which consumers wish to buy, and (2) the continuing sequence of investment and productivity increase which accommodates this demand and generates rising incomes.

Chapter 5

Other countries, other systems

5.1 Maintaining growth

5.1.1 The early leaders

The highest income country in the world in 1900 was the United Kingdom. The U.K. had led the world into economic growth some 150 years earlier and in 1900 was still riding high based on its textile and engineering industries. The top income countries at that time are shown in Table 5.1.

Table 5.1 Highest income countries in 1900
GDP per capita, 1990 dollars.

World rank		GDP per capita	Difference from #1
1	United Kingdom	4,492	
2	New Zealand	4,298	-4%
3	United States	4,091	-9%
4	Australia	4,013	-11%

Source: Data from Maddison (2006b).

Australia and New Zealand produced foodstuffs and agricultural products for the British market, earning high incomes by doing so; the United States was emerging as a leading agricultural and industrial country in its own right although per capita incomes were still below British levels.

A century later, though, the picture was very different – see Table 5.2. Although all four countries had grown substantially, the rankings had changed with only the United States, now at number one, still in the top four.

Table 5.2 Ranking in 2003 of the early leaders
GDP per capita, 1990 dollars.

World rank		GDP per capita	Difference from #1
1	United States	29,037	
5	Australia	23,287	-20%
13	United Kingdom	21,310	-27%
21	New Zealand	17,564	-40%

Source: Data from Maddison (2006b).

The early leader, the United Kingdom, had dropped to number 13 with average income 27% below the new leader while New Zealand had dropped to number 21 at 40% below. Australia had not fallen far in the rankings but its income level was now 20% below the United States.

This history shows that growth does not just happen. The United States and Australia were able to maintain their growth over the 20th century but the United Kingdom and New Zealand, despite growing rapidly in the 19th century, failed to maintain their growth and fell behind the new leaders.

5.1.2 Growth in the 20th century

All four countries grew over the century but the growth record shows definite differences. Table 5.3 indicates the trends.

Table 5.3 Growth rates over the 20th century
Average annual growth rates in constant dollar GDP per capita

	U.K.	New Zealand	United States	Australia
1900-1938	0.9%	1.1%	1.1%	1.0%
1938-1948	0.7%	0.7%	4.0%	1.7%
1948-1973	2.3%	2.4%	2.5%	2.5%
1973-1991	1.7%	0.5%	1.8%	1.5%
1991-2003	2.3%	2.2%	2.0%	2.7%
1900-2003	1.5%	1.4%	1.9%	1.7%

Source: Data from Maddison (2006b).

Britain grew relatively slowly through the 1930s. Further differences emerged during World War II. The United States handled the war and early post-war years well; the United Kingdom handled this period less well. New Zealand followed the U.K. with slower growth. Growth rates were then similar until the oil price shock of 1973 precipitated the end of the post-war industrial boom. The following years also saw widespread efforts to reduce inflation. Growth slowed after 1973 but New Zealand's growth was particularly slow. New Zealand in the period 1973 – 1991 went through a period of massive government intervention in the economy followed by several years of unwinding these controls so as to return to a market system. After 1991, New Zealand returned to the trend growth rate.

There are two types of differences in these growth patterns – differences across time and differences across countries. We consider first whether growth differed over time, referring to Table 5.4.

Table 5.4 Median growth rates
Median growth rates in GDP per capita

1900-1938	1.0%
1938-1948	1.2%
1948-1973	2.4%
1973-1991	1.6%
1991-2003	2.3%

Growth rates were modest up to World War II and again after the 1973 oil shock and the following inflation. These were all periods of instabilities and economic shocks of one form or another. The median growth in all these periods was, roughly, 1.3% a year. Periods of stability, after World War II and after 1991, saw systematically more rapid growth, at around 2.3% a year. The implication is that major disruptions take around 1.0 percentage points off of the typical growth rate of GDP per capita, reducing the rate by more than one third.

The severity of economic fluctuations was much lower in the second half of the century. The standard deviation of growth rates from 1900 to 1948 was 5.8%, considerably larger than the median growth rate of around 1.0%. After 1948, the standard deviation fell to 2.5%, which was only slightly larger than the median growth rate. This improved stability probably reflected the development of Keynesian and monetary economics and the parallel development of effective government stabilization policies. The implication in turn is that improved stability after World War II helped to increase the average rate of economic growth. This conclusion is reinforced by noting that the slow growth period after 1973 was also a time of inflation, oil price shocks and the consequent efforts to restabilize these economies.

There also are clear differences across the four countries. The United Kingdom, and its farming supplier, New Zealand, appear not to have handled their economies well up to and including during World War II and grew less rapidly in this period. The United States, in contrast, appears to have handled its economy well over this time and accelerated away from the other countries. The four countries then grew in parallel until around 1973. New Zealand's growth in the period 1973-1991 was noticeably slow. This appears to have been related to the introduction of widespread government controls over the allocation of resources and the management of the economy. The implication is that government policy can make a substantial difference to growth rates.

5.1.3 The growth implications

There are three broad implications from these growth comparisons. First, the underlying growth trends of GDP per capita of the four countries have been similar at between 1.5 and 2% a year. Second, deviations from the underlying growth paths have not been made up; after a deviation on either side of the trend, countries have returned to their trend growth rate but not to their earlier growth path. Third, appropriate government policies are needed to maintain reasonably stable growth.

All four countries experienced broadly similar growth rates apart from isolated episodes in which a country experienced either unusually rapid or unusually slow growth. The similarities are not surprising as all four countries have been subject to similar pressures, such as two World Wars and the Great Depression, and the oil price and other shocks of the 1970s; they have similar language, institutions and economic systems; and they are closely connected through international trade. The different growth outcomes result from isolated periods of departure from trend. The United States grew unusually rapidly over the World War II period. Australia has had the same growth trend as the U.S. but never caught up after America's wartime spurt. The United Kingdom grew less rapidly than the others through the 1930s then again performed poorly, economically, during World War II, pulling New Zealand with it. Then New Zealand went through an experiment with massive government interventions in the 1970s and 1980s. After these deviations, growth in all countries returned to pretty much the same growth trend.

A country never recovers from a major event moving it off of its growth trend. After a temporary (of the order of 10 years, not one year) departure into unusually rapid (or unusually slow) growth, countries then resume their typical growth rate but from a higher (or lower) starting point, never giving up (making up) the temporary deviation. For these high income countries established in economic growth, steady application of the right policies is required in order to allow long term growth. The right policies seem to be to let markets operate and to stabilize spending growth by means of appropriate monetary and fiscal policies.

5.2 Coat-tail growth

Britain and then the United States have led the world in economic growth. Table 5.5 shows the four early leaders in 1900 and then their growth over the 20th century.

Table 5.5 Growth of early leaders over the 20th century

	GDP per capita in 1900		Growth rate
	Rank	\$(1990)thous	20th Century
United Kingdom	1	4.5	1.5%
New Zealand	2	4.3	1.4%
United States	3	4.1	1.9%
Australia	4	4.0	1.7%

Source: Data from Maddison (2006b).

It is striking that two other countries, Australia and New Zealand, had income levels comparable to Britain in 1900 and have grown almost as rapidly as the United States since then. And, the western European countries have grown at the same rate as the early leaders, although from lower initial levels of income.

Australia and New Zealand are examples of what we call "coat-tail" growth – they shared in the rapid growth of the leading countries by supplying raw materials to those leading countries. Australia supplied wool and wheat; New Zealand supplied wool, meat and dairy products to the British market. In essence, these countries exploited their comparative advantage in farming to feed Britain. This allowed these countries to share in the high incomes of Britain, and later the United States, and to grow alongside the leaders, to ride on their coat-tails.

The economic structures of the four countries reflect the nature of coat-tail growth. Table 5.6 shows the production structure of GDP in 2007.

Table 5.6 GDP by industry, 2007
Percent of GDP

	Australia	New Zealand	United Kingdom	United States
Agriculture, forestry and fishing	2	5	1	1
Mining and quarrying	8	1	2	2
Manufacturing	10	14	11	12
Electricity, gas and water utilities	2	3	3	2
Construction	8	5	8	5
Services	70	71	76	79
GDP	100	100	100	100

Sources: Australian Bureau of Statistics, Australian National Accounts, Industry gross value added. Statistics New Zealand. National Accounts, Contribution to GDP by industry. U.K. Office of National Statistics. Gross Domestic Product by gross value added. U.S. Bureau of Economic Analysis, National Economic Accounts.

Australia has slightly more agriculture and substantially more mining than the leaders, Britain and the United States. (Although Australia's early growth was based on agriculture its recent growth has been based on the export of minerals to the growing east Asian countries.) New Zealand has more much agriculture than the leaders. The high shares of agriculture and mining reflect the growth path taken by these two coat-tails countries.

The rest of the economic structure is relatively similar across all four countries. This appears to be the production structure associated with a modern high income country. The exception is that Australia and New Zealand have a lower share devoted to services. Growth in the leading countries tends to be concentrated in services so it is not unexpected that services are relatively smaller in Australia and New Zealand to allow for more production to take place in the primary industries.

There is a general similarity in the production structures of all these countries. They have grown at similar rates and their production structures are distinguished only by the effects of comparative advantage and international trade.

There is a question, though, as to whether in the long term coat-tail countries can continue to match the growth rates of the leading countries. This is because of the sorts of products which the coat-tail countries export to the leaders – these products tend to be foods and raw materials. Demand for these products tends to grow with population rather than with incomes. Demand in the leading countries tends to shift towards sophisticated manufactures and, in particular, to services; these are not intensive in inputs of materials. Although countries like Australia and New Zealand have enjoyed more than a century of rapid coat-tail growth, it is uncertain whether they can continue to grow at these rates.

5.3 Communism

5.3.1 Communist government

Several countries in Europe and Asia had communist governments for part of the 20th century. The question arises as to whether communism is compatible with economic growth. This really involves two questions, the first referring to government, the second to economic management. In the present section we look at communism itself - communist party control of the organs and processes of government.

The Soviet Union was formed in 1922 and dissolved in 1990. As the first available economic information is for 1928 we look at Soviet growth for the years 1928 – 1989. The average growth rate for real GDP over these years was 3.6% and for per capita GDP 2.7%. This growth in GDP per capita is consistent with economic growth.

China, which still has a communist form of government, has achieved rapid growth in recent years. The average rate of growth in GDP over the years 1978 (the beginning of the agricultural reforms) to 2010 has been 9.9%. This is similar to Japan's growth over its post World War II growth spurt when average growth from 1950 to 1973 was 9.3%. Chinese growth has been comparable to the rapid growth achieved by a leading democratic country.

Neither of these growth rates has continued over a sufficiently long period to demonstrate that communism is compatible with economic growth. For example, Britain has achieved sustained growth for more than 250 years while the United States has achieved sustained growth for some 150 years. Chinese growth over 35 years is less than the life cycle of a major new product in Britain or the United States. The Soviet Union had a lifetime of just 62 years, again less than the life cycle of British cottons or American automobiles.

The growth in Soviet and Chinese GDP might well have been due to catching up – copying technology and products from leading countries, such as the United States, and undertaking heavy investment to make these products for domestic use (in the Soviet case) or domestic investment and export (in the case of China). Nonetheless, both countries experienced ongoing growth in GDP per capita.

This history does not prove that communism is consistent with growth as the time spans were too short to form a conclusion on this. At the same time, though, this history shows that communist government is not necessarily inconsistent with economic growth as both countries experienced growing GDP per capita for several decades.

5.3.2 Government control of the economy

The next question is whether extensive government control of the economy allows economic growth. By extensive government control we mean that the government, rather than individuals coordinated by the market, makes the key allocation decisions – essentially, the government decides what is to be produced. For example, the Soviet model had central planning whereby government plans, such as a sequence of Five Year Plans, set production targets which producing units were required to meet and which were used to determine the allocation of resources.

It is clear from the growth statistics in the previous section that GDP per capita did increase in these two centrally directed economies. Therefore, our question must be rephrased to ask whether there was a growth rate penalty associated with using the government rather than the market to make allocation decisions.

China switched from a communal, planned agricultural system to a market-led system beginning in 1978. Agricultural output responded with rapid growth. Justin Wifu Lin (1992) has studied the performance of Chinese agriculture over the course of this "decollectivization". Using Lin's numbers we estimate that agricultural output 10 years after decollectivization was 36% higher than it otherwise would have been. If this increment were assumed to apply to an entire economy being decollectivized and instead spread over 50 years the increment to growth would be 0.6% a year. This provides our first estimate of the growth effect of using government rather than market allocation mechanisms.

New Zealand experimented with widespread government controls over resource allocation decisions over the years 1973-1984. The controls were then dismantled over the years 1985 – 1991. During the years of control, New Zealand's rate of growth in per capita GDP was 0.7% less than that of neighboring Australia whereas previously and subsequently the two countries had similar growth rates. The implication is that the widespread interference in market allocation took 0.7% off of the annual growth rate.

We next compare the growth of three eastern European countries which were brought into Soviet-style central planning (the former Czechoslovakia, Hungary and Poland) with three western European countries which used market systems (Austria, Denmark and France).

This comparison is over the period 1937 – 1989. The three centrally planned countries had growth rates which were lower by 0.6% a year.

Finally, we look at the record of the Soviet Union and seven east European countries in what was called the "eastern bloc". Average growth rates over the post World War II period, 1948 – 1989, are shown in Table 5.7. The difference in the trend growth rate, market vs central planning, was 0.7%.

Table 5.7 Relative growth with central planning
Average annual growth in GDP per capita

USSR, 1948 - 1989	2.7%
7 eastern bloc countries, 1950 - 1989	2.7%
29 western European countries, 1948 - 1989	3.4%
Difference, west over east	0.7%

Source: Data from Maddison (2006b).

Each of these examples shows a partial although significant reduction in growth associated with government control over resource allocation. Table 5.8 summarizes the growth differences between government and market allocation mechanisms.

Table 5.8 Growth effect of government allocation
Reduction in growth of GDP per capita compared to market system

	Growth with planning	Growth reduction	Relative effect (1)
China	2.9%	0.6%	17%
Eastern bloc	2.7%	0.7%	20%
Eastern Europe	2.1%	0.6%	22%
New Zealand	0.9%	0.7%	45%
Weighted average	2.8%	0.6%	18%

Note (1): Growth reduction / (Growth with planning + Growth reduction)

The reduction in the growth rate was similar across the various examples at around 0.6 percentage points. The relative reduction varied but the population-weighted average was around 18%. The implication is that the use of central planning or other government allocation mechanisms reduced growth rates but only by about one fifth. Growth was still possible even with government direction. We note, first, that this is not the full economic growth effect as the time periods involved are too short to make any firm conclusions about sustained economic growth.

There are further considerations which suggest that the relative reduction observed under central planning will underestimate the full economic effects. First is the problem of quality. Centrally planned economies are notoriously bad at producing good quality goods and services and also are bad at producing the goods and services which people want. The reason is simply that there is no mechanism for consumer preferences to be reflected in production and resource allocation decisions and there is no accountability mechanism to enforce quality. The measurement systems which underlie the GDP numbers do not fully pick up these quality issues. Second is the role of investment and defense. Communist central planning tended to favor heavily the production of investment goods and spending on defense. This production might have boosted the recorded output of the economy but did little to help consumers. For example, Abram Bergson (1972) calculates that (for 1955 and valued in dollars rather than rubles) consumption was only 55% of GNP in the USSR compared to 67% in the United States. As personal consumption and government services to the people are the aims of economic activity, the communist bias towards investment and defense means that the economic cost of central planning was even greater than the numbers given above.

We can indicate the effect on material standards of living as follows. Say the United States and a planned economy started off with the same levels of GDP per capita and GDP per capita in the U.S. grew at its actual historical rate of 1.9% a year while a centrally planned economy grew at 0.6% less or 1.3% a year. Consider a time span of 150 years, roughly the time since the United States started on rapid growth. After this time, GDP per capita in the planned economy would be 58% less than in the United States. If the consumption share of GDP was as Bergson estimated then the material standard of living in the planned economy would be 66% less than in the U.S. Living standards in the U.S. would be three times the level in the planned economy. And that is without taking account of the higher quality of goods and services and a more desired range of goods and services available in the U.S. Allowing for quality and choice, it is quite plausible to think that living standards in the U.S. would be four times or more higher than those of the planned economy.

But even this is not the end of the story. Where would the new products and new processes come from in the centrally planned system? A market system such as the United States has built-in incentives for the creation of new products and better processes; a centrally planned system has no such incentives. The government might tell people to come up with "the next big thing" but this is unlikely to be effective. The Soviet Union got by for as long as it did by copying western ideas, products and technologies. It is unlikely that a centrally planned system in isolation could even sustain any economic growth for 150 years.

We conclude that the capitalist, market economic system in the long term is likely to be many times, probably an order of magnitude, more effective than the centrally planned economic system in generating growth and higher incomes for its peoples.

In fact, we think it unlikely that a centrally planned economy would even make it into the long term. If people within such an economy have any contact with the rest of the world they will realise how low their standard of living is. They will struggle to get out from under government control. The Soviet Union lasted for almost 70 years but with today's worldwide communications channels, the life expectancy of extensive government control is likely to be much less. Only the continuing application of force against its citizens (such as in the Democratic People's Republic of Korea – North Korea) would be able to keep such a government in power.

5.4 Empire

5.4.1 Past empires

We look at three of the largest empires in history – the Roman Empire, the Spanish Empire and the British Empire. These were so extensive that it was said that "the sun never sets" on the Spanish and then the British Empires. There is no question but that empires could be made to work.

But, all empires ultimately have faded away. What does this say about the empire as a form of economic organization? Have empires been successful economically?

5.4.2 The course of empires

The pre-eminent power in the ancient (western) world was Rome. Although Rome started as a republic, and took on an imperial structure only with the rise of Augustus in 27BCE, the Roman economic system was always run on imperial principles. Rome conquered territories by force, managed them by force and expropriated food, labor and resources from these territories. Empire worked for Rome in the sense of raising the living standards of its citizens (at the expense of its colonies). However, government by force meant that the Empire collapsed when that forced weakened. Living standards of Roman citizens peaked during the reign of Augustus; although the Empire continued for a further 400 years it neither expanded nor grew in that time. The Empire was static.

The Spanish Empire was powerful in the 15th, 16th and 17th centuries. Spain led the colonization of the Americas and even the Philippines. Spain acquired its Empire by force. Spain's primary interests in managing its territories were to spread the influence of Roman Catholic Church and to extract treasure, particularly precious metals. Spain experienced relatively rapid economic expansion in the 16th century with GDP per capita increasing at an average rate of 0.3% when western Europe managed only 0.1%, although Britain also managed 0.3%. Spain's expansion appears to have been driven by monetary expansion with both production and prices rising as a result of increased spending. Spain's Empire hardly brought large economic gains. And Britain achieved similar growth without, at that time, having an empire.

The British East India Company was granted a Charter by the Queen of England in 1600 to trade in cotton and other goods with India and neighboring regions. The Company in effect ruled India after its forces won the Battle of Plassey in 1757. The Indian Rebellion of 1857 led the British Government to take over the administration of India, turning the subcontinent into a British colony. The British ruled India until they departed, giving India and Pakistan independence, in 1947. In view of the huge population of India, British rule over India was probably the largest example of empire the world has ever seen.

India did not develop under the East India Company as its traditional products, such as hand-made cottons, simply were sold into the British market. Most earnings went to the trader, not the producers. Things hardly changed when Britain was running the country – it was treated as a source of materials and as a market for Britain's new textile and engineering industries. Table 5.9 shows Indian growth trends. Per capita GDP increased not at all under the East India Company and only slightly under British rule. Britain was growing steadily but this growth did not spill over to India. World growth was accelerating but India did not even keep up with that. India did not gain from being a colony.

Table 5.9 Growth in India

Average growth rates of GDP per capita

	1700 to 1870	1870 to 1947
India	0.0%	0.2%
United Kingdom	0.6%	0.9%
World Average	0.2%	1.1%

Source: Data from Maddison (2006b).

Britain gained control over India by force and retained control by civil government underpinned by force. This was costly to Britain. As Indian resentment intensified it became obvious to Britain that ever increasing expenditures and force would be needed to retain India as a colony. A simple benefit-cost analysis would have shown Britain that continuation of the Empire was inefficient. Britain finally realized this and walked away from its Indian and other colonies.

Britain earlier had had a troubled experience with the colonies it established in America. Britain ultimately was forced to accept that it was not possible to maintain control over these areas. The subsequent relationship between the United States and Britain was based on trade, not force. This new relationship has proved to be amicable and mutually advantageous.

Britain also had settled other relatively empty lands – Australia, Canada and New Zealand – and made these parts of the Empire. However, trade not force was the basis of these relationships. Britain granted these colonies self-government as soon as they requested it. These countries continued a mutually beneficial relationship with Britain by trading – foodstuffs and materials for manufactures and financial services.

5.4.3 Inefficiency and efficiency

The Roman Empire worked because the production expropriated from its territories was greater than the cost of maintaining the Empire. In the end, though, Rome tired of carrying this cost and let the Empire wither away. Spain and Britain learnt that a force-based empire was economically inefficient; they ultimately walked away from their colonies. It was only the trading-based portion of the British Empire which survived and even here the imperial relationship was disbanded.

The lesson learned by Britain and others was that force-based empires were not worthwhile even on economic grounds. Clearly empires are disadvantageous for the colonies but also they are not worthwhile for the imperial country. The one part of the old imperial relationships that was worthwhile was trade. Trade is a win-win situation and both sides, Britain and Australia for example, gained. The political leaders finally realized that international relationships based on trade are superior to those based on force. This realization was given a firm practical basis with the General Agreement on Tariffs and Trade (GATT), signed in 1947, part of the efforts of world leaders to construct a better world after the horrors of World War I, the Great Depression and World War II.

International trade has emerged not only as an efficient basis for international relations but also as a great enabler of economic growth. Trade has allowed the suppliers of materials to grow, riding on the coat-tails of high income countries. Trade has also allowed lost cost producers to export commodity manufactures to high income countries and thereby to grow in a catch-up fashion.

5.5 Japan

5.5.1 The growth record

Japan grew extremely slowly until the mid-19th century. Production did increase but population grew correspondingly so that per capita incomes hardly moved. Japan, using western technologies, then started to industrialize. Growth accelerated. From 1870 to 1941, GDP per capita increased at the rate of 1.9%. Even so, by the time of Japan's entry into World War II, its GDP per capita was only 35% of that of the United States.

World War II not only took a significant human toll but also left Japan with little capital stock in many of its cities. Japan entered the post war world with considerable human capital and labor but with severely depleted infrastructure and manufacturing capital. Assisted by foreign aid, Japan commenced reconstruction; growth resumed and by 1953 Japan had passed its pre-war level of GDP per capita. Rapid growth continued for two decades until the oil price shock of 1973; the oil price shock raised the cost and prices of Japanese exports, thereby slowing demand growth. GDP per capita had increased at an average of 8.1% a year from 1950 to 1973. Growth continued but now at a slower rate, 3.0% a year from 1973 to 1991. Growth slowed abruptly in 1991 when domestic demand dropped as a result of the collapse of a financial bubble and at the same time export demand slowed as Japan saturated its existing markets. In the two decades since 1991, GDP per capita has grown at a rate of just 0.7% a year.

5.5.2 Manufactures and exports

Japan depends heavily on manufacturing - manufacturing generated 29% of GDP in 1991. This is an unusually large share; for example the United States' figure is only 12% and this is typical of most high income countries. Accordingly, where manufacturing went, so did the Japanese economy.

Japanese manufacturing grew rapidly with the post war reconstruction and with rising exports. GDP originating in manufacturing increased at an average rate of 7.1% a year for more than 40 years, from 1955 through 1998. Figure 5.1 shows this growth. The associated logistic model, also shown in the graph, suggests that the rapid growth days were over by the 1990s as markets for Japanese goods, at home and abroad, were becoming saturated.

Figure 5.1 Manufacturing GDP, Japan
Constant prices of 1990

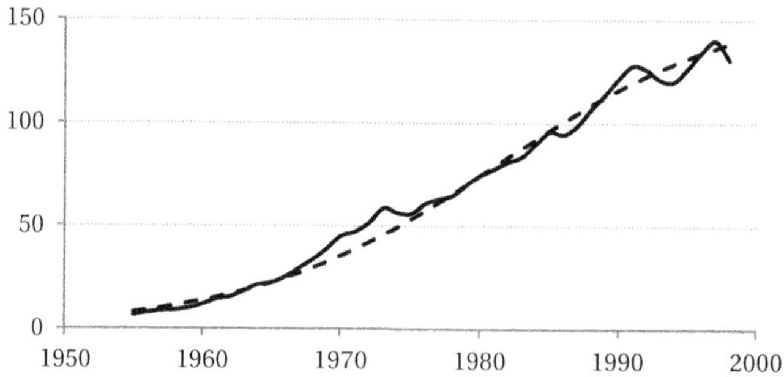

Source: Data from Economic and Social Research Institute, Cabinet Office, Government of Japan.

The importance of exports to Japanese growth can be seen from Table 5.10. Exports led growth with investment following close behind. Personal consumption and government consumption have increased but these have followed the general rise rather than leading it.

Table 5.10 Growth rates in final demand, Japan

	Private consumption	Investment	Government consumption	Exports	GDE (1)
1960-1991	5.5%	7.5%	4.6%	9.6%	5.9%
1991-2010	1.0%	-1.4%	2.4%	4.4%	0.6%

Note (1): GDE is Gross Domestic Expenditure. All indicators are in constant prices.
Source: World Bank, World Development Indicators.

Exports grew rapidly until around 1990; export growth then slowed as Japan had saturated many markets and as competition from newly industrializing countries was taking away Japan's pre-eminence. The collapse of a credit bubble left households and businesses laden with debt; subsequent efforts to reduce this debt caused a slowdown in domestic spending. The result has been that Japanese growth slowed to a crawl.

5.5.3 The growth process

Japan, after World War II, acquired western financial capital and technical knowledge and applied its own management and labor to achieve rapid growth. Japan found large markets by producing both for its own reconstruction and in producing simple manufactured goods for export to high income countries. Japanese goods initially competed on price. Simply penetrating and gaining market share in other countries provided rapid growth to Japan even though these other countries themselves may not have been growing rapidly. In time, Japanese manufacturers were able to move into higher value products, such as automobiles and consumer electronics, which generated new rounds of growth. However, Japanese manufacturers in the 1990s ran into problems – their markets in higher value goods were approaching saturation, so growth was slowing, while their markets in lower value goods were being taken over by low cost export competitors. Japan was unable to put together a new generation of rapid growth products. When Japanese industrial products and consumer electronics had reached maturity, Japan had no further growth engine and the country moved from a growth leader to a growth laggard.

5.6 Republic of Korea

5.6.1 The growth record

The Republic of Korea (South Korea) had an unstable and often violent history until the end of the Korean War in 1953. Reconstruction after the war led to some growth but it was only in 1967 that GDP per capita regained pre-war levels. Coincidentally, in 1967 the government introduced a development plan stressing investment and exports. A central part of this plan was the making available of low cost financial capital to designated industries and companies. The initial emphasis was on basic metals and chemicals. Over time, South Korea has gradually moved from this base into higher value goods for export.

This strategy of industrializing via cheap capital and cheap labor, and to produce for export, has been effective. Table 5.11 shows that GDP per capita, already growing up to 1967, accelerating to the rapid rate of 6.0% over the past 40 years.

Table 5.11 Growth rates, South Korea

	Population	GDP	GDP per capita
1953-1967	2.6%	5.8%	3.1%
1967-2010	1.1%	7.2%	6.0%

Sources: Data from Maddison (2006b). World Bank, World Development Indicators.

5.6.2 Manufactures and exports

South Korea's growth has been led by manufacturing. Constant price value added in manufacturing increased at an average rate of 11.4% from 1967 to 2010. Figure 5.2 shows this growth along with the fitted logistic curve. The logistic model suggests that South Korea is only part way through its present growth stage.

Figure 5.2 Manufacturing GDP, South Korea

Value added in 2005 US$ billion

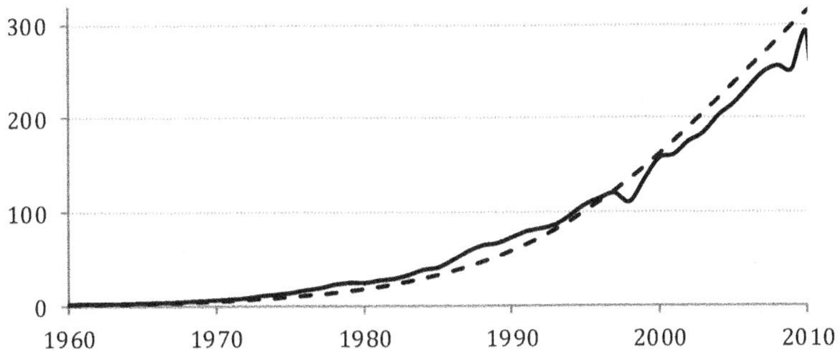

Source: World Bank, World Development Indicators.

The market for these manufactures has been in exports to higher income countries. Domestic consumption has grown but has followed the overall growth in the economy, not led it. Table 5.12 shows the growth rates for 1967 to 2010.

Table 5.12 Growth in expenditures, South Korea
Average growth rates in constant price expenditures, 1967 - 2010

Household consumption	6.1%
Capital formation	8.1%
Government consumption	5.5%
Exports	15.1%
Gross Domestic Expenditure	6.9%

Source: World Bank, World Development Indicators.

5.6.3 Growth strategy

South Korea followed a deliberate growth policy; this policy has succeeded in generating rapid growth for more than 40 years. The strategy was to provide massive financial capital to manufacturing industries to invest in production for export. This has used existing technologies and exploited South Korea's cost advantage (in capital costs and labor costs) to get into existing markets in other countries and rapidly penetrate these markets.

The logistic model suggests that this strategy will continue to work for another decade or so. At some point, though, South Korea will have reached the limits of its existing export markets and will face increasing competition from new, low cost exporting countries. Continuing growth will then depend on South Korea boosting domestic consumption as well as finding or developing new products which it is able to sell into the markets of higher income countries.

5.7 China

5.7.1 Early China

China in the year 1000 was possibly the most advanced economy in the world. The next thousand years saw China move forward in punctuated advances. Periods of geographic and economic expansion were interrupted by periods of invasion, civil war, struggles for power and restrictive government policies. Production expanded during the periods of tranquillity but this was absorbed by population growth and not reflected in income growth. China was an example of a Malthusian system. Maddison (2006b) estimates that population in 1950 was more than 9 times higher than in 1000 (an average growth rate of 0.2% per annum) while per capita incomes were the same as in 1000.

5.7.2 Government policies

Mao Zedong and the Communist Party were victorious in the civil war of the 1940s, proclaiming the People's Republic of China in 1949. The government then channelled investment into infrastructure and manufacturing. GDP increased rapidly. Government policy beginning in 1958, the "Great Leap Forward", collectivized agriculture and instituted controls over agricultural production and trading. There followed a reduction in agricultural production, a massive fall in GDP and a significant loss of life due to starvation. Production had just stabilized when the "Cultural Revolution", launched in 1966 as a class struggle to reinvigorate the communist ethic, caused a decade of further social turmoil and economic disruption. Government policies began to change only after Mao Zedong's death in 1976. Agriculture was released from control, the decollectivization policy, leading to a surge in agricultural production. Capital and resources were directed into manufacturing but now manufacturing was directed to investment within China and to production for export. Incomes began a rapid growth which still continues.

Table 5.13 shows the different growth rates during these different stages of government policy. The effect of replacing private economic incentives with government or communal management is clear. Equally clear is the effect of re-introducing private incentives after 1976.

Table 5.13 Growth of GDP per capita in modern China
GDP per capita is in constant dollars of 1990.

	Change event	GDP per capita	Growth rate (1)
1950	Start of the People's Republic of China	448	5.6%
1958	Start of the Great Leap Forward	690	1.0%
1966	Start of the Cultural Revolution	746	1.3%
1976	Death of Mao Zedong, start of markets	853	6.6%
2003		4,803	

Note (1): Average growth rate until the next event or date..
Source: Data from Maddison (2006b).

5.7.3 Growth in China

Government-directed investment in the 1950s led to rapid growth in manufacturing, construction, transport and communications. There was, though, no or even negative growth in agriculture for the two decades of collective management of farms. It was not until collectivization began to be removed in 1978 that agricultural output surged. Justin Wifu Lin (1992) calculates that agricultural output increased by almost 60% between 1978 and 1984. He attributes half of the increase to decollectivization and half to more inputs, in particular of capital and chemical fertilizers.

World Bank data show that industrial output accelerated in 1984 and has since been increasing at more than 10% a year. Initially, most of this increase went into investment. But a new trend started around 1990 - the rapid growth of exports of manufactured goods. China, exploiting its low costs (from low cost finance and low cost labor), broke into established markets in high income countries. In the 20 years after 1990, constant price GDP increased at an average rate of 10.5% a year, led by exports at 17.0% and manufacturing at 12.5%. Supporting activities – construction, services, transport and communications - have been growing at around 10% a year, in line with GDP; agriculture has grown at just 4.0% but even this has exceeded population growth.

China's growth has been based on two types of markets – the domestic market for investment and world markets for low and medium valued added manufactured goods. Table 5.14 shows how China is emphasizing these markets; this contrasts with the structure of the United States where personal consumption is much more important. (Expenditures do not add to 100% as imports are omitted from the Table.)

Table 5.14 Final demand in China and U.S.A.
Expenditures as percent of GDP, 2010

	China	USA
Private consumption	48%	71%
Investment (1)	48%	12%
Exports	30%	13%
Government (1)	13%	21%

Note (1): Government gross capital formation is in Government for the U.S.A. but in Investment for China.
Source: World Bank, World Development Indicators.

Production in China is heavily weighted to agriculture and manufactures, as shown in Table 5.15.

Table 5.15 Final production in China and U.S.A.
Value added as percent of GDP, 2011

	China	USA
Agriculture	10%	1%
Manufacturing	47%	22%
Services	43%	77%

Source: Data from CIA World Factbook.

China does not have to invent new production mechanisms or new products/markets, it just has to devote more labor and capital to producing the sorts of goods for markets in the west in which it can compete on price. China is on a rapid growth path but in a catch-up manner. It is exploiting its low costs to enter existing markets in high income countries for low value added tradeable goods.

5.8 Catch-up growth

Japan, South Korea and China have used what we call "catch-up" growth. This is where a low income country penetrates the markets of higher income countries using low priced manufactured goods. These exports then grow rapidly in the large markets of high income countries.

This growth is led by low value added goods which compete solely on price. Prices are low because of low labor costs. In addition, and perhaps surprisingly, these countries often have low capital costs. Government provision or arrangement of financial capital to selected manufacturers supplies these producers with cheap capital. The capital might be sourced from domestic savings, from credit creation or from international capital flows.

Different countries have followed this strategy using different goods. A traditional path is to export textiles and clothing. Another path, followed by Japan for example, is to export simple consumer goods. Yet another strategy, followed by South Korea, is to export basic manufactures such as chemicals and steel. The common thread, though, is that these countries use established technologies, supply their own low cost inputs, and use international trade to enter established markets in higher income countries. Their low prices allow them to penetrate rapidly in these markets.

The country can grow rapidly until it has saturated its chosen markets for simple goods. Continued growth then depends on moving into more sophisticated goods and repeating the strategy of entering markets in high income countries and competing on price. Japan executed this strategy successfully for several decades, moving into increasingly sophisticated consumer and producer goods. South Korea also has been successful in this strategy for two decades, moving from producer materials into, for example, sophisticated consumer electronics and electronic components. China too has started to embark on this upgrading strategy.

There is a question, though, as to how long this strategy can work. Japan appears to have reached its limits in continuing to expand its exports of manufactures – although it has large export businesses it has been unable to maintain a rapid growth in exports. Most demand in high income countries is for services and the catch-up countries have been unable to export services, partly because they tend to be poor in producing services and partly because many services are difficult to export. Continued rapid growth in a catch-up country will depend on catering to rising domestic consumption and in continually moving into more and more sophisticated manufactures.

This catch-up growth has some similarities to the process described by Moses Abramovitz (see Abramovitz (1986) and Abramovitz and David (1995)). Abramovitz describes a catch-up process wherein productivity growth rates vary inversely with productivity levels. This process implies that a lower income country can grow rapidly, adopting the technologies pioneered elsewhere, but that growth slows as productivity and incomes converge to those enjoyed by the high income countries.

Our characterization of catch-up growth has the low income country producing low-technology goods and, by exploiting its low cost structure, penetrating world markets for these goods by virtue of low prices. The low income country then moves on, once its initial markets have been saturated, to repeat the process with slightly more complex goods. The process involves using existing technologies, not developing new technologies. Successive stages in this process use successively more complex technologies. And, the process slows as the growth country runs out of products to make and sell to the high income leaders. This can generate a convergence-like outcome. All these steps are similar to the Abramovitz characterization. Our characterization though involves market processes - cost advantages, international trade and price-based market penetration - rather than simple movements to higher levels of technology.

Chapter 6

Effects of economic growth

6.1 Population

6.1.1 The Malthusian trap

The British writer Thomas Malthus (1798) argued that population will expand until, forced by famine and disease, it converges on the limit represented by the supply of food. He further argued that population inevitably would converge onto this limit as the inherent tendency is for population to increase geometrically (in essence at a constant rate of growth) while food production tends to increase arithmetically (in essence at a constant annual increase in terms of, say, tons per acre). Malthus' theory implies that income per capita will remain constant over the long run.

Malthus' theory was broadly consistent with the world he had observed. Figure 6.1 shows that in England incomes and population had moved broadly in parallel from 1200 until his time of writing in the late 18th century. Although Malthus probably did not know this, other countries such as China had exhibited this same behavior. Nor did Malthus recognize that Britain by 1798 had broken through the food constraint and per capita incomes were beginning a continuing increase.

Figure 6.1 Population and income growth
Series scaled to 1600 = 1

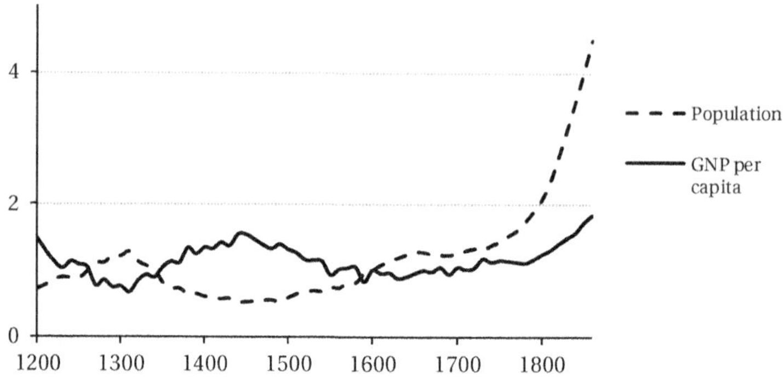

Source: Data from Clark (2009).

There is, for almost this entire period, a close relationship between population and income. The two diverged beginning in the 14th century. Early in the century, population was expanding rather more rapidly than income. This came to an end in mid-century with the arrival of the Black Death (bubonic plague), killing more than 50% of the population. Income per capita then increased, as the capital/labor and land/labor ratios increased. It took until 1650 for population to increase back to its pre-plague peaks. Population and incomes resumed their parallel increase until they began to diverge sometime in the 18th century. The correlation between population and incomes was sufficiently close that it is understandable how Malthus reached his conclusions.

Something changed early in the 18th century, around 1725. Total production and incomes started to increase and continued to increase. Initially, population also increased but in time production growth outstripped population increase. This divergence has continued to the present day. Population in England was no longer constrained by income. England had launched onto a path of economic growth with steadily rising levels of income per capita. It had escaped the Malthusian trap.

This was the first, and enormously important, effect of economic growth. Population was no longer tightly limited by famine and disease; population could grow and average incomes also could increase over the long term.

6.1.2 Population

Population has increased in a distinctive way since the British economy broke out of the Malthusian trap. Initially, population increased almost as rapidly as incomes but then incomes continued to increase while population growth slowed.

Figure 6.2 shows the main drivers of population change since 1550. The crude birth and death rates (rates per 1,000 of the population) are 20 year moving averages centered on the year shown. GDP per capita and population are scaled to fit on the same axis as the birth and death rates.

Figure 6.2 Population drivers

Data for England and Wales

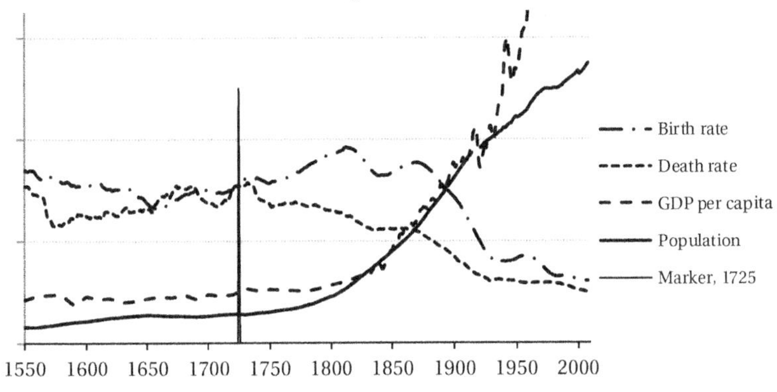

The Figure shows relative changes only as all series are scaled to fit on the graph.
Sources: Data from Mitchell (1988), Clark (2009) and Maddison (2006b).

Population growth initially reflected a decline in the death rate, beginning around 1725 when per capita incomes began to increase.

The birth rate then rose for around 100 years before starting to decline rapidly from the late 19th century. The result was that population rose rapidly, in parallel to incomes, until the late 19th century then continued to increase but at ever slower rates.

6.1.3 Children

The crude birth rate in England evolved in a distinctive way. Figure 6.3 shows that the rate increased steadily from 1700 until around 1820 and then started to decline. The decline after the early 19th century followed a logistic curve, shown in the Figure, accelerating over the course of the 19th and then into the 20th centuries before levelling off to the present day rate of around 12 births per 1,000 population.

Figure 6.3 Crude birth rate
England and Wales. Births per 1,000 population

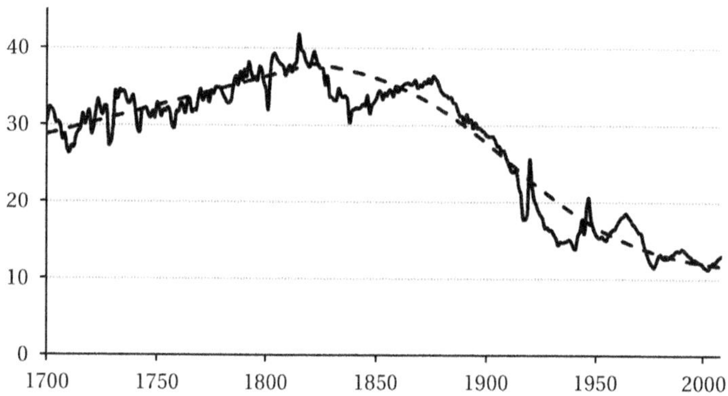

Source: Data from Mitchell (1988).

The first century of economic growth saw an increase in the birth rate but the birth rate began to decline around 1820; the decline became rapid after 1880. Drastic changes in behavior were taking place. Figure 6.4 shows some related factors.

Figure 6.4 Birth rate and related factors
Data for England and Wales

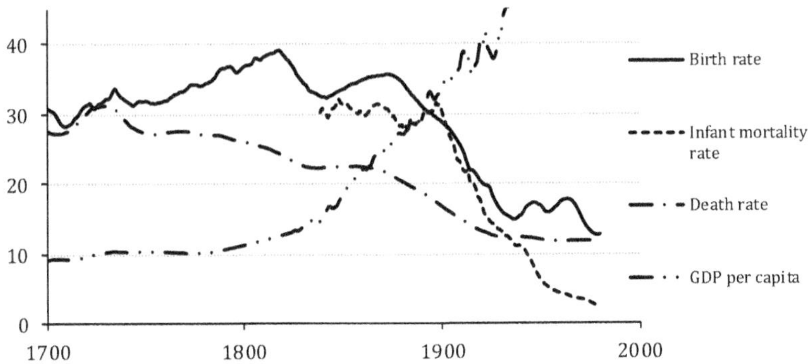

The graphed series show moving averages - 10 year moving averages for Birth rate, Death rate and GDP per capita, with 5 year moving averages for Infant mortality. The series for Infant mortality and GDP per capita are scaled to fit on the graph; this preserves their relative changes although their absolute numbers have no direct meaning.
Sources: Data from Mitchell (1988), Clark (2009) and Maddison (2006b).

The start of the long decline in the birth rate does not correlate with the rise in incomes, which had been rising rapidly since around 1820, but rather with the accelerating decline in the death rate, which started around 1875. The infant mortality rate began to plummet around 1900 but the rapid decline in the birth rate started before this.

A plausible explanation as to what was going on here is that, with the declining death rate, families needed to have fewer births in order to have at least two children survive to adulthood and to look after their parents in old age. The need for private provision for old age was further reduced by government programs, particularly under the Old Age Pensions Act 1906, but this would have accentuated a trend which had begun a generation earlier. The decline in the death rate started to slow around 1930 and the birth rate finished its precipitous decline around this same time. This adds further weight to the argument that having children previously was a form of saving for old age.

The cost of having children rises with income. This is the cost to the family in spending time in looking after children rather than in paid work or leisure and also the cost of feeding, housing and educating children. The introduction of compulsory education and, in recent decades, the trend to tertiary education raised the direct cost of parenthood over and above the opportunity cost of time spent caring for children. These forces would make children a normal economic good – when the cost goes up people have fewer children. Although this might seem cold and calculating it is consistent with the facts and also with the plausible notion that having children is ultimately a matter of individual choice.

These behavioral factors can be formalized by means of a statistical model explaining the birth rate in terms of per capita income and the death rate. A simple model, fitted to the above data for the period 1730 – 2003, implies that the elasticity of the birth rate to average income is -0.11 and to the death rate is 0.74. (Elasticity is the percentage change in the birth rate when the explanatory factor, such as the death rate, changes by 1%.) The birth rate is more sensitive to the death rate than to income. However, the rise in income has been far larger than the fall in the death rate so the overall effect is that the decline in the birth rate has been due more to higher incomes than to a lower death rate.

The trend in births is better expressed in terms of the "total fertility rate", the average number of children born to a woman over her lifetime. There is only limited historical data on fertility rates so we start with the rate for 1900. The decline in the fertility rate in the United Kingdom is from 3.5 in 1900 to 1.9 in 2010. As the population replacement fertility rate is 2.1, the decline in births has been such that population growth has become negative. Birth patterns are now such that the population is expected to decline over time; only immigration can offset this trend and lead to an increasing population.

Other countries also have followed this same population path. The decline in birth rates which has accompanied economic growth has been such that population numbers are levelling off and even starting to decline. Every high income country shows this same relationship between income and fertility. Figure 6.5 shows the relationship for 2010. The solid line in the Figure is a constant elasticity, or double log, relationship from income to fertility. (To clarify, GDP per capita in the graph goes to $60,000 only; this excludes five countries but these countries are on the same trend line as in this Figure.)

Figure 6.5 Fertility rate relative to income

Fertility rate and GDP per capita, $'000. 2010. 183 countries

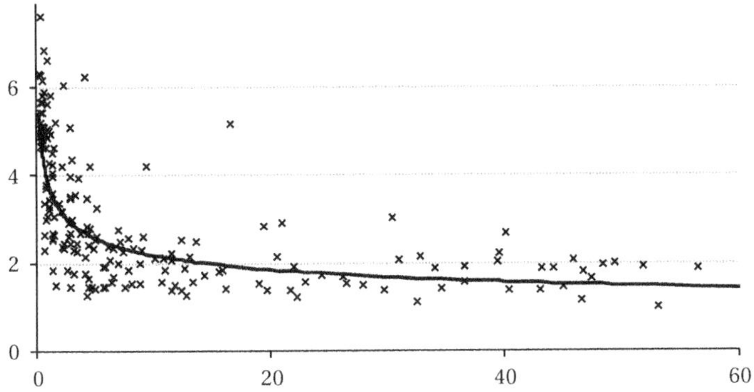

Source: Data from *World Development Indicators*, The World Bank.

This cross-country comparison suggests this general pattern: fertility rates decline as income increases until per capita income reaches $15,000 and then level off at less than 2.1. The fertility rate for most high income countries is less than the replacement rate of 2.1.

Actual population change reflects immigration as well as birth and death rates. Immigration means that some countries, in particular the United States, are continuing to increase in numbers despite having high incomes. But many countries have not had large net immigration and the population slowdown can be seen clearly. Figure 6.6 shows the population trends in Belgium, Germany and Japan. We have selected these countries as they are not or no longer experiencing large scale immigration, as Japan is Asian and Germany is European and as Belgium is a small economy.

Figure 6.6 Population growth in three countries
Population in each country in 2008 = 1

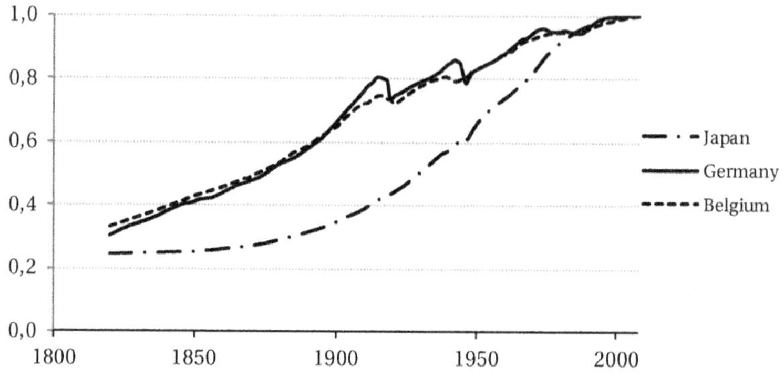

Source: Data from Maddison (2006b).

Each graph shows the same pattern – population has increased and then levelled off. Each growth path follows a logistic path reasonably closely. It might be coincidence that population growth has a logistic shape but it more likely that high income fertility practices are the result of behavioral choices which are adopted gradually; the logistic model captures well such a process of behavioral adjustment.

The conclusion is that economic growth has transformed the reproductive behavior of society. Economic growth has transformed society from high to low fertility; this has led to declining birth rates such that fertility converges to a level around or even below the replacement rate of 2.1.

6.1.4 Health

One of the most significant effects of economic growth has been an improvement in health. The death rate has declined and, the opposite side of this, life expectancy has increased dramatically. Table 6.1 shows the broad features of these changes for Britain where death rates have declined by two-thirds and life expectancy has more than doubled since the start of economic growth.

Table 6.1 Health indicators, England and Wales

	1750	1913	2000
Deaths per 1,000 of population	27.3	13.8	10.2
Life expectancy at birth, years	35	54	78

Deaths are for England and Wales; Life expectancy for 1750 is for England and Wales, data for later years is for U.K.
Sources: Data from Mitchell (1988), Government Actuary's Department (2006) and Office for National Statistics (2009b).

The history of the death rate is shown in Figure 6.7. GDP per capita has been scaled to fit on the same axis as the crude death rate. The markers are at 1725, when per capita incomes started their long upward trend, 1875, the start of the era when clean water was piped to urban households, when hygienic waste disposal began and when pasteurization of milk and other liquid foods began, and 1945, when modern pharmaceuticals started to become available.

Figure 6.7 Death rate and income

Deaths per 1,000 population. Index of GDP per capita

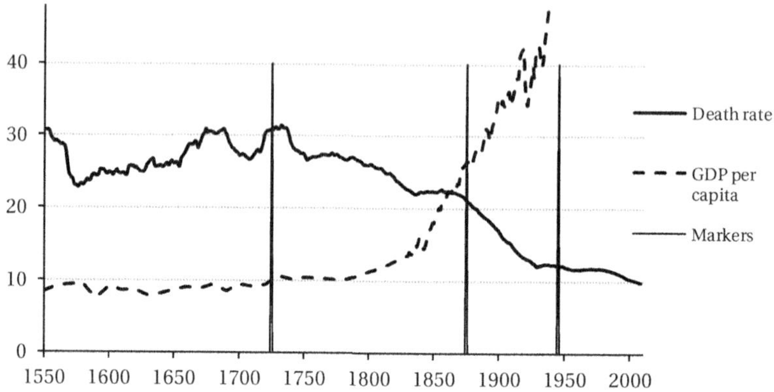

Death rate for England and Wales. GDP per capita for England then U.K.

Sources: Data from Mitchell (1988), Clark (2009) and Maddison (2006b).

The death rate had been level, although with fluctuations, before economic growth began around 1725. The death rate then began a long decline, a decline that is continuing to the present. The onset of this decline coincides with the increase in incomes above a basic level and the continuing decline has closely followed the increase in per capita incomes.

Economic growth led to better nutrition, better clothing, better personal hygiene and better housing. In the late 19th century some of the fruits of higher incomes were spent on providing sewerage and clean water systems to the urban population; this practically eliminated the waterborne diseases, cholera and typhoid fever, which were then widespread. Beginning late in the 19th century there were improvements in living conditions - replacing dirty, damp, overcrowded housing – which helped reduce the incidence of tuberculosis, previously one of the leading killers. These changes reflect the gains from economic growth. The remaining potential cause of reduced mortality is the introduction of modern medicine -

vaccinations, antibiotics and other medicines, improved preventive care and improved hospital care. However, these medical changes began in earnest only after World War II. The correlation of the death rate with income is so strong and extends over such a long period of time that we are led to the conclusion that economic growth has been the root cause of the improvement in health showing up as the declining death rate. If we oversimplify somewhat and attribute the change up to 1945 as reflecting economic growth alone and the change after 1945 as reflecting medical care alone it follows that 85% of the total reduction in the death rate has been due to economic growth.

This conclusion is consistent with the seminal medical work in the field by Thomas McKeown (1976) who argued that the greater part of the fall in mortality in the 19th century was due to improved environmental conditions (nutrition, housing, sanitation) and not to medical developments.

It could even be argued that the development of the modern pharmaceutical and health care systems has been enabled by the human and material resources generated by decades of economic growth. But, whichever way we look at it, it is clear that one of the benefits of economic growth has been the enormous improvement in health and life expectancy which has occurred since growth began almost 300 years ago.

Economic growth has changed the nature of ill health - the infectious diseases of two centuries ago have largely been defeated and have been replaced by illnesses associated with lifestyle and with old age. In the England of 1800, the most prevalent disease was tuberculosis and there were also widespread outbreaks of cholera, typhoid, smallpox and other infectious diseases. These diseases were, over time, all but eliminated as housing, nutrition, sanitation and water quality improved and vaccination was introduced. In recent decades, the main health risks have become those associated with lifestyle factors, such as obesity and smoking, and with longevity. For example, 69% of deaths in England and Wales in 1997 were due to cancers or diseases of the circulatory system whereas the figure in 1880 was only 10%. To some extent, people have used the gains from economic growth in ways which increase their health risks.

There also is a feedback from better health to better economic performance. Rising incomes allow better nutrition, better sanitation and better medical care; these contribute to economic growth as there are more people, more energetic workers, and more older and experienced workers. The health effect is that labor input increases and human capital increases. Fogel (1993) estimates that improved gross nutrition accounted for roughly 30 percent of the growth of per capita income in Britain between 1790 and 1980. While we are not sure about this 30% contribution – we found that more capital per worker, new products, more productive technologies and more productive management and organization account for most of the growth in incomes – there can be no doubt that improved health made a significant contribution to economic growth in Britain.

6.2 Higher incomes

6.2.1 In Britain

This section looks at the growth in incomes and spending over the past 300 years. In this, we look just at Britain. This is for two reasons. First, Britain was the first country to experience economic growth so we have a longer period, almost 300 years, to examine. Second, British data is relatively good so we can go back to the early days of growth and investigate quantitatively what has happened. We look at total income and total spending, household income and household spending, consumption of food, consumption of housing, investment by households and then the growth of government activity. Finally, we look at changes in the distribution of income.

6.2.2 Growth

Incomes in Britain had been growing slowly, around 0.2% a year, for centuries but growth accelerated beginning around 1725. Since that time, GDP per capita has grown at an average of 1.0% a year. Faster growth has a large effect when compounded over time - constant price GDP per capita in 2010 was 20 times larger than in 1730.

Gross Domestic Expenditure measures final demand spending. This expenditure is the point of economic activity as spending converts income and production into goods and services that people can enjoy. There is data on the expenditure side of the British economy since only 1830. The pattern of spending, indicated in Table 6.2, has changed greatly.

Table 6.2 Composition of aggregate spending

Shares of Gross Domestic Expenditure

	Personal Consumption	Government Purchases	Investment	Net exports
1830	90%	6%	6%	-2%
2003	63%	21%	16%	-3%

Sources: Data from Mitchell (1988) and U.K. National Accounts.

At the start of the growth process, personal consumption absorbed almost all, over 90%, of economic output. Although consumption has grown over the past two centuries, it has not increased as rapidly as government purchases or investment. Investment creates the physical plant and equipment that contributes to production in the future. The increasing capital-intensity of production has meant that an increasing share of production has been devoted to investing for the future. It is just consumption and government purchases which represent spending to cater to the present satisfaction of wants. (Government purchases are goods and services used by the government to produce public services, these purchases do not include spending on income transfers.) Economic growth has been used to support more personal consumption but an even more rapid growth in government activity.

6.2.3 Household income

The average wage in an English household in 1730 was 16 pence per day. Allowing for days worked, this was just over £20 per annum. Allowing for general inflation since that time, this is equivalent to £75 per week in 2003. The actual income per household in 2003 was £574 per week, 8 times the earlier income.

In addition, households had considerably more leisure time in 2003. Average hours worked fell from 2,892 a year in 1750 to 1,640 in 2003, freeing up around 24 hours a week. And, the increase in life expectancy from around 40 to around 80 years allows older members of households either to work for longer or else have more leisure time. Valuing these time-related effects at the average wage, we estimate that the effective income, combining both money income and more leisure of households was, in 2003, 15 times higher than in 1730.

Allowing for both money income and leisure gains, the average household became better off by 1.0% for every year since 1730. Households gained from economic growth by having more purchasing power and also in having more leisure in which to enjoy their new purchasing power. Households chose to split the benefits of economic growth roughly equally between more money income and more leisure.

6.2.4 Household spending

Household money income in terms of purchasing power increased 8-fold from 1730 to 2003. The composition of spending changed greatly. Households did not just scale up their initial spending; they directed most of the increase to entirely new types of spending. Table 6.3 shows these changes.

Table 6.3 Household weekly spending, 1730 and 2003

	Spending in 1730		Spending in 2003		Increase
	£ 2003	Share	£ 2003	Share	2003 / 1730
Food	40	54%	43	7%	6%
Alcohol	5	6%	6	1%	22%
Housing, household operation	12	17%	163	28%	1206%
Clothing	9	12%	22	4%	146%
Basics		89%		41%	
Transport, communications	0	0%	70	12%	New
Tobacco	0	0%	5	1%	New
Entertainment, travel	1	1%	98	17%	12926%
Services	5	7%	38	7%	616%
Savings	3	4%	33	6%	1155%
Other		12%		43%	na
Income taxes	0	0%	96	17%	New
Total	75	100%	574	100%	661%

Sources: Data from Clark (2009) and Office for National Statistics (2004).

Spending in 1730 was dominated by survival – buying food, shelter and clothing - with little left over for other purchases. 89% of spending went on these basics. Alcohol is included in basics as alcohol, primarily beer, was a food more than a recreational purchase. The largest element in discretionary spending was personal services. About 3% of income was left over and saved.

Purchases of basics declined from 89% of household spending in 1730 to 41% in 2003. Within this, the amount, not the share but the amount, spent on food and alcohol has hardly changed. The share of clothing in the budget has declined sharply. The increase in spending has been directed elsewhere – to housing and to new types of spending.

Spending on housing and household operation has risen dramatically. Housing has long since ceased being a basic purchase. People today buy larger and better equipped houses and operate these houses to a higher level of comfort and convenience. Some of this housing-related spending goes to devices which replace household labor, releasing time for leisure and entertainment activities.

Then there are several entirely new categories which have absorbed a large part of the increase in spending; these are transport and communications, entertainment and travel, and taxes. Most of the increase in taxes went to finance new types of government activities – education and health services and income support transfers.

This represents a huge re-allocation of personal spending. Reduced (relative) spending on food and alcohol has released 52% of the household budget. Spending on items which did not exist in 1730 – mechanical transport and communications, entertainment and travel, and income taxes - has absorbed 46% of the budget. There has been an enormous shift from basics to entirely new goods and services.

Then there is the whole issue of retirement. Organized retirement in the modern sense did not exist in the 18th century as most people did not survive to an advanced age. Preparation for infirmity or old age was primarily a matter of having sufficiently large families that those children who survived to adulthood could look after surviving parents. This has changed dramatically. Not only are family sizes smaller but also children are no longer expected to provide total care for aged parents. Instead, retirement is catered for financially by personal savings (6% of the 2003 budget) and from government transfers (out of the 17% of income which now goes to income taxes).

The dramatic change in household budgets reflects a hierarchy of wants - once the basic needs are provided, spending moves towards new and discretionary areas. Economic growth has allowed households to purchase these new types of goods and services and has released time, from paid work as well as household chores, for the enjoyment of these new goods and services.

6.2.5 Food

Economic growth has resulted in people today being far better fed than in the old days. Limited nutrition in modern Britain is a thing of the past. (If there is inadequate nutrition it is a matter of personal choice rather than economic necessity.)

Expenditure on food and drink, after inflation is taken into account, changed hardly at all between 1730 and 2003 – people still spend the same amount on food and drink. However, prices of foods have fallen dramatically. The basket of foods shown in Table 6.4 today costs only 16% of its cost in 1730. Productivity increases in food production have allowed relative prices to decline by an average of 0.7% a year.

Table 6.4 Change in prices of principal food items

Prices are in 2003 £. Weights are expenditure shares in 1730.

Food	Unit	Price in 1730	Price in 2003	Ratio (1)
Cheese	250g cheddar	4.17	1.26	0.30
Eggs	1 dozen	16.94	1.68	0.10
Butter	250g	7.59	0.82	0.11
Milk	1 pint	1.73	0.34	0.20
Beef	Stewing steak/kg	16.93	5.96	0.35
Lamb	Shoulder/kg	17.69	4.70	0.27
Potatoes	1 kg	3.62	0.59	0.16
Bread	1 kg	6.21	0.71	0.11
Average				0.16

Note (1): Price in 2003/ price in 1730.

Sources: Data from Clark (2009) and Office for National Statistics (2006b).

Keeping spending on foods the same with prices falling means that the quantity of food bought by each household has increased; in fact it has increased six-fold. Calorie intake has increased but only by 50%, from around 2,200 per person per day early in the 18th century to around 3,300 today. There has been a big change in diet. Table 6.5 shows that there has been a large shift away from fats and starches and towards vegetables, meat and drinks. The modern household not only eats more but also better than its ancestor.

Table 6.5 Change in diet

Share of expenditure for the average household, England

	18th C	2003	Change % of total
Starches, sugars, fats, beer	0.68	0.30	-38
Meats, fish	0.15	0.24	9
Dairy	0.12	0.11	-1
Vegetables except starches, fruits	0.01	0.15	14
Drinks except beer	0.02	0.16	14
Salt, spices	0.02	0.04	2
	1.00	1.00	0

Sources: Data from Clark (2009) and Office for National Statistics (2004).

The availability of cheap foods has led everyone to eat more than their ancestors and has led some people to over-indulge. The body mass index (BMI), although imperfect, is used as an indicator of the health effects of weight. A BMI of 25 is regarded as the upper limit for a normal, healthy person; higher BMIs are regarded as overweight (up to 30), obese (over 30) or very obese (over 40). 54% of English adults surveyed in 1993 had a BMI in excess of 25. And the weight situation is changing. By 2009, 64% had a BMI over 25 with 38% overweight, 23% obese and 2% very obese. Carrying too much weight creates health risks. For example, the risks of coronary artery disease increase and of type 2 diabetes increase rapidly as BMI rises. A very obese person has a life expectancy 11 years shorter than the average person with a healthy BMI.

Economic growth has resulted in more food and a wider range of foods becoming available and accessible to everyone. Everyone is better off is this sense. Some people have chosen to indulge in a way which is injurious to their future health. Present gratification has, to some extent, outweighed future costs. But this present-future dilemma is part of human nature. Economic growth has made these opportunities available; it is part of the market system that people are free to decide how to make use of these opportunities and how to manage their own lives.

6.2.6 Housing

Economic growth has brought about huge changes in household accommodation. Not only do households now spend much more of their budget on housing but also the nature of their accommodation has changed dramatically.

The first change has been in tenure - there has been a huge increase in ownership. Table 6.6 shows the move from rented towards owner-occupied accommodation. Today, around two-thirds of people own their dwelling. The move to ownership took place over the 20th century. It has recently stabilized at around 67 – 69% (in the U.K. as well as many other countries).

Table 6.6 Housing tenure in U.K.

Share of households owning their residence

19th C	< 10%
1914	10%
1945	40%
1971	49%
2001	69%

Sources: Data from Hicks and Allen (1999) and Office for National Statistics (2010a).

Next, the size of the typical house has increased – new houses have become progressively bigger. The typical house in the mid-18th century was around 400 square feet (sq ft). Houses in the new towns were only slightly bigger, around 450 sq ft. As the industrial towns became established house sizes increased so by 1900 the typical size was 760 sq ft. The size continued to increase over the 20th century reaching 1,230 sq ft by 2008. (House size has not increased as much as household spending – average floor area has increased at 0.4% a year since 1730 while spending has increased at a 0.7% rate.)

The amenities of housing have changed markedly, especially involving water and energy. The typical house in the mid-18th century was a rural or village cottage, made of local materials (whether brick, stone, rock, wood or mud) and with two rooms. This house provided shelter from the elements and contained a fireplace for cooking and heating. The amenities, other than the fire, were candles for lighting, utensils for handling food and a container for water. Water was carried in from outside of the house and waste was carried out for disposal. Piped supply of clean water and piped removal of sewage was introduced late in the 19th century. The modern flush toilet (developed by a John Crapper (real name Thomas Crapper), who improved an earlier design by adding the ballcock mechanism to control cistern filling) greatly added to the convenience. Toilet facilities were moved from an outhouse to a room inside the house. Gradually, the bathroom changed to contain both washing and toilet facilities. After the introduction of water heating, washing facilities became more elaborate, containing bath and hand basin with, later on, showers becoming popular. As house sizes continued to increase it became common to have two bathrooms and to put toilet facilities into separate rooms.

Changes in energy supply allowed equally dramatic changes in housing amenities. Cooking was originally done over a wood or coal fire. The town houses of the 19th century took advantage of Britain's new industries by using coal ranges – cast iron structures with a coal firebox heating a cooking surface and possibly also an oven. Later in the century town gas became available. This gas was produced in central stations from the partial combustion of coal and was piped to households. Gas was used for cooking and lighting. Water heating became possible using either pipes through the coal range or a gas heater.

Equally profound changes followed from the development of electricity service. Generation began late in the 19th century but reticulation to households was a drawn out process. By 1930 only 38%

of U.K. households had electricity supply but this share rose to 71% by 1940, 87% by 1950 and 98% by 1970. Electricity supply provided lighting and then power to the whole range of electrical appliances which were developed over the 20th century. Finally, natural gas became available, completely displacing town gas and being used particularly for cooking, water heating and space heating.

Housing today has all the basic amenities, or what are now regarded as necessities of life, as shown for the U.K. in Table 6.7.

Table 6.7 Penetration of basic amenities, 2008

Safe water	99.9%
Safe sewerage	99.7%
Electricity supply	> 99%
Lighting	100%
Hot water	99.6%
Cooker	99.5%

Source: Data from Office for National Statistics (2013).

Electricity supply has allowed the use of all manner of electrical appliances which have transformed modern household life. These appliances add to the convenience and comfort of life or else save time in doing household work. The penetration of major appliances in the U.K. is shown in Table 6.8.

Table 6.8 Penetration of convenience amenities, 2008

Refrigerator, freezer	>99%
Telephone	>99%
Clothes washer	96%
Central heating	95%
Microwave oven	92%
Tumble dryer	59%
Dishwasher	37%
Small kitchen appliances	varies
Small household appliances	varies

Source: Data from Office for National Statistics (2013).

In addition, there are huge numbers of appliances used for entertainment – radios, televisions, music players, video players, computers, electronic games and so on. And, households are today wired extensively to take advantage of modern communications – the telephone and the internet.

Last but not least are the effects of the automobile. The automobile has revolutionized the location of housing, creating the suburb. Housing in the suburbs in turn has adapted to the automobile by including one or more garages and hardtop parking spaces.

6.2.7 Investment by households

Households in 1730 did virtually no capital spending but today the situation is very different. Table 6.9 shows the details. Purchases of physical capital are particularly important in housing and transportation.

Table 6.9 Capital structure of household spending, 2003

Average weekly spending by households, £

	Current	Capital	Capital share
Housing	53	79	60%
Household goods & services	8	22	73%
Transport	33	27	45%
Communications	10	1	6%
Entertainment	64	10	13%
All household expenditure	436	138	24%

Source: Based on data from Office for National Statistics (2004).

Purchases of physical capital goods and equipment accounts for 24% of today's household spending. For the economy as a whole, the share of investment (gross fixed capital formation) in GDP is around 16%. The household sector is comparable in capital-intensity to the overall economy. Household activity has been transformed by capital just as the overall economy has been. The only real difference is that the production of services by household capital is hidden as these services are not bought and sold in the market place whereas the output of industrial and commercial capital is traded.

Viewing the broad range of assets shows the modern household is particularly capital-intensive in the broadest sense - where capital is viewed as investing in assets which will yield a stream of services in future years. Households add to their financial assets by direct saving and also by their claims on government retirement programs. We indicate this by applying to household taxes the share of these retirement programs in total government expenditure. In addition, households are heavily engaged in the accumulation of human capital through formal education. We indicate this in a similar way. The resulting pattern of household investment is shown in Table 6.10.

Table 6.10 Investment by households, 2003
Share of household spending directed to asset accumulation

Investment in plant and equipment	24%
Direct saving	6%
Retirement saving through taxation	3%
Investment in human capital by education	13%
Total investment share of household spending	46%

Source: Based on data from Office for National Statistics (2004).

Almost half of household spending is, in one way or another, directed to investment. This investment adds to capital which generates income, either monetary income or income in kind. Income in kind is particularly important, covering services such as accommodation from owner-occupied housing, time released by household appliances, mobility gained from owning cars, and entertainment services from personal equipment.

The modern household is one of the most capital-intensive areas of the economy. The age of capital which has transformed the economy has similarly transformed the household.

6.2.8 Government activity

Government spending in Britain has evolved enormously since 1730. Table 6.11 indicates the changes.

Table 6.11 U.K. government spending, 1730 and 2003

	1730 £ mn	2003 £ bn
Defense	2.4	30
Transport		15
Health		66
Education		53
Protection		24
General government	0.9	12
Interest	2.3	21
Other spending	0.1	53
Purchases	5.7	274
Welfare		66
Pensions		80
Transfers	0	146
Defense/GDP	4%	3%
General govt/GDP	1%	1%
Interest/GDP	3%	2%
Other purchases/GDP	0%	19%
Govt purchases/GDP	8%	24%
Transfers/GDP	0%	13%

Sources: Data from Chantrill (2011), Clark (2009) and U.K. National Accounts.

Government purchases have risen from 8% to 24% of GDP. Defense, government administration and interest have retained their relative size but several new areas of activity have emerged – purchases relating to transport, protection and, most of all, education and health care have risen from nothing to account today for around 19% of the economy.

There has been an even greater increase in government transfers. These transfers, which are mainly welfare and retirement benefits, today are equivalent to 13% of GDP. These transfers redistribute income, they do not create income; as such they are not part of GDP. Transfers modify the distribution of income which emerges from the operation of the productive economy. These transfers are a form of government activity unknown in 1730.

One of the main things that people have chosen to do with the fruits of economic growth has been to increase the size and scope of the government. Entirely new government services, such as education and health care, and entirely new government activities, such as income redistribution, have emerged and grown to massive proportions.

6.2.9 Income distribution

Any society has an uneven distribution of income with some people at low incomes, most in the middle, some with high and a few with extremely high incomes. The Italian economist Vilfredo Pareto in 1897 made the observation that the distribution of income and wealth in a country tends to have a particular shape. One characteristic of the original "Pareto curve" was that 80% of the land was owned by 20% of the people, the famous 80/20 rule. This shape has been found to describe the general pattern of the distribution of income which emerges from a market economy. Income distribution has more recently been analyzed in terms of the better-fitting "log normal" statistical distribution. Many features of human, biological and natural life are characterized by the normal statistical distribution or bell curve. Income distribution though typically exhibits a pattern where the logarithm of the relative frequency is normally distributed.

The income distribution of the U.K. in 2011-12, shown in Figure 6.8, exhibits the typical log normal shape.

Figure 6.8 Income distribution in UK, 2011-12

Number of taxpayers, mn (vertical) vs income per taxpayer, £ (horizonal)

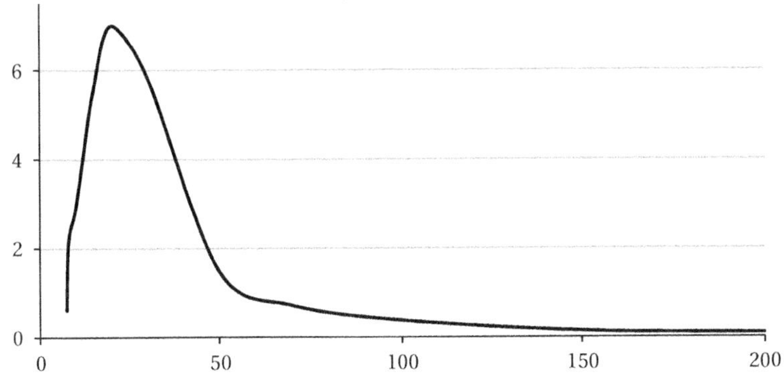

There were also 81,000 taxpayers with incomes above £200,000.

Number of taxpayers in millions. Before tax income per taxpayer in thousand £.

Source: Data from HM Revenue & Customs (2014).

The market economy has produced economic growth and has lifted much of the world out of poverty. A consequence, though, is this particular form of income distribution. This market distribution of income has come to be seen as socially undesirable. With the rise of government power, government mechanisms have been put in place to modify the market income distribution. This movement to government redistribution of income as an explicit policy goal took place in several stages. We now outline the evolution of income redistribution measures in Britain.

First came measures to help people at the very bottom end of the income distribution – the very poor. The Poor Law passed in the reign of Elizabeth I in 1601 remained in force for more than two centuries. This law made each parish responsible for supporting the needy in its community. This support was by payments to the needy, funded by taxes on the wealthier landowners of the parish. New legislation in 1834 added workhouses to the support system. These workhouses provided accommodation, meals and employment. It has been estimated as much as 5% of the population may have been housed in workhouses (see Fraser (2009)). *Oliver Twist* and other novels by Charles Dickens offer a particular view of these workhouses.

Next came monetary payments to defined categories of people. These payment schemes started in 1908 with the first pensions. Subsequently, unemployment, widows and orphans benefits were added, pension benefits were extended, sickness/disability benefits were introduced and then benefits were introduced for low income single parents. Benefits in kind started with government-subsidized housing after World War I and were extended to services such as free health care and free education in the welfare state legislation introduced after World War II.

The introduction of the personal income tax transformed the ability of the government to redistribute income. The first income tax (on high incomes only) was introduced to help pay for the wars against Napoleonic France. The income tax was introduced permanently in 1842. Again, only the highest incomes were taxed; the tax was primarily to gather revenue, not to redistribute income. A general income tax was introduced in 1908 but with only two rates – a standard rate and a higher rate in high incomes. The standard rate was 6% at the outbreak of World War I and 30% by the end of the War. The move to progressive tax rates – where the rate increased steadily as taxable incomes rose – began in earnest after the introduction of the welfare state after World War II. In recent decades, the progressive personal income tax has become a strong tool for taking income away from people with higher incomes.

The situation today is that the government modifies the market income distribution by a range of measures to provide income, whether in money or in kind, and to take away income, through taxes. Table 6.12 shows the effect of these government mechanisms in modifying the income distribution in the U.K. in 2010-11.

Table 6.12 Effects of government redistributions, 2010-11

Average annual income per household, £ thousands

Quintile group	Bottom	2nd	3rd	4th	Top	All
Original income	5.1	11.8	22.5	39.6	81.5	32.1
+ Cash benefits	7.0	8.3	6.7	4.1	2.1	5.6
+ Benefits in kind	7.7	7.6	7.5	6.8	5.8	7.1
- Direct taxes	-1.3	-2.5	-4.8	-9.0	-19.7	-7.5
- Indirect taxes	-3.4	-3.7	-4.8	-6.0	-8.3	-5.3
= Final Income	15.2	21.4	27.1	35.5	61.4	32.1
Final / Original income	3.00	1.82	1.20	0.90	0.75	1.00

Source: Data from Office for National Statistics (2012a).

The principal mechanism for getting income to low income households is government benefits with cash benefits and benefits in kind approximately equal in importance. The principal means of taking income away from high income households is the tax system with income taxes more important in this than indirect taxes.

The result is a considerable flattening of the income distribution. Average income in the lowest quintile is increased by 200% by these redistributive policies while average income in the top quintile is reduced by 25%. The lowest quintile gets its average income increased from 16% to 47% of the national average while the top quintile is reduced from 254% to 191% of the national average.

In addition, the aim of the original Elizabethan Poor Law, of protecting the extremely poor, remains. Today it is called providing a safety net. Benefits in cash and benefits in kind, including subsidized housing, education and medical care, allow those at the bottom of the income distribution to share in the economic growth of their country.

Government programs for redistributing income can substantially modify the distribution which emerges from the market system. There is a balancing act to be done as too much redistribution destroys the economic incentives on which economic growth depends. However, modern social democratic governments appear to have achieved some kind of balance that satisfies social pressure for less inequality while preserving the conditions needed for economic growth. Those at the bottom of the income distribution have been taken care of sufficiently that they are better off to go along with the system than to try to overthrow the system. The Marxist-style potential for class warfare has been nullified by these measures to ensure that everyone benefits from economic growth.

In the fullness of time, all incomes increase as a result of economic growth, as a result of more and better capital, increasing labor skills, productivity increase and the competition for hiring labor. Not everyone's income goes up by the same proportion, not everyone ends up on the same income but economic growth gives everyone a higher income. In the jargon, economic growth is not a zero sum game, where one person becomes better off as a result of someone else becoming worse off; economic growth is a positive sum game, where everyone becomes better off. Redistributive policies simply take some of the sharp edges off of the distribution of the gains but economic growth generates gains, and large gains, for all.

6.3 Education

6.3.1 Before growth

Pre-industrial Britain was dependent on agriculture and its supporting industries. Literacy was not essential for many of the laboring activities in these industries. Table 6.13 shows the occupational structure in 1759, based on Lindert and Williamson's Social Tables, shown in Mitchell (1988). If we assume that the literacy rate for high title, professions and commerce was 100%, for agriculture was 75%, for industry was 50%, for military was 25% and for the remaining categories was 0% then the overall literacy rate would have been 50%. The actual literacy rate was slightly over 50%. This structure therefore provides a plausible picture of literacy in England before the start of economic growth.

Table 6.13 Families in England and Wales, 1759

High titles and gentlemen	18,070	1%
Professions	57,000	4%
Military and maritime	86,000	6%
Commerce inc tradesmen	200,500	13%
Industry and building	366,252	24%
Agriculture exc laborers	379,008	25%
Laborers	240,000	16%
Cottagers and paupers	178,892	12%
Vagrants	13,418	1%
Total	1,539,140	100%

Source: Data from Mitchell (1988).

The first factories were cotton mills which began to appear in the 1770s. At the same time, activity in the iron and coal industries began to accelerate. This growth in industry pulled in labor to provide muscle power and to tend machines. There was no need for the operatives in the new industries to be literate.

By 1800, education remained in its pre-industrial form. There were no government schools, there was no general education, there was just education provided by churches and in private schools. Education was an expensive service which was out of the reach of the growing class of industrial families.

6.3.2 Provision of education

The development of the education system was led by the government although it took more than 100 years to establish the modern system of free, universal primary and secondary education, aiming to make the adult population literate and numerate.

The new industries of the 1800s employed thousands of men, women and children. Hours for all workers were long and employers paid scant regard to the welfare of the workers. This led to pressure from workers, as well as public spirited citizens, to improve working conditions, particularly for women and children. This pressure led to a sequence of legislation intended to improve working conditions and, as part of this, to provide education for children.

The Factories Act 1802 prohibited the employment of children under 9 years, limited the work-day of older children and required factory owners to provide children with instruction in reading, writing and arithmetic during their first four years of work. This Act had no effective enforcement mechanisms but it did establish standards which set the direction for future reform. The Factories Act 1833 introduced further restrictions on hours and conditions and it required that children aged 9 to 13 have two hours of education per day. The Act took the first step towards enforcement with provision for routine inspections of factories.

The Elementary Education Act 1870 created the concept of compulsory elementary education for children. The Factory Act 1878 formalized compulsory elementary education of children and prohibited the employment of children so that these children could instead enrol in schools. Another Act in 1891 required that publicly supported schools provide free elementary education to every child who enrolled. Compulsory education was subsequently extended to the secondary or high school level. The required age of attendance was raised to 11 years in 1893 then progressively to 16 years by 1973.

Government funding began in 1833 with some grants to church schools. Funding was gradually extended as universal compulsory schooling was introduced and state schools became fully funded by the government. Over the 20th century, extended government funding allowed college/university and vocational institutions to offer subsidised education. In recent decades, government funding has become available for pre-school education.

6.3.3 Content

Compulsory elementary education in Britain has always focused on literacy and numeracy, covering the fundamentals of reading, writing and arithmetic. This education has always been secular; religious education, such as learning religious texts or studying religious doctrine, has never been a significant part of compulsory education.

In more recent times, the elementary school curriculum and in particular the secondary/high school curriculum has been expanded to cover a range of intellectual areas. The present curriculum in publicly funded schools in England is made up of 12 subjects - the core subjects of English, Mathematics and Science are compulsory for all students up to age 16, with some choice possible in the other subjects of Art and design, Citizenship, Design and technology, Geography, History, Information and communication technology, Foreign languages, Music and Physical education.

Compulsory education has always been directed at the intellectual side of education, endeavoring to provide the knowledge and skills for thinking and communication. After leaving compulsory education, young people may pursue further and more specialized education. There are two main strands to further education. One is to more advanced intellectual study; this is provided in tertiary institutions (colleges, universities and polytechnics). The other direction is vocational or trade education which combines on-the-job and classroom training. Adult education is available for adult students to pursue further learning and practice in either intellectual or practical subjects.

Finally, there has been growth in recent years of pre-school education. These institutions are not directed to education as much as to the social development of children. They also provide child care, which assists households in which the primary caregiver is in paid work.

6.3.4 Inputs

Government spending on education in the U.K. today accounts for some 6% of GDP. In addition, households spend around 1% of their income on direct education payments. Education in total absorbs around 7% of total income, making it one of the largest industries in the modern economy. The growth in government spending on education over the past 200 years is shown in Figure 6.9.

Figure 6.9 Government education spending as % GDP

Sources: Data from Mitchell and Deane (1971) and Chantrill (2011).

There has been an upward trend in the relative size of the education industry. The main reason is the gradual expansion of coverage of education. Starting in the 19th century with elementary education then moving to compulsory secondary education and more recently to available pre-school, tertiary and adult education, more and more of the population has been brought under the coverage of the education system.

6.3.5 Outputs

Indicators of student participation in the U.K. are shown in Table 6.14.

Table 6.14 Participation in Education, U.K.
Data for 2008 except 2009 for tertiary education

Enrolment rate, pre-primary	81%
Enrolment rate, primary	100%
Enrolment rate, secondary	93%
Higher education initial participation rate, 18 years	22%
Male to female ratio, primary education	1
Male to female ratio, initial tertiary education	0.67

Source: Data from *World Development Indicators*, World Bank.

Education in the U.K. has succeeded in its objective of including everyone in its target demographic set, the resident population aged 5 to 16. Education outside this age range is voluntary. The participation rate in secondary education is 93%; as it is less than 100% it means that a number of people are leaving school at 16 rather than choosing to complete high school. The initial participation rate in higher education of 18 year olds is lower, at 22%. This is the fraction of secondary school completers who go straight on to higher formal education. At the other end of the age range, fully 81% of pre-school children are enrolled in formal education/care establishments. For the population as a whole, 22% are engaged in formal education of one form another, in either part-time or full-time study or training. There is no evidence to suggest gender inequality in terms of access to education.

Educational attainment is summarized in Table 6.15.

Table 6.15 Educational attainment of the U.K. population
Population of working age, highest education. 2003

Degree or equivalent	16%
Other higher education qualification	9%
"A" level or recognized trade qualification (1)	24%
Secondary School certificate (2)	22%
Other qualification	14%
No qualification	15%
Total	100%

Note (1): "A" level is a secondary school completion qualification gained by examination.

Note (2): Pass in the mid high school level General Certificate of Secondary Education.

Source: Office for National Statistics (2011).

Only 71% of the working age population has completed compulsory education in the sense of passing the secondary school examinations taken around age 15. This means that 29% of the working age population does not have a recognized qualification at the mid secondary school level. Although the education system has been successful in getting young people into instruction it has not been so successful in getting these people up to the target level of educational achievement. (The picture is complicated by immigration as some of the working age population might not have received their formal education in the U.K.)

The International Adult Learning Survey (IALS) was sponsored by the OECD. IALS endeavored to compare functional literacy across 20 countries. IALS presented results on a scale of 1 to 5 where level 1 is viewed as functional illiteracy, where a person's information acquisition and cognitive skills are below the "minimum for coping with the demands for everyday life and work in a complex, advanced society". The results for level 1 literacy for the working age population in the U.K. and a number of high income countries are shown in Table 6.16.

Table 6.16 % of adults with Level 1 functional literacy
Data for 1994 - 1998 from the International Adult Literacy Survey

	Prose	Document	Quantitative
U.K.	22	23	23
U.S.A.	21	24	21
Australia	17	17	17
Germany	14	9	7
Netherlands	11	10	10
Sweden	8	6	7

Source: Data from OECD (2000).

These survey results suggest that the education systems in high income countries have been able to get at least 75% of their populations to a level of workable literacy. The non-English speaking northern European countries, such as Germany and Sweden, have only 10% of their population shown as functionally illiterate. This is consistent with the idea that different education systems might be able to improve the quality of basic education although there remains a core of people who are not responsive to formal education.

6.3.6 The principles

Education policy has evolved in Britain (and in most high income countries) to reflect these principles:

(1) Compulsory education of children up to a set age such as 16 years;

(2) Universal education – all children participate regardless of gender, ethnicity, income or class;

(3) Free education – governments support this education so that there are no core charges to students;

(4) Intellectual education – the central purpose of this core education is to promote literacy, numeracy and knowledge or skills in other intellectual areas; there might be some vocational training but it is not central to the curriculum. Education is secular, there is no role for the teaching of religious beliefs or religious texts.

(5) Subsequent education – more advanced intellectual education and, separately, vocational instruction are available subsequent to the compulsory core education and on a voluntary basis.

6.3.7 Benefits from education

There are several types of gain, private and as well as public, from education.

(1) The private economic gains from education are the higher net incomes and consumption which arise from having more human capital and from being more productive.

(2) There are private non-economic but nonetheless significant benefits from being able to understand and participate in the literature, arts, science and other achievements of the western and other great civilizations of the world.

(3) There are public economic gains from having more productive, more creative people who drive the economy forward to everyone's benefit.

(4) There are public gains from the improvements to health, security, social interaction and governance arising from a more educated, more responsible and more thoughtful populace.

It is not easy to put monetary values on many of these gains but it is possible to quantify the direct income gains resulting from education. Table 6.17 shows rates of return on investment in education to the secondary level and to the tertiary level as calculated by the OECD. The private rate of return compares the additional net income received by a holder of the qualification, relative to someone without this qualification, to the expenditure made by the student in getting the qualification. The public return compares the additional gross income to the total cost associated with getting the qualification.

Table 6.17 Rates of return on investment in education
For U.K., 2006.

	Private return	Public return
Men		
Upper secondary qualification	13.5%	10.1%
Tertiary qualification	11.2%	10.4%
Women		
Upper secondary qualification	10.5%	21.9% (1)
Tertiary qualification	8.8%	9.5%

Note (1): This is the OECD number; it is somewhat out of line with the corresponding rates of return for other countries.
Source: Data from OECD (2011b).

The return on core investment, such as to completing high school, generally exceeds the return to tertiary education but both core and tertiary education investment are productive. Both private and public rates of return exceed 10%. The FTSE100 index of prices on the London Stock Exchange increased at an average rate of 5.9% for the 25 years through 2010; adding in say 2.5% for dividend yield gives an indicative return of 8.5% before fees and taxes. It is difficult to compare average returns to education at one point in time to returns on financial investment covering many years. It appears, though, that the direct returns from education are at least as good as the returns on other forms of investment available to an individual.

6.4 Time

6.4.1 Hours worked

In 1730 England, the typical worker was an agricultural laborer. He worked 285 days a year, an average of 5.5 days each week, and an average of around 10 hours per full workday. This adds up to 2,890 hours worked a year. Leisure time was around 5 hours per working day (leaving 9 hours a day for sleep and personal care), some general holidays, together with some of Saturday and all of Sunday.

Work patterns changed with the emergence of manufacturing – the working year got longer. Industrial workers had Sundays off and four general holidays a year (Good Friday or Easter, May Day, All Saints' Day and Christmas Day) but otherwise worked around 12 hours a day. The length of working days in the textile mills is indicated by some of the Factory Acts. For example, the Act of 1819 limited children of 9 to 16 years to a maximum of 12 hours work a day; the Act of 1844 limited the workday for women to 12 hours; and the Act of 1847 limited the workweek of women and children to 58 hours, in effect a 10 hour day. Work hours for women and children were reduced through legislation but working hours for men were reduced mainly by pressure from trade unions. Union activity gradually reduced the work week but it was not until the 20th century that the 40 hour week became standard. In addition, the number of general holidays increased, paid vacation time was introduced and paid sick day entitlements were introduced. These changes, going on for more than 150 years, have led to an average working year of around 1,640 hours. This is the working year produced, for example, by working for 43 weeks, 5 days a week and 7.5 hours a day. Figure 6.10 shows the evolution of the working year. It appears that the working year has levelled off – there has been little reduction in the past 40 years.

Figure 6.10 Average work year, England

Average hours worked each year

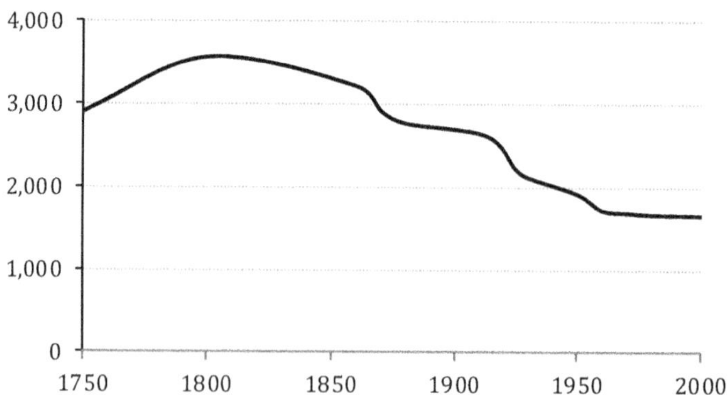

Sources: Data from Office for National Statistics (2006c) and Voth (1997).

The initial change, with the emergence of new employment opportunities in manufacturing, was for longer working hours. Workers apparently responded to these opportunities by willingly taking on more work – the income effect dominated the substitution effect in the supply of labor. Gradually though, as wages increased, the substitution effect came to the fore – workers wanted more leisure time in which to enjoy the goods and services they could buy with their higher incomes.

Hours worked in a year have fallen in all countries which are now viewed as industrialized. Maddison (2006a) has assembled data going back to 1870 for seven of these countries. This is shown in Figure 6.11. The rate of decline in the work-year has been 0.5% a year in every country except Japan where it has been 0.4%.

Figure 6.11 Annual hours worked per person employed

Source: Data from Maddison (2006a).

The simple elasticity of hours worked to income in these seven countries is -0.3, or for every 1% rise in average incomes the annual work year declines by 0.3%. There is a similar relationship across countries at a given time. We used data from the OECD for 34 countries to relate the working year in 2003 to GDP per capita; the simple elasticity was -0.2. Either way, across time or across countries, people have tended to work fewer hours as their income rises. One way that workers have enjoyed higher incomes has been to take more leisure.

6.4.2 Retirement

Another increase in leisure time has followed from what is now a standard feature in the household life cycle – having several healthy years of retirement time. Life expectancy in the mid-18th century was less than 40 years. Few workers could look forward to retirement; even the notion of retirement was unknown to the majority of the population. Retirement from paid work is an important consequence of economic growth. The additional life expectancy is the result of better nutrition, better water supply and waste disposal, better public health, better medicine and better health care, all made possible by economic growth.

Today, workers retire in their 60s and can look forward to several years of good health and enjoyment of leisure time. The remaining life expectancy for 65 year old males in England in 2008-2010 was 18 years. This means that workers today can enjoy 18 years of life after leaving paid work; 10 of these years were classed as being free from a limiting chronic illness or disease (see Office for National Statistics (2012b)).

It is difficult to overstate the significance of this gain. It is as if every person were given an extra decade of leisure combined with good health and an income sufficient to pursue their main interests during this time. Obviously this is not immortality but being given a decade for free is a useful step in that direction.

6.4.3 Leisure

Economic growth has released huge amounts of time from daily work and chores. People today have considerable time available for activities which they choose to do as opposed to have to do to survive. Table 6.18 shows the change from the mid-18th century for British households.

Table 6.18 Use of time in Britain, hours per day

	Mid 18thC	2005
Men		
Personal essentials	10.5	10.5
Paid work	7.9	4.5
Remaining time	5.6	9.0
Increase in remaining time		3.4
Women		
Personal essentials	10.5	10.5
Housework	8.8	3.0
Remaining time	4.8	10.5
Increase in remaining time		5.8

Personal essentials covers sleep, meals and personal hygiene.
Remaining time covers childcare and household work (for men), paid work (for women) as well as discretionary activities.
Sources: Data from Clark (2009) and Office for National Statistics (2006c).

Before industrialization, the average man worked in agriculture for an average of around 8 hours a day. With industrialization and the later move toward services, the average working day fell to only 4.5 hours (this is the average over 365 days of the year). The time remaining after paid work and personal essentials increased by 3.4 hours a day.

This is additional leisure time, available for use however the man wishes to use it. We do not have use of time information for earlier centuries but there are detailed statistics for recent years. Table 6.19 shows the average use of time for British men in 2005.

Table 6.19 Use of discretionary time, British men

Average hours per day, 2005.

Housework, childcare	1.9
Study	0.2
Social, volunteer work	1.5
Sport, outdoor, culture	0.3
TV, video, audio, computer	3.1
Reading	0.4
Travel	1.5
Total	9.0

Source: Data from Office for National Statistics (2006c).

Men today spend 3.1 hours a day watching TV or using electronic entertainment devices. These devices were not available in the 18th century; this use of time is entirely new. We do not know how much time men spent on social and educational activities in the 18th century but we do know that they spent no time on electronic entertainment. To oversimplify slightly, men gained a lot of time from working less on their jobs (3.4 hours a day) and have spent this time watching TV and using electronic entertainment equipment.

Women have gained even more discretionary time than men. Women have gained almost 6 hours a day by spending less time on housework and on child care. There is no less housework to be done but capital equipment has been developed to allow this work to be done in much less time. The most important change was the combination of piped water, electricity and the washing machine – these changes mechanized laundry. Also, cooking, water heating and space heating by electric or gas appliances released time from gathering fuel and tending fires. And a multitude of other appliances have mechanized most other housework.

We estimate that women used their increased discretionary time as shown in Table 6.20.

Table 6.20 Time use by working age women

Average hours per day, British women 25 - 64, 2005

Time released from housework	5.8
Additional or new time spent on	
Paid work	2.2
Childcare	0.5
TV, video, audio, computer	2.4
Reading	0.4
Other	0.2
Total	5.8

Source: Data from Office for National Statistics (2006c).

The big changes have been in TV and in paid work. Watching TV or using electronic entertainment equipment is a new activity, compared to previous centuries; this is now the primary use of leisure time. The other large change is the movement of women into the labor force and into paid work. Few women were in paid work in the 18th century. With the growth of textiles and other manufacturing, young women took on paid work but typically ceased this work on marriage. Today, all women can participate in paid employment. Although women work on average fewer hours than men there is now little difference between the sexes in participation in paid work.

There have also been major changes involving the time of young adults and of older people. 16 – 24 year olds have much more discretionary time today; their main uses for this additional time are TV, computers and electronic entertainment (2.7 out of 5.4 hours), study (1.2 hours) and more sleep (0.5 hours). Large numbers of older people are a new phenomenon as life expectancy has increased so much; these people have large amounts of leisure time available as generally they are not engaged in paid work.

The average amount of time, after personal essentials, paid work and housework, in the 18th century was around 5.2 hours a day. Allowing a further 2.0 hours for chores around the house and 0.7 hours for sickness, the time available for individual choice activities might have been around 2.5 hours a day. This might be viewed as leisure time. This time has today increased to 8.0 hours a day, an increase of 220%. Leisure and choice activities in all their forms are now people's largest set of waking activities. Economic growth has taken the modern society from being a work-first to a leisure-first society.

The growth in leisure is also reflected in the modern pattern of household spending. We estimate that 24% of the increase in household spending since the mid-18th century is associated with leisure activities. Current consumption (spending excluding asset purchases) on housing, household goods and services, communications, food, alcohol and tobacco today comes to £126 per week. Expenditure associated with leisure, comes to £119 a week. People now spend approximately as much on leisure as on food and shelter.

6.4.4 Choices open to women

Women have gained particularly from economic growth. Not only have all incomes increased over time but also women have gained from a vastly expanded set of opportunities arising from having more discretionary time.

Family sizes today are smaller. The crude birth rate (the number of live births per 1,000 people) has fallen from over 30 before industrialization to around 10 today. The fertility rate (the average number of births over the lifetime of each woman) is now less than two. The reasons probably have to do with savings and with income. Children are no longer needed as the primary form of saving for old age. At the same time, higher incomes have meant that the cost of having children (the opportunity cost of the time needed to look after children and the monetary cost of bringing up children) has greatly increased. The development of new methods of contraception, such as the hormonal contraceptives introduced in the 1960s, have helped women control their family size. The result has been that women today have less time absorbed in looking after children; they have more time available for other activities.

The next major change in women's economic position has come about from changes in the way household services are produced. Before the start of economic growth, the production of most goods and services was labor-intensive. This included the production of services within the home, services such as food preparation, clothes management and household management. Simply put, women did most of the work inside the household and they did it manually. With economic growth, the household has become capital-intensive. For example, 24% of household spending today is directed to the purchase and maintenance of physical capital. This capital provides accommodation services and also provides services around the house. Many of these services allow household tasks to be performed quickly and easily. Time has been released from housework. As women have traditionally performed most housework, household capital has created time for women.

Table 6.21 shows the holdings of major appliances in U.K. households. More than 99% of households have equipment to assist with the basic household services.

Table 6.21 Use of major appliances, 2008

Penetration, % of U.K. households

Cooker	>99
Water heating	>99
Clothes washer	96
Central heating	95
Refrigerator	94
Vacuum cleaner	94
Microwave	92
Dishwasher	37
Tumble dryer	59

Source: Data from Office for National Statistics (2010b).

The largest single time saver has been the washing machine. Washing clothes and textiles used to be the largest use of household time, taking more than four hours a day. Today, washing takes only 0.2 hours a day. The washing machine has released four hours a day.

Before economic growth, women spent an average of 8.8 hours a day on work in the home; in 2005 only 3.0 hours a day were needed. The changes – smaller families and the arrival of household equipment – have created 5.8 hours a day in additional usable time for women. Women now can choose how to spend this additional available time. They have chosen to spend 2.8 hours (around half of the time) on entertainment in the form of watching TV, enjoying other electronic entertainment devices and reading, and 2.2 hours (around 40% of the time) on paid work.

The time pattern of married women's participation in the labor force is shown in Figure 6.12. The smooth line is a logistic model fitted to the participation rate data.

Figure 6.12 Labor force participation rate, married women, U.K.

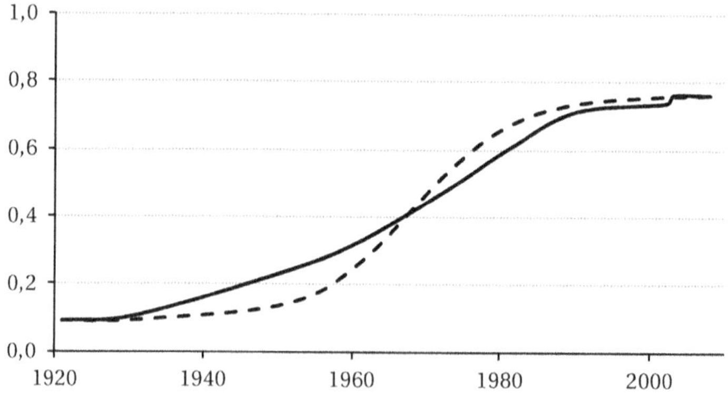

Sources: Data from Costa (2000) and Office for National Statistics (2009c).

The time pattern of the move of women into paid work is closely linked to the introduction of labor-saving appliances. Figure 6.13 shows the time pattern of women moving into paid work and the adoption of the washing machine. Young women have long been active in the paid labor force but it was only from the 1950s that married women began to enter (or re-enter) the work force in large numbers. This coincides with the widespread adoption of the washing machine. The result is that 76% of married women now do paid work. (This number is approaching the labor force participation rate of 16 – 64 year old males which is around 80%.)

Figure 6.13 Women's paid work and adoption of washing machines

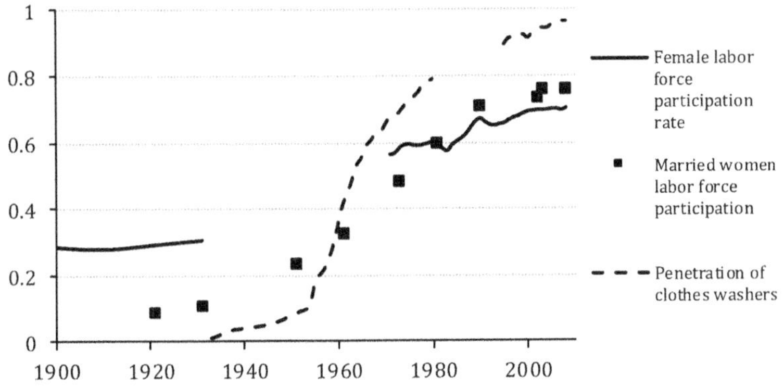

Sources: Data from Office for National Statistics (2004) and (2009c), Bowden and Offer (1994), Killingsworth and Heckman (1986) and Costa (2000).

Economic growth has brought large benefits to both men and women in better health, longer lives and higher incomes. But economic growth has benefited women in particular by allowing them greater choice over family size, freeing up time from work inside the home and giving them the income and ability to choose how to enjoy this additional time. One way in which women have chosen to use this freedom is to enter into paid work. They have done so to such as extent that women's labor force participation rates are now almost the same as men's. Economic growth has created a considerable degree of gender equality.

6.4.5 Creating time

Economic growth has increased life expectancies, has created retirement time, has released time from work and chores, and has provided people with money and good health to use this time for their own enjoyment. This has transformed life today, compared to 1730. There have been three key changes:

- people are living longer and can expect one or more decades of retirement during which they have the money and health to pursue their personal interests;
- the working year, for those in employment, has become much shorter, people in paid work now have considerable leisure time, and money, available to pursue whatever their personal interests might be;
- the working day required for household and family chores has become much shorter, releasing this time for people (and typically these are women rather than men) to pursue their personal interests.

In these ways, economic growth has done something miraculous – it has created time.

6.5 Mobility

6.5.1 Industrialization

Movement has been transformed since the start of industrialization. Movement of goods and people by muscle power or wind power has been supplemented by engine-powered vehicles. Mechanical and electrical power has enabled movement over water, on the land and in the air. In recent decades, movement of information has emerged, adding electronic modes to the mobility revolution. Table 6.22

summarizes the technologies which have come into use to move people, goods and information.

Table 6.22 Types of mobility

Mode	People	Freight	Information
Coastal shipping	Yes	Yes	
Ocean shipping	Yes	Yes	
Urban rail	Yes		
Busses	Yes		
Long distance rail	Yes	Yes	
Cars	Yes		
Trucks		Yes	
Aircraft	Yes	Yes	
Elevator	Yes		
Postal service			Yes
Radio, television			Yes
Telecommunications			Yes
Internet			Yes

The first type of benefit from the industrialization of movement has been reduction in the cost of movement. It is now affordable to move goods anywhere in the world. And, people can afford to travel anywhere in the world. In addition, the time required for movement has been slashed. Pre-industrial movement, such as by horse or by sailing ship, could reach anywhere on Earth but this movement was slow as well as costly. Delivery of a cargo of wheat from Australia to England by sailing ship took more than six months for the round trip. Industrial transport has developed in ways specialized to the need, and can today move goods and people speedily, and information instantly, anywhere in the world. Reduction in cost has allowed old markets to expand, reduction in time and money cost has allowed entire new markets to develop. For many types of goods, the world has been transformed into almost a single marketplace; for many types of information, the world has been transformed into a single village.

6.5.2 Transport has become cheaper

The cost of internal movement of goods can be indicated by what has happened in the United States. The (constant dollar) price of railroad transport has declined at an average of 1.9% a year since 1890. The decline in overall freight transport costs must have been even more rapid as the growth of truck, water-borne and pipeline transport must reflect the fact that these modes were even cheaper than railroads in the majority of instances. The move to containerization has accentuated these cost reductions. Overland freight transport costs today are less than 10% of their level 100 years ago.

Shipping costs have also fallen dramatically. Ships have become more efficient. Steam powered, steel ships started reducing shipping costs in the 19th century. More recently, costs have continued to decline through the development of ever larger, diesel-powered ships. These ships have become specialized - some move solely containers, others are bulk carriers designed to move a particular commodity, such as oil or iron ore or wheat. In view of the economies of scale in shipping, the trend has been to ever larger ships. Modern bulk carriers, for example, can carry as much as 400,000 metric tons deadweight (DWT) while the largest container ships can carry more than 18,000 containers (twenty foot equivalent units, TEUs). In addition, containerization has made cargo handling more efficient. Led by Malcolm McLean in the United States, shipping containers were developed as a means of avoiding break-bulk handling of goods. It is estimated that containerization reduced the cost of loading or unloading a ship by more than 95%.

These huge productivity gains in moving goods have contributed to rising real incomes and economic growth in high income countries. In addition, these gains have facilitated the growth of international trade and helped enable the growth of developing countries.

6.5.3 International trade

The growth of world trade in goods depends on transport – of raw materials to production facilities (such as Australian ores to Chinese mills) and of produced goods to consumers (such as Chinese textiles to American consumers). International trade benefits all parties involved -

in this example Australia, China and the United States all gain. The basic theory was worked out by David Ricardo more than 150 years ago. The practicalities have been demonstrated time and again, beginning (in the industrial age) with the United States exporting raw cotton to Britain and Britain then exporting cotton textiles to the world. Indeed, this international trade in cotton and cotton goods was an essential feature in the emergence of economic growth. Newly industrializing countries today, countries such as China and South Korea, import raw materials and export goods to high income countries; international trade is essential to the spread of growth.

Figure 6.14 uses data from Maddison dividing the world into six areas – western Europe, Western offshoots including the United States, the Eastern bloc and the former USSR, Asia, Latin America and Africa – and relating growth in merchandise exports to growth in GDP per capita over four periods – 1870 to 1913, 1913 to 1950, 1950 to 1973 and 1973 to1998. The straight line in the Figure is simply a linear regression through these 24 data points.

Figure 6.14 Exports and GDP growth

Growth rates, GDP per capita (vertical), merchandise exports (horizontal)

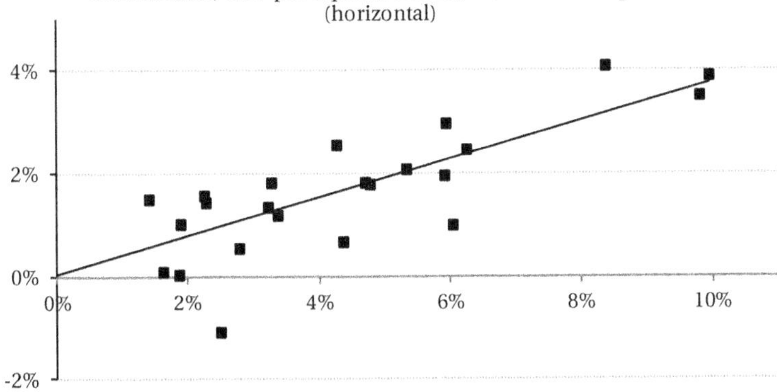

Sources: Data from Maddison (2006a) and (2006b).

There is a clear relationship between exports and growth. Exports have led growth in western Europe and most of the European offshoots. In recent decades, exports have led growth in Asian countries. Growth in the United States has not been led by exports but imports from materials producers and from low cost manufacturing countries have helped to sustain its economic growth. Conversely, low growth countries have generally been associated with low involvement in international trade.

Exporting is the typical way in which catch-up and coat-tail growth countries have achieved their growth. And improved transportation has been vital to this export growth. In this way, efficient transportation has played a vital role in enabling international trade and economic growth.

6.5.4 Cars

The United States today has more than 0.8 motor vehicles for every man, woman and child in the population or 1.1 vehicles for every adult. Roughly 10% of GDP is spent on purchasing, owning and operating motor vehicles. The automobile plays a large part in modern life.

Clearly, people like to own and use cars. But, purchasing and operating a car is expensive so people can express their preference for cars only as incomes rise. There is a strong linkage from income to vehicle ownership. Figure 6.15 shows a graph of car ownership compared to income for 156 countries in 2007. The highest income country is Monaco where average income is over $169,000 and where there are 0.87 vehicles per person.

Figure 6.15 Vehicle ownership vs income

156 countries, 2006 - 2008

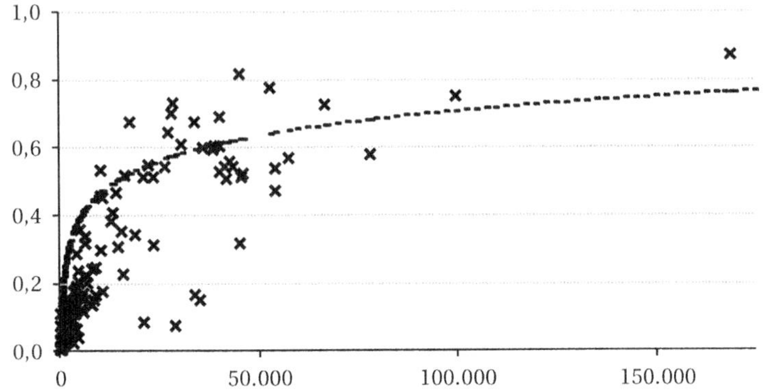

Horizontal axis: income per person, U.S. dollars.

Vertical axis: vehicles per person.

Source: Data from *World Development Indicators*, World Bank.

The crosses are the income-ownership observations. The dashes are the predicted ownership rates for different incomes, generated by fitting a semi-exponential model. As incomes rise, car ownership initially rises very rapidly; as incomes rise past $15,000 the rate of vehicle ownership continues to increase but not as rapidly. At high incomes, the rate of ownership seems to level off at around 0.8 per person which is around 1 vehicle per adult. The average elasticity is 0.6 – on average every 1% increase in income leads to a 0.6% increase in vehicle ownership (although the elasticity falls for higher incomes).

People everywhere love their cars. But what do they do with their cars? Table 6.23 shows what people used their cars for in Britain in 2009.

Table 6.23 Nature of travel in Britain, 2009

	Share of trips	Cars as % trips
Commuting	15%	67%
Business	3%	78%
Education/escort education	11%	42%
Shopping	20%	63%
Other escorting people	9%	84%
Personal business	11%	65%
Leisure, social	27%	69%
Other including just walk	4%	1%
All purposes	100%	63%

Source: Data from U.K. Department for Transport (2010).

63% of all British travel is done by car. The main uses are for commuting, shopping and leisure/social activities. The car has become an integral part of just about everything that people do outside of the home. Even education now depends on the car (taking the kids to school). And, activity inside the home also depends on the car as earning income (business), obtaining goods (shopping) and leisure/social activities make so much use of the car.

6.5.5 The shape of cities

Industrialization created factory towns. Production was drawn towards resources and took place in large factories. People moved from the countryside to the towns for work. Support services grew to sustain the manufacturing and the workers. Towns grew into cities. People moved initially by walking but as cities grew the need for mass transport became apparent. Horse-drawn streetcars met the need. Later, steam railroads, electric streetcars and electric rail served to move people between home and work. The cities continued to grow.

Transport costs were minimized by having production, particularly of service and entertainment activities, concentrated in the core and residences spread around the core. Land in the core could be used most efficiently by building up rather than out. Taller buildings became feasible with the introduction of elevators. Early elevators were hydraulic, coming into use beginning in the 1850s after the invention of the safety elevator by Elisha Otis. The first electric elevator was built by Werner von Siemens in 1880. Electric elevators, in conjunction with steel framed buildings (the steel framed "skyscraper" was pioneered by the Home Insurance Building constructed in Chicago in 1885) removed the height constraint. Central cities became increasingly dense.

The central city depended on the surrounding residential areas for its customers and its workers. The residential areas were linked to the center by public transport. Then, the nature of the city changed as the automobile allowed the city to spread through low density housing. The suburb had arrived. The adoption of the automobile and the rise of suburbs were a major feature of human geography in the 20th century. Figure 6.16 shows that around 80% of the U.S. population now lives in metropolitan areas, up from around 25% at the start of the century, and that most of this growth took place in the suburbs. This development was due to the mobility conferred by the automobile.

Figure 6.16 U.S. residential patterns and vehicles

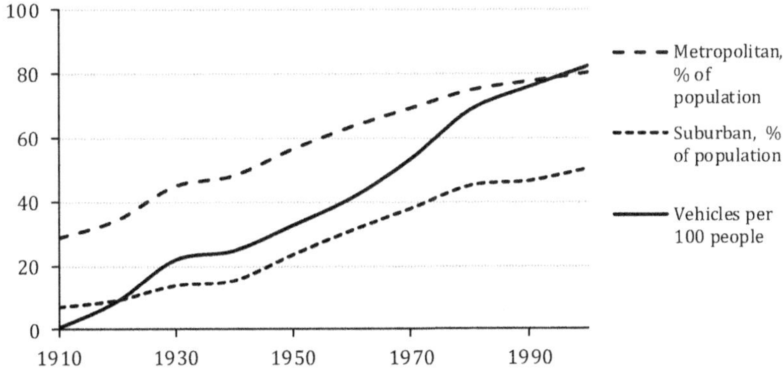

Sources: Data from U.S. Census Bureau, Historical Statistics of the United States and annual Statistical Abstracts, U.S. Census Bureau (2002) and Highway Statistics, U.S. Department of Transportation.

6.5.6 Travel

Personal travel modes have developed since reliance on muscle power – first by railroads, busses and ships, then by car and finally by aircraft. Decreasing prices combined with rising personal incomes have greatly expanded the distance accessible for mass travel. Leisure travel was originally to nearby cities or resorts, then to the entire country, then to neighboring countries and today it is easy to travel to anywhere in the world. People in high income countries today can enjoy travel to participate in different climates, cultures, societies, geographies and recreational activities anywhere in the world.

Figure 6.17 shows the growth in airline passengers passing through U.K. airports. Air travel was uncommon prior to World War II. The rapid growth in air travel started in the 1950s and accelerated in the 1960s. This coincides with the introduction of gas turbine aircraft (a pivotal event was the introduction of the Boeing 707 in 1958). The steady improvement in aircraft transformed the economics of air travel, bringing prices down to levels which could be afforded by a mass market.

Figure 6.17 U.K. airline passengers

Passengers through U.K. airports, year 2000 = 100

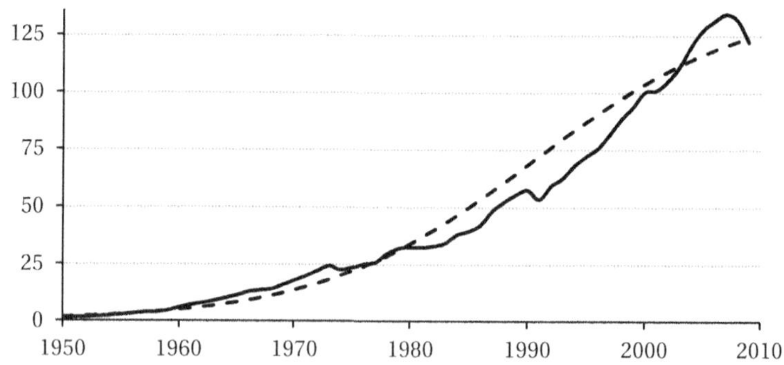

Source: Data from Air Traffic at UK Airports, UK Department for Transport.

These time and cost savings expanded the market for domestic travel and created new markets for international travel. Domestic travel in the U.K. grew at a 4.7% average rate from 1978 to 2002 while international travel has increased at a faster rate, 5.9%. Growth in air travel for the U.K. has followed a logistic curve; this curve suggests that growth is now slowing as markets approach saturation. The existence of these large markets reflects the personal benefit, as well as the economic contribution, provided by the emergence of low cost travel.

6.5.7 Moving information

Information initially was moved by sending messengers. It was cheaper to send documents but it was not until postal services were organized that economies of scale came into play and brought the price down to accessible levels. The telegraph then cut the time and money cost of sending written information. The telephone made it possible to send voices and have an interactive conversation. The 20th century saw telephone service became cheaper and, in high income countries, ubiquitous. Services which could be conducted by conversation, without face to face contact, increasingly were carried out over the telephone. This allowed many types of customer inquiries, customer support, routine transactions and routine administrative functions to be carried out by telephone; the location of these services became a matter of choice for the provider as they were no longer tied directly to the customer. Radio and television allowed information to be broadcast cheaply. Finally, digitization of telephone services and the arrival of the internet allowed video and documents, as well as voice, to be moved instantly, essentially to anywhere in the world.

6.5.8 Shrinking the world

A consequence of economic growth has been to create mobility on a scale previously unimaginable. Goods can be moved anywhere in the world in a time scale measured in weeks. People can travel anywhere in the world on a time scale measured in hours. Information can be moved anywhere in the world on a time scale measured in seconds.

This mobility has greatly reduced costs of production and supply. Customers everywhere gain from lower prices while countries can use international trade to move into economic growth. The gains in incomes and purchasing power are huge. Consumption opportunities have been enhanced as people can now travel anywhere rapidly and affordably. And, people's lifestyle opportunities have been enhanced by their greater ability to reside where they wish, carrying out many of their communications at low cost and instantly by telephone and internet.

6.6 Urbanization

6.6.1 Rural starting point

Britain, before the industrial age, was a rural country. Most people lived in the countryside or in towns directly servicing the rural economy. Using Lindert and Williamson's (1982) social tables, describing families in England and Wales in 1759, we estimate that around 73% of the people were linked directly to the land and agriculture. The main exception was London, the largest town, which for centuries had been the seat of government and the center of trade and commerce.

A survey of houses in England, carried out in 1662 to provide information for a hearth tax, identifies the population distribution. The 10 largest towns are shown in Table 6.24. Seven of the 10 largest towns serviced the surrounding agricultural or extractive activities.

Table 6.24 The 10 largest towns in England in 1662

Rank	Town	Activity
1	London	trades, commerce, government
2	Norwich	wool, wheat
3	York	wool
4	Bristol	port
5	Newcastle	coal
6	Exeter	wool
7	Ipswich	wool
8	Great Yarmouth	port, fishing
9	Oxford	education
10	Cambridge	education

Sources: Data from *List of towns and cities in England by historical population*, Wikipedia, viewed 10 July 2011.

6.6.2 Economic development

Pre-industrial Britain was rural because agricultural productivity was so low that most of the population was engaged in producing the basics needed for food and clothing. Then, beginning in the 18th century, agricultural productivity began to rise; this increased the food supply, sustaining higher incomes and a larger population. Some of this higher income was spent on manufactures, in particular cotton goods. Breakthroughs in production technologies for textiles, iron and steam power led to reductions in the cost of producing manufactures. Lower prices fed back to further increases in demand for goods in Britain and in exports to other countries. Manufacturing started on a path of rapid growth. Britain came to export manufactures and import foodstuffs and materials. Servicing industries such as transport, finance and insurance developed to sustain the growth in trade.

There are economies of scale in exploiting mechanical power and in using machinery so the factories of the new manufacturing were large. In turn, these factories tended to be geographically concentrated. Cotton production concentrated around Manchester as this region had access to water and coal (for power) and to a port (for shipping the raw cotton and the finished product). Wool processing was concentrated in west Yorkshire because of the damp climate and also access to water and coal resources. Iron production concentrated around Birmingham as this region had access to suitable coal and to iron ore.

Old villages grew and new towns emerged, based on these new industries. People came to where the work was. The towns grew with an industrial heart surrounded by residential areas. Cities emerged. These cities specialized in particular industries, such as cotton processing, or economic function, such as transport hubs. The cities grew in number and size. Urbanization had arrived. In 1700, 13% of the population of England lived in towns of 10,000 or more; by the turn of the 20th century this proportion had risen to 67%.

Figure 6.18 shows the close relationship between the change in economic structure, from primary industry to manufacturing industry, and urbanization. (Urbanization is measured by the percentage of the population living in areas which are defined by the census agency as being urban.) Industrialization created and drove urbanization.

Figure 6.18 Urbanization and economic structure, U.K.

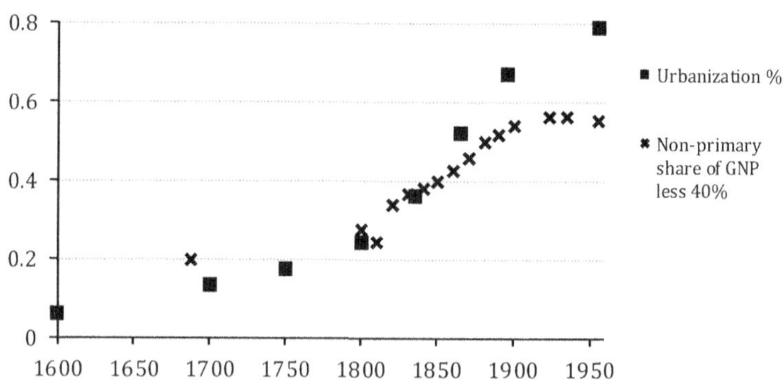

Sources: Data from Mitchell and Deane (1971), Mitchell (1988) and Szreter (2011).

6.6.3 Growth of the cities

Table 6.25 shows the 10 largest towns in 1910. The list is a little artificial as it is based on administrative boundaries rather than economic boundaries. As a result, the sizes of several textile areas in England's northwest and metals areas in the midlands are understated. Nonetheless, the pattern is clear – the large towns are now based on manufacturing or transport. The only exception is London which picked up manufacturing which wanted to be close to the customer, to go with its traditional commercial and government activities. Rural and natural resource centers, which in 1662 took seven of the top 10 positions, no longer feature in the top 10.

Table 6.25 The 10 largest towns in Britain in 1901

Rank	Town	Activity
1	London	manufacturing, commerce, government
2	Glasgow	engineering
3	Liverpool	port, textiles
4	Manchester	cotton goods
5	Birmingham	metal products
6	Leeds	woolen goods
7	Sheffield	steel products
8	Bristol	port
9	Bradford	woolen goods
10	Plymouth	port

Sources: Data from *List of towns and cities in England by historical population*, Wikipedia, viewed 10 July 2011.

Population growth in the new cities is shown in Figure 6.19. These growth paths all have the same shape – the S shape of the logistic curve. The reason is that the industry underpinning each city itself grew along a logistic path – becoming established then growing rapidly and finally saturating its markets and levelling off.

Figure 6.19 Growth of cities in Britain

Cities excluding London. Population in thousands.

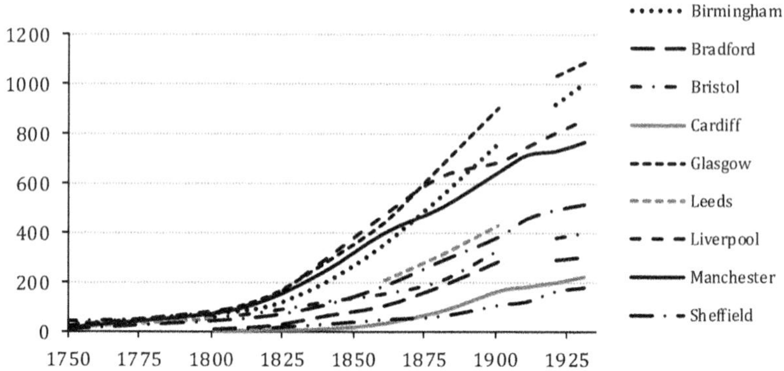

Sources: *List of towns and cities in England by historical population*, Wikipedia, viewed 10 July 2011.

London has always been the largest town in Britain. English government has been relatively centralized, based on London, for a thousand years. Before industrialization, people were so dispersed that even London accounted for just 7% of the population (this was in 1662). With industrialization and then with the growth in services, London has grown substantially, today accounting today for around 20% of the population.

London's recent growth has reflected several new trends. First, there has been a steady increase in the size and role of the government. London, as the capital city in a highly centralized governmental system, hosted much of the growth in the public sector. Second, the structure of the economy has moved from manufacturing to services. Services follow people and many services must be produced directly with the customer. London, as the largest city, has attracted much of the growth in service industries. In addition, London, building on its historical role in providing financial services to British manufacturing and the British Empire, has developed as one of the leading financial centers of the world. Finally, urbanization has taken on a growth of its own as people discover the social, cultural and intellectual benefits of living in a large city. London, already the largest city and offering a wide range of social and cultural choices, has increased its attractiveness as people relocate for lifestyle reasons.

Industrialization created urbanization. The move to services continued the trend as service industries were pulled towards customers whereas manufacturing had been pulled towards physical resources. A new set of cities grew, away from the old manufacturing areas. The trend to urbanization then continued as people took advantage of the social and cultural benefits of living in a large city. So urbanization, which had risen to 67% of the population by1900 continued to increase, reaching 89% by 2000.

6.6.4 General trend to urbanization

This same trend towards urbanization has been repeated in many other countries. The path to urbanization followed by the United States is shown in Figure 6.20. Urbanization in the United States proceeded in parallel to industrialization then continued as services replaced manufacturing as the leading growth industries. The drive to urbanization has been accentuated by lifestyle choices as people like to live in cities. As with most behavioral changes, the move to urbanization has closely followed a logistic path.

Figure 6.20 Urbanization ratio, U.S.

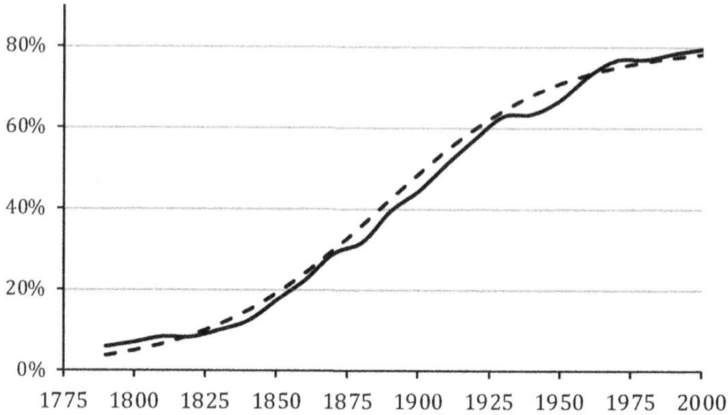

Sources: Data from U.S. Census Bureau, Historical Statistics of the United States and annual Statistical Abstracts.

Other countries have also seen a move to greater urbanization. Urbanization in high income countries is driven by the economic and social wishes of their people. In many low income countries, the appeal of urban living has attracted people to the cities even though there might not be an economic base for this internal migration; in these cases, urban concentrations exist only because governments make available the necessities of food, fuel and water. Either way, urbanization is now widespread. The World Bank estimates for urbanization are summarized in Table 6.26. (The definitions used in each country are used in compiling this Table so urbanization does not have a consistent definition.)

Table 6.26 World Bank urbanization indicators, 2010

	% of population living in urban areas
South Asia	30%
Sub-Saharan Africa	37%
East Asia and Pacific	46%
Middle East and North Africa	58%
OECD	77%
Latin America and Caribbean	79%
Selected countries	
China	45%
Germany	74%
U.S.A.	82%
Australia	89%
U.K.	90%

Source: Data from *World Development Indicators*, World Bank.

Less than 10% of the population in pre-industrial Britain lived in urban areas. Now 51% of the world's population lives in urban areas and even in low income countries the urban share typically exceeds 30%. In high income countries, 80 – 90% of the population live in urban areas. The appeal of living in cities, originally based on economic forces, has now been magnified by social and cultural factors. The economic surplus created by economic growth has sustained this rise in urban living. Cities are one of the major consequences of economic growth. As so many people have chosen to live in cities, cities must be regarded as one of the benefits of economic growth.

6.7 Natural Resources

6.7.1 Coal

Coal was the energy source that powered the Industrial Revolution in Britain and has underpinned industrialization in many other countries since then. Is there sufficient coal to sustain the continuing demands placed on it?

Consumption of coal in the U.K. increased for many years, first as coal fuelled industry and transport, then as coal fuelled the new industry of electricity generation But demand has more recently fallen away as the industrial intensity of the economy has declined (with the move to services) and as electricity generation has moved towards nuclear and natural gas. Figure 6.21 shows that coal, once a pillar of the British economy, now has almost disappeared. This disappearance is entirely due to changes in demand patterns, not to any exhaustion of the resource.

Figure 6.21 U.K. production of coal
Million tons a year

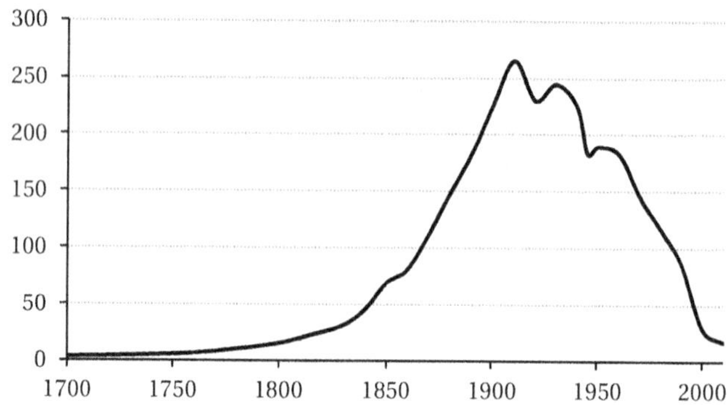

Sources: Data from Mitchell (1988) and BP (2011).

As Britain has shifted away from heavy industry other countries have entered that phase of industrialization. The United States, Europe, Japan, South Korea, India and China are major users of coal for metallurgical (principally steel-making) and steam (principally electricity generation) purposes. World demand for coal has continued to increase; for example, demand has increased at an average of 1.9% a year since 1965.

World consumption of coal (all types - anthracite, bituminous, sub-bituminous and lignite) in 2010 totalled 7.3 billion tonnes. This may sound like a lot of coal but reserves were up to the job. World proven reserves were 861 billion tonnes, equivalent to 118 years of consumption at current rates. And, the reserves are widely spread. The top 10 reserve countries and reserve lifetimes at current production rates are shown in Table 6.27.

Table 6.27 Coal proven reserves and lifetimes
10 largest proven reserves of coal and world total

	Reserves Bn tonnes	Years at current rates
U.S.A.	237	241
Russian Federation	157	495
China	115	35
Australia	76	180
India	61	106
Germany	41	223
Ukraine	34	462
Kazakhstan	34	303
South Africa	30	119
Colombia	7	91
World	861	118

Source: Data from BP (2011).

The world has ample proven reserves of coal. If shortages were to loom and prices went up, no doubt more reserves would be found and more reserves would pass into the proven category. We are not going to run out of coal.

6.7.2 Aluminum

Aluminum is a metal in increasing use because of its lightness, compared to steel, and resistance to corrosion. Bauxite is a mined mineral; bauxite in turned into alumina by a chemical process known as the Bayer process; and in turn aluminum is made from alumina by electrolysis.

Annual consumption of bauxite is around 200 million tonnes. World proven reserves are around 27 billion tonnes. The U.S. Geological Survey (2009) places estimated reserves at up to 75 billion tonnes. At present consumption rates, proven reserves will last for 132 years while estimated reserves would last 366 years. There is no imminent shortage of bauxite. And, even if a shortage threatened, rising prices would create new sources of supply. The U.S. Geological Survey says most aluminum-producing countries "have essentially inexhaustible sub-economic resources of aluminum in materials other than bauxite" (see USGS (2009), p28).

6.7.3 Oil

Oil is one of the key inputs to the modern economy, used as a transportation fuel, for heating and as a chemical feedstock. The price of crude oil has been subject to massive shocks in recent years, shown in Figure 6.22. Does this mean that the world is running out of oil and that economic prosperity is thereby under threat?

Figure 6.22 Crude oil prices

2010US$/barrel

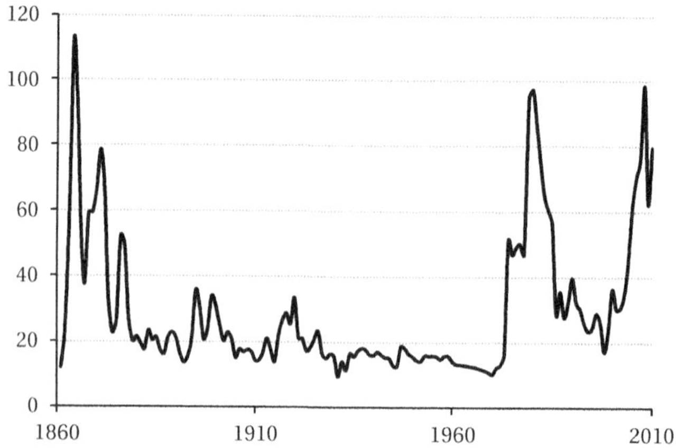

Source: Data from BP (2011).

Consumption of oil has kept climbing despite the price shocks, as seen in Figure 6.23. But the growth in consumption is more complex than it seems. Although consumption has risen compared to the past it has fallen compared to where it would have been if earlier trends had continued. The growth trend up to 1973, the year of the first oil shock, was 7.5% a year; the growth trend since 1973 has been 1.0%. In the 1980s, as the price shocks of the 1970s were working through people's decision-making, consumption actually decreased.

Figure 6.23 World oil production

Million barrels

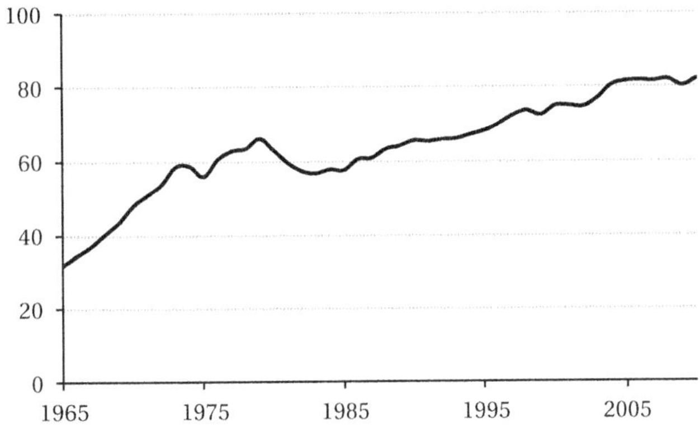

Source: Data from BP (2011).

Even so, the world is consuming 80 million barrels a day of oil and rising. Can this be sustained? The world in 1980 had 668 billion barrels of proven reserves. Since then, the world has consumed 764 billion barrels. But in 2010 proven reserves were 1,383 billion barrels. The world has added twice as much in proven reserves over this time as it has consumed. The lifetime of proven reserves, the number of years that current rates of production can be sustained from current proven reserves, has been increasing, as shown in Figure 6.24.

Figure 6.24 Lifetime of world oil reserves

Reserves/current production, years

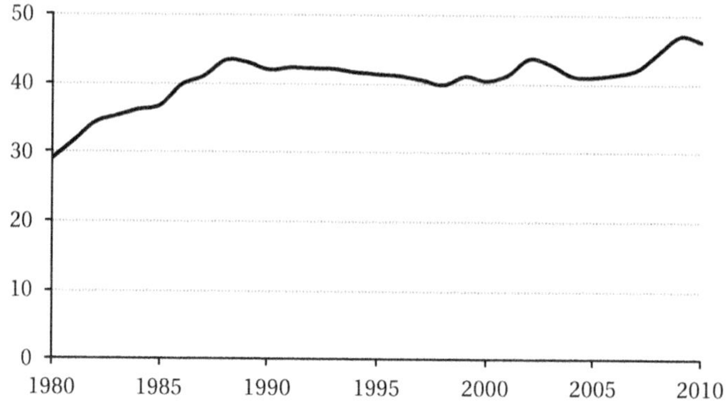

Source: Data from BP (2011).

The world now has proven reserves equal to 46 years of current production. If production were to increase at 1.0% a year, the growth rate of the past 30 years, these reserves would still be sufficient for 38 years. If reserves were to come under pressure then the likelihood is that prices would rise. Rising oil prices lead to changes on the demand side and on the supply side. On the demand side, customers use less oil. They do this in two ways – they use less oil directly, for example by switching to more fuel-efficient vehicles, and they use less oil indirectly, for example by switching spending from goods to less oil-intensive services. On the supply side, rising oil prices lead oil companies to expand their exploration, to improve their exploration and recovery technologies, and so to increase their production.

Figure 6.25 shows the declining oil-intensity of the U.S. economy and also shows the declining oil-intensity of motor vehicle use.

Figure 6.25 Oil-intensity of the U.S. economy
1973 = 1

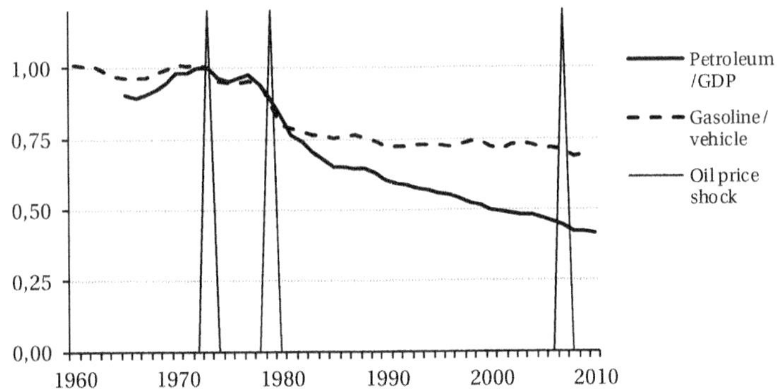

Sources: Data from U.S. Bureau of Economic Analysis, National Economic Accounts; Federal Highway Administration, U.S. Department of Transportation and U.S. Energy Information Administration.

This graph is based on 1973, the year of the first oil price shock. Since then, the U.S. economy has reduced its oil-intensity by 60%. Part of the reduction has come from reduced fuel use in vehicles – by driving less and by using more fuel efficient vehicles. Driving less happens straight away but improving the efficiency of vehicles takes time as it takes 15 or more years to turn over the vehicle stock, replacing less with more efficient vehicles. In the 20 years after the first oil shock, average fuel used per vehicle declined by more than 25%.

Rising oil prices lead consumers to redirect their spending towards goods and services which are low in oil content and so are now relatively less expensive. These changes are superimposed on the steady shift in spending away from goods (which tend to be more oil-intensive) to services (which generally have low oil-intensity). Figure 6.26 shows the trends in the composition of U.S. personal consumption expenditure. There is a systematic shift from goods to services purchases as incomes increase. The shift in spending accounts for more than half of the reduction in the oil-intensity of the U.S. economy since the first oil shock in 1973.

Figure 6.26 Composition of U.S. consumption spending

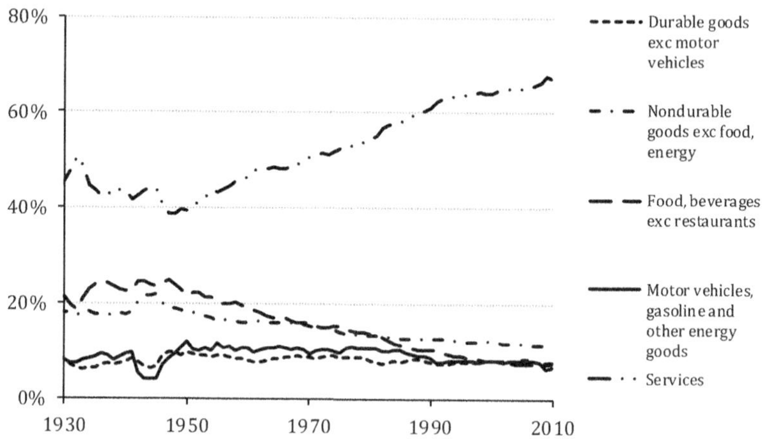

Source: Data from U.S. Bureau of Economic Analysis, National Economic Accounts.

Different mechanisms are at work on the supply side. We consider what has happened in ExxonMobil Corporation, one of the largest oil companies. First, an increase in the price of oil makes current production, coming from existing reserves, more valuable. The earnings of the company therefore move with the oil price. Figure 6.27 shows how the rate of return on equity, ROE, has broadly tracked the oil price.

Figure 6.27 ExxonMobil ROE and the oil price

Rate of return on equity (ROE) and price of oil, scaled to 1990 = 1

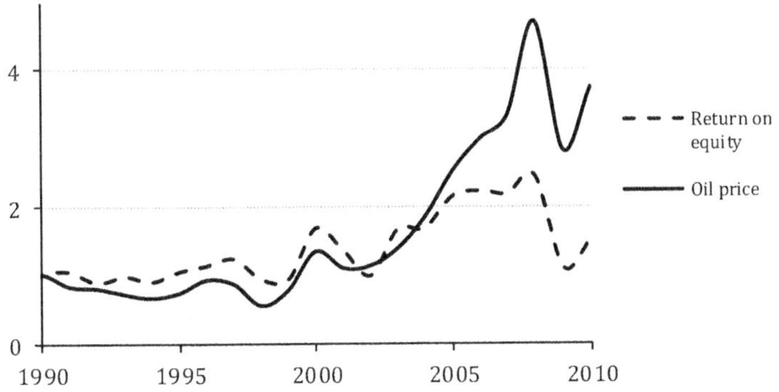

Sources: Data from U.S. Energy Information Administration and Summary Annual Reports, ExxonMobil.

Rising prices are to some extent a windfall for owners of existing reserves but they also increase the prospective return on exploration, incentivizing exploration and development. ExxonMobil over the five years to 2010 spent on upstream exploration and capital works the equivalent of 77% of earnings. Reserve replacement over these five years was 139% - every barrel produced was accompanied by an increase in reserves of 1.39 barrels. In this way, reserves actually increased.

ExxonMobil (2011a) states that the exploration resource addition cost was \$0.87 per oil-equivalent barrel and that the earnings per oil-equivalent barrel produced were \$14.85. At a discount rate of 10% (taken from ExxonMobil (2011b)) the breakeven time horizon for exploration is 54 years - it is worthwhile incurring the exploration cost now in order to generate the specified earnings up to 54 years in the future. This sort of calculation places a limit on exploration activity as it is not worthwhile identifying resources which will not be used until the far distant future. It so happens that ExxonMobil's proven reserves of oil-equivalent resources (liquids and natural gas) are 52 times current production rates. (This analysis oversimplifies the situation somewhat as it omits development and production costs.)

Superimposed on the exploration incentives of higher prices are the productivity incentives flowing from higher prices. Higher prices for crude oil have stimulated improvements in the technologies used in exploring for and producing oil. Advances in seismic data acquisition and field modeling techniques since 1973 have greatly improved the identification of new reserves. Advances in drilling technology which allow a single well to host a number of angled or even horizontal wells branching off at depth, have reduced the costs of production. And, the development of hydraulic fracturing has expanded the range of geological formations which can sustain production. The U.S. Energy Information Administration (2012) estimates that finding costs in constant dollars per barrel have declined at an average of 6% a year in the 20 years after 1977.

The world is using more and more oil but is not about to run out. In fact, proven reserves are increasing more rapidly than production. Economic growth, although intensive in oil, is not about to be stifled by shortages of oil. The mechanism which ensures this outcome is the price system. As cheap oil is used up, prices rise (or, equivalently, those countries controlling large volumes of supply raise their offer prices). The result is that demand is reduced, compared to its previous trend, while additional exploration and development is stimulated, increasing reserves. The international oil system has been operating like this for more than 100 years; there is every reason to think that it will continue to work in these ways. Although the days of cheap oil may be over there is no reason to think that oil will cease to be available to meet the world's demand.

6.7.4 The Limits to Growth

The Club of Rome described itself as "a group of world citizens, sharing a common concern for the future of humanity." The Club of Rome came to international prominence with its book *The Limits to Growth*, Donella Meadows et al (1972). Although this book is now many years old, it is worth examining as it typifies the predictions made by those who do not recognize the adjustment mechanisms inherent in the market economic system.

The Limits to Growth argued that the world would run out of resources, such as minerals or oil, in the foreseeable future with dire consequences for our economic well-being. The argument was that as resource reserves were strictly finite and consumption was growing exponentially, reserves would be depleted in the foreseeable future. (This is the Malthusian argument in modern clothes.) The argument for petroleum illustrates the method: petroleum reserves were then 31 times current annual consumption, consumption was growing at 3.9% a year so reserves would be exhausted in 20 years. As the first oil shock soon followed its publication, *The Limits to Growth* appeared to have presciently identified a fundamental threat to the western way of life.

In fact, the modern economy did not come to an end in 20 years. It is easy to say this in hindsight as we are now more than 20 years later with still higher levels of consumption. But it was equally possible in 1972 to see that *The Limits to Growth* was wrong. There is nothing wrong with the mathematics in *The Limits to Growth* but there is everything wrong with the two central numerical assumptions involved – that reserves are fixed and that the consumption growth rate is fixed. These fixity assumptions rule out all flexibility and adaptation. Adaptation is what a market economy is good at. The mechanism is simple – increasing scarcity will lead to rising prices which will in turn lead to increased supply and reduced demand (compared to the previous trends). Supply of resources will increase by the development of more costly (previously uneconomic) reserves and by technical improvements which extend the economic extraction frontier. Demand will decrease because customers will improve the efficiency with which they use the resource and because consumers will shift their purchases to goods less intensive in the now more expensive resource.

The market system will prevent a resource crisis because price signals will lead people to change their behavior to ease any incipient shortage. Prices might rise but we will not run out of resources. The history of oil since 1972 amply illustrates these mechanisms. Prices have risen, more resources have been established, production has risen and the oil-intensity of the western world has decreased. Certainly prices are higher (6 times higher in 2010 than 1972, measured in inflation-adjusted dollars) but reserves which in 1972 were 31 times current consumption have now increased to 45 times present consumption.

6.7.5 Resources and growth

Physical resources such as metals, minerals and fuels are essential to the functioning of the industrial economy. Obviously the total supplies of these resources are finite. But there remain large reserves, some proven, some known but not proven and some not yet discovered, of these resources. As existing mines are depleted and prices rise, production will move on to extracting more remote or lower grade, and so higher cost, resources. Or, new exploration and improved discovery and extraction techniques may yield additions to proven reserves at even lower cost. The trend in supply costs will be the result of a race between opposite forces – depletion of existing low-cost reserves and improvement in technology which lowers the cost of adding to proven reserves.

For the past 100 years, improved exploration and improved technologies have dominated the effects of depletion. Figure 6.28 shows the prices of industrial commodities in the United States. The price index is for raw materials through 1912 and industrial commodities beginning in 1913. The trend has been downwards. The cost of basic commodities has been declining despite increasing quantities of these materials being used.

Figure 6.28 Prices of industrial commodities
For the United States. Constant dollars, 2005 = 1

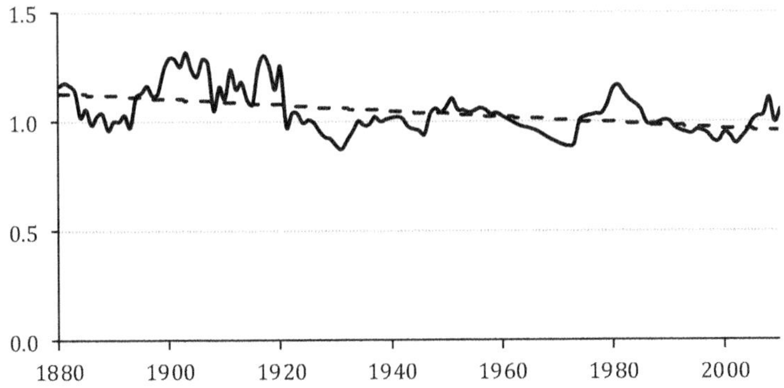

Sources: Data from U.S. Bureau of Economic Analysis, National Economic Accounts. U.S. Census Bureau, Historical Statistics of the United States. U.S. Bureau of Labor Statistics, Producer Price Index-Commodities.

Economic growth has not been and will not be stopped by lack of resources. If existing resource supplies become scarce then prices will rise. One the supply side, higher prices will stimulate the use of previously uneconomic reserves and will also encourage technological improvements which lower the cost of finding, extracting and processing resources. On the demand side, higher prices will stimulate greater efficiency in resource use and will motivate a shift away from consumption of goods intensive in the resource. As long as markets continue to operate and are allowed to operate, there will be sufficient resources. Prices may increase but resources will be available to sustain economic growth.

6.8 Local environmental effects

6.8.1 The problem

Modern economic production and consumption activities frequently create significant effects on the environment. Can economic growth coexist with reasonable environmental quality or does growth inevitably come at the cost of serious environmental degradation?

The environmental problem arises because a pure market system allows unrestricted discharges into the environment, such as into the air. Producers and consumers treat the environment as a free good and, as it is costly to limit or prevent discharges, have no incentive to limit their emissions. In simple markets, there is no mechanism to make producers and consumers take account of the environmental costs of their actions. There is, as a result, no balancing of the cost savings from being able to emit with the social and health costs resulting from the emissions.

There are several kinds of local environmental effects arising from production and consumption activities in a modern economy. These potential problems are associated with discharges of chemicals or particles into the air, discharges of chemicals or other materials into waterways, and dumping of chemicals or other materials on the land.

We look in these next sections at local as opposed to international environmental effects. Local effects are those contained within the country generating the emissions, for example emission of particulates by burning fuels in the Midwest. We look in later sections at emissions with significant international or global impacts, for example emissions of greenhouse gasses. For local emissions, we look in detail at the history of air pollution in the United States; we then apply the conclusions from this examination to other types of local environmental effects.

6.8.2 U.S. Clean Air Act

By the 1960s, air pollution was seen as a significant problem in many parts of the United States. There were visual and health effects from the smog over Los Angeles and other large cities. There was worry about acid rain in areas with heavy industry and coal-fired electricity generation. There was worry about the health risks of lead in the atmosphere. And particulates in the air were seen as a health problem as well as degrading visual amenity.

Air pollution aroused so much concern that people turned to the political system to try to get change. The United States government entered the picture with environmental regulations. The original Clean Air Act was passed in 1970; significant amendments were passed in 1977 and 1990. The Environmental Protection Agency (EPA), the operating agency to administer the Act, was created in 1971.

The EPA targeted six types of air emissions which were seen as creating significant health and environmental risks – carbon monoxide (CO), nitrogen oxides (NOx), lead, ground level ozone, sulfur dioxide (SO_2) and particulate matter (initially particulate matter of 10 or more micrometer diameter with an additional standard subsequently introduced for particulates of 2.5 to 10 micrometer diameter). The EPA set standards for each of these, typically maximum levels of ambient concentrations. The EPA then endeavored to enforce these standards through a variety of mechanisms. These mechanisms were:

(1) Carbon monoxide. The principal source is combustion of fuels, particularly in motor vehicles. The EPA set standards for CO emissions from light vehicles and required vehicle manufacturers to meet these standards. It was up to the manufacturers to work out how to do this. Manufacturers have used various approaches to reducing emissions, such as catalytic converters on exhaust gasses, fuel management, combustion management and reduced vehicle weight.

(2) Nitrogen oxides. The main source is fuel combustion, particularly in motor vehicles. One way of meeting the EPA standards has been to use catalytic converters on exhaust gasses from gasoline engines. As lead in fuel is harmful to the converters, there has been a mandated phase-out of leaded fuels.

(3) Lead. Use of lead in gasoline has been phased out and use of lead in residential paints has been prohibited.

(4) Sulfur dioxide. The principal source was the burning of fuels, particularly coal, for electricity generation and in heavy industry. Standards were set for emissions at the plant level. Tradeable emission permits, around the target level, were then allocated. This introduced a market mechanism, allowing emitters to work out and follow the least cost way of meeting the targets – whether to purchase/use emission permits or to reduce emissions and sell the excess permits. Utilities and industrial sites have reduced SO_2 emissions by a combination of exhaust gas treatment, switching to lower sulfur coal and switching from coal to other energy sources.

(5) Particulate matter. Airborne particulates are difficult to limit in view of their many sources, such as combustion, agricultural tilling, construction, mining, road surfaces and wind erosion. EPA has introduced a number of measures to reduce particulates the two principal ones being corporate average fuel efficiency (CAFE) standards for automobiles and emission standards for electricity generation plants (which utilities typically have met by exhaust gas filtering).

The EPA approach has been to set performance standards relating to the principal types of air emissions, then to use specific mechanisms to try to force compliance with the standards. Three types of mechanisms have been used - outright bans (for example of lead in gasoline and residential paint), setting mandatory discharge or performance standards (for example for automotive and power plant particulate emissions) and a market mechanism (such as tradeable SO_2 emission rights). Apart from banning lead, the EPA has left it to manufacturers to decide how to meet the standards.

6.8.3 Air quality improvement

Emissions of carbon monoxide have fallen substantially with the introduction of standards for motor vehicles. Emissions per capita in 2008 were down to 25% of their level in 1970. Emissions of nitrogen oxides have also declined - emissions per capita in 2008 were down to

41% of the 1970 levels. Some of the decline is due to regulatory action although some would have resulted from reduced use of gasoline due to higher fuel prices. We estimate that 20% of the reduction in emissions of nitrogen oxides has been due to price effects and 80% to the regulations.

Emissions of lead have virtually been eliminated. The critical change was the replacement of leaded by unleaded gasoline. This switch depends on the retirement of older automobiles and their replacement by new models with catalytic converters and other emission improvements. It takes 15 - 20 years to turn over the light vehicle fleet; correspondingly, it took 20 years for lead emissions to fall to minimal levels. Emissions per capita in the 1990s were 99% lower than in 1970.

Figure 6.29 shows emissions of sulfur dioxide since 1900. The level of emissions had been increasing over the 20th century although the intensity had not. Soon after the introduction of standards and regulations in the early 1970s, the level of emissions began a steady decline while the intensity of emissions declined even more rapidly. SO_2 emissions per capita in 2008 were only 24% of the level in 1970.

Figure 6.29 U.S. emissions of sulfur dioxide

All indicators scaled to 1970 = 1

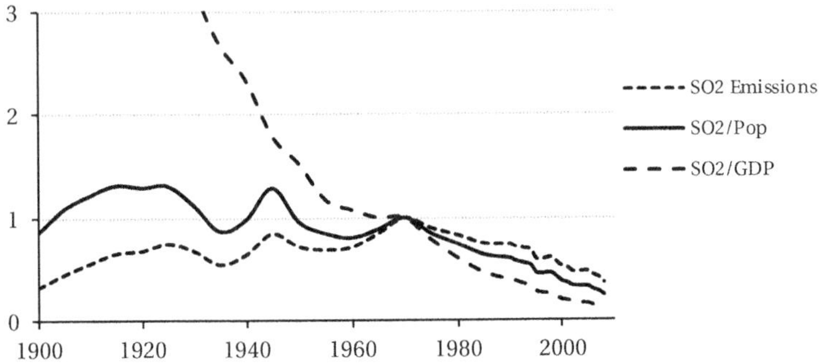

Sources: U.S. Environmental Protection Agency (1998). U.S. Bureau of Economic Analysis, National Economic Accounts. U.S. Census Bureau, Historical Statistics of the United States and annual Statistical Abstracts.

Particulates are more difficult to manage in view of the variety of sources, only some of which are controllable. Particulate emissions from industry can generally be managed but emissions from other sources are more difficult to restrict. Nonetheless, the introduction of standards and regulations on industry and vehicles has had a large effect in reducing the level of emissions. Particulates per capita in 2008 were down to 28% of their 1985 level.

6.8.4 Effective environmental management

The United States has been successful in improving its air quality and maintaining this improved quality. This was done by government intervention. The market does not attend to emissions as it is cheaper for producers to use the atmosphere as a dumping ground than to restrict emissions. Government action is needed to force or induce producers to change their designs and processes so as to reduce emissions. The experience of the United States is that appropriate government actions can exert force or provide inducement sufficient to achieve targeted standards of air quality.

This experience shows also that a particular condition must be fulfilled if government action is to be effective. This condition is that the source of emissions and the costs imposed by these emissions are both within the jurisdiction of a single government unit. Action by the state of California achieved considerable success in limiting photochemical smog (due primarily to nitrogen oxides) in the Los Angeles Basin. However, acid rain (from sulfur dioxide emissions) is different as the sources of the problem tend to be in states upwind of the states suffering the consequences. State-level action is not effective in these conditions. Only national action is effective as both emitters and sufferers are within the same jurisdiction which is that of the U.S. government. Thus, it was only when the United States government swung into action in the 1970s that air quality policy on a broad front became effective.

This history shows that most types of emissions can be brought down to acceptable levels. The best method of control is to force or induce emitters to meet certain standards and then leave it to emitters to work out how to do this. With the exception of banning lead in certain uses, the EPA did not tell producers how to achieve the reductions – it told them what they had to achieve, not how to achieve it.

Different control mechanisms are suited to different emission situations. As a general rule, inducement is better than force. Sulfur dioxide reductions were achieved by inducement – creating tradeable emission permits which then led to a market in these permits. This approach works if there are a relatively small number of large emitters which was the case for sulfur dioxide. The total level of emissions is limited to the sum of the permit quantities so any target level of emissions can be achieved. These "cap and trade" permits are efficient as emission reductions are achieved in the least cost way – if a producer can limit emissions for less than the market cost of permits, it will make the emission reductions, leaving high cost producers to pay the price for buying the right to emit. There is nothing wrong with trading these rights to emit as their total quantity has been set to the target level by the EPA.

If there are large numbers of small emitters, though, a tradeable permit system would be cumbersome and costly to administer. The EPA avoided this practical problem by identifying the principal types of emitters and imposing standards on the design of the equipment causing the emissions. The largest single source of emissions of carbon monoxide, nitrogen oxides and particulates is motor vehicles. Having identified this source, the EPA imposed standards on emissions per vehicle. As there are relatively few vehicle manufacturers, it was feasible to monitor compliance at the manufacturer level rather than at the (millions of) points of use.

A further control mechanism, although one not used in the United States, is to tax emitting activities. For example, a sales tax on gasoline, such as $1 per gallon, would induce vehicle owners to change their behavior so as to reduce their gasoline purchases. Owners might shift to more fuel-efficient vehicles, they might reduce their driving distances and they might change their driving behavior (such as speed and acceleration). Using the price system in this way leaves it to the operator to work out whether to and how to reduce emitting activity;

this inducement approach generally is more efficient than forcing people to change their behavior in specified ways.

6.8.5 Other environmental effects

The approach followed by the EPA has succeeded in limiting air pollution to what are regarded as acceptable levels. This approach relies upon government regulation to introduce disciplines and incentives which are absent in a simple market. The policy approach sets specific standards for emissions or for ambient quality and introduces a range a targeted measures to try to enforce compliance with these standards. This approach has been used successfully also to handle water pollution and to manage dumping on land.

The one area where little has been done is to use government power to try to control the visual impact of economic activity. As there is no consensus on visual standards, there has been no widespread political drive for government intervention. Private decisions and the market generally have been left to deal with visual features. (We contrast this with the policies followed in Britain where governments have followed so called "town planning" policies under which governments may restrict the types of economic activities which may be carried on in specified locations and may even impose restrictions on aesthetics.)

6.8.6 Economic effects

Markets by themselves do not allow for the environmental effects of production and consumption. These effects, by the 1970s, were reaching levels regarded by many people as unacceptable. The United States government stepped in with mechanisms which ultimately succeeded in reducing atmospheric pollution and pollution of fresh water to what were regarded as acceptable levels.

The next question is whether these environment improvements are compatible with economic growth. The rate of economic growth almost certainly is reduced by the environmental improvements as some resources are used to clean up emissions and as some production is configured away from the previous, least cost (but dirty) methods. How large is this growth penalty?

The long term economic growth path shown in Figure 6.30 places the years of active environmental clean-up in some kind of perspective. The graph is of the logarithm of constant dollar per capita GDP of the United States from 1820 to 2003. We use logarithms as a straight line in a semi-log graph corresponds to a constant rate of growth; this makes it easy to see if growth trends have changed.

Figure 6.30 Logarithm of GDP per capita
Log of constant dollar U.S. GDP per capita, 1820 = 1

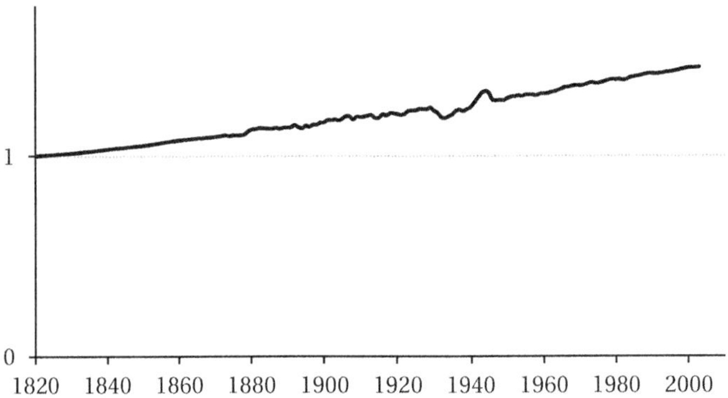

Source: Data from Maddison (2006b).

The growth path looks remarkably constant - the long term growth rate is 1.8% and the fit of constant rate growth to the actual path is close. The blips in the growth path are associated with the Great Depression of the 1930s (down) and World War II in the 1940s (up), not with the introduction of environmental regulations in the 1970s. In fact, the trend growth rate from 1820 through 1970 is 1.7% while the trend rate after 1970 is 2.0% so the growth rate increased after the introduction of strong air quality regulations.

This does not prove that environmental regulation is good for growth as the correct comparison is between the growth which did occur and the (unobservable) growth which would have occurred in the absence of the regulations. However, this does demonstrate that environmental protection does not prevent economic growth; the two can coexist. It also suggests, although does not prove, that the growth cost of environmental protection is relatively modest. Modern societies have made the choice that it is better to lose a little bit of growth (whether 0.01% or 0.1% or 0.5% a year is not known) in order to protect environmental quality. Economic growth, with the right policies, appears to be compatible with national environmental quality.

6.9 Broad environmental effects

6.9.1 The commons and externalities

"The Tragedy of the Commons" is a term coined by ecologist Garrett Hardin (1968). The tragedy of the commons has come to refer to the situation in which multiple, independent, uncontrolled users of a common resource over-exploit the resource, leading to its long term deterioration or even demise.

The commons originally were shared lands in England on which anyone could carry out their own activities, such as collecting firewood, grazing animals or growing vegetables. The danger arises from the incentives created in this situation. The individual user has no incentive to allow for the future as his actions today have no discernible effect on his future ability to enjoy the resource. There certainly is no incentive to invest in the land as the individual will not benefit from his investment. And, even the short run incentives are inefficient. It is in the interest of an individual user to keep increasing his use of the resource until his additional benefit equals his additional short run cost. The short run additional cost is small so the user is encouraged to, say, collect more wood as long as there are trees to be cut. This will degrade the longer term productive capacity of the resource. Taking this example to the extreme all the trees will be cut down so there will be no firewood next year.

The commons problem in England was overcome by enclosure – the movement in the 18th century whereby common land was converted to private ownership. But the problem remains whenever individual players benefit from using a resource today but do not have to take account of the consequences of their actions for resource productivity in the future.

A related problem is that of externalities. External effects, whether benefits or costs, are effects of production or consumption which are not charged for. As there is no charge, external effects do not enter the decision calculus of players. The result for external benefits is that the level of the activity is too low; for external costs, activity is pushed too far and other people have to carry the external costs. Markets are inefficient in managing the production or consumption of goods with significant external effects. The market outcome will be for too little production of goods with significant external benefits and too much production of goods with significant external costs.

We look in this chapter at four examples of the problem of commons and externalities which have emerged in recent decades as a result of economic growth. These examples are the Atlantic cod, fisheries management in New Zealand, global warming and ozone holes. These provide two examples of successful management of the problem and two examples of non-management of the problem. We then relate these problems to economic growth and examine some of the implications for economic growth.

6.9.2 Atlantic cod

The cod was prolific in the western Atlantic, particularly on the Grand Banks and Georges Bank, as well as in the eastern Atlantic, particularly in the North Sea. Large catches were taken for hundreds of years. Catches increased over the course of the 20th century with the development of more effective fishing technology and, in the western Atlantic, as vessels from European countries began to operate in addition to American and Canadian vessels. However, the resource could not sustain the intensity of the fishing effort. Catches began to decline and the decline was rapid – landings of cod in Canada went from 269 thousand tonnes in 1968 to just 120 thousand tonnes in 1975. The governments of the United States and Canada began to act. For example, the United States in 1976, through the Magnuson Act, excluded foreign fishing in its Exclusive Economic Zone (EEZ). However, the authorities tended to yield to pressure from domestic fishers to allow high ongoing catches; as a result there was continuing decline in the stock and in catches. The western cod fisheries proceeded to collapse. The resource was all but destroyed. The cod resource in the eastern Atlantic similarly has been fished intensively. Efforts by some organizations to limit catches were over-ruled or ignored by other countries. The annual catch has fallen steadily.

Figure 6.31, compiled by the Food and Agriculture Organization, shows these developments – the essentially complete collapse of the cod resource in the northwest Atlantic with the cod resource in the northeast heading in the same direction.

Figure 6.31 Capture of Atlantic Cod, 1950 - 2005

Annual capture in million tonnes

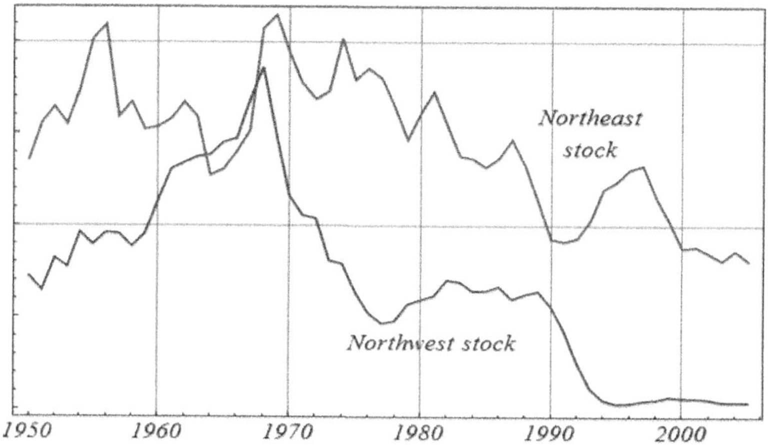

Source: This graph is from the FAO Fishery Statistics programme (FIGIS Online). It was downloaded from wikipedia File:Atlantic cod capture 1950 2005.png on 28 September 2011.

The fate of the Atlantic cod is a prime example of the tragedy of the commons. The incentive for individual operators was to keep increasing their annual catch. This is exactly what happened. When the catch rate exceeded the reproduction rate of the cod, the stock began to decline and, with it, the catch. There was no effective control over capture rates and so no mechanism to allow for the future. Even when government controls began to be introduced, their objectives tended to emphasize the protection of the local industry rather than the protection of the resource. This situation of no control over much of the resource and myopic management of that part of the resource which was under control allowed short term interests to prevail; the tragedy of the commons was played out.

6.9.3 New Zealand fisheries management

New Zealand is a small country (population around 4 million) in the south western Pacific Ocean. Because of it elongated north-south shape, New Zealand has a long coastline. Consequently, New Zealand's EEZ, extending 200 nautical miles into the ocean, covers a vast area, an area of around 4.5 million square kilometers. New Zealand was well aware of the tragedy of the commons and the potential for destruction of its fisheries resources by uncontrolled fishing. This led the New Zealand government to pioneer efforts to manage its fisheries on a sustainable basis.

Fisheries management in New Zealand's EEZ takes place on a species and area basis. The system encompasses some 95 species and 10 areas within the EEZ. Each stock has a total allowable catch which is the best feasible scientific assessment of the total annual catch which can be taken sustainably from the stock. Tradeable quotas are then defined in terms of percentages of the total allowable catch. The quotas generate equivalent Annual Catch Entitlements (ACE) for each species/area. ACE amounts not used may be sold while catches in excess of ACE may be covered by purchased ACEs or, failing this, by paying a charge (akin to a fine) to the government. To try to deal with the problem of inaccurate reporting of catches, the New Zealand government stations observers on fishing boats. The prime duty of the observers is to record independently catch amounts, by-catches (catches of species for which the fisher has no ACE), and catches of marine animals and birds. To try to deal with the problem of unauthorized boats fishing in the EEZ, New Zealand uses aerial and ship surveillance.

This fisheries management system has been designed to avoid the tragedy of the commons. It appears to work reasonably well in managing New Zealand's fisheries resources. Allowed catches are set with the aim of sustaining the resources in perpetuity. Active monitoring takes place to try to ensure that allowed catches are respected and to minimize collateral damage to the fauna. Finally, quota and ACEs are tradeable to try to ensure that fishing is done as efficiently as possible.

New Zealand's experience suggests that efficient management of the commons is possible. Of course, efficient management requires well designed and well implemented policies but this appears to have been achieved. New Zealand's experience also draws attention to the fundamental problem of managing the commons – efficient management requires that the common resource be under the control of a single entity which has both the incentive and power to manage the resource for the long term. New Zealand's EEZ, large though it is, covers only a small part of the Pacific Ocean – most of the rest of the Pacific has no effective governing body and is not managed on a sustainable basis.

6.9.4 Greenhouse gasses and climate change

Human activities like the combustion of fossil fuels and the burning of wood or forests release carbon dioxide. The concentration of carbon dioxide in the atmosphere has increased from 280 parts per million (ppm) at the start of industrialization to over 380 ppm today. Carbon dioxide is a greenhouse gas - it traps (some of) the solar energy which warms the Earth's surface and is re-radiated from the surface in infrared wavelengths. This greenhouse mechanism is expected, theoretically, to result in a warming of the Earth's atmosphere. Observations show that the temperature of the Earth's surface has indeed been increasing. Figure 6.32 shows a broad correlation between carbon dioxide concentrations and surface temperature. This type of correlation, combined with an associated theoretical causal mechanism, suggests that economic activity, via emissions and the greenhouse effect, is likely to be making the planet warmer and, as a result, may be creating climate change.

Figure 6.32 Correlation of CO_2 and temperature

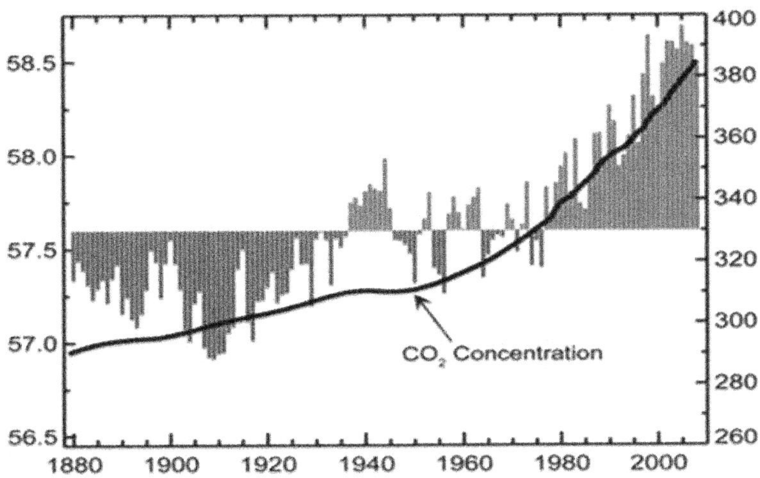

Left hand scale: Mean global surface temperature, degrees F.
Right hand scale: CO_2 concentration, parts per million (ppm)
Source: National Oceanic and Atmospheric Administration (2011).

Figure 6.33 gives a longer time perspective, going back almost one million years. This Figures uses carbon dioxide measurements obtained from ice cores taken at the Vostok Station in the Antarctic.

Figure 6.33 Atmospheric carbon dioxide concentration

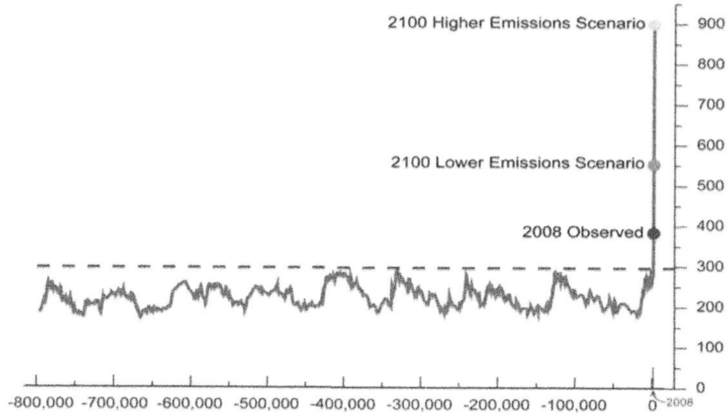

Horizontal axis: years before the present.
Vertical axis: CO_2 concentration, ppm.
The future emissions scenarios are as reported by the National Climatic Data Center, National Oceanic and Atmospheric Administration.
Source: National Oceanic and Atmospheric Administration (2014).

This long term record shows that there have been carbon dioxide cycles, not a steady upward trend. The main cycle appears to have a periodicity of around 100,000 years. Atmospheric temperatures, inferred from the same ice samples, show an almost identical path, cycles and all. These main temperature cycles appear to be Milankovitch cycles, due to characteristics of the Earth's orbit around the Sun. In addition, there are cycles in solar activity which affect the intensity of solar radiation reaching the Earth. Information on these solar or sunspot cycles goes back only for a few hundred years but it appears that these cycles, with a periodicity of around 11 years, also are correlated with temperature cycles.

These data, and the associated Milankovitch and solar mechanisms, provide natural explanations for the observed long term changes in

Earth's temperature. These explanations do not involve man-made emissions of carbon dioxide. However, we have now gone past the natural peak, of around 300 ppm, in carbon dioxide concentrations. We have concentrations never experienced in the past million years and they are projected to increase substantially in the decades ahead. And, there is a well-recognized mechanism, the greenhouse effect, linking increasing concentrations of greenhouse gasses in the atmosphere to increasing atmospheric temperatures.

There has been an increase in temperature since 1980 which cannot be explained by natural mechanisms. The most plausible hypothesis, and the only hypothesis which is consistent with both theory and observations, is that anthropogenic (man-made) emissions of greenhouse gasses have caused this recent rise in temperature. The effects of man-made emissions are superimposed on the natural processes driving temperature change. The carbon dioxide graph in the previous Figure is now in uncharted territory. The implication is that increasing concentrations of greenhouse gasses due to economic growth are causing warming and climate change and we do not know where these processes will take us.

The next question is whether continuing increases in atmospheric and surface temperatures, leading to climate change, matter.

Global warming has both benefits and costs. The main benefit is that economic growth can continue as it has been, with production and consumption activities continuing to emit large quantities of greenhouse gasses. However, there are significant costs and considerable risks associated with global warming and climate change.

There appear to be two principal costs. First, higher temperatures mean that more energy goes into climatic processes, causing a greater frequency of extreme weather events. These are storms, floods, droughts and winds. These events will affect lives, property and economic and social activities. In addition, higher temperatures might reduce the productivity of the Earth's principal crop-growing areas. Second, a rising sea level (due to melting snow and ice cover of land

and to the expansion of sea water) will affect lives, property, economic activity and social activity in coastal areas and in low lying countries.

Then there are the risks. There could be a spread of diseases associated with warm, wet conditions. Ecosystems will change and the location of species will change. The system of ocean currents could change. The ocean current most at risk appears to be the Gulf Stream; if the Gulf Stream were to diminish the climate of Europe would become markedly colder. Then there is a risk that the permafrost in high northern latitudes will melt, releasing large amounts of methane gas. Methane has a greenhouse effect some 20 times greater than that of carbon dioxide. This would significantly accelerate global warming. Finally there is a catastrophic risk. If adverse feedback mechanisms come into play, there is the possibility of a runaway greenhouse effect. The planet Venus gives an example of a runaway greenhouse process, making life as we know it impossible. This appears to have a very low but nonetheless non-zero probability.

Global warming and climate change are exacerbated by economic growth. This climate change appears set to impose costs and create risks for everyone on Earth. It is potentially a serious problem. Will global warming be stopped? Probably not – this is a tragedy of the commons situation. Individual countries will not act to reduce their emissions as they suffer the costs of adjustment and reap no benefit. There is no effective international government to require all countries to act to reduce greenhouse gas emissions. The power framework does not exist to force remedial action or to force individuals to take account in their decision-making of the global consequences of their actions.

The Kyoto Protocol was adopted in 1997 under the auspices of the United Nations. 37 industrialized countries and the European Union, but not the United States, committed to reducing their emissions of greenhouse gasses to specified levels, related to their 1990 emissions, for the period 2009 - 2012. Emissions have not been reduced to their target levels. Furthermore, nothing has followed the Kyoto Protocol to apply after 2012. The Kyoto Protocol might have helped (or then again it might have made little difference) but it certainly did not solve the climate change problem.

Our existing institutions have proved unable to deal with the problem of climate change. Greenhouse gas emissions are outside of the market system and their effects are outside the control of national governments. Climate change might be manageable in the future but new mechanisms, based on a new international power structure, will be needed if effective action is to be taken. The likelihood of this happening is uncertain. For the foreseeable future, climate change is a cost, and a possibly a large cost, of economic growth.

6.9.5 Ozone holes

Ozone in the upper atmosphere is important as it provides a shield against ultraviolet (UV) wavelengths in solar radiation. UV radiation reaching the Earth's surface causes increased risks to human health (risk of skin cancers and cataracts in particular), to the health of non-furry animals such as whales, and to vegetation.

Some industrial chemicals, when released into the atmosphere and after rising to the upper atmosphere, deplete the ozone layer. This process had been known for some time. A compilation of research by the National Academy of Sciences in 1976 focused attention on the ozone depletion hypothesis and highlighted the role of chlorofluorocarbons (CFCs). The U.S. responded by banning the use of CFCs as aerosol propellants in spray cans. But a report by the British Antarctic Survey (see Farman et al (1985)) shocked the scientific community as it identified observationally a large decline in ozone density in the upper atmosphere over the Antarctic. This was the Antarctic "ozone hole"; another ozone hole was subsequently found over the Arctic. The Antarctic hole was extensive, expanding in the summer months as far north as New Zealand. Now theory was matched by observation. Halogens (primarily CFCs, freons and halons) were clearly identified as the cause of the problem. These halogens were used primarily as refrigerants and aerosol propellants.

Led by the U.S., the larger industrialized countries began discussing ways of regulating the production of ozone-depleting substances. This led to the Montreal Protocol (in 1987 with amendments in the 1990s) in which signatory countries (ultimately 196 in number) agreed to phase out the production of these substances. The phase-out of CFCs, for all except specified special cases, was completed before 2000 with the phase-out of the other substances proceeding on a slower schedule. The offending chemicals have now been replaced as refrigerants and aerosol propellants by other, non-ozone-depleting, chemicals. Although polar ozone appears no longer to be decreasing, the long life of halogens in the polar regions means that it will take decades for the ozone holes to recover; in particular it is estimated that the Antarctic ozone hole will take until 2100 to recover. Nonetheless, the ozone hole story is a case of the international community coming together to take effective action against an international environmental problem.

The policy response to the ozone holes was both prompt and effective. Such unity of purpose and resolution of action is unusual if not unprecedented for international action on an environmental issue. Why did it happen?

It appears that the cause was essentially commercial, operating through the following sequence: (1) Production of the offending halogens was dominated by a few companies, mostly based in the United States; (2) the principal halogens were going to come out of patent protection so the prospect was that these chemicals would become commodities with small profit margins; (3) banning these chemicals would require that substitutes be found, playing to the strengths of the leading producers; (4) these substitutes would have patent protection and so carry high margins; (5) accordingly, it was in the interest of the large chemical companies to overturn the status quo and support moves by their governments to require the replacement of the identified chemicals. Mostafa Tolba, former head of the U.N. Environment Programme, is quoted (from Mackenzie (1990)) as saying: "the chemical industry supported the Montreal Protocol in 1987 because it set up a worldwide schedule for phasing out CFCs, which [were] no longer protected by patents. This provided companies with an equal opportunity to market new, more profitable compounds."

Under this plausible scenario, the interest of the chemical companies (in shifting to more profitable products) coincided with the interest of governments (responding to environmental concerns). Governments could make everybody happy, an appealing situation for politicians, and so acted with alacrity. These conditions were sufficient to get effective international action on a global environmental problem. However, the occurrence of conditions making for a perceived win-win situation is most unusual. The ozone hole story is not typical in dealing with widespread environmental dangers.

6.9.6 The problem

The conventional way of managing activity with significant external costs is for governments to enter the decision process and either by inducement (charging for external harm or creating a market in the environmental effect) or force (regulation) to get decision-makers to take account of the full costs of their actions. But this approach is feasible only if the government can control the cause of the problem and can be held accountable for its effects. Environmental effects whose effects lie within the jurisdiction of a single country can be dealt with by the government of that country. However, there is no effective government which can intercede to deal with super-national effects. (A partial exception to this is that the European Union can exercise some control over the European countries.)

Action to deal with ozone holes, where effective international action did occur, was the result of most unusual circumstances where there were no barriers to international cooperation – everyone perceived themselves to be winners from collective action. In most cases, though, there are some perceived winners and some perceived losers so it is not possible to get international unanimity; this makes effective international action difficult if not impossible. New Zealand's management of its fisheries is an object lesson in managing common resources but the limited extent of this jurisdiction means that most of the world's oceans are outside of effective management and that the tragedy of the commons remains.

The mismatch between the extent of effects and the extent of management power is the inherent problem in dealing with environmental effects which transcend national boundaries. The areas at risk include the oceans, the atmosphere and space. Examples are the depletion of off-shore fish species, dumping toxic wastes into the oceans or emitting dangerous gasses into the atmosphere. There is no effective mechanism to stop the problem from happening - to get people to take account of the full effects of their actions and so limit the effects to an efficient level. Also, there is no mechanism to secure a clean-up of the damage after it has happened.

6.9.7 Super-national environmental effects of growth

Economic activity, in particular industrial activity, is imposing costs on and creating risks for the global environment. Potentially, every country and every person in the world is affected. National environmental effects can be managed effectively but our institutions cannot effectively deal with international environmental effects. These effects, the accumulation of three centuries of economic growth, are now reaching serious levels. This is a clear disadvantage of economic growth. This is not to say that economic growth is undesirable but it is to say that this is a significant cost resulting from economic growth and that there is a need to strive for more effective international institutions to deal with these problems.

6.10 Well-being

6.10.1 Does economic growth help?

Economic growth has brought large increases in incomes. People have chosen to spend their higher incomes on better food and housing, on entertainment and mobility, and on more leisure time. The nature of work has changed with the widespread substitution of physical and human capital for manual labor. By individual actions and through their governments, people have made enormous gains in health and education. Many aspects of the environment have been improved; for example, clean water supplies have been established and disease vectors have largely been eliminated. Other aspects of the environment though have suffered, such as pollution of the air and water. And there are uncertainties about the effects of income – is it absolute income that matters or is it relative income? And, does working and living in a consumer society create stresses that negate the gains from higher incomes? Does economic growth provide unequivocal gains or does it present us with a Faustian bargain?

What, then, is the record of economic growth in improving people's well-being? We have examined already the general effects of economic growth in increasing incomes; we have examined also its record in improving health, longevity, housing, leisure, education and consumption opportunities. Almost all these effects appear to be positive, to make people better off, not just financially but in the sense of moving them to a preferred position. What we need now is some way of combining these effects and assessing whether economic growth has improved people's lives.

6.10.2 Surveys of well-being

Studies of well-being address the question of whether higher incomes improve people's well-being. Most of these studies are based on the premise that people are the best judge of their own well-being. Sample questionnaires have been used to record the degree of subjective (self-assessed) well-being. These assessments then have been related to the incomes of the people or groups involved.

An early analysis, which established a benchmark in the field, was by Richard Easterlin (1974). Easterlin suggested the presence of a satiation effect – satisfaction does not increase much after a reasonable standard of living has been achieved. This has become known as the "Easterlin paradox" – that some economic growth is good but that, after a point, it doesn't really help. A related idea, raised for example by Easterlin (1974) and Richard Layard (2005), is that in higher income societies it is relative income that matters to people, not their absolute level of income.

Subsequent investigations, though, have revised these conclusions. A comprehensive examination is that by Betsey Stevenson and Justin Wolpers (2008) who conclude that increases in income are clearly associated with increases in self-assessed well-being and that there is no satiation effect. Furthermore, Stevenson and Wolpers conclude that absolute income is the principal economic force driving self-assessed well-being; relative income might be relevant but it is secondary at most.

Stevenson and Wolpers use data and models across people (in the same country at one point in time), over time (for people in the same country) and across countries to investigate the well-being-income relationship. They find a consistent pattern from all three approaches – that there is a statistically significant relationship between income and well-being. They find that this relationship is semi-logarithmic - it is between well-being and the log of income. The coefficient of log income varies between different data sets but it is centered on 0.4.

The semi-logarithmic relationship is particularly important. This specification means that (1) increasing income is associated with greater well-being, (2) each additional dollar of income is associated with a declining, although positive, increase in well-being, (3) each one percent increase in income is associated with a constant increase in well-being, and (4) each one percent increase in income is associated with a less than one percent increase in well-being and this percentage declines as income increases.

On the relationship between economic growth and well-being, Stevenson and Wolpers (2008, page 1) conclude ". . . we find economic growth associated with rising happiness." This implies simply that more is better; economic growth, by increasing people's incomes, moves people to a preferred situation. This does not necessarily mean that people just want money but it does mean that people enjoy the things that go with or are made possible by higher incomes. By generating higher incomes, economic growth increases well-being.

6.10.3 The OECD better life approach

A different approach to analyzing well-being has recently been carried out by the OECD which constructed the so called "Better Life Index". This is an index covering 11 dimensions of the human condition – housing, income, jobs, community, education, environment, civic engagement, health, life satisfaction, safety and work-life balance. Indicators for each of the 11 dimensions were measured for various countries. The performance in each of the 11 dimensions was, for each country, combined using equal weights to give an indicator of "life satisfaction" (OECD (2011a)). Life satisfaction is related to household income for 26 OECD countries in Figure 6.34. The smooth line is life satisfaction which we have modeled in terms of the logarithm of income. (There is no scale on the Life satisfaction axis as the absolute value of this index is arbitary.)

Figure 6.34 Life satisfaction vs income

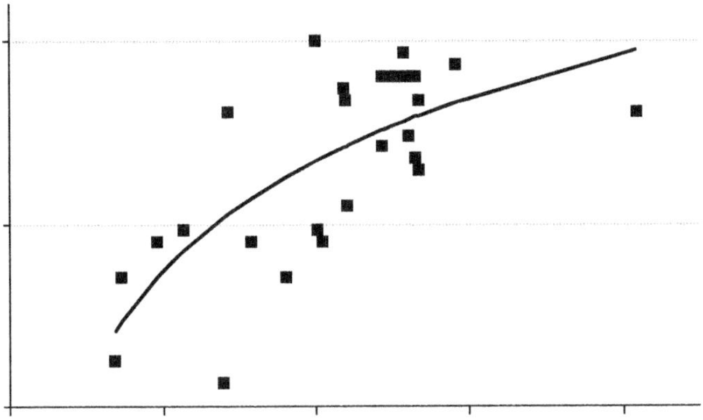

This graph covers 26 OECD countries in 2009.
An index of life satisfaction is measured on the vertical axis.
An index of household disposable income is measured on the horizontal axis.
Source: Our semi-logarithmic model fitted to data from OECD (2011a).

There is a clear relationship between the average income of a country and its Better Life Index. The line of best fit is curved in a semi-logarithmic way (just as in Stevenson and Wolpers). This semi-log relationship implies that each 1% increase in income is associated with a less than 1%, and also diminishing percentage, increase in life satisfaction.

The OECD approach is objective, to the extent that it uses clearly measureable indicators, but ultimately subjective in that it assumes that these indicators are directly related to well-being and that each indicator carries the same weight. It is different to but not necessarily better or worse than Stevenson and Wolpers. However, the nature of the conclusions is the same – more income (and the things that go with higher income) is better than less income, there is no evidence of a satiation effect but there does seem to be something akin to diminishing marginal utility of income – the percentage gain in the quality of life from each 1% increase in income is less than 1% and declines as income increases.

6.10.4 Economic growth is good

It is important to recognize what these investigations into well-being show and what they do not show. They do not suggest that money brings happiness; they do not suggest that money is the most important thing in life. They do suggest that money, or more precisely a person's income or purchasing power, is one of the things which contributes to that person's satisfaction with life; purchasing power may or may not be the most important contributor to satisfaction – there is no claim either one way or the other on that point – but it is a contributor. And, the most important implication of these studies is that more income is preferred to less income – people gain more satisfaction if their purchasing power increases.

In virtually all countries, higher income is associated with greater satisfaction. Absolute income is strongly linked to self-assessed well-being. Relative income matters but increases in absolute income over time dominate any relative income effect. There is no evidence of satiation – more continues to be better. However, the contribution to well-being of continuing increases in income does diminish. This is the semi-logarithmic effect – successive 1% increases in income increase well-being but by diminishing amounts.

The conclusion, combining all the effects of economic growth, the good and the bad, by the people who experience this growth, is unequivocal: people gain from economic growth.

Chapter 7

Past theories of economic growth

7.1 Adam Smith

Adam Smith's book, *An Inquiry into the Nature and Causes of the Wealth of Nations*, published in 1776, was the foundation of modern economics. Smith was writing at a time when Mercantilism was the prevailing philosophy, guiding thinking on economics and government policy. Mercantilism in effect equated a nation's wealth to the money and treasure it owned. Smith argued instead that the wealth of a nation was its ability to produce useful goods and services. *The Wealth of Nations* was devoted to exploring what generated this wealth and how it could be increased. The wealth of a nation is its total production (what would be known today as Gross Domestic Product) and not the value of its treasure.

Smith recognizes that the modern economy is based on specialization and exchange. Book III, Chapter I, titled "Of the Natural Progress of Opulence" includes:

> "The great commerce of every civilized society is that carried on between the inhabitants of the town and those of the country. It consists in the exchange of crude for manufactured produce, either immediately, or by the intervention of money, or of some sort of paper which represents money. The country supplies the town with the means of subsistence and the materials of manufacture. The town repays this supply by sending back a part of the manufactured produce to the inhabitants of the country. .... The gains of both are mutual and reciprocal, and the division of labour is in this, as in all other cases, advantageous to all the different persons employed in the various occupations into which it is subdivided."

Specialization allows the division of labor. This is the key to increased production. From Book I, Chapter I:

> "The greatest improvement in the productive powers of labour, and the greater part of the skill, dexterity and judgement with which it is anywhere directed, or applied, seem to have been the effects of the division of labour."

Smith lists three causes for the greater productivity flowing from the division of labor:

- improvements in productivity from experience or learning by doing, "the improvement of the dexterity of the workman necessarily increases the quantity of the work he can perform; and the division of labour, by reducing every man's business to some simple operation, and by making this operation the sole employment of his life, necessarily increases very much the dexterity of the workman."
- the saving of time which would be "lost in passing from one sort of work to another"; and
- the application of capital or "every body must be sensible how much labour is facilitated and abridged by the application of the proper machinery."

Smith even mentions (still in Book I, Chapter I) three ways in which productive innovations are made. First, workmen come up with ideas for better ways of working:

> "A great part of the machines made use of in those manufactures in which labour is most subdivided, were originally the inventions of common workmen, who, being each of them employed in some very simple operation, naturally turned their thoughts towards finding out easier and readier methods of performing it."

Second, specialized equipment manufacturers improve the design and performance of their machines:

> "Many improvements have been made by the ingenuity of the makers of the machines, when to make them became the business of a peculiar trade;"

And third, inventors come up with new machines:

> "and some [improvements have been made] by those who are called philosophers or men of speculation, whose trade it is not to do any thing, but to observe every thing; and who, upon that account, are often capable of combining together the powers of the most distant and dissimilar objects."

The greater the division of labor, the more productive the economy. The division of labor though is limited by the extent of the market. From Book I, Chapter III:

> "As it is the power of exchanging that gives occasion to the division of labour, so the extent of this division must always be limited by the extent of that power, or, in other words, by the extent of the market."

Changes which increase the extent of the market therefore allow further increases in productivity. Smith notes several ways in which a market can be extended; he notes the favorable effects in expanding the market of improvements in transport (for example in Book I, Chapter III); he notes the unfavorable effects of restrictions on international trade (for example in Book IV, Chapter II); he notes the problems caused by restrictions on employment and restrictive work practices (for example in Book I, Chapter X); and he stresses the detrimental effect of monopolies (for example in Book I, Chapter VII).

Smith recognizes that the division of labor involves specialization and that in turn it requires an efficient system of exchange. Money is the key to effective exchange as it supplants barter and minimizes transaction costs (Book I, Chapter IV). Smith identifies the existence of capital and the source of capital as savings – that part of income which is in excess of consumption (Book II, chapter I). (These are the modern words for Smith's arguments; Smith never mentions transaction costs, income or consumption.)

He suggests that output depends on labor and capital inputs (see Introduction and Plan of the Work): The annual consumption of a nation is determined

> "first by the skill, dexterity and judgement with which its labour is generally applied; and secondly, by the proportion between the number of those who are employed in useful labour, and that of those who are not so employed. . . . The number of useful and productive labourers . . is every where in proportion to the quantity of capital stock which is employed in setting them to work, and to the particular way in which it is so employed."

Smith's first concern is with production and productive effectiveness. For this production to be economically efficient it must be directed to what people want to consume. Smith recognized the role of markets in allocating resources in a useful way. He even appears to be groping towards a simple model of supply and demand (in Book I, Chapter VII). He develops the concept of natural price, a sort of long run competitive equilibrium price, and shows that an increase in demand will lead to higher prices which will stimulate supply with competitive forces then driving the market price back to the natural price.

Smith goes on to explore the market system. The crucial concept here is "the invisible hand". The key paragraphs describing the power of the market are (from Book IV, Chapter II):

> "Every individual is continually exerting himself to find the most advantageous employment for whatever capital he can command. It is his own advantage, indeed, and not that of the society which he has in view. . . . But the study of his own advantage naturally, or rather necessarily leads him to prefer that employment which is most advantageous to the society. . . . every individual . . endeavours . . to employ his capital . . so to direct that industry that its produce may be of the greatest value . . . and by directing that industry in such a manner as its produce may be of the greatest value, he intends only his own gain, and he is in this, as in many other cases, led by an invisible hand to promote an end which was no part of his intention."

Smith linked the pursuit of self interest in production to the public interest in producing the right things. This idea of "the invisible hand" is the intellectual precursor to the systematic study of the market leading ultimately, although this took almost 200 years, to the concept of general equilibrium and proof of the welfare properties of a competitive equilibrium (see, for example, Kenneth Arrow (1951)).

Adam Smith was not concerned with economic growth per se; indeed, the concept of economic growth was unknown when he was writing. Smith was tackling the pressing problem of his time – rejecting society's emphasis on treasure and instead trying to clear the decks for people to get on with production and increasing production. He was concerned with (in modern jargon) maximizing GDP, the production of goods and services which people wanted. In investigating how to maximize production, Smith identified the central roles of incentives, self-interest, competition, money and the market; he also investigated the role of capital and productivity. Smith's intellectual approach laid the foundation for modern economics. Although unforeseen by Smith, the forces unleashed by incentives, competition and free markets have been vital to economic growth.

7.2 David Ricardo

David Ricardo, an English political economist, published *On the Principles of Political Economy and Taxation* in 1817. This book set out what has become known as the law of comparative advantage. Ricardo showed that there is mutual benefit from trade, regardless of absolute productive potential, as long as each party concentrates on the activities in which it has a relative advantage – the product for which it has a lower opportunity cost. This is the underlying efficiency argument in favor of specialization and trade. It applies to free trade among all trading parties whether individuals, businesses or countries.

England at the time protected its agriculture from import competition by means of tariffs, the "Corn Laws". These tariffs raised the price of all food as well as creating rents (higher incomes) to landowners; indeed, the purpose of the Corn Laws was to protect English agriculture and to raise the incomes of landowners. Ricardo opposed these restrictions on international trade for two reasons, one to do with comparative advantage and the other to do with investment. The comparative advantage argument was essentially that England should concentrate on what it did well (at the time textiles and metal goods) and import what others did relatively well (in particular foodstuffs). He also argued that the Corn Laws caused less-productive domestic land to be worked and rents to landowners to increase. Thus, income would be directed more toward rural landlords and away from the emerging industrial capitalists. Since landlords tended to spend on conspicuous consumption rather than investments, Ricardo believed that the Corn Laws were restraining the growth of the British economy. Ricardo provided the intellectual firepower to the argument against the Corn Laws. The Corn Laws were eventually repealed although only in 1846, many years after the publication of his book. (And it is more likely to have been political machinations rather than dispassionate intellectual argument which prevailed in the repeal of the Corn Laws.)

International trade, allowing comparative advantage to find expression, went on to become one of the essential features of British economic growth. Britain produced coal, iron and steel, it imported cotton and foodstuffs, and it exported textiles, transportation equipment and machinery. Britain depended on foreign markets for sales of the textiles and metal goods on which its growth was based just as it depended on foreign producers for many of its raw materials.

More recent examples of rapid economic growth - in countries such as Australia, Canada, China, Japan, New Zealand, Singapore, South Korea and Taiwan – similarly depended on international trade. Australia, Canada and New Zealand grew on the back of trade with Britain and the United States. The east Asian countries have grown by catching up, exploiting their cost advantages to supply American and European markets while buying equipment and services from these high income countries.

Ricardian comparative advantage (and its cousin, the Heckscher-Ohlin theorem) provided the theory while the experience of Europe and the United States provided the practical demonstration of the benefits of free markets and international trade. Free markets and international trade have been central in enabling the economic growth of the past 200 years.

7.3 Karl Marx

Karl Marx was a German philosopher who, having been hounded out of various European countries, ended up in London where he wrote his most influential economic works. The first volume of his *Capital* was published, in German, in 1867. Marx's subsequent work on *Capital* was published posthumously by his friend and patron, Friedrich Engels, as Volumes II and III.

The heart of *Capital* is Marx's labor theory of value. Marx attributed prices to the labor contained in the good or service being sold. But, labor content, even if indirect labor is taken into account, does not account for the entire price. The difference between the labor content and price was termed by Marx "surplus value". This surplus value is what today we would call profits plus interest plus tax. As there were no company income taxes or general sales taxes in Marx's time, this surplus value was income to capital.

This surplus Marx viewed as being created by labor but not paid to labor. Labor created the value but was paid only the amount needed to subsist. The presence of a "reserve army of the unemployed" would hold wages down to the survival level. This surplus value was seen by Marx as evidence of exploitation – exploitation of the proletariat by capitalists or "the dictatorship of the bourgeoisie". Marx viewed the prevailing capitalist system as being run by the wealthy business classes for their own benefit with their wealth being based on expropriation of this surplus value. This created one of the destructive pressures inherent in capitalism. Marx termed this the dialectic of "class struggle", pitting labor against capital.

These tensions would be heightened by the tendency of the rate of profit to fall. Marx argued that the growth of capital relative to labor would reduce the rate of profit. Any attempt to raise profits by investing still more would accelerate this process in a vicious circle of diminishing returns.

Competition among capitalists would grow so fierce that most would fail, leaving only a handful of monopolists controlling nearly all production. Marx saw this as one of the contradictions of capitalism - competition, instead of benefiting consumers, in the long run would create monopolies, harming those consumers.

These internal tensions would result in the destruction of capitalism.

This was part of the evolution of society through six stages – primitive communism, slavery, feudalism, capitalism, socialism and communism. Primitive communism was based on self-sufficient villages without a market economy. Slavery was based on landowners also owning labor. Feudalism was an agricultural economy wherein the masses worked on rented land. Capitalism encompassed agriculture, manufacturing and services with production based on workers employed by capitalists - the owners of land and physical capital. Socialism featured social ownership of the means of production. The socialist state served to take control of capital and the means of production. This would be "the workers' state" or "workers' democracy" or "dictatorship of the proletariat".

Pure communism was the utopian final stage. Pure communism would emerge when the productive power of the economy was so great that there would be freedom from need, freedom from wage labor and freedom from private property. In this classless society, production and consumption would be fully socialized, relationships between people would be based on free association and free access to goods. This would be an age of superabundance in which everyone's needs would be satisfied and so there would be no internal tensions and even no need for government. Among the features of pure communism is "from each according to his ability, to each according to his need".

This was Marx's theory of economic growth. The high income countries of the day, such as Britain and Germany, had long since passed through the initial stages of growth and were well into the age of capitalism. The later stages, of socialism and communism, would arrive in the future the result, Marx argued, of the tensions already contained in the capitalist system. The final stage, pure communism, would feature superabundance in which everyone had all the economic goods they wanted. Economic growth would (somehow, it was not explained how) proceed into the long term when incomes would be so high that no-one would have to do wage labor. (The slight drawback to this theory was that Marx never explained the economic mechanisms whereby this utopia would emerge or operate.)

Marx's economic predictions did not come to pass. The capitalism of 19th century Britain evolved into new system with a hugely expanded role of government. But this was a new creature – government became involved in providing infrastructure, public goods and an income safety net but not in social ownership of the means of production. The modern welfare state was not envisaged by Marx. Britain did experiment with socialization of the large scale industrial system (under Clement Attlee, Prime Minister 1945 – 51) but this public ownership was later dismantled (under Margaret Thatcher, Prime Minister 1979 – 90). Communism was tried by several countries, most notably in the Soviet Union. This communism was imposed by political dictatorship on essentially feudal societies; it did not evolve from capitalism and socialism. The leap from feudalism to a communist economy was not successful. Communism in the Soviet Union, for example, for decades was kept in place by political and police force but even so it finally collapsed. This collapse was the result of worker and citizen displeasure, the same sorts of pressures from within which Marx had prophesied would destroy capitalism in fact came to destroy communism.

Socialist revolutions have occurred in many countries but not where Marx predicted. Marx predicted that socialism would emerge in high income capitalist countries but, in fact, socialism was forced on many low income countries, closer to feudal than capitalist in nature. These revolutions unwittingly condemned the masses to continuing poverty and political dictatorship. These revolutions failed to create the classless society, failed to create a high income economy and failed to create personal freedoms.

Marx's system fares just as badly at a theoretical level. Marx did not understand markets. He did not have the tools of marginal analysis, embodied for example in demand and supply curves or partial and general equilibrium analysis, with which to understand prices. His surplus value corresponds essentially to income to capital or profit; profit is now known to be the residual between price and expenses, it is a consequence rather than a cause of price. Economic growth increases the demand for labor and the market price of labor; growth also increases the wage rate which can be negotiated through collective bargaining. The result of these developments has been that wages and labor income have increased over time, not, as Marx would have it, decreased. Labor has done well out of economic development just as has capital. Both labor and capital have an interest in maintaining the capitalist system, not in overthrowing it by (physical or political) force.

Marx did not properly analyze incentives. Profit is needed to generate investment; everybody gains from the resulting growth. The incentive is to get on board the growth train, not to derail it by force. Industries which have been socialized have been found to perform poorly and this too is due to incentives - the incentives created for sloth, resistance to change, featherbedding, lack of investment and inattention to quality. And, pure communism will not work simply because of the incentives – if consumption is independent of income, where is the incentive to work or to invest and so produce the goods which everyone wants to consume?

Marx's view of economics was fundamentally flawed and his predictions bound to fail.

Nonetheless, Marx's theories were hugely influential. A number of revolutionary governments, including Russia, the Soviet Union and China, found in Marx an intellectual way of legitimizing their power, of justifying government control of the economy and society. A large part of 20th century world history was influenced by Marx's ideas. Ultimately though the inherent failings in Marxism came to the fore; it was essentially the matter of incentives and economic stagnation which undid the Soviet Union as well as Chinese central control of the economy.

7.4 John Maynard Keynes

John Maynard Keynes was an English economist and government adviser, prominent in the years from World War I until his death in 1946. His *General Theory of Employment, Interest and Money*, published in 1936, established what came to be known as macroeconomics. Keynes was concerned with the problem of a country's overall stability. He solved analytically the determination of the level of aggregate income; this analysis could then be applied to the design of stabilization policy.

Keynes' concerns can be understood from a glance at Figure 7.1. This shows constant price GDP for the United Kingdom for the years 1830 to 1938 and current dollar Net National Income per capita for 1855 to 1938. The economy followed a relatively steady growth path until World War I. For the rest of the period though the trend was lost, production quantities and prices and so real incomes moved in unprecedented swings.

Figure 7.1 U.K. economic growth and stability

Indexes of constant price GDP and current price Net National Income per capita

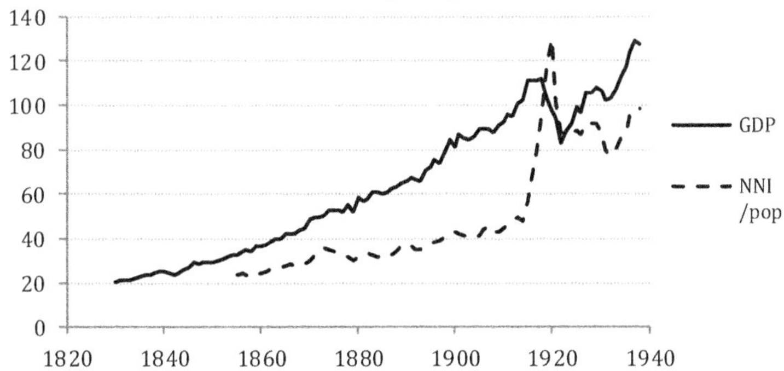

Source: Data from Mitchell and Deane (1971).

This history suggests why no-one previously had been too worried about economic stability. Production and incomes had been increasing relatively steadily since 1831 or even earlier (1831 is the earliest year of this annual data series) until World War I. There had been minor variations but the broad picture had been one of steady growth. It so happens that this growth was unprecedentedly rapid (the average annual growth rate from 1830 to 1913 was 2.0%) but the point here is the relative stability of the growth path rather than the growth rate. Until 1913, then, there was not really a macroeconomic stability problem. Beginning in 1914, however, a variety of problems arose. The rapid increase in production and inflation in World War I, the instabilities in Germany and Europe in the 1920s then the Great Depression of the 1930s shook the European world to the core. Economic stability was now recognized as the pre-eminent economic problem of the age.

Traditional economics was unable to explain these events. Classical doctrine, such as Say's Law, held that as long as prices including wages were flexible, the market would establish full employment equilibrium. This view was that "supply creates its own demand"; as such the productive potential of the economy, or supply, was seen as the driving force in determining economic performance. Keynes turned the logic around – demand was now the driving force. The interaction of aggregate demand and aggregate supply will lead to a macroeconomic equilibrium which may or may not involve full employment of resources. Insufficient demand, regardless of supply, could lead to an unemployment equilibrium.

The core Keynesian ideas can be expressed in terms of the following concepts. (Keynes gave a verbal presentation of these ideas; the expression in mathematical form and the emphasis on the equilibrium condition came later as people such as John Hicks (1937) and Alvin Hansen (1941) refined Keynes' ideas.) The core variable is total income, referred to as Y. Consumption spending depends on income; investment spending depends on the interest rate; government spending, exports and imports are taken as given in the simple model. Total spending is:

$$\text{Spending} = C + I + G + X - M$$

The core idea is the equilibrium between spending and income (or demand and supply); income adjusts until:

$$Y = \text{Spending}$$

The simple model can readily be extended to include taxation so that consumption depends on disposable income (which is income less taxation, $Y - T$). This model can be solved for the equilibrium Y, giving the total value of income, spending and production. Demand or spending is the key driving force. In turn, resource use, such as employment, follows from total production which is the same as total income. If the willingness to spend is low it is possible to have a stable equilibrium with less than full use of resources.

Two things followed from this view of the world. First, it was possible to understand that the economy could, and how it could, become trapped in a situation of less than full resource use. Second, the Keynesian approach provided a framework for designing government policy to try to alter the level of economic activity. To move the economy out of a low employment equilibrium, such as the Great Depression, the prescription was to use appropriate fiscal policy (more G and less T in this model) and appropriate monetary policy (lower interest rates in this model).

Keynesian theory is concerned with determining the level of economic performance at one point in time rather than with growth of the economy over time. The application of Keynesian theory to date has been concerned with the design of stabilization policy and with short term forecasting of general economic conditions.

However, Keynesian economics can help with economic growth. Growth is helped by total demand increasing at a moderate rate. Moderate growth in spending helps avoid inflation (when rising asset prices divert investment into asset plays and away from productive capital formation). Moderate growth in spending helps avoid depressions (when low demand discourages investment and discourages new product development). And moderate growth in spending helps to increase demand, including demand for new types of goods and services. It is no coincidence that the strong economic growth of the United States and Europe since World War II took place in a favorable macroeconomic environment of (for the most part) steadily rising spending and modest inflation. Helping create a stable macroeconomic environment with moderate spending growth is the important contribution that Keynesian economics has made to economic growth.

7.5 Milton Friedman

Milton Friedman led the development of monetary economics. (See, for example Friedman (1959) and (1968), and Friedman and Anna Schwartz (1963).) Initially focussing on the supply of money but later encompassing also banking and the supply of credit, monetary economics examines the influence of money and credit on aggregate economic activity.

Monetary economics has led to the rise in the use of monetary policy whereby a country's central bank influences the availability and cost of credit so as to try to manage the growth in spending. In turn, the growth in spending influences inflation and the growth in constant price production and incomes.

Monetary economics is not a theory of growth. However, like Keynesian economics, monetary economics has underpinned the development of government stabilization policies which have diminished macroeconomic instabilities, creating conditions which are conducive to growth. In particular, monetary policy has been effective in combating inflation – an enemy of growth – and in ensuring that total spending increases at a moderate rate. To promote these objectives, many countries have established central banks to manage monetary policy independent of political interference. As fiscal policy (government spending and revenue) operates through government revenues and expenditures and can be directed to objectives other than economic stability, an independent monetary policy has often carried the burden of economic stabilization.

7.6 Wassily Leontief

Wassily Leontief developed input-output or inter-industry economics, starting with his 1941 work - *The Structure of the American Economy, 1919–1929.* The input-output model divides the economy into industries and is based on actual transactions between these industries. For example, the 2009 Input-Output Accounts for the United States have 70 inputs (provided by 66 industries as well as non-comparable imports, labor, capital and sales taxes) supplying outputs to 72 users (each of the 66 producing industries as well as six types of final demand - personal consumption, private fixed investment, change in private inventories, exports, comparable imports, which are a negative use, and government purchases). The Leontief model works as:

(1) Inputs. Production in each industry is represented by a fixed proportions model of its purchases from other industries and from primary inputs such as capital services and labor. Therefore, the input to industry j from source i is $A_{ij} \times X_j$ where X_j is the output from industry j and A_{ij} is the input-output coefficient.

(2) Demand. The demand for the output from each industry is the sum of its inputs to other industries and final demand for its products. Demand for output from industry i is $\Sigma_j A_{ij} \times X_j + Y_i$ where the summation term covers inter-industry demand and Y_i is total final demand for product i.

(3) Equilibrium. Demand must equal supply for every industry. (This is a static, linear, general equilibrium model.) The equilibrium condition implies:

$$AX + Y = X$$

where A is the matrix of input-output coefficients, X is the vector of industry outputs and Y is the vector of total final demands. Solution of this system of equations gives the set of industry outputs:

$$X = (I - A)^{-1} Y$$

This is the central Leontief result. As A is known from the data and Y is the target set of final outputs; the model solves for the set of required industry output levels. Inter-industry transactions are then found as AX.

(4) Accounting. The industry outputs, X, are gross outputs. The national income aggregates such as GDP are based on value added which is, for each industry, gross output less intermediate purchases. The national income aggregates can be derived directly from the table of input-output transactions – GDP is the sum of value added across industries and Gross Domestic Expenditure is the sum of the final demands.

The Leontief model is not a model of economic growth, rather, it deals with the structure of the economy at a given time. (Dale Jorgenson has extended the Leontief model in several ways, including to introduce prices and considerations of growth; see, for example, Edward Hudson and Jorgenson (1974).) However, the Leontief model provides a framework for analyzing the interactions between industries. A growth industry will pull many industries along in its wake both by purchasing inputs from the other industries and by generating income which is then spent across the entire economy. The Leontief model traces these links between spending and industry outputs.

7.7 Simon Kuznets

Simon Kuznets (1973) viewed economic growth as "a long-term rise in capacity to supply increasingly diverse economic goods to its population, this growing capacity based on advancing technology and the institutional and ideological adjustments that it demands."

Kuznets was a leading figure in developing national income accounting in the United States. He also investigated economic development and growth using quantitative data to supplement the traditional qualitative analysis.

Kuznets identified six characteristics of modern economic growth. (1) There is rapid growth in income per capita and population. (2) There is rapid growth in productivity. (3) There is structural change such as the shift from agriculture to manufacturing to services, the shift of production from individuals to companies and the shift of labor from self-employed to employee. (4) The structure of society changes as a result of education, secularization and urbanization. (5) The world becomes more interdependent. (6) Economic growth has been limited to a minority of the world's population.

The fact that only some countries have achieved growth shows that growth is not automatic. Kuznets argued that conditions necessary to allow growth include a flexible social and political framework, and incomes above some floor level. The central feature of growth, once it starts, is productivity growth. In turn, productivity growth results from innovation. Kuznets places the driving force behind innovation in science (see Kuznets' (1973)):

> "some new major growth source, some new epochal innovation, must have generated these radically different patterns. And one may argue that this source is the emergence of modern science as the basis of advancing technology - a breakthrough in the evolution of science that produced a potential for technology far greater than existed previously."

This is a self-sustaining process:

> "Mass application of technological innovations, which constitutes much of the distinctive substance of modern economic growth, is closely connected with the further progress of science, in its turn the basis for additional advance in technology. . . "

Kuznets also was concerned with income distribution. Economic growth brings about a decline in the relative position of some groups - farmers, small scale producers and landowners – and an increase in the position of other groups - owners of produced capital, managers and entrepreneurs. Kuznets looked at the evolution of income distribution and postulated what has become known as the Kuznets curve – as growth proceeds the inequality of income distribution at first increases and then, as average incomes continue to increase, begins to decrease.

Kuznets attributed economic growth to continuing technological advance. In turn, technological advance was based on science. Scientific knowledge is available to all so presumably the answer to the question of why only some countries move into economic growth is that the social structure, personal skills and attitudes in some countries are permissive of growth whereas in others they work to prevent growth.

However, Kuznets did not link his arguments into a consistent theory of growth. It was too easy just to attribute growth to science. What gives rise to scientific advance? Is scientific advance the cause of growth or the result of growth? What causes scientific advance to be translated into technological advance? Why do people behave in a way that generates growth? What are the practical mechanisms of growth? Kuznets did not create a practical view of the growth process. But, Kuznets greatly advanced the measurement of growth, and clarified the social characteristics and social effects of economic growth.

7.8 Walt Rostow

Walter Whitman Rostow (1960) set out a structured picture of the growth process with countries going through five stages of development. The growth process is led by a small number of industries; it is not a broad, economy-wide process although subsequent advances do spread through the economy. Rostow's five stages are: (1) Traditional society, (2) Preconditions for take-off, (3) Take-off, (4) Drive to maturity, and (5) Age of High mass consumption.

Stage 1 - Traditional Society. Traditional societies are marked by their pre-Newtonian understanding and use of technology. Attitudes, behavior and organization are static – resource allocation and productive activities follow traditional patterns based on agriculture. Production is labor-intensive and incomes are close to subsistence.

Stage 2 - Preconditions for take-off. Rostow distinguished between two cases – Britain, the first industrial country, and other countries which followed the path pioneered by Britain.

> "The preconditions for take-off were initially developed . . in Western Europe of the late seventeenth and early eighteenth centuries as the insights of modern science began to be translated into new production functions in both agriculture and industry, in a setting given dynamism by the lateral expansion of world markets and the international competition for them. . . . . Among the Western European states, Britain, favored by geography, natural resources, trading possibilities, social and political structure, was the first to develop fully the preconditions for take-off. . . . . The more general case in modern history, however, saw the stage of preconditions arise not endogenously but from some external intrusion by more advanced societies."

More specific elements in the preconditions seem to be a rise in secular education, increasing specialization in production, improvement in agriculture and in transport infrastructure, the emergence of an entrepreneurial class, the beginnings of capital mobilization (the establishment of banks and currency) and an increase in investment.

Stage 3 – Take-off. Here, "Growth becomes its normal condition. Compound interest becomes built, as it were, into its habits and institutional structure." Growth is led by a small number of industries and is concentrated in a small number of regions within the country. This growth is probably in manufacturing. This growth reflects the interaction of demand and supply. New capital and new technology is employed to produce certain goods more efficiently but there has to be a demand for these goods.

> "The stages-of-growth also require, however, that elasticities of demand be taken into account, and that this familiar concept be widened; for these rapid growth phases in the sectors derive not merely from the discontinuity of production functions but also

> from high price- or income-elasticities of demand. Leading sectors are determined not merely by the changing flow of technology and the changing willingness of entrepreneurs to accept available innovations: they are also partially determined by those types of demand which have exhibited high elasticity with respect to price, income, or both."

Feedback loops reinforce and spread growth. Profits from the expanding industries are invested so capacity continues to expand. Rostow sees productive investment increasing from less than 5% to more than 10% of national income. Rising incomes are then spent, stimulating the growth of other new industries. Growth spreads over industries and regions. The new class of entrepreneurs expands while political and social institutions change to accommodate change and the new creators of wealth. Take-off occurs when industry-led growth becomes common and society is driven by economic processes and not by traditions.

Stage 4 - Drive to Maturity. Rostow characterizes the drive to maturity as:

> "After take-off there follows a long interval of sustained if fluctuating progress, as the now regularly growing economy drives to extend modern technology over the whole front of its economic activity."
>
> "Formally, we can define maturity as the stage in which an economy demonstrates the capacity to move beyond the original industries which powered its take-off and to absorb and to apply efficiently over a very wide range of its resources - if not the whole range - the most advanced fruits of (then) modern technology. This is the stage in which an economy demonstrates that it has the technological and entrepreneurial skills to produce not everything, but anything that it chooses to produce."

The economy changes now on a broad front, incomes and wages increase, and living standards improve across the board.

Stage 5 - High Mass Consumption. The entire society has unprecedented levels of purchasing power. Personal incomes are high, people have the ability to purchase a wide range of goods and services, consumers concentrate on durable goods and on services, and governmental activity expands as collective wants share in the productive abundance.

The nature of government activity also changes:

> "In addition to these economic changes, the society ceased to accept the further extension of modern technology as an overriding objective. It is in this post-maturity stage, for example, that, through the political process, Western societies have chosen to allocate increased resources to social welfare and security. The emergence of the welfare state is one manifestation of a society's moving beyond technical maturity."

Rostow describes and systematizes the growth process followed by the leading industrialized countries. Furthermore, he provides several important insights into how the growth process works.

Rostow stresses the roles of technology and investment but makes it clear other changes in behavior and institutions also are essential. He does not, though, investigate which institutional changes are necessary for growth and which are the result of growth. Nor does he investigate how or why technology and productivity increase. His stages seem to be a mixture of describing the results of growth and searching for the causes of growth.

Perhaps his most important insight was that growth operates at the industry level, not the economy-wide level. Rostow stresses that the take-off to growth is concentrated in a small number of industries and only later, once the transition to growth has been completed, does the economy move forward on a broad front. At the industry level he identifies the vital role of new technology in creating new products or in making existing products cheaper. He identifies the interaction between supply (new technology and more capital leading to lower prices) and demand (increasing due to lower prices and to higher incomes) and saw that growth involves demand and not just production and technology. He also considers the feedback loops whereby growth in these leading industries spreads to the rest of the economy.

However, the development of growth theory had started on a different direction by the time Rostow's book was published. This new direction stressed mathematical elegance rather than a concern with the causes and mechanics of growth. Rostow's work passed out of, or perhaps never got into, the mainstream of economic thought.

7.9 Modern growth theory

7.9.1 Frank Ramsey

Frank Ramsey (1928), a mathematical philosopher at Cambridge University, was the first to formulate a mathematical model of economic growth. Ramsey applied a one-sector model to the question of optimal behavior – what was the optimal consumption/saving plan over an infinite decision horizon?

Ramey's approach can be expressed as follows. Output of the single good at any time is a function of capital stock and labor input at that time; output is split between consumption and investment; income is split between consumption and saving; therefore investment is equal to saving; the change in capital stock is investment less depreciation. This will model economic growth once the time sequence of the consumption/saving split is determined.

Ramsey approached the saving choice through utility maximization: households choose their savings plan so as to optimize their utility. Ramsey assumed that utility was bounded above (which is needed for there to be a determinate solution to the infinite-horizon optimization problem) at a "bliss" level. He then formulated the decision problem as choosing savings behavior so as to minimize the present value of the shortfall between actual utility and the bliss level.

This model was solved through the calculus of variations and yielded a result which came to be called the Ramsey rule – the optimal savings plan is such that the "rate of saving multiplied by the marginal utility of consumption should always equal bliss minus the actual rate of utility enjoyed" (Ramsey, p547). Ramsey's article included an equivalent rule which he attributed to discussions with John Maynard Keynes and which came to be called the Keynes-Ramsey rule - "the marginal utility of consumption falls at a proportionate rate given by the rate of interest" (Ramsey, p546).

Ramsey's interest was in describing household behavior but in doing so he formulated the first modern growth model. However, Ramsey did not investigate the growth properties of the model. Nor, initially, did anyone else. Ramsey's approach lay unrecognized for many years. Perhaps people were too concerned with pressing economic issues – such as the roaring 20s then the Great Depression then World War II. Or, perhaps economists did not understand the use of advanced mathematics in a discipline in which analysis had been verbal or graphical.

It was not until Robert Solow (1956) formulated a simple one sector growth model directed to "explaining" aggregate economic growth that the study of growth moved into the mainstream of economic thought. (Subsequent work in the Ramsey tradition, the so-called "Ramsey-Cass-Koopmans" models, and in the Solow tradition, the so-called "golden rule" and "turnpike" models, did bring some sort of convergence of the two approaches to the question of optimal growth.)

7.9.2 The stylized facts

The efforts of Solow and others in the 1950s to model economic growth were shaped to a considerable extent by a set of "stylized facts", general patterns observed in the records of some countries which have experienced sustained economic growth. For example, Nicholas Kaldor (1957) noted six "remarkable historical constancies revealed by recent empirical investigations". These stylized facts were:

(1) The shares of national income received by labor and capital are roughly constant over long periods of time;

(2) The rate of growth of the capital stock is roughly constant over long periods of time;

(3) The rate of growth of output per worker is roughly constant over long periods of time;

(4) The capital/output ratio is roughly constant over long periods of time;

(5) The rate of return on investment is roughly constant over long periods of time;

(6) Real wages increase over time.

7.9.3 The Solow Growth Model

"Modern growth theory" is based on models following from Robert Solow's 1956 paper. The approach has evolved considerably since Solow's original formulation but this theory retains the Solow view of the world. The expression of the Solow model in the present section draws on that of David Romer (1996). The model today referred to as the Solow model is based on the production function:

$$Y(t) = F(K(t), A(t) \times L(t)) \quad (7.1)$$

where

Y = output in constant prices
K = capital quantity input
L = labor quantity input
A = effectiveness of labor
t = time

$A \times L$ is the effective labor input or labor in effectiveness terms. The level of technology, represented by $A(t)$ is thus labor-augmenting or labor-embodied (also known as Harrod-neutral). Capital-augmenting or capital-embodied technological progress (known as Hicks-neutral progress) is ruled out by this specification. This feature of no capital-augmenting technical progress corresponds to the capital-output ratio ($K(t)/Y(t)$ or K/Y) being constant over time which is consistent with the stylized facts.

The model assumes that capital and effective labor are the only constraints on output so that demand for output is not a constraint nor is the availability of natural resources. All capital and labor inputs are assumed to be used just as aggregate demand is assumed to equal potential supply. The model is not concerned with macroeconomic stability or with the demand side of the economy.

The production function assumes constant returns to scale in its two arguments, capital and effective labor inputs, so:

$$F(c \times K, c \times A \times L) = c \times F(K, A \times L)$$

Using this assumption of constant returns, equation (7.1) can be written with the arguments expressed per unit of effective labor:

$$Y / A \times L = F(K/(A \times L), 1)$$

or $$y(t) = f(k(t)) \qquad (7.2)$$

where $y = Y/(A \times L)$ and $k = K/(A \times L)$.

This production function is assumed to have these features:

(1) $f(0) = 0$ if there are not inputs there is no output;

(2) $f'(k) > 0$ the marginal product of capital per unit of effective labor is positive so the input of more capital causes output to increase. It is assumed also that $\lim_{k \to 0} f'(k) = \infty$ and that $\lim_{k \to \infty} f'(k) = 0$ (the Inada conditions).

(3) $f''(k) < 0$ the marginal product of capital per unit of labor declines as capital per unit of labor increases.

Labor quantity and the level of technology, or labor effectiveness, are assumed to grow at constant rates. In continuous time, these growth assumptions are:

$$L^{\bullet}(t) = n \times L(t) \quad \text{or } L^{\bullet}/L = n$$

$$A^{\bullet}(t) = g \times A(t) \quad \text{or } A^{\bullet}/A = g$$

where n and g are externally given (exogenous) growth rates and a dot next to a variable denotes the time derivative so that, for example, $L^{\bullet}(t) = dL(t)/dt$.

The model assumes that output is divided between consumption and investment (all in constant prices):

$$Y = C + I$$

The fraction of output devoted to investment (or, in this simple model, saved) is constant at an externally given value s (the saving share). Therefore,

$$I(t) = s \times Y(t)$$

and $$C(t) = (1 - s) \times Y(t)$$

Investment adds to the capital stock but at the same time capital depreciates at rate δ. The change in the capital stock is:

$$\begin{aligned} K^{\bullet}(t) &= I(t) - \delta \times K(t) \\ &= s \times Y(t) - \delta \times K(t) \end{aligned}$$

This completes the specification of the model. The next step is to solve for the economic growth path predicted by the model. The model treats the growth of effective labor as given and the investment share in output as given; accordingly, the only things left to determine are the behavior of capital and of output. Furthermore, as the production function links capital and effective labor to output, it is only capital that really emerges from the model. Thus, solving the model boils down to solving for the time behavior of capital, whether K or k. The growth of capital per unit of effective labor is given by:

$$k^{\bullet}(t) = s \times f(k(t)) - (n + g + \delta) \times k(t) \qquad (7.3)$$

This is the fundamental equation of the Solow model. It describes the change over time in capital per unit of effective labor. This change is the net effect of investment during time t which is found as the part of output that is invested, $s \times f(k(t))$, less the capital absorbed in maintaining the capital:labor ratio for an expanding input of effective labor, $(n + g) \times k(t)$, and less the capital lost to depreciation, $\delta \times k(t)$. The investment per unit of effective labor needed to maintain the existing level of capital per unit of effective labor is termed the breakeven level of investment. Equation (7.3) implies that k increases when actual investment exceeds the breakeven level, falls when actual investment is less than breakeven and remains the same when the two are equal.

Figure 7.2 shows actual investment and breakeven investment as functions of k(t). Breakeven investment is a straight line as it is proportional to k(t). The graph of actual investment follows from the model's assumptions about the nature of the production function. As $f(0) = 0$ so the graph starts from the origin. The Inada conditions imply that $f'(0)$ is large so the $s \times f(k)$ line must be steeper than the $(n+g+\delta) \times k(t)$ line for small values of k(t). The assumptions also imply that $f'(k(t))$ falls steadily, ultimately towards zero, as k(t) rises. Therefore, the actual investment line must cross the breakeven investment line from above then continue to increase but at an ever-decreasing rate. The cross-over level of capital per unit of effective labor is denoted by k*. The assumptions ensure that k* exists and is unique.

Figure 7.2 Investment in the Solow model

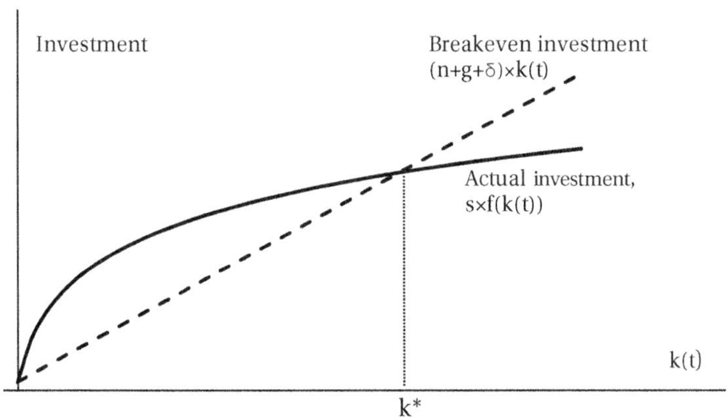

The behavior of $k^{\bullet}(t)$ is shown by means of the phase diagram in Figure 7.3. This shows the implications of the investment components in equation (7.3) and Figure 7.2 in terms of the change in capital per unit of effective labor.

Figure 7.3 Capital dynamics in the Solow model

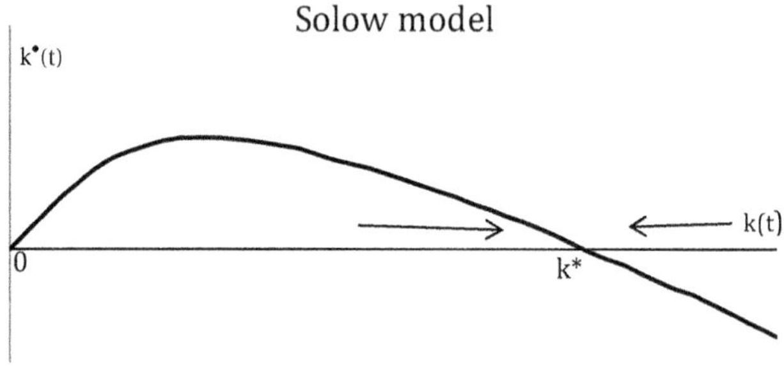

If k(t) is less than k*, actual investment exceeds breakeven investment and is positive; k(t) approaches k*. Similarly for other values of k(t). The implications are that k(t) converges to k* from any starting point and that, once k(t) = k*, it will not move from k*.

The Solow model implies that there is a unique growth path to which the economy will converge. Everything on this path grows at a constant rate – it is a steady path. This steady growth path is consistent with the stylized facts. The crucial growth rates are of total income, Y, which grows at the rate n + g, and income per capita, corresponding to income per unit of labor, Y/L, which grows at rate g. Living standards grow at the externally given rate of increase in labor effectiveness, g, or, in the jargon often surrounding the model, with technical progress.

The share of output saved, or directed to investment, does not affect the balanced growth rate. However, an increase in the saving share will raise the level of output between the two corresponding growth paths. From equation (3), an increase in the saving share when the economy is initially on a balanced growth path, will mean that $k^{\bullet}(t) > 0$. The economy will then converge to a new balanced growth path with higher

k^*. Growth rates on this higher balanced growth path will be the same as before but the levels of output, consumption and capital will be higher. An increase in the saving rate will increase the rate of economic growth in the short run but not in the long run, once the economy is on its new balanced growth path. From a policy point of view, investment will not buy economic growth although it will buy a short term acceleration in growth. From the point of view of understanding actual economic growth (at least as represented by the Solow model), more investment is not the cause of economic growth.

Although balanced growth rates are not affected by the saving/investment rate, s, the levels of output and consumption are affected. This gives rise to the question: for which saving rate is consumption per worker highest? The consumption maximizing saving rate has come to be called the "golden rule". Balanced growth will satisfy the golden rule when the capital/labor ratio has a particular value which can be found from the features and parameters of the model. On the golden rule growth path, the competitive interest rate, which is the marginal product of capital less the depreciation rate, is $n + g$, which is equal to the rate of growth of output. Whether any particular specification of the model has a balanced growth path that satisfies the golden rule depends on the numerical features of the model. There is no mechanism to drive the balanced growth path to the golden rule path if the two paths are different.

The Solow model has been extended to allow for household behavior in the form of the consumption/saving choice. This has the effect of modeling the saving rate rather than having it fixed externally. Modeling the saving rate involves defining household welfare, as a function of consumption, then allowing households to plan their consumption over time so as to maximize the present value of the future time stream of welfare. The growth patterns predicted from this class of model have been termed "optimal economic growth".

The optimal growth path with endogenous saving behavior has an associated balanced growth path with the same features as in the simpler form of the Solow model; in particular, output increases at rate $n + g$ while income per worker and consumption per worker increase at rate g. This optimal growth path coincides with the earlier golden rule path if the household discount rate is zero. If the discount rate is positive, probably a more likely situation, there is less saving so the balanced growth path is below the golden rule path.

The economy can have an initial position which may be away from the balanced growth path but the optimal growth path converges to the balanced path. If the planning horizon is finite, the optimal growth path moves along the balanced path and then, late in the planning period, departs from the balanced path to move to the target terminal position. If the planning horizon is infinite, the optimal path converges to and then travels along the balanced growth path. This dynamic behavior is illustrated in Figure 7.4. This is known as "turnpike" behavior – regardless of the starting and finishing positions, the optimal growth path always involves getting onto, moving along, then if need be getting off, the turnpike, the balanced growth path. There is only one optimal long run growth path for the economy.

Figure 7.4 Turnpike behavior of the Solow model

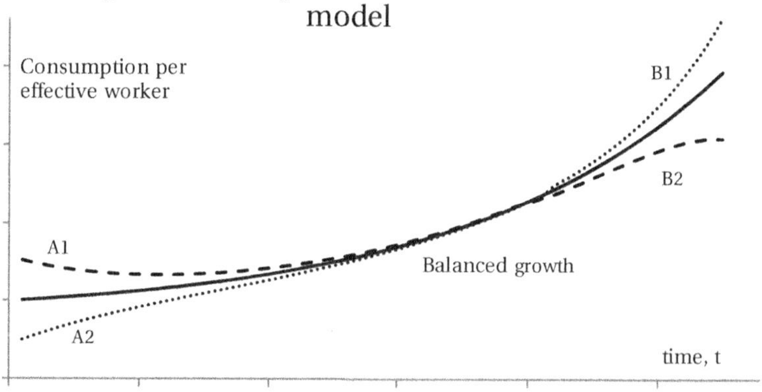

The labor/leisure choice can also be brought into the model. Optimal growth in this case has households making two types of decisions; the first involves the time pattern of consumption, which is the saving decision, while the second is the labor/leisure decision, which determines the supply of labor. Households make these decisions in order to maximize the present value of their future stream of welfare (where welfare results from consumption of goods and consumption of leisure). The resulting growth path has the same properties as the growth path in the simpler Solow model – an optimal growth path exists and, for long time horizons, it exhibits turnpike behavior (the optimal path converges to and travels along a balanced growth path). The turnpike has the usual features; in particular, output grows at rate n + g while income and consumption per worker each grow at rate g.

This completes the development of the Solow model in its basic form. It is an elegant theoretical framework which provides insights into economic growth in this stylized world (sometimes referred to as "Solovia"). The main conclusions from this class of model can be summarized as follows.

(1) Existence. There is a balanced long term growth path.

(2) Uniqueness. There is only one balanced growth path. Output grows on this path at the constant rate n + g while output per unit of labor, typically interpreted as income per capita, grows at rate g.

(3) Stability. The economy converges to this balanced growth path. With household decision-making, the economy exhibits turnpike behavior – the growth path always moves towards then travels along the same balanced growth path.

(4) Optimality. The balanced growth path is the optimal path in terms of household welfare.

(5) Investment and capital. The balanced growth path has a constant capital:output ratio and constant capital per effective worker. Balanced growth rates do not depend on saving/investment behavior although an increase in the investment share will move the economy to a higher growth path and, during the transition period, will increase the growth rate.

(6) Source of economic growth. The long term rate of growth in output per worker is equal to g, the growth rate of labor

effectiveness. Thus long term growth depends entirely on increasing labor effectiveness, what has come to be referred to as technical progress. g is external to the model.

7.9.4 Extensions to the Solow approach

The core Solow model concluded that increasing productivity, rather than more capital and labor, is the source of long run economic growth - the long run growth rate in output per worker is equal to g, the rate of increase in labor effectiveness.

Theoretical work then shifted to try to make the model more general and in particular to explore the source of productivity advance. Capital began to receive more attention with modeling to allow the effectiveness of capital to increase and then to allow for human as well as physical capital. Subsequently, attention shifted to so called "endogenous technical change" or "endogenous growth theory", trying to model the technology term A(t) - to explain the crucial but fixed, exogenous g parameter of the core Solow model.

Endogenous saving

Ramsey's early (1928) paper featured a representative household formulating a saving plan to optimize utility over an infinite horizon. This approach was extended by David Cass (1965) and Tjalling Koopmans (1966), resulting in the Ramsey-Cass-Koopmans class of models. These models incorporate exogenous technical change, the A variable of the Solow model. If A increases at rate g, there exists a steady state growth path with per capita income increasing at rate g. This provides a behavioral interpretation for savings in Solow-type models.

Learning by doing

Observed productivity improvements in several industries show that labor effectiveness often increases as a function of cumulative output. This has been termed "learning by doing", following the initial work by Kenneth Arrow (1962). Learning by doing has been incorporated into the Solow model by driving labor effectiveness off of the total capital stock with the growth rate $A^{\bullet}(t) = \varphi \times K^{\bullet}(t)$. If φ is less than one, which appears to be the most plausible case, there is a balanced growth path for Y at a rate which is a function of n, the rate of growth of population.

Capital-embodied technical change

Capital-embodied technical change has new capital goods being more effective than existing capital. The improvement in effectiveness proceeds at a constant rate. The capital stock existing at any point in time, therefore, is made up of units of different vintages, each vintage having its own effectiveness. Solow (1960), in his original capital-embodiment paper, derived an aggregate production function in which the quantity of capital K(t) in the simple model is replaced by an index of effective capital input. Edmund Phelps (1962) constructed a growth model with both capital-embodied and disembodied technical progress. This economy converges to a steady growth path whose growth rate depends on both embodied and disembodied rates of improvement. As in the initial Solow model, the steady state growth rate is not influenced by the share of output devoted to saving and investment although the level of the growth path is higher for higher saving shares.

These vintage models assume that the capital:labor ratio can be varied, even for the existing capital stock. A more realistic assumption may be the so called "putty-clay" world in which new capital can be designed for any capital:labor ratio (it is flexible, like putty) but once produced it is locked into its particular ratio (it is inflexible, like baked clay). (See, for example, L. Johansen (1959) and Robert Solow (1962).) However, C.J. Bliss (1968) showed that steady growth in a putty-clay model is possible if and only if technical progress is labor-augmenting at a constant rate. This suggests that the capital-embodied form is at best a partial generalization of the initial Solow model.

Human capital

Modern economies are characterized by considerable human capital, the value of the abilities and skills which result from the learning and experience of workers. Indeed, the total value of human capital appears to be of similar magnitude to the total value of physical capital while income to human capital appears to be similar to income to physical capital and possibly larger than income to unskilled labor. It seems important, therefore, to introduce human capital into models of economic growth.

The Solow model can be extended to cover human as well as physical capital. Two examples are Robert Lucas (1988) and Gregory Mankiw, David Romer and David Weil (1992). Production now becomes a function of human capital, physical capital and unskilled labor; investment is directed to the two different types of capital at fixed investment shares; and technology still augments the input of unskilled labor. This economy converges to a balanced path. The key features of this growth path are the same as in the simple Solow model - the growth in output per worker is g, the rate of increase in labor effectiveness and an increase in the investment rate, for either human or physical capital, leads to a higher growth path but does not change the steady state growth rate.

Endogenous technical change

Endogenous technical change expresses labor effectiveness as a function of other variables in the model. Paul Romer (1986) created a model in which the level of labor effectiveness, A, follows from the stock of capital. (This is an example of the so called "AK" models.) This introduces a complexity as firms carrying out research generate external effects – advances in technology from which everyone benefits. If there are constant total (internal and external) returns to capital there is a steady growth rate which depends on other parameters in the model such as the rate of time preference and the size of the economy (represented by the number of firms).

More general models were then developed, for example by Paul Romer (1990), Gene Grossman and Elharan Helpman (1991), and Philippe Aghion and Peter Howitt (1992). A(t) here is "produced" by the input of capital and/or labor. This is seen as a proxy for productivity improvements flowing from research and development activity. The economy now has two sectors, one producing finished goods and services, Y(t), and the other producing improvements in labor effectiveness. Available capital and labor are allocated between these two sectors. This economy has a steady state growth path at rate g where g is now a function of other parameters in the model. This g increases with the productivity of research and with the size of the economy, and decreases with the rate of time preference. The balanced growth path is not affected by the share of capital which is invested nor is it affected by the fractions of capital and labor devoted to R&D although these parameters do affect the level of the growth path. The nature of these conclusions is similar to the properties of the initial Solow model.

7.9.5 Assessment of Solow-type models

The theory of economic growth based on Solow-type models is a magnificent intellectual construct. It is an elegant framework, encompassing the main aggregate indicators of economic growth and giving the impression of great precision. But, how well does the model explain the origins and processes of economic growth in the real world?

The central conclusion of these models is that the essence of economic growth lies in productivity growth rather than in more inputs of basic resources. We now examine the Solow model in which economic growth (in Y/L) comes entirely from increases in labor effectiveness, the A(t) term. A(t) is external to the Solow model, its numerical values or numerical features are entered into the model by assumption. The model can be made to fit the data by selecting A(t) appropriately but this means that the model "explains" growth only in a tautological sense. The model can describe after the fact the growth performance of a country but cannot predict growth other than by assuming that previous trends will continue. Crucially, the model does not explain – it does not have or cover causal mechanisms which can account, before the fact, for the level and growth in A(t). Even with endogenous technical change, the growth rate g is a mechanical function of other parameters in the model and these may or may not have any relationship to the practical features of the economy.

Many presentations of Solow-type models have viewed g, or increases in labor effectiveness, as technical progress. However, our review of actual growth suggests that technical progress is complex and certainly is not a simple labor-augmenting process. Innovation in economic growth is of two kinds – there are new products for which there are large potential markets and there are efficiency improvements in the production of existing products. Demand for new products pulls the economy forwards; productivity improvements in existing production allow income per capita to increase and also release resources to allow the growth of the new industries. These changes take place in a complex way at the industry level, not at the economy-wide level. Innovation in successful new products has nothing really to do with improving productive efficiency, it has everything to do with coming up with new products which consumers want to buy. And, improvement in existing industries appears to have more to do with management and capital, physical capital and human capital, than with simply making labor more productive.

Similarly, there has been a widespread tendency to associate g with science and research. The driver of growth is the creation of (a sequence of) new products for which there are huge potential demands. These new products are innovative but the nature of the innovation is that they satisfy a (large potential) demand which was previously not being catered to, not that they necessarily follow from research. These new products may have something to do with research but are much more likely to have much more to do with practical engineering and design and then with good marketing. Productivity improvement in established industries similarly is essential for growth. Although there may be some research-led process improvements, most process improvements appear to be incremental improvements to existing processes, led by managers and engineers rather than by fundamental researchers.

We turn now to a basic scientific test of a theory – does it generate practical predictions which square with the facts and, if it does, does it provide the best explanation of the facts of all the theories which square with the facts?

Solow-type models conclude that a country cannot invest its way to long term economic growth. All versions of the model say that the long term balanced growth rate is independent of the share of income which is invested even though the level of income on the growth path is directly related to the investment share. This prediction corresponds to what was learnt so painfully by the Soviet Union and by Mao Zedong's China – a government can force investment but cannot force long term growth. It is possible, though, that a sufficient explanation of the economic failure of the Soviet Union and of Mao Zedong's China lay in the adverse incentive structures of those countries. It is not necessarily the case that the economic failure of those countries demonstrates the veracity of Solow growth models.

The economic growth literature has considered the question of convergence as an empirical test of Solow models. Convergence refers to actual growth paths approaching the steady state growth path for the country. Tests of convergence have looked at whether growth rates of lower income countries are more rapid than growth rates of high income countries. There is little evidence of convergence in the basic Solow model (see, for example, Robert Summers and Alan Heston (1991)). However, a Solow-type model which includes human capital generates cross-country results which are consistent with convergence as predicted by the model (see, for example, Mankiw et al (1992)).

This test for convergence provides some practical support for Solow-type models. However, this does not appear to be definitive support as there could be a different explanation for the more rapid growth of low income countries. This alternative possible explanation is the operation of comparative advantage - low income countries import capital goods and management services from and export low value manufactures to the high income countries. The exporting countries grow rapidly as they penetrate the large markets in the high income countries and then move on to export slightly higher value goods. As their advantage in manufactures diminishes, their growth rate slows, converging towards the growth rate of their high income markets. This is similar to catch-up growth discussed in other chapters, the process by which, for example, several east Asian countries have achieved rapid growth over the past half century.

We now look at the growth predictions of Solow-type models and ask whether these are realistic in terms of the experience of the United States. Table 7.1 shows the predicted growth rates for a steady growth path for an economy calibrated to the U.S. The data is from Jorgenson (2005); we calibrate a Solow-type model to this data by using the data values for the two basic, and exogenous, growth rates, n and g. The other growth rates in Solow steady state growth follow from n and g.

Table 7.1 Growth on the balanced growth path

	Solow model		Actual	Difference
Y	n + g	2.58	3.46	34%
Y/L	g	1.36	2.24	64%
Y/K	0	0	0.17	nm
K/L	g	1.36	2.07	52%
K	n + g	2.58	3.29	27%
L	n	1.22	1.22	nm

Inputs of labor (L) and capital (K) are of quantities; n is the growth rate of input of Labor quantity; g is growth not due to input quantities; nm is not meaningful.

The final column of this Table shows the relative differences between the predicted and actual growth rates. The growth difference for Y/K is not meaningful because the reference point is 0; for L the difference is not meaningful because the two rates are the same by assumption. The differences which can be tested are all considerable. (The differences are still larger if the model is formulated in terms of the input of factor services rather than factor quantities.)

The differences are so large that it is difficult to think that the economy implied by the Solow model is consistent with the facts. Another way of looking at this is to suspect that the "stylized facts" underlying the specification of the Solow model are not really the facts that characterize the United States economy.

These Solow-type models operate at the economy-wide level. Their conclusion is that productivity improvement is at the heart of the growth process. However, they have not really delved into the mechanics of the growth process such as the changing structure of a growth economy and what drives growth. Productivity advance permits growth but does it drive growth? There is a need to get down to a more detailed level where decisions are made about spending, production, new products and new processes. This suggests that an industry-level approach to growth would be better suited to examining the growth mechanisms. Also, it suggests that demand and spending need to be brought into the picture. After all, spending comes first – Keynes taught us that production responds to demand rather than creates demand. The theory of growth would gain from considering demand and supply, spending and production, as equal parts of the broad picture rather than focussing just on production.

Our conclusion is that Solow models represent a huge step in looking at economic growth but that they are just the first steps, not the last word. The models fit actual growth paths by assumption rather than by explanation. We need to extend these models if we are to gain a better understanding of the causes and mechanisms of growth. Two particularly promising directions to extend the conventional theory are (1) to operate at the industry level, arriving at GDP through aggregation rather than as the sole level of analysis, and (2) to consider demand and bring spending onto center stage alongside production.

7.10 Growth accounting

7.10.1 Growth accounting

The Solow representation of the economy can be applied to measure the sources of growth – how much came from labor input, how much from capital input and how much from everything else, the residual.

This residual in the growth accounting context is Total Factor Productivity (TFP).

In a simple approach to growth accounting, such as used by Kendrick (1961 and 1973), the data or growth variables are the number of workers or, preferably, hours worked (denoted by L), capital stock (K), GDP in constant prices (Y), population (Pop) and factor input (I, where I is the composite of labor and capital inputs). Using a simple, Cobb-Douglas production function with constant returns to scale we can indicate the growth of factor input as:

$$gr(I) = b \times gr(K) + (1-b) \times gr(L)$$

where gr( ) denotes the growth rate and b is the elasticity of output to capital. Everything else follows by arithmetic. Total Factor Productivity is the growth residual so:

$$gr(TFP) = gr(Y) - gr(I)$$

$$gr(Y) = gr(TFP) + b \times gr(K) + (1-b) \times gr(L)$$

$$gr(Y/L) = gr(TFP) + b \times gr(K/L)$$

and growth in GDP per capita is:

$$gr(Y/Pop) = gr(TFP) + b \times gr(K/L) + gr(L/Pop)$$

The economic growth rate depends on the growth of productivity, increases in capital per input of labor (the capital:labor ratio) and changes in hours worked per person. Capital and labor in this simple approach refer to quantities; the quality increases in these inputs are subsumed into productivity advance.

This approach can decompose the actual growth in production into its sources. Table 7.2 does this for growth in the United States since World War II. This Table is based on the results of Jorgenson (2005).

Table 7.2 Growth accounting for the U.S., 1948 - 2002

	Growth rate	Contribution to growth	Share of growth
Capital stock per person hour	2.05%	0.85%	39%
Total Productivity	1.36%	1.36%	63%
GDP per person hour	2.21%	2.21%	102%
Labor hours per capita	-0.04%	-0.04%	-2%
GDP per capita	2.17%	2.17%	100%

Source: Data from Jorgenson (2005).

GDP per capita grew at 2.2% a year; this was enabled by more capital per worker (which contributed 0.85 percentage points of this growth) and productivity growth (contributing 1.36 percentage points); a reduction in hours worked per person subtracted slightly from the overall growth rate. Total productivity in this Table incorporates both TFP and the effects of improved qualities of capital and labor inputs. Income growth, in essence, came from more capital and increasing productivity.

7.10.2 John Kendrick

John Kendrick carried out a pioneering growth accounting for the United States. Kendrick's method was straightforward, measuring just input quantities and calculating TFP as the residual, analogous to the simple procedure set out in the previous section. Kendrick's results are summarized in Table 7.3.

Table 7.3 Kendrick's growth accounting, 1899 - 1966

	Growth rate	Contribution to growth	Share of growth
Labor quantity	1.5%	1.1%	32%
Capital quantity	2.6%	0.6%	19%
Factor input	1.8%	1.8%	51%
Total factor productivity	1.7%	1.7%	49%
Output	3.5%	3.5%	100%

Sources: Data from Kendrick (1961) and (1973).

These results show that fully half the growth in GDP came from unknown sources – the residual or TFP. They also suggest that capital has an important but secondary role in growth. Kendrick's results suggest that the Solow approach is not particularly effective in revealing the sources or nature of growth as 71% of the growth in GDP per worker comes from TFP, which is unexplained.

7.10.3 Dale Jorgenson

Dale Jorgenson has led the recent development of growth accounting. Jorgenson has developed theoretically well founded procedures for measurement and aggregation. Jorgenson separates capital and labor input into quantity and quality components with overall input being the input of effective services, the combination of both quantity and quality. Input qualities therefore are tracked explicitly, not incorporated with everything else in the residual.

Jorgenson (2005) presents results for a growth accounting for the United States for the years 1948 – 2002. These results are summarized in Table 7.4.

Table 7.4 Contributions to U.S. growth, 1948 - 2002

	Growth rate		Contribution to GDP growth		
	% pa	% pa	% pa	% pa	% of total
GDP	3.46		3.46		100%
Input of labor services	1.81		1.05		30%
Quantity		1.22		0.71	
Quality		0.58		0.34	
Input of capital services	4.13		1.75		51%
Quantity		3.29		1.39	
Quality		0.84		0.36	
Total Factor Productivity	0.67		0.67		19%
Input quantities			2.10		61%
Input qualities			0.69		20%
Total Factor Productivity			0.67		19%

Source: Data from Jorgenson (2005).

GDP growth averaging 3.46% a year was generated by more input services (2.80%) and an increase in Total Factor Productivity of 0.67%. Taking both quantity and quality into account, 81% of economic growth came from more inputs. Productivity increases were important but not overwhelming. Rising input quantities generated 61% of GDP growth while input qualities accounted for 20%. Capital, quantity together with quality, was the principal source of growth, accounting for 51% of the total.

Jorgenson's accounts give a more thorough summary of the growth record and how this growth was sustained in terms of inputs and productivity. His analysis of labor quality and capital quality has been able to reduce substantially the growth residual, attributed simply to productivity growth, in Solow-type models. The residual accounted for just under half of GDP growth in Kendrick's accounts; Jorgenson has reduced this to less than one fifth.

7.10.4 Assessment of growth accounting

Growth accounting helps clarify what sustained the growth in production. But it is based on supply; it does not ask why these goods and services were produced. This is looking backwards at the results of growth and how final outputs were produced; it does not reveal the causes of growth.

This is like looking at a business' accounts and trying to work out why the business performed well. For example, the Coca-Cola Company (see Coca-Cola Annual Report for 2012) earned $9 billion for shareowners but the accounts do not show how it generated these earnings. In a mechanical sense the company obtained revenues and paid expenses as set out in the accounts. But, these financial results do not reveal that Coca-Cola has developed new products and sophisticated marketing techniques which have created substantial value for its labor and capital.

Just like a business' accounts, growth accounting records the results but does not explain the causes of growth. In fact, much of the growth is due to the unexplained residual although Jorgenson has succeeded in measuring the increases in labor and capital quality and in allowing for the changing mix of production, greatly reducing the unexplained residual in production growth. Growth accounting, like Solow-type models, provides insights into how production was sustained but does not consider why production increased or what was produced. We must look elsewhere for the drivers of economic growth and the mechanisms of economic growth.

7.11 Economic theory in the world

Economic theory tends to follow changes and problems in the real world - theory is developed to try to understand these events and, possibly, to help resolve these practical problems.

Adam Smith, the founder of economics, was trying to get people's thinking straight on the very nature of economics. He saw that the objective of business and government commercial policy should be production and income, not the holding of treasure. Smith was writing in 1776, as the Industrial Revolution was taking hold. He provided an intellectual justification for industry, markets and the pursuit of income. Possibly due to Smith but more probably due to the irresistible force of human initiative in a capitalist system, Britain let the free market reign and economic growth proceeded at an accelerating pace.

In Britain after the Napoleonic Wars, international trade emerged as a contentious political issue. Tariffs were forcing up the price of food imports, helping landowners but harming the workers. David Ricardo's treatise appeared in 1817, making the intellectual case for free trade. But, the issue was decided by politics rather than by dispassionate analysis when, after decades of debate, the Corn Laws were repealed in the 1840s. In the following half century Britain reached the zenith of its economic success. Under a regime of free trade, Britain exported its textiles and machinery while importing foodstuffs; trade-related industries such as shipping, insurance and banking also thrived.

The next stage in economic thought was the "marginal revolution", led by British thinkers such as Alfred Marshall (1890). These developments led to the concept of demand and supply, the partial equilibrium model which remains at the heart of microeconomics. These developments extended the understanding of the market system and buttressed support for the market and the unrestricted capitalism which drove the British economy through the Industrial Revolution and to its height in the years before World War I.

The first half of the 20th century was dominated by conflict and instability. World War I involved unprecedented human losses. The Great Depression involved unprecedented economic losses. Economic recovery was spurred by Franklin Delano Roosevelt's New Deal policies but it was only with World War II that the United States returned to full employment. Post war reconstruction led Europe and Japan back to full employment. Keynes' theory, published in 1936, provided the intellectual framework needed to understand macroeconomic instability. In the 1950s and 1960s governments began to use this theory to try to promote stability. Friedman's theories led to the development of active monetary policies; these were deployed beginning in the 1980s in the pursuit of stability. The result has been a more steady (than historically) growth path over the past 60 years.

With this new era of economic expansion, interest turned to trying to understand economic growth. Development economics, with low income countries trying to get onto their own growth paths, heightened this interest. And the importance of growth was further accentuated by the Cold War, the struggle for supremacy between the Soviet Union and the United States, where economic strength was the basis both of military power and of political popularity.

The course of events clarified economic thinking. The Cold War ended - the Soviets lost. Centrally planned economies stagnated while the market economies of the West surged ahead. A number of countries in Africa and South America started to grow after governments stabilized their economies and allowed markets to operate. And, several east Asian countries moved onto rapid growth trajectories by producing manufactured commodities for export to the high income countries. Economic growth in the high income countries continued, led by the United States.

Research into growth theory took two different paths. The process path described the growth experience of the high income countries and tried to identify the structures and processes involved. Kuznets and Rostow followed this approach. The mathematical approach, led by Solow, sought to capture the growth process in simple equations involving aggregate economic indicators. The mathematical approach soon gained the upper hand; this approach became the standard theory of economic growth.

There is no question but that actual economic developments have prompted the development of economic theories. But the reverse path, of economic theory changing the real word, has been less well travelled. Adam Smith, Ricardo, the development of neoclassical economics and even growth theory have not lead to any specific real world successes. The main lesson from the real world has been that markets work. The development of theory has provided intellectual support and justification for the market economy. The exception concerns economic stability – the theories inspired by Keynes and Friedman have led to governments achieving some success in avoiding major macroeconomic instability.

Economic growth has continued in the leaders – Britain, the United States and what Maddison (2006b) calls "western offshoots". Some other countries in east Asia and South America have achieved rapid growth. But these achievements owe much to the operation of markets and international trade and apparently little to growth theory. The Soviet Union and Maoist China provided case studies of how not to grow – by denying the use of markets – at great cost to their citizens. The undoubted economic growth successes of the past century have not achieved their success by using growth theory.

One reason for the lack of practical effect of growth theory may be that established theory, typified by the Solow model, essentially describes the results of growth. Established theory does not come to grips with the causes of growth. Growth theory is still searching for foundations in practicality and trying to understanding the process of economic growth.

Chapter 8
The mechanics of growth

8.1 Breaking through constraints

Economic growth, the sustained increase in GDP per capita, started in England in the first half of the 18th century. Britain led growth for some 150 years until the United States took over leadership around the turn of the 20th century; the United States has continued to lead growth since then.

Before England showed the way, several countries had experienced increasing incomes but their expansion had been halted when they ran into constraints they could not overcome. Ancient Rome grew wealthy by conquering neighboring lands and expropriating their surplus production and population, but Rome's income growth ended when its territorial expansion ended. Spain grew wealthy on the basis of monetary expansion but its income growth ended when its resources became fully employed. The Netherlands exploited its superior (shipbuilding, navigation and trading) technology to build an international trading empire but its expansion stopped when it had saturated its particular markets. China, for centuries the most successful nation, advanced by applying its superior (organizational and agricultural) technologies to new lands but each expansion led to a Malthusian equilibrium wherein rising population used up the additional production.

The central feature of the world before Britain's Industrial Revolution was the inability to break through an economic constraint which had become binding. Production and incomes would increase until a production constraint or market saturation was reached; growth then stopped as production was held in check by this constraint and incomes just bounced along this ceiling. Incomes could be higher than previously or in other countries, such as with the Netherlands, as a major new technology or set of resources was exploited but income growth ceased when this exploitation had reached its full extent. Britain's achievement was to break through successive production and market constraints. For the first time in history, expansion continued as one constraint after another was reached and overcome. The United States took over the economic leadership in the 20th century and it too has seen a succession of new industries and production improvements, breaking through successive constraints on demand and production, pulling the economy ever upwards.

Something happened in 18th century Britain and later in the United States which allowed these countries to break through growth constraints. Breaking through constraints in consumption and production subsequently became almost routine. To understand growth we need to work out how and why this happened.

8.2 Industry growth

Although economic growth is conventionally viewed at the aggregate level, such as in terms of GDP per capita, economic processes actually operate at the level of individual markets. Markets are where consumers and producers come together and transactions take place. These markets are the highest level at which economic activity can be observed and measured directly. Aggregate expenditure, production and aggregate income are artificial concepts even though they can be calculated as the summation of individual transactions.

The most useful level at which to consider economic growth is the industry. Although an industry is an aggregate of individual transactions these transaction are closely related. Suppliers in an industry make similar products, have similar production activities, similar production technologies and similar sales processes. On the other side of these markets, customers will be expressing similar needs. Changes take place at the industry level and growth takes place at the industry level. Therefore, we look to individual industries in our investigation into economic growth.

Different industries perform in very different ways. In particular, the growth features of different industries can be vastly different. Table 8.1 shows the growth rates for constant dollar GDP originating in United States industries. Although these data go only through 1966 they do cover the decades when the United States became well established on a path of sustained growth, the same years which saw the great industrial expansion of the United States.

Table 8.1 Growth of U.S. Industries, 1899 - 1966

Average growth rates of value added in constant dollars

Lumber and products	0.8%
Farm segment	0.9%
Leather and products	1.2%
Mining	2.6%
Textile mill products	2.8%
Beverages	3.0%
Contract construction	3.1%
Trade	3.3%
Finance and services	3.3%
Food and kindred products	3.3%
Tobacco products	3.3%
Apparel and related products	3.4%
Furniture and fixtures	3.4%
Transportation	3.4%
Economy, GDP	**3.5%**
Primary metal industries	3.7%
Stone, clay, glass products	3.8%
Machinery, nonelectric	4.3%
Printing and publishing	4.4%
Instruments	4.8%
Fabricated metal products	4.8%
Paper and allied products	5.0%
Petroleum and coal products	5.9%
Transportation equipment	6.4%
Chemicals and allied products	6.5%
Communications and public utilities	7.4%
Rubber products	7.5%
Electric machinery	7.6%

Sources: Data from Kendrick (1961) and (1973).

Although the economy grew at an average of 3.5% a year, not all industries grew at this rate. In fact, there was a wide range of growth rates. For the 27 industries in the Table growth rates ranged from less than 1% to more than 7%. These different growth rates lead to large differences in industry size. For example, growth for 70 years at the slowest rate, for Lumber products, means that the industry ends up 73% larger than it started while growth for 70 years at the rate for Electric machinery increases the size of the industry by a factor of 173, a change 100 times larger.

Most industries grew at around the overall economic growth rate of 3.5% a year – 15 of the 27 industries grew at rates between 2.5 and 4.5%, or the average growth rate of 3.5% plus or minus 1%; 18 grew at the GDP growth rate plus or minus one standard deviation. But some industries grew much more rapidly. Six of the 27 industries grew more rapidly than one standard deviation above the GDP growth rate, or more than 5.3% a year, over the 67 years covered in the Table.

The vastly different behavior of different industries reinforces our view that understanding economic growth requires us to approach growth at the industry level where all these spending and production changes are taking place.

Something causes a few industries to show sustained, rapid growth while more industries grow more or less at the average rate. Understanding economic growth requires us to understand why different industries grow at different rates and, in particular, why some industries grow rapidly over long periods of time.

8.3 Different types of industry growth

All main industries were shown in Table 8.1 although the goods producing industries are more specific or detailed than the service industries. We can separate the 27 industries into three categories.

(1) Leading or growth. Six industries grew rapidly, at more than one standard deviation above the average rate. Three of these had large sales into final demand (final demand comprises

finished goods and services for consumers, investment, governments or export). These were transportation equipment, electrical machinery, and communications and utilities. Final demand industries purchase inputs from other industries, the intermediate goods industries. Those intermediate industries supplying the rapidly growing final industries themselves experienced rapid growth. For example, transportation equipment pulled petroleum products and rubber products along rapid growth paths. Chemicals also grew rapidly in part by supplying the growth industries. The rapid growth industries are those industries associated either directly or indirectly with new growth products supplying final demand.

(2) Mainstream. Established industries tend to grow in line with the overall economy. These are industries such as food, beverages, apparel, furniture and transportation. These appear to be pulled along by the general rise in incomes and spending.

(3) Decline. Then there were a few slow growth industries, industries such as lumber, farms and leather goods. These industries face saturated or even declining markets and therefore grow only slowly. They are in relative decline although not necessarily in absolute decline.

This growth structure is summarized in Table 8.2. This Table shows the three types of industry; it also shows the relative size of each type. The sizes are estimates for 1938, close to the mid-point of the 1899 – 1966 time coverage of Kendrick's data. The growth rates are from the previous Table. The growth categories are defined by the GDP growth rate plus or minus one standard deviation. By far the largest part of the economy, some 90%, falls into the middle category, growing broadly in line with the economy as a whole. The leading, or rapid growth industries, occupy rather a small part of the economy – only 5% of value added is in these rapid growth industries. Similarly, declining industries account for an even smaller part of the economy.

Table 8.2 Industry growth structure

	Growth rate	Growth rate	Size, % of GDP
Leading	> average + 1×SD	>5.3%	5%
Mainstream	average + or - 1×SD	1.9% to 5.3%	93%
Declining	< average - 1×SD	<1.9%	2%

The key to economic growth in the United States over the years 1899 - 1966 was rapid and prolonged growth in three finished goods industries - transportation equipment, electrical goods and communications. These industries accounted for a relatively small part of the economy. However, their rapid growth also pulled along their supplying industries so their growth effect widened. In turn, the increase in incomes led to spending increasing on a broad front.

Production capability was able to expand in line with the rising level of spending. This was the supply side of the economy where increases in capital input, labor input and productivity sustained the growing demand and generated rising incomes. The result was sustained economic growth.

We turn now to investigate the causes of the growth in the types of final demand which led this growth process.

8.4 The growth path for leading industries

Our review of growth in Britain and the United States showed that virtually every leading industry followed a S shaped growth path. In the present section we illustrate the growth process for two leading industries – cotton production in Britain and household purchases of electricity in the United States.

Figure 8.1 shows the growth of the first modern manufacturing industry – British cottons. The industry got started in the 18th century, grew rapidly in the 19th then peaked early in the 20th century.

Figure 8.1 Value of British cotton output
£ million

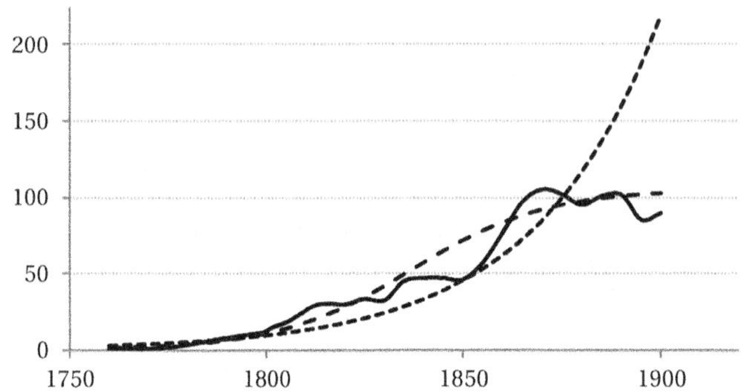

Source: Data from Deane and Cole (1969).

The Figure shows actual output, the line with irregular growth, along with two smooth growth curves, one a logistic curve and the other exponential. It is clear that this market growth is much better described by a logistic curve; the S shape of the logistic curve picks up the actual life cycle of the industry.

Figure 8.2 shows a different type of product – consumption of electricity per household in the United States. Use of electricity follows the same life cycle as cotton in Britain – slow to start with, followed by rapid increases in adoption and finally with adoption reaching saturation. The logistic curve in the graph closely fits the actual process of adoption of electricity by U.S. households.

Figure 8.2 Electricity use per residence, U.S.

Average, thousand kilowatt hours per annum

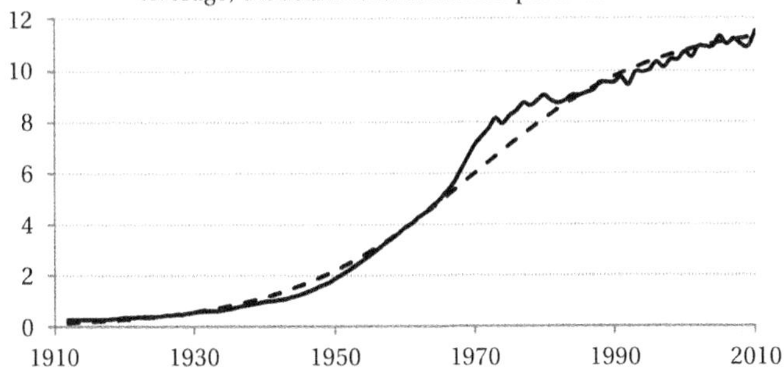

Sources: U.S. Census Bureau, Historical Statistics of the United States and annual Statistical Abstracts.

These growth paths, and the growth paths of all the leading industries, span many decades. British cottons took around 150 years to reach market saturation while U.S. electricity took around 100 years. Some other industries took less time; for example, automobiles in the United States took around 75 years to reach maturity. Also, the numerical features of the growth path, such as gradients and ceilings, differ between industries. But what does not differ is the shape of the curve, the S or logistic shape. The key feature of the logistic curve is that growth initially is slow, in terms of quantity purchased, followed by rapid adoption and finally, as the market becomes saturated, growth slows and even ceases.

8.5 The logistic model

The growth of leading industries follows a logistic path. The logistic model can be derived from an adoption or contagion process. Here, an encounter between a "have" and a "have not" has a particular probability of passing on the feature. Say an encounter between an existing consumer and someone who does not purchase the good has probability "h_1" of converting the non-consumer to being a consumer.

If "p" is the proportion of the potential market which purchases this particular good then:

$$dp / dt = h_1 \times p \times (1-p)$$

describes the rate of change in the proportion which are actual consumers. Solving this differential equation gives:

$$p_t = \frac{1}{1 + e^{-(h_0+h_1 t)}}$$

The starting and ending values of p depend on the parameters h_0 and h_1. If $-h_0$ is large and h_1 is positive then p(t=0) is close to 0 while p(t large) is close to 1. The coefficients h_0 and h_1 might be functions of other variables, such as price or income, but we use only the simple form of the model in which they are constant.

If the good involved is a flow variable, such as purchases of a food item during a year, and the size of the potential market is M then the quantity of purchases or sales during time t is $M \times p_t$. If the good involved is a stock variable, such as ownership of an automobile or the proportion of households connected to the electricity supply, then p_t is a proportion, the market penetration at time t.

The logistic model produces a S shaped growth path. Figure 8.3 shows the example of the growth path over 100 years for a model with h_0 = -390, h_1 = 0.2 and a potential market size of 100.

Figure 8.3 Example of logistic growth

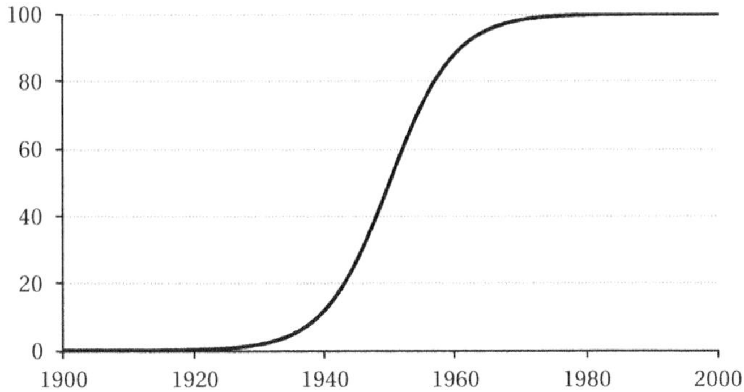

The rate of growth in the quantity purchased or owned (for a flow and a stock good, respectively) is greatest at the start of the process, in year 1901 in this graph. Growth in the annual number of sales is greatest at the mid-point when p = 0.5, which is around 1950 in the example. Sales or market penetration approaches a ceiling, in this example of 100, as time moves on. This corresponds to a mature market or to market saturation. The coefficient h_1 determines the speed of adoption – the larger is h_1, the greater the rate of adoption and the sooner the market reaches saturation.

The logistic model fits observed growth patterns. It not only reproduces the S shape observed in markets but also it has an economically reasonable behavioral basis in the sense of product adoption.

8.6 Creating industry growth

Economic growth is driven by a small number of leading industries. The leading industries in Kendrick's data for the United States were motor vehicles, electrical goods and communications. More recently, leading industries have included computers, entertainment and health care. We come now to the crucial question – what is the key feature which creates a leading industry? This is crucial as the continuation of economic growth depends on a country having a succession of leading industries.

These leading industries have followed a logistic growth path characterized by introduction, slow take off, rapid growth then saturation. These industries have also experienced growth in productivity. However, this productivity growth is not sufficient to sustain the rapid increase in production; these industries need more and more inputs to enable their growth. The distinguishing feature of the leading industries is logistic growth; this comes only from demand considerations. It is demand or something on the demand side of the market which holds the key to the growth of leading industries.

More precisely it is the interaction of innovation and demand. Growth industries come from the introduction of a new or vastly improved good or service for which there is a huge potential market. It is not innovation by itself, it is innovation in the sense of creating something which customers really want. It could be process innovation which vastly reduces costs, permitting such a large reduction in prices and expansion of supply capability that a mass market is created. It could be design innovation, creating a good or service which is far superior to existing ways of providing customer benefits or which creates a new type of customer benefit. It could be technical innovation which creates a product which provides an entirely new type of benefit to customers. Or it could be some other type of innovation, as long as it creates a new/improved product which is highly desired by large numbers of customers and so which will have a huge potential market.

An innovation may involve a good or it may involve a service; the form doesn't matter but meeting a customer need matters. Innovation doesn't necessarily have anything to do with science or invention. Being new and different does not necessarily create innovation. Novelty or invention is not innovation. Innovation does involve novelty but it must lead create something needed by customers and by large numbers of customers.

The emergence of a growth industry results from a number of forces coming into play. The conditions needed for a growth industry are:

(1) There is a new or a vastly more attractive product,

(2) People, whether individuals or businesses or governments or foreign buyers (exports), must want to buy these products, there must be a large potential demand or market,

(3) Potential customers must have or be able to get the money to buy these products, to convert their desire for the product into actual purchases.

New products are created by product innovation – a good which provides a new service to customers. The innovation might be in design, using existing technologies and materials in new ways, or it might result from new technologies or new materials. Whichever way, the product allows customers to meet a need which previously could not be met. In fact, consumers previously might not even have known they had this need.

More attractive products can gain their appeal in several ways. The most obvious is for the product to meet an existing need but in a much cheaper manner. Cheaper products are created by process innovation, making the product in a different, lower cost way. Or the product might save time in use or it might be much more convenient to use. Or, the product might work a whole lot better than existing products, meeting the user's need but in a far superior way. Or, the product might meet an entirely new need, one which previously was not being satisfied or even one of which consumers were unaware.

Table 8.3 sets out some examples of major innovations which have created growth industries in the past. Some of the classifications might seem arbitrary, such as the telephone being an improvement compared to telegraph rather than a new product, but the point is that some major innovations have been entirely new products while others have been vastly superior ways of meeting existing customer needs.

Table 8.3 Innovation - examples of growth products

	New product?	Major improvement?	Nature of the improvement: Cut price	Cut time	Perform
Cotton cloth, Britain		Y	Y		
Railroads		Y	Y	Y	
Automobile		Y		Y	Y
Electric light		Y	Y		Y
Electric motor		Y	Y		Y
Telephone		Y		Y	Y
Washing machine		Y		Y	Y
Electric range		Y	Y	Y	Y
Radio	Y				
Motion pictures	Y				
Television	Y				
Antibiotics	Y				
Vaccinations	Y				
Business computers		Y	Y	Y	Y
Credit cards	Y				
Personal computers	Y				
Video games	Y				
Internet	Y				
Cellphones		Y			Y

New product refers to a product providing a new type of service to the customer. Major improvement refers to a product performing an existing service but in a far superior way.

A product innovation or improvement is just the first step in fuelling growth. The next requirement is that the new product must satisfy a customer need - it must be useful and desirable. In addition, the potential market must be large to sustain a growing industry. Innovation or improvement is not enough, the product must also be wanted by large numbers of customers.

Marketing is a vital part of creating demand and a large market. Marketing informs customers of the product and its benefits, helps persuade potential customers that they need the product and makes it accessible and easy to purchase. Even new products which were so attractive that they virtually sold themselves – like cotton goods in Victorian England and telephone service in early 20th century America - needed effective marketing to convert people's desires into actual purchases.

Then there is the necessity of having to pay for the new product. A small ticket item, such as a motion picture ticket, can readily be accommodated in consumers' budgets but the purchase of a big ticket item, such as an automobile, generally requires credit. The availability of consumer and business credit is vital to the growth of industries selling expensive goods such as automobiles, consumer electronics and household major appliances.

Only when all these conditions are present will a product innovation or major improvement create a growth industry. Industry growth is a complex process; consumer behavior, marketing and financing all are vital to an innovative product creating a growth industry.

8.7 The consumer society

Continuing growth depends on growth in final demand. In a catch-up economy, this demand growth can come from exports to higher income countries. But, in a frontier economy, such as the United States, this growth can come only from consumer expenditure. Government purchases cannot lead growth for long periods of time (as the government deficit and government interest payments would grow so much as to undermine the economy) nor can business investment lead growth (as business investment ultimately follows, not leads, the growth in consumer demand).

But how can consumer demand keep increasing when people's basic needs have already been met? The answer is that needs are elastic. People's wants get converted to needs and their spending, consumer demand, keeps increasing. More simply, the answer lies in the emergence of a "consumer society". This is an economy in which people purchase what they want to have, as opposed what they really need to have. Equivalently, people's needs continue to expand to encompass the latest goods and services.

Victor Lebow (1955) famously characterized the consumer society as:

> "Our enormously productive economy demands that we make consumption our way of life, that we convert the buying and use of goods into rituals, that we seek our spiritual satisfactions, our ego satisfactions, in consumption. We need things consumed, burned up, worn out, replaced and discarded at an ever-increasing rate"

There is no need to introduce morality into the argument. It is not necessary to go as far as identifying spiritual satisfaction with consumption or to stress discarding goods; all that is needed for the modern economy is that consumers wish to consume more and are willing to buy new types of goods and services. In a word (or three), the consumer society is equivalent to: more is better.

The notion of the consumer society has attracted much criticism but it is difficult to see any problem as long as one respects the individual and the right of the individual to carry on his/her life as he/she sees fit. To criticize the consumer society requires that the critic's values take precedence over the values of millions of individuals and the decisions, including economic decisions, of these individuals.

The consumer society emerged in Britain with the Industrial Revolution. Consumer demand increased for clothing, for bigger and better houses, for household supplies, for better food, for travel, for education, for health care, for books and for myriad new goods. On the one hand, this spending helped drive the economy upwards; on the other hand, this is how people spent the rising incomes generated by economic growth. Rising consumer spending and purchases of an ever increasing range of goods and services similarly has characterized the United States since it took over economic leadership around the turn of the 20th century.

The necessary conditions for a consumer society are:

(1) A flow of new goods and services that appeal to most consumers; this is product innovation;

(2) The desire of consumers to purchase these new goods and services; this desire is heightened by marketing; and

(3) Lending that allows consumers to spend on these new and on existing goods and services in excess of their current incomes; this is the growth of consumer credit.

The starting point is innovation. This is not to be equated to innovation in a technical sense, it is innovation in the sense of creating something new which is useful to or desired by customers. Some industries are launched into growth by process innovation – production advances which drastically reduce the price of existing products, opening up a mass market for the product. For example, process innovations in cotton manufacture launched the Industrial Revolution. The more typical starting point, though, is product innovation. This is the development of a product which provides a new or vastly improved service to the consumer, as the automobile provided personal mobility, the telephone allowed personal conversations regardless of distance and radio allowed mass entertainment regardless of location. The benefits of major product innovations are so great and apply to so many people that mass markets develop. In turn, product refinements keep expanding these markets.

A new product, or even a cheaper or better version of an existing product, is of value only if people want to buy it. Marketing is the art of stimulating demand for a product. Marketing has emerged as a mainstream production service as specialist businesses as well as in-house specialists work to increase demand. Marketing has evolved from a product focus to a customer focus. The product-focused approach can be summarized by the well-known concept of the "4 ps" – product, promotion, price and place. These were having a desirable product, well-advertised so that people were aware of it, at an affordable and attractive price, and readily available to potential buyers. This has been superseded by the customer-focused approach – solution (the product satisfies a customer need), information (making the customer aware of the product and how it meets their needs), value (price relative to the need being met), and access (availability, ease of transaction and delivery).

Three elements in marketing which have seen huge development over the past century are design, advertising and retailing. Design – so as to make a product provide new services, work better and be easier to use - has advanced enormously. Advertising has become more sophisticated, more persuasive and more pervasive, especially as new media and new forms of communication have developed. Finally, retailing has changed hugely with the development of mail order, department stores, shopping malls, supermarkets and now on-line (internet) shopping.

Finally, growth requires the economic ability for people to purchase additional goods and services. Consumer spending cannot grow if people simply spend out of their current incomes. Growth requires that some customers spend more than their current income. Finance or credit provides the means of doing this. There has always been a finance industry providing credit to businesses and to governments. But, in the long run, government spending cannot continue to increase more rapidly than the economy and business spending follows, rather than leads, consumer spending. The type of credit needed to support consumer spending is consumer credit – lending to individuals or households to support their spending. The development of consumer credit has been a central feature of economic growth in the United States. Consumer credit is now available in a multitude of forms such as personal loans, mortgages, hire purchase or loans secured by an asset such as an automobile, and credit card finance. Consumer credit has been an essential element in sustaining the rise of the consumer society.

8.8 Example - automobiles

The development of the consumer society and the rise of a growth industry are well illustrated by the growth of the automobile industry in the United States. From the start of the industry around the turn of the

20th century to its peak around 1970, automobiles were one of a handful of industries which led U.S. economic growth. In this section we look at the rise of automobiles as an example of the life cycle of a growth industry.

The early industry comprised a multitude of small producers experimenting with technology and design. It was clear that there was a vast potential market for automobiles but no-one was really in touch with that market until Henry Ford introduced the Model T. Ford's breakthroughs were technical but were driven by marketing objectives:

- Design a simple car which provided personal transportation with reasonable reliability;
- Organize production, such as standardized parts and then the moving assembly line, to drive down costs;
- Pass the cost savings on to customers in the form of lower prices; keep improving the efficiency of production and keep reducing prices;
- Establish a retailing network to make the purchase of Model Ts widely accessible.

The Model T was a price-driven car. It led a rapid expansion of the market for automobiles and quickly dominated that market. For almost two decades the Model T reigned supreme. But the market for a low-priced, no frills car became saturated. The automobile market then moved to a new stage – features, all related to providing additional value to the customer, took precedence over low price. Ford gave way to Chevrolet.

This new era was led by General Motors under the leadership of Alfred P. Sloan Jr. In doing this, Sloan invented the modern business corporation and modern techniques of doing business. Sloan brought the consumer society to a new level. Sloan has documented his approach in his classic book, *My Years at General Motors.* The key features of modern marketing pioneered by General Motors were:

- Regular improvement in the mechanical quality of the car,

- Styling introduced as a core part of product design,
- Regular improvement of the comfort and convenience features of the car,
- Annual model change,
- Establish a retail network of franchised dealers to sell and service cars,
- Dealers accept trade-ins of used cars as part purchase of new cars,
- Offer finance to dealers to purchase cars,
- Offer finance to customers to buy cars,
- Segment the market into different brands, "a car for every purse and purpose",
- Price differentially between the brands,
- Market research, focus groups, consumer research,
- Advertising across the media,
- Advertise the customer benefit rather than the product.

In addition, Sloan established the framework for the modern business corporation. Separate lines of business - such as the Chevrolet brand, the Buick brand, the Cadillac brand, automotive parts, diesel engines, aircraft engines, railroad locomotives, the finance business, etc. – were decentralized into separate divisions. The divisions went about doing their own specialized business but were coordinated by the center by means of monitoring against budgets/business plans while also the center raised and allocated capital and carried out common functions.

The early leader in automobiles, Ford, was a production-focused organization which, by virtue of its low price strategy, established the mass market for cars. General Motors took over the leadership of the automobile industry by being a customer-focused organization. In doing this, General Motors pioneered the techniques of modern marketing, modern organization and modern business. (It is ironic that just a generation after Sloan's retirement General Motors had ossified and, being unable to adapt to changing market conditions, lost its industry leadership to more customer-focussed businesses).

8.9 Sequence of leaders

Continuing growth needs a sequence of leading industries, a sequence in which new growth industries emerge to take over from older growth industries which are reaching maturity as their markets become saturated. The consumer society generates demand for new products; individual creativity in pursuit of profit generates a supply of new products.

Figure 8.4 gives an illustration of the industry growth sequence. The industries and growth rates are based on the experience of the United States. These growth rates are of contribution to GDP or value added in constant dollars. The growth rates themselves are based on the actual record but have been altered slightly so as to illustrate more clearly the growth process.

Figure 8.4 Industry growth sequence

These rates are based on fact but accentuated so as to illustrate the growth process

Growth rate Industry growth	Relative to GDP	1880 to 1900	1900 to 1920	1920 to 1940	1940 to 1960	1960 to 1980	1980 to 2000	2000 to 2020
7.0%	3.5%						Computers	
6.5%	3.0%			Vehicles				
6.5%	3.0%			Electrical equipment, appliances				
6.0%	2.5%				Telecommunications			
5.5%	2.0%						Entertainment	
5.0%	1.5%						Health care	
4.5%	1.0%			Metals				
4.0%	0.5%					Chemicals		
4.0%	0.5%	Railroad services						
This is the average GDP growth rate, 3.5%								
3.0%	-0.5%				Clothing			
3.0%	-0.5%				Furnishings			
2.5%	-1.0%				Construction			
2.5%	-1.0%				Food			
1.0%	-2.5%							Vehicles
1.0%	-2.5%						Electrical equipment	
This is zero growth								
-1.0%	-4.5%					Railroad services		
-2.0%	-5.5%				Leather goods			

Sources: Based on data from Kendrick (1961). U.S. Census Bureau, Historical Statistics of the United States. U.S. Bureau of Economic Analysis, National Economic Accounts.

Railroads were an early growth leader but subsequently fell into decline. Telecommunications was another early leader but this industry has kept growing and remains a leader to this day. Motor vehicles and electricity/electrical equipment began rapid growth early in the 20th century and continued to grow rapidly until the 1970s; these industries then fell back to slow growth. New growth leaders emerged in the 1960s and 70s – computers, entertainment and health care; these continue as growth leaders today, 50 years later. The industrial growth leaders in the first half of the 20th century purchased steel and other inputs; this is illustrated by the growth of metals at above average rates. Chemicals are shown to illustrate the supply industries feeding into the more recent growth leaders. There are then several large industries growing at rates around or slightly less than the economy-wide average of 3.5%. These are illustrated by clothing, furnishings, construction and food. Demand for the products of these industries reflects growth in income and population. Their markets have long been saturated and their demand grows just in line with overall income and overall spending. Then there are two industries in decline with negative growth. Railroads illustrate an early growth industry whose products have been superseded by newer technologies while leather illustrates an industry which has been bypassed by both changing technologies and changing consumer preferences.

This Figure illustrates the hierarchy of industry growth paths – leading industries growing rapidly, their supplying industries growing more rapidly than the overall economy, income-driven industries growing more or less in line with the economy, then a few industries in relative or even absolute decline. Just as important, the Figure illustrates the succession of leading industries. Telecommunications has been growing through the entire period. The motor vehicle and electrical industries, which led the economy for decades, peaked and then slowed, while new industries such as computers and entertainment commenced their rapid growth. There has been at least one complete turnover of leading industries. It has so happened that this turnover saw manufacturing industries such as motor vehicles, replaced by service industries such as entertainment. This has been widely characterized as moving from an industrial to a post-industrial economy or from a manufacturing to a service economy. What matters from the point of economic growth though is that one set of leading industries has been replaced by a new set and that growth continues.

Today's leading industries, such as entertainment, computers and health care, still have some way to run if their life cycles are anything like previous leaders'. New leading industries, such as internet-related services, might just be starting. But, as long as there is a succession of leading industries (and as long as the productive capacity of the economy can keep expanding) economic growth will continue.

8.10 Sustaining the leading industries

Growth in the leading industries is driven by demand. However, the increasing demand must be matched by a corresponding increase in production. How is this growth in production achieved? Again, we look at the growth of the transportation equipment industry in the United States to understand the supply side of leading industry growth.

Table 8.4 summarizes Kendrick's data for output and input growth over (most of) the years when automobiles were a leading growth industry. Production increased rapidly, at an average rate of 6.4% a year. This requires that production capability, the combination of inputs of labor and capital and of productivity, must also have increased at a rate of 6.4%. The Table shows that productivity was increasing rapidly but not rapidly enough to sustain the whole increase in production. Factor inputs, inputs of labor and capital, also had to increase. Productivity growth accounted for a little over half of the growth with increasing inputs accounting for the remainder.

Table 8.4 Manufacture of transportation equipment
Average annual growth rates, 1899 - 1966

Output	6.4%
Labor hours	2.8%
Capital input	4.3%
Factor input	3.0%
Total Factor Productivity	3.3%

Sources: Data from Kendrick (1961) and (1973).

Productivity growth alone cannot account for the growth in production in the leading industries. Although productivity typically assists their growth, these industries still need increasing inputs of capital and labor. In transportation equipment, increasing production sucked in labor and capital from the rest of the economy; resources were shifted towards this growth industry.

In general, there is no "free lunch". Growth of the leading industries typically benefits from productivity growth in these industries themselves but still requires resources from the rest of the economy. Some of these inputs are of intermediate goods, as the growth industries pull their supplying industries along after them. And, some of these inputs are labor and capital; these are obtained by diverting labor and investment to the growth industries and away from uses elsewhere in the economy.

8.11 Capital

Capital is vital to production in all industries. For example, the 1998 U.S. Input- Output Accounts show that input of capital services ranged from 9% of industry purchases (for education and health care) to 43% (for finance, insurance and real estate); capital services averaged 20% of inputs across all industries. Labor averaged 31% of purchases across all industries while purchases of intermediate goods and services together with indirect taxes made up the remaining 49% of inputs.

Physical capital is not as important as labor at any point in time but capital has played a greater role in growth. This is in part due to the use of more capital relative to labor. Jorgenson (2005) calculates that, for the U.S. for 1948 – 2002, capital stock increased at 3.3% a year while labor hours increased at only 1.2%; capital per labor hour was increasing at 2.1% a year. In addition, much technical progress and process innovation has been embodied in capital. Our review of growth in Britain and the United States showed that in industry after industry, process innovation was embodied in new types of machines, equipment and structures. Jorgenson estimates that capital quality increased at 0.8% a year. Combining the growth in capital stock and capital quality, the total growth of capital input was 4.1% a year. This capital growth was significantly more rapid than GDP which increased at 3.5% a year. Capital services were the most rapidly growing of all inputs.

Table 8.5 shows some of Jorgenson's results about U.S. growth from 1948 to 2002. Fully 60% of GDP growth has been associated with capital in one form or another. 40% of total growth has come from more physical capital with 10% coming from each of human capital (better quality labor due to more training and experience of workers) and capital quality (better quality physical capital due to embodiment in new capital of more productive techniques).

Table 8.5 Contributions to supply growth

U.S. growth, 1948 - 2002

	% pa	% of total
Labor quantity	0.71	20%
Human capital (Labor quality)	0.34	10%
Capital quantity	1.39	40%
Capital quality	0.36	10%
Total capital	2.09	60%
Total Factor Productivity	0.67	19%
GDP	3.46	100%

Source: Jorgenson (2005).

The contribution of capital to GDP growth has been more important than Total Factor Productivity – increased quality and quality of capital have been the principal sources of increases in productive potential. Despite all the attention given to innovation and productivity, capital, in terms of quantity as well as quality, has been the real driver of growth in supply.

8.12 Process innovation

Product innovation underlies the emergence of growth industries. However, there is a second type of innovation which also is vital to economic growth – process innovation. In simple terms, product innovation is creating new, high demand products while process innovation is about increasing productivity in established industries. Both types of innovation are crucial; furthermore, they are complementary. Product innovation leads growth but these leading industries absorb resources; these resources are released by process innovations in mainstream or even declining, industries. In addition, established industries make up the great bulk of the economy and process innovation, by increasing productivity, allows production to increase more rapidly than the quantities of input of labor and capital. The dual effect of this is that incomes increase.

Process innovation increases the efficiency of production within a business. This increase in productivity is equivalent to reducing costs. Efficiency in production, cost reduction and productivity improvement are different ways of viewing the same thing. Businesses want process innovation as it reduces costs while the economic benefit is increased productivity and increases in potential GDP and total incomes.

Process innovation can be either incremental or disruptive.

Incremental innovation is the gradual improvement of existing processes. This is the kind of improvement which increases productivity by perhaps 1% a year. Economies of scale and learning effects are examples of these improvements. Or, the improvement might simply come from managers and engineers steadily working to improve efficiency. The result is for more or less steady increases in production efficiencies. At the economy-wide level, this implies a slow but steady increase in productivity.

Some examples of continuing incremental improvement in efficiency come from the evolution of engines. The power per liter of engine displacement of Ford automobiles increased at an average rate of 2.5% a year from 1909 to 2010; the average tractive effort of steam locomotives in the U.S. increased at an average of 1.6% a year from

1905 to 1965; the average horsepower of diesel locomotives increased at a trend of 1.6% a year from 1970 to 2009; aircraft fuel efficiency in the U.S., measured by revenue passenger miles per gallon, increased at 2.6% a year from 1960 to 2009; and the thermal efficiency of atmospheric steam engines in Britain increased at 2.7% a year from 1712 to 1776. These are engineering gains rather than gains in economic efficiency; the gains in economic efficiency would be smaller as these engineering gains are likely to have been achieved at the cost of more capital input. But, these improvements illustrate the gradual, even steady, evolution of effectiveness within a particular technology.

Disruptive innovation is when a major new process, technology, material or procedure comes along, allowing large increases in efficiency. It generally takes time for the new feature to be adopted. This might be because of the time taken for managers to become aware of the innovation or to become convinced of its value; or, it might be because the new process needs to be incorporated in new equipment or in new human skills and it takes time for these investments to be made and new capital and skills to replace old. Adoption of the innovation is likely to follow a contagion process so we would expect to see the typical logistic pattern of gradual initial uptake then rapid and widespread adoption leading to saturation when pretty much everyone is using the new approach.

We saw this logistic adoption pattern repeatedly in our review of economic growth in Britain and the United States. One example is in Figure 8.5 which shows the adoption of new materials – first iron and then steel – in British shipbuilding. The adoption clearly follows the S shape of the logistic process. Iron had clear advantages over wood in shipbuilding but it took time for people to recognize the advantages and learn how to use iron. It took about 35 years for iron to supersede wood. Then low cost steel started to become available. The advantages of steel over iron were so great and the transition from using iron to using steel so easy that that, once steel became plentiful, it took just 10 years for steel to take over the market.

Figure 8.5 Hull material of new British ships

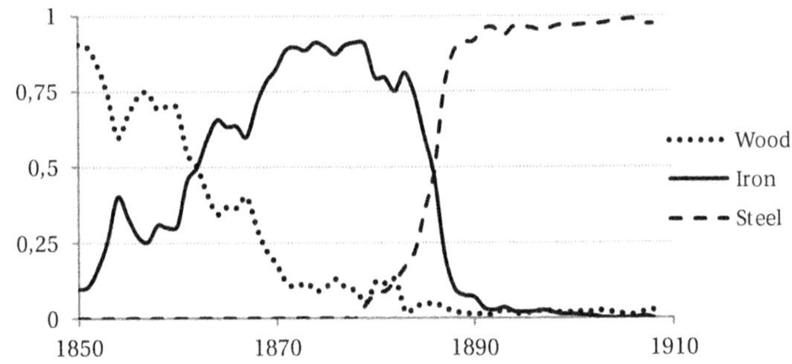

Source: Data from Mitchell and Deane (1971).

Adoption of genetically engineered (GE) crops in the U.S. followed a similar logistic path. As the transition to GE crops was straightforward, involving just the use of different seeds, the adoption of the new technology was rapid. For example, herbicide resistant (HT) cotton went from 1% to more than 80% of the market (acreage planted in cotton) in just 10 years.

Most process innovation is probably incremental in nature with disruptive innovation occurring in just some industries and infrequently. The crucial effect of process innovation is increasing the efficiency of production in existing industries. This is the source of most of the increase in Total Factor Productivity and, in turn, a major source of increases in production. Kendrick's numbers for 1899 – 1966 imply that 49% of production (GDP) growth came from TFP improvement. Jorgenson (2005) has a more refined methodology; he calculates, for 1948 – 2002, that TFP improvements contributed 19% of overall growth. However, Jorgenson calculates that improving quality of capital and labor input contributed a further 20% to growth. Process innovation is likely to be embodied in better capital and better labor, as well as greater TFP, so in total process innovation may have sustained somewhere between 19% and 39% of GDP growth.

8.13 Productivity in industry growth

Conventional growth theory has searched for mechanisms to explain productivity growth. Productivity growth at the economy-wide level, such as TFP, has been viewed as proceeding at a steady rate – exponential growth. Three of the mechanisms which have been considered to try to explain this growth are learning-by-doing, economies of scale, and investment in human capital. In this section we explore these approaches and relate them to the nature of economic growth operating at the industry level.

We first consider steady productivity growth and what this implies for an industry's growth path. We take an industry in which producers keep improving their efficiency at a steady rate and market demand has constant elasticities. In this simple model AC is unit cost which declines at the steady rate "c", P is price, Pop is population, Q is quantity produced and Y is GDP. The assumptions of the model are:

$$Pop_t = (1 + n) \times Pop_{t-1}$$
$$Y_t = (1 + a) \times Y_{t-1}$$
$$AC_t = (1 - c) \times AC_{t-1}$$
$$P_t = (1 + m) \times AC_t$$

so $$\Delta P_t / P_{t-1} = -c$$

Price markup over cost $= m$
Price elasticity of demand $= -e_p$
Per capita income elasticity of demand $= e_Y$
Population elasticity of demand $= 1$.

Growth in this model proceeds as:

$$\Delta Q_t / Q_{t-1} = e_p \times c + e_Y \times (a - n) + n$$

Production grows at a steady rate. As an example, if efficiency improves at 2% a year, the price elasticity of demand is 0.5, the income elasticity of demand is 0.6, population grows at 1% a year and GDP grows at 3.5% a year then production in this industry increases at 3.5% a year. This model generates steady or exponential growth. By varying the numerical assumptions, the growth rate will vary but the growth rate is always exponential.

Leading industries do not grow exponentially, they grow along logistic paths. Growth mechanisms in conventional models, which are exponential in nature, therefore cannot deal with the leading industries. However, these mechanisms might be able to shed light on productivity increase in the mainstream industries which do grow exponentially.

We now examine learning-by-doing, economies of scale, and investment in human capital to see what sort of industry growth is implied by each of these processes.

Some industries exhibit learning-by-doing or learning curve or experience curve effects whereby costs decline as a function of cumulative production. For example, a rule of thumb in aerospace construction is that each doubling in cumulative production of airframes leads to a 15% reduction in marginal cost (see Federation of American Scientists). A simple learning curve cost model is:

Q_t	=	production in year t
MC(n)	=	marginal cost, the added cost of producing unit number n
X_t	=	cumulative production through year t, $X_t = \Sigma Q_t$
$MC(X_t)$	=	$MC(0) \times X^{-c}_{t-1}$

Coefficient "c" in this model is the learning percent; it would be 15% in the airframe example. We introduce this into the earlier constant elasticities model. The resulting industry growth approaches an exponential path. With the numerical parameters used in the previous section, the production growth rate approaches 2.5% which is less than the growth of the economy, 3.5% a year.

Many industries exhibit economies of scale whereby average cost decreases as a function of the magnitude of output. This is current output not the cumulative output which is involved with learning effects. We use a simple market model to examine the effects of economies of scale; the demand features are the same as those above while average cost depends on the scale coefficient "c" as:

$$AC(Q_t) = (Q_t / Q_0)^{-c}$$

so $$\frac{\Delta AC(Q)}{AC(Q)} \Big/ \frac{\Delta Q}{Q} = -c$$

Each 1% increase in the annual quantity produced leads to a 100×c% reduction in average cost. If income and population are growing at constant rates, this industry shows exponential growth. With the numerical parameters used earlier and a scale coefficient of 10%, the industry growth rate is around 2.6% a year, somewhat less rapid than GDP growth of 3.5%.

Investment in human capital will increase input efficiency and possibly also total factor productivity. This will accelerate the reduction in production costs and so prices. In the simple constant elasticity market model considered above, a doubling of the rate of productivity improvement will increase the steady growth rate, from 3.5% to 4.5%, but it remains an exponential growth path.

These three mechanisms for productivity improvement generate exponential growth. As such, they are not relevant to the leading growth industries but they may well be relevant to the mainstream industries which make up the great bulk of the economy.

8.14 What drives innovation

Innovation is driven by people or businesses seeking to increase their incomes.

Product innovation seeks to design, produce and market a new product for which there is a large potential demand. The aim is to come up with a product hit, "the next big thing". Most product innovations fail but a few succeed and a very few succeed in a big way. It typically is individuals or maybe two people working together who lead the search for radical new products. (It then takes teams of people to translate the original vision into a practical product.) Existing businesses typically focus on incremental improvements to existing products or on introducing new products related to existing ones. The incentives facing existing businesses work against threatening existing success by heading off into the unknown; these incentives work in favor of building on existing success, a process of incrementalism. (Clayton Christensen (1997) characterizes this as "the innovator's dilemma".) In contrast, the incentives facing individuals do not tie them to the past – they have no existing business to lose and every incentive to throw the dice for a big win.

Process innovation is different, it seeks to ease or even break through a production constraint. In the small, process innovation seeks successive incremental improvements in efficiency. In the large, process innovation seeks radical new processes which will reduce costs significantly. Process innovation tends to come out of existing businesses as managers and engineers seek to increase earnings by reducing costs. Sometimes, although infrequently, an individual working alone or heading a small team will create a new product or process which substantially reduces costs in existing businesses. This individual might then be able to grow a large business by selling to existing producers.

Innovation is spurred by market opportunity, not by technological advance. Technical progress and research do not guarantee economic innovation although business people may later see a way of exploiting commercially a new technology. It is more likely that technical progress will be stimulated by trying to meet a market opportunity or to release a production constraint.

8.15 Some innovation leaders

Another perspective on innovation comes from looking at recent growth companies. A recent article in FORTUNE magazine (March 18, 2013) listed the world's 50 most admired companies, based on a survey of executives, directors and analysts. It is striking that the growth of each of the top 10, such as Apple or Disney or Federal Express, was due to the vision and leadership of one or (with Google) two people.

The success of these prominent companies tells a lot about the nature of economic innovation. Individuals are generally the key innovators. The creativity and vision of one or two people can lead to a growth company or even a growth industry. However, the early vision is necessary but not sufficient for success. A team or even a large company is needed to convert the successful initial innovation into its fully developed form. The initial vision must be converted into a useful product, it must be marketed, it must be produced and it must be delivered. These are the work of a team and possibly a large team. Workers, finance, equipment, advertising and more must be organized. Business leadership is required and management is required. Leadership tends to be provided by the innovator, management and execution by people brought on board as the innovator builds up the business.

These innovators tend to start off alone. It is only later, as their product is taking off, that they create a business to go around the product. The business comes later, after the innovation or at least after the original insight. The big product innovations tend not to come out of established businesses. Christensen (1997) gives a cogent analysis of one possible reason – established companies are happy to make incremental improvements to their products but are reluctant to risk their markets and earnings by coming up with totally innovative competing products. Also, established businesses may not see the attraction of trying to come up with an entirely new product. On the opposite side, someone with a great idea, an idea for "the next big thing", will always be tempted to go it alone, even if he/she works for an established producer. The reason is simply one of incentive – the idea of working 80 hours a week and risking much in order to gain fame and fortune for oneself is much more attractive than the idea of doing it for one's employer.

Successful innovation involves coming up with a new type of product (such as Walt Disney or Google) or a much better version of an existing product (such as IBM or Starbucks) which appeals to large numbers of customers. But, there is a lot needed to make this happen. The creativity and vision of one or two people starts the process but these must be followed by hard work, good business leadership, good management and the efforts of whole teams of people.

8.16 Innovation Hall of Fame

Economic growth emerged in England in the early 18th century. Britain led growth until around the turn of the 20th century. Leadership then passed to the United States. Many people have played important roles in the growth process. Some of these roles have involved product innovation – new products which have created new, growth industries; some of the roles have involved process innovation – new processes which have made production of established goods much more efficient.

Most of these people are unknown to history and even those who are known are too numerous to mention. Nonetheless, we select here a few people whose contributions have been so enormous that their roles demand to be recognized. This is a subjective list but we feel that the names on this list would be on any such list of the movers and shakers of economic growth.

Successful innovation generally takes the efforts of a whole team of people, bringing all manner of skills to the task of converting the original vision into a practical product. However, the crucial starting point is one (or sometimes two) visionaries who conceive of the idea of the breakthrough product; these visionaries are the people who have led innovation.

English agriculture. This is where it all started. Advances in agricultural productivity created the discretionary income which then created the market opportunities, for manufactures, which drove the Industrial Revolution. There were many separate advances in agricultural productivity, each building on what had gone before. We mention just one person to indicate the advocacy and adoption of change in agricultural practices. This person is Charles Townshend, known to his contemporaries as "Turnip" Townshend. Townshend was a leader in popularizing the four-field crop rotation system – growing wheat, barley, turnips then clover; the turnips and clover renitrogenated the soil at the same time as providing food for livestock and avoiding the need to keep land fallow.

Cotton. The mechanization of cotton processing was the change which started the Industrial Revolution. This change process took more than a century. Cleaning and spinning were mechanized first (by the 1770s), weaving was mechanized in many subsequent steps (by 1850) and coloring was transformed last. Many people made important advances in developing the cotton industry. We mention just one, Richard Arkwright. Arkwright invented a spinning frame, the first mechanically-powered equipment which could spin cotton. Arkwright also refined early carding machines (for cleaning and preparing the cotton for spinning). Then, Arkwright brought these elements together in the first modern factory – the water-powered cotton mill at Cromford, England.

Iron. Abraham Darby (around 1707) developed a process for using coke to make cast iron. This was at the now-famous Coalbrookdale blast furnace in England. This process sought to use coke (from abundant coal) instead of charcoal (from scarce wood) as the source of carbon and energy in making cast iron. Darby also developed new types of molds and casting techniques for making cast iron utensils and implements. However, Abraham Darby's process was not economic. It fell to his son, Abraham Darby II, to improve the technology sufficiently to break the cost barrier in making pig iron using coke (around 1755). This ushered in the age of abundant and cheap iron.

Steam engine. Thomas Newcomen, an ironmonger, invented the first practical steam engine around 1712; it was an atmospheric, reciprocating engine used for pumping water out of mines. Incremental improvements raised the power of the Newcomen engine sufficiently that, late in the 18th century, the steam engine began to be used in the new cotton mills and iron works. But the breakthrough to the modern steam engine was made by Richard Trevithick (in the early 1800s) who introduced the high pressure boiler. The high pressure engine, as it developed over the ensuing decades, had the power to drive the increasingly large and complex factories of the Industrial Revolution and the efficiency for mobile applications, introducing mechanical transport (railroads and steamships) to the world.

Railways. George Stephenson and his son Robert established the railway as a technically and commercially viable business. George Stephenson designed the Stockton and Darlington Railway (early

1820s) for moving coal. This was followed by the Liverpool and Manchester Railway (opened in 1830) for which George designed the road and Robert designed the locomotives, the *Rocket* followed by the *Planet.* The L&MR, the first economically viable railway, pioneered both freight and passenger rail service.

Steamship. Isambard Kingdom Brunel pioneered the steamship. Brunel didn't invent anything but he brought together all the components - the steam engine, iron (for the hull) and the marine screw (propeller) - to build the *Great Britain,* launched in 1843; the *Great Britain* successfully established steam power for marine transport (in this case on the Bristol to New York trade).

Steel. Henry Bessemer learned metallurgy working at his father's foundry. He made his first fortune by mechanizing the manufacture of bronze powder used in making gold paint. Bessemer began experimenting with furnaces in his efforts to improve the manufacture of plate glass. Bessemer moved on to tackle the problem of reducing the cost of making steel. After several years of experimenting, Bessemer in 1856 introduced a new type of furnace, the "converter" which produced steel by blowing air though molten pig iron. This allowed steel to be made from inexpensive pig iron. With the Bessemer converter and subsequent furnace improvements, steel became plentiful and cheap. Steel took over from iron; the age of steel had begun.

Infrastructure. New systems were needed to allow the growth of the cities created by economic growth; these were infrastructure systems such as roads, sewerage systems, clean water supply, urban transport and urban energy supply. We mention one leader – Joseph Bazalgette, an engineer who conceived, designed and supervised the construction of London's sewerage system. This system, opened in 1865, transformed the health and quality of life of the residents of London. And, by designing in massive overcapacity, Bazalgette laid an essential foundation for decades of growth in the London metropolitan area.

Steam turbine. Charles Parsons gained a college degree in mathematics before doing an apprenticeship in marine engineering. Parsons in 1884 joined a ship engineering business to head the development of electrical equipment. Later in 1884 he took out a patent on a steam turbine. He then designed an electrical generator which he drove off of the turbine. The steam turbine found widespread use in marine propulsion. Its main effect though has been to revolutionize electricity generation. The steam turbine, initially using coal but later using other sources of heat, freed generation from the constraint of finding suitable rivers (for hydro generation). By breaking the supply constraint in generation, the steam turbine allowed the growth of the electricity age.

Electricity. Michael Faraday discovered the scientific basis of electromagnetism. James Clerk Maxwell expressed Faraday's discoveries in tractable analytical form. Years later it was Nikola Tesla who established the principles of practical electricity – alternating current (AC), AC transmission and the AC motor. However, it was George Westinghouse who put all the pieces together to construct the essence of the modern electrical system. Westinghouse refined the design of AC transformers, developed the electricity meter, constructed multiple voltage AC networks, bought patent rights to Tesla's motor and introduced this motor, developed the steam turbine (having purchased the rights from Charles Parsons) and used stream and water generation. Westinghouse, by making electricity accessible to customers, laid the foundations of the electricity industry.

Telephone. The principles of the telephone and the basic instrument were developed in the 1870s, led by people such as Alexander Graham Bell. However, to be useful, the telephone needs a network with many customers. The person who led the creation of a nationwide telephone system in the United States was Theodore Vail, president of the American Telephone and Telegraph Company in the years 1885-89 and 1907-19. Vail's approach of "one policy, one system and universal service" led to a standardized, integrated system with a uniform numbering plan. Vail also led the company into a public utility stance by entering into a regulated monopoly arrangement with the U.S. Government and with state governments.

Automobiles/Production. Henry Ford introduced many of the central features of industrial production – a product which met core customer needs, standardized parts, mass production using a moving assembly line, constant searching for efficiencies that reduced costs and allowed prices to be reduced. Ford applied this approach most famously to the automobile but also to tractors and airplanes. Ford pioneered the mass production of complex machines with the objective of driving prices down so as to build a mass market.

Management. Alfred P. Sloan Jr, a long-time CEO of General Motors, developed the modern business organization (central policy setting and control, central allocation of capital, divisional operations) and also much of the practice of modern business – product innovation, market segmentation, advertising, customer research, styling, model changes and customer finance. He led General Motors as a multinational producer and marketer of motor vehicles - automobiles, trucks, busses, aircraft engines and locomotives – to become one of the largest organizations in the world. Sloan pioneered modern management, building an effective organization to meet and extend customer needs.

Electronics. The transistor was invented at Bell Labs in the late 1940s. The transistor, a device which can amplify and switch electrical current, is the building block of electronic devices such as computers, video equipment, audio equipment, telephone switches, telephone handsets, industrial control devices and so on. Integrated circuits put multiple transistors onto a single semiconductor chip. Integrated circuits were invented by Jack Kilby at Texas Instruments and Robert Noyce at Fairchild Semiconductor in 1959. Integrated circuits, which are vastly cheaper than discrete transistors, provided the cost-performance breakthrough which made modern electronics possible. A subsequent breakthrough came from extending the integrated circuit to encompass the entire central processing functions of a computer, the microprocessor. A particularly successful family of microprocessors was invented by Ted Hoff at Intel in 1971.

Computers. Thomas J. Watson Jr led the International Business Machines Corporation (IBM) as it moved into the age of electronic computers. The critical step was the System/360, introduced in the 1960s. The System/360 was a family of general purpose computers with standardized software and peripherals. Establishing a software standard allowed users to move between computers, for example by purchasing a more powerful computer, and also allowed software to be written that could be used on any IBM or compatible computer. The System/360 and subsequent generations of computers led to the widespread adoption of computers in business, government and research.

Retailing. Richard Warren Sears started a mail order business in 1888. The strategy of offering a wide range of good quality goods at reasonable prices and accessible to all, urban and rural, was successful and the business grew rapidly. The Sears catalog became a mainstay of American life, particularly in rural areas. The range of products covered is indicated by the fact that the 1895 catalog was 532 pages in length. With the rapid growth of cities, the focus of general retailing moved to department stores. The first Sears Roebuck retail store was opened in 1925 in Chicago. Further stores in cities, suburbs and, later, malls followed. Sears Roebuck was for several decades the largest retailer in the United States. Sears' insight was the power of reliability and accessibility. The mantle of largest retailer subsequently passed to Wal-Mart Stores. Founded by Sam Walton in 1962, Walmart has grown to become the largest retailer in the world; this growth has been due to the consistent application of one idea – organize operations, purchasing and everything else in order to offer the lowest possible prices. Sam Walton's insight was the power of low prices.

Marketing. Asa Griggs Candler in 1888 purchased the rights to a flavored, carbonated soft drink. That drink was Coca-Cola. Through skilful marketing – product, packaging, distribution, promotion and advertising – the Coca-Cola Company grew to one of the largest consumer goods companies in the world. Coca-Cola established what became known as the brand and showed how to manage the brand. Marketing and branding became a foundation of the consumer society which has powered economic growth ever since.

Finance. John Pierpont Morgan started the investment bank J.P. Morgan & Co in New York in the 1870s. J.P. Morgan was instrumental in forming the General Electric Company (GE) and financed the formation of the United States Steel Corporation. J.P. Morgan was a leading player in the financing and governance of many companies in the early years of commercial and industrial growth in the United States as well as a leading player in underwriting government bonds.

Economics/stabilization. John Maynard Keynes published *The General Theory of Employment, Interest and Money* in 1936, setting out a theory of the determination of aggregate features of the economy, such as income, employment and total production. This theory laid the foundation of "Keynesian" economics which provided governments with the intellectual framework to design policy to try to stabilize the level of economic activity and avoid repeats of episodes such as the Great Depression. Stabilization ideas were later enhanced by applying the monetary ideas of Milton Friedman. As a result, the years since World War II have seen considerably less volatility than previous eras. We have estimated earlier that this greater stability has increased average rates of economic growth by around 0.8 percentage points a year. Then, as the role of governments was steadily expanded, the voice leading the call for moderation was that of Milton Friedman. Friedman argued that the size of government should be moderated and that governments should focus on core public objectives, leaving people free to make their own choices in other areas.

International trade. Part of the growth of the high income countries and most of the catch-up growth of low incomes countries has been due to international trade. International trade allows the principles of comparative advantage to be expressed. Also, international trade creates market access whereby low income but industrializing countries can move onto a rapid growth path. International trade since World War II was hugely facilitated by the General Agreement on Tariffs and Trade (GATT). The GATT was signed in 1947 and lasted, with modifications, until it was replaced by the World Trade Organization in 1993.

Movement of goods. Malcolm McLean in the 1960s led the introduction of the shipping container. Shipping containers vastly reduced the cost of handling and moving goods. This was a vital enabling factor in the growth of international trade which assisted the growth of high income countries and permitted the growth of newly industrializing countries.

Highways. The Interstate Highway System created for the United States a single network of high speed, high capacity roads. The total length of the system is around 48,000 miles. The Interstate System was championed by President Dwight D. Eisenhower. The Interstate System contributed to the mobility of the population and to the growth of the motor vehicle industry as well as increasing productivity throughout the economy.

Entertainment. Walt Disney in the 1920s cofounded a movie studio which grew into one of the largest entertainment companies in the world. Disney led the development of animation in movies (creating, among other things, the character of Mickey Mouse), produced a wide range of movies, led the creation of theme parks, such as Disneyland, and later moved into recorded audio and video entertainment. Disney pioneered many products which filled the leisure time of generations of young people.

Hospitality. Ray Kroc joined the McDonald brothers' hamburger business in 1954 as a franchise agent; he later bought out the brothers' interest. Kroc proceeded to transform the business. Kroc applied the assembly line approach – break the business into minute separate operations, each carried out by unskilled workers, develop standardized ingredients and procedures to achieve complete consistency and minimum cost then pass on low cost to customers in the form of low prices. Kroc also applied modern marketing techniques to develop a brand - differentiate the product by means of packaging, service and extensive promotion while franchising outlets to get maximum accessibility and keeping control of product and service quality. Kroc led the development of the modern, mass market hospitality business.

Credit card. Ralph Schneider and Frank McNamara in 1950 created a general purpose charge card, the Diners Club card, which allowed a single card to be used for purchases from different merchants. In 1958 the Bank of America launched a card which provided credit for purchases made on its card. This developed into the Visa system. Visa and other leading credit cards are widely accepted by merchants, offer the convenience of having a single card and not using cash, allow delayed payment and also allow for credit. Credit cards have been important in sustaining the growth in consumer spending.

Personal information technology. Steven P. Jobs helped create and market the Apple II, the first commercially successful personal computer. Jobs went on to lead the development of a succession of personal computers, music players and cellphones. Jobs focused on software which would make personal electronic equipment useful and easy to use. By placing the customer first and making information technology work for the customer, Jobs was the leading figure in bringing personal information technology to the people.

These people were all innovators – they did things in new and different ways. What distinguishes them, though, is that their innovations brought huge benefits to their customers. Customer benefits could take different forms, whether cost reductions (such as Richard Arkwright or Henry Bessemer) or creating accessibility (such as George Westinghouse or Richard Sears) or creating entirely new products (such as George and Robert Stephenson or Walt Disney or Steve Jobs). The benefits could even be intangible, such as Alfred P Sloan Jr or the people at Coca-Cola or J.P. Morgan who helped improve business practices. It is not innovation itself which is important, it is the type of innovation. These people created things which were of great benefit to large numbers of people. Creating large potential markets allowed the emergence of new, large and rapidly growing industries. These are the industries that lead economic growth. Similarly, cost reducing innovations allow production to expand to meet increasing demands and also allow incomes to increase.

8.17 Demand and supply

Demand must equal supply for each industry. The quantity of transactions in each market moves to whichever is less – demand and production (for goods) or demand and production capacity (for services). If desired demand and intended supply are unequal then adjustments begin, driving the two into balance. These adjustments will be some combination of price changes, changes in production levels and, in the longer run, changes in production capacity. In the long run, demand is always the driver with supply adjusting to match demand – supply does not create its own demand, supply adjusts to match demand.

The primacy of demand was one of Keynes' insights. Overturning the received wisdom that supply dominated, Keynes argued that demand determined the overall level of economic activity and that an overall equilibrium with less than full utilization of resources was possible if demand (spending) was insufficient to make use of all productive capacity.

Similarly, we argue that in the context of economic growth demand comes first. We argue that demand comes before supply not that demand is more important than supply. Production in each market will reflect demand in that market. Over time, productive capacity in the industry will be changed to bring production into line with demand. This is the opposite of the conventional wisdom whereby the long term growth path is determined by production capacity with the growth of GDP matching the growth contribution of capital plus the growth contribution of labor plus the growth in Total Factor Productivity. Growth in supply is enabling but growth in demand is driving.

Supply adjusts to match demand industry-by-industry by the movement of inputs. Purchases of intermediate inputs – finished or semi-finished goods and services used in producing other goods and services – adjust by the growing industry purchasing more of these goods and services. Increasing purchases of raw materials might require investment in resource extraction or primary processing in order to increase the output of these materials. Then there will be adjustments in the input of labor and capital to each industry. These adjustments will take time. Unskilled labor is relatively mobile so this input usually adjusts quickly, for example with hiring and/or higher wages attracting workers to growth industries. Skilled labor might take longer to adjust as it might be necessary to train workers in the particular skills needed in growth industries and for them to gain experience in using these skills. Adjusting capital input also might take longer. However, much existing capital stock is relatively mobile – buildings can be used for different purposes, trucks and transportation equipment can be switched to work for different customers and some types of equipment similarly can be switched. But, the need for switching is likely to be limited. New capital typically can be constructed relatively quickly. This is a matter of redirecting new investment from existing industries to growth industries.

However, we do not minimize the importance of supply. Supply expansion is essential to sustain growing levels of spending and demand. This is the enabling role of supply. And, supply has another hugely important role – supply growth, whether from more capital or increasing productivity, is the source of rising incomes.

GDP originating in an industry is the value added created by that industry. Value added essentially is income. Income is the principal source of spending; the remaining source of spending is new credit but overall this is far smaller than income. There is a circular flow - spending calls forth production, spending is revenue to producers, the portion of revenue left over after paying for intermediate inputs is value added, value added is income to owners of capital and suppliers of labor, these owners/suppliers then spend (out of) their incomes and new credit, and so on. Rising GDP is, equivalently, rising income which, with credit, enables rising spending.

Increasing GDP per capita comes out of the supply side of the economy. We denote the quantity of GDP originating in industry i as Y_i and its growth rate as $gr(Y_i)$. GDP originating is the same as value added or income generated in industry i. A first order expansion of a constant returns to scale production function for industry i gives:

$$gr(Y_i) \quad = \quad b_i \times gr(K_i) \; + \; (1 - b_i) \times gr(L_i) \; + \; gr(TFP_i)$$

where K_i is the input of capital services to industry i, L_i is the input of labor and TFP_i is Total Factor Productivity in industry i. This implies that income per unit of labor (whether people or person hours) grows as:

$$gr(Y_i) - gr(Li) = b_i \times gr(K_i/L_i) + gr(TFP_i)$$

Here is the source of increasing average incomes – more capital per unit of labor and increasing productivity.

Table 8.6 shows the source of growth in average income for the United States over the period 1973 – 2002. Total factor productivity has been the principal source of growth in average income (71% of the total) with more capital per worker about half as important (contributing 29% of the growth).

Table 8.6 Sources of growth in average income
For U.S. 1973 - 2002.

	Growth rate	Contribution to growth	Share of growth
Capital stock per person hour	1.2%	0.5%	29%
Total Factor Productivity	1.1%	1.1%	71%
GDP per person hour	1.6%	1.6%	100%

Source: Data from Jorgenson (2005).

Demand and supply conditions each are essential for growth. On the demand side, there must be a sequence of product innovations giving rise to growth industries. On the supply side, productive capacity must expand in order to sustain the rising level of spending. Increasing productive capacity comes from higher productivity, more capital and more labor; these simultaneously create the rising incomes which are the payoff from economic growth. Demand or spending growth comes first but supply growth is just as important. Each is necessary for economic growth, neither is sufficient alone but together they are sufficient.

8.18 Creative destruction?

Joseph Schumpeter (1942) applied the term "creative destruction" to the changing production structure involved in economic growth. Schumpeter in fact took the concept from Carl Marx but applied it more carefully to the process in growing economies whereby old industries decline to make way for the new.

Schumpeter's creative destruction is one view of how productive capacity shifts towards the growth industries. However, we suggest that the term destruction overstates the severity and difficulty of changing the productive structure. Our review of growth suggests that production adjustment is gradual with few existing industries being destroyed. It is more the case that old industries grow less rapidly or, in more extreme cases, old industries gradually fade away by their productive capacity not being replaced.

Table 8.1, above, showed a few slow growth industries rather than any industries in absolute decline. The slowest growth industry was Lumber and lumber products with a growth rate, 1899 – 1966, of 0.8% a year. This was when the overall U.S. economy grew at 3.5% a year and the most rapid growth was in Electric machinery at 7.6%. The slow growth in demand for Lumber meant that purchases of labor, capital and intermediate goods by the Lumber products industry did not have to expand rapidly, leaving a larger share of these inputs available for more rapidly growing industries. In fact, most of the (slow) increase in output of the Lumber industry came from increasing productivity (TFP grew at 1.4% a year) while capital input increased at a 1.0% rate and man-hours declined at a 0.8% average rate.

Even if an industry entered absolute decline – decreasing in terms of its quantity of output – the adjustment is gradual. Capital stock wears out and, if demand for the product declines, this capital is unlikely to be replaced; it is likely that new investment will not be made; the industry will get by with old capital and old productive processes. Production levels and productive capacity will gradually decline. Labor will be released or departing workers might not be replaced, and purchases of materials will decline. The industry will shrink by non-replacement of capacity with inputs diminishing by attrition. It is more likely that resources will be released in a relative sense than an absolute sense. Even if actual inputs decline, it is more likely to be by non-replacement than by scrapping or dismissals. In the case of the Lumber products industry, capital input actually increased, although slowly, and labor input decreased at just 0.8% a year; this reduction in labor input is less than the normal loss of labor due to voluntary departures and retirements.

Economic growth requires that growth industries be able to expand their production to meet rapidly growing demand. Movement of resources to growth industries typically takes place by directing new labor and new investment to other industries, not by moving resources out of slow growth or declining industries. "Creative destruction" appears to overstate the severity of the adjustment process although there is no question but that growth requires the continuing restructuring of the economy.

8.19 The mechanics of growth

The growth economy drives forward on two fronts – demand and supply. Demand is spending on new products and additional spending on existing products. Supply increases to meet these demands. Supply expands by using more labor, more capital and by improvements in production effectiveness. And production expansion also is the source of income growth.

Both demand and supply growth processes take place at the industry level. Overall performance, such as growth in GDP or average incomes, is the summation of industry activity; economy-wide performance does not exist in its own right.

Growth industries involve new products for which there is a large (potential) consumer demand. These industries follow a logistic, S-shaped, growth path characterized by introduction and initial acceptance, rapid growth as a mass market emerges then slowing growth as the market becomes saturated. Continuing economic growth requires a succession of successful new products so leadership passes from established, maturing to new, growth industries. Demand for the products of mainstream industries increases as a result of rising incomes and increasing population. A few industries face slow growth of demand and so enter into relative or (less frequently) absolute decline.

Supply, or productive capacity, increases to meet the growing demand. Investment in more and better capital is the most important source of growth in production capacity. This investment includes human capital – better educated and more experienced workers. Also vitally important is also improvement in Total Factor Productivity – gains in production capability which are not embodied in either capital or labor.

Equally important, production increases create rising incomes. More capital per unit of labor and increasing Total Factor Productivity are the sources of rising average incomes (GDP per capita).

There is a circular flow. Spending stimulates production, production generates income, income and credit then allow higher spending. Spending leads the growth process but supply growth, coming principally from more capital and increasing productivity, is essential both to sustain the increasing spending and to generate rising incomes. Also essential is an increasing supply of credit to allow the growth in spending.

An essential part of supply growth involves flexibility, the redirection of resources to growing industries. The growth industries absorb labor, capital and other inputs; these inputs come either from new investment and new labor not claimed by existing industries or from inputs released by productivity improvements in existing industries. The industrial structure of the economy changes continually as spending increases differently across industries and as productivity increases differently across industries.

Innovation is an essential feature of economic growth. Growth industries are created by visionaries creating new products for which there are large consumer markets. Although only a miniscule proportion of new products succeed in this way, they have been sufficient to create a succession of growth industries. Productivity improvement likewise is created by innovation but this is process innovation – better methods of organization or production which reduce costs. Process innovations generally involve incremental improvement in existing businesses although sometimes a new process is developed which provides a radical improvement in production efficiency. The motivation for all these innovations is profits. Innovation is commercially driven, not technologically driven. New products and new processes might involve new technologies but the economic need or opportunity always comes first with the technology pressed into service if it fits or even is developed to address an identified need.

Chapter 9

Extending the theory of economic growth

9.1 Three types of growth

There are three types of economic growth – "frontier" growth, "coat-tail" growth and "catch-up" growth. Coat-tail growth and catch-up growth are relatively easy to accomplish if conditions are right and the right policies are followed; frontier growth is extremely challenging.

Frontier growth is to lead the world, to develop the products which people want to buy and which lead spending and production upwards, and to keep increasing productivity in the established industries. Only two countries have achieved this – Britain from the early 18th century to around the end of the 19th century and the United States since that time. Britain led the world into industrialization with the development of the cotton, iron, railroad, steel, steamship and mechanical engineering industries. The United States passed Britain early in the 20th century with industrial growth based on motor vehicles and electrical goods. When these industries flagged, new growth industries emerged to take their place; these were industries such as consumer electronics, information technology, health care, communications and finance. The really difficult challenge is to have a succession of rapid growth industries. This needs a succession of products entering or creating large and rapidly growing markets. The United States has so far been successful in achieving this sequence of major new products. At the same time, the United States has steadily increased the productivity and capacity of its established industries so as to sustain the increasing level of spending. The United States has for a century been pushing out the frontier of economic activity. This not only has produced rising standards of living for Americans but also has pulled many other countries along their own growth paths using the coat-tails and catch-up mechanisms.

Coat-tail growth is where a country produces goods needed by rapidly growing countries and exports into these growth countries. The supplying country rides the coat-tails of the larger client, pulled along by demand in the client country. Of course, the exporting country must have the natural resources, the capital and the human resources to supply competitively into the client country. Examples of this over the past 150 years have been the nations supplying foodstuffs to Europe and the United States, countries like Australia, Canada and New Zealand. Examples in more recent times are countries like Australia and Brazil which supply raw materials to rapidly industrializing countries, and countries like Saudi Arabia and Norway which supply oil to world markets.

Catch-up growth is where a low income country penetrates the markets of higher income countries based on low costs and low prices. The low income but growing country takes technologies, products, management systems, marketing structures and possibly even finance from higher income countries and sells (exports) into the higher income countries, exploiting its low cost structure. Japan, South Korea and recently China are examples of countries which have followed this strategy.

9.2 Overview of the theory

We now set out our theory of frontier economic growth. This is not a mathematical model, although parts of it are expressed in mathematical form, but rather a logical model which sets out a combination of elements which appear to be necessary and, together, sufficient for economic growth. This is economic growth in the sense of sustained increases in constant price GDP per capita.

Our theory is based on our analysis of the causes and nature of the frontier growth which has been experienced in Britain and then the United States since economic growth began early in the 18th century.

The bones of the theory are set out in the present section; the details are in later sections in this chapter. The core features are:

(1) Pre-conditions. There are several essential pre-conditions to economic growth – there must be a market economy; people must be able to participate freely in economic life; prevailing attitudes must place the individual, and not a state or a religious entity, at the center of people's value systems; there must be civil and legal security so that people can work and receive the benefits of their efforts; people must be able to keep enough of their income as to create effective economic incentives; there must be flexibility in spending, working and production activities; and there is the need for large markets in which producers are free to compete.

(2) The potential growth rate. Potential GDP increases as a result of more inputs of labor and capital and increasing productivity across the many industries which make up the economy.

(3) Productivity. Increasing productivity may be associated with labor, with capital, or may be separate, taking the form of increases in Total Factor Productivity. Increased labor quality results from more human capital which comes from education and training of workers as well as workers gaining more experience. Increased capital quality comes from incorporating process improvements in new capital. Increased Total Factor productivity comes from process improvements – changes in production practices or technologies which increase production efficiency – or even from economies of scale. Most process improvements come from incremental improvements in management and operations; some process improvements come from innovation – adopting new and more efficient production technologies.

(4) Demand growth. Aggregate demand or spending needs to increase at the potential growth rate, such as around 2.5 – 3.5% a year, plus inflation. The long run source of spending growth is consumer spending and this needs an expanding supply of consumer credit. People must also want to keep spending – there

must be a consumer society. At the same time, inflation needs to be kept under control to avoid the distorting resource allocation effects of high inflation; this probably requires the rate of inflation to be kept in the range 1 - 2%. Keeping total spending increasing in the target range is the job of government stabilization policy. As fiscal policy typically is precluded by government revenues and expenditures being directed towards other objectives, the burden falls on monetary policy - the central bank must keep the growth in credit within an appropriate range.

(5) Growth industries. Product innovation is the development and introduction of new goods or services which are desired by customers. Successful innovation involves a product with a vast potential market which creates a new industry and launches that industry onto a rapid growth path. This growth follows a logistic path – this is a life cycle with a few early adopters followed by widespread adoption and rapid growth until finally the market becomes saturated and growth slows. The growth cycle for a major new product typically takes 50 - 80 years.

(6) Succession of product innovations. A handful of major innovations will create leading industries which pull the economy along for the duration of their growth life cycles. Continuing economic growth depends on a sequence of major product innovations creating a succession of growth industries.

(7) Mainstream industries. Most of the economy is made up of established industries. Final demand for their output increases as a result of income increases and price changes; intermediate demands – purchases by other industries – increase through the standard input-output process.

(8) Declining industries. There are a few slow growth industries; demand for their outputs increases only slowly or even declines as their markets become saturated or through low income elasticities of demand or by being superseded by substitute products.

(9) Restructuring. Change is constant. Resources, in particular labor and capital, gradually move from slow to rapid growth industries. The principal mechanism is for new labor and new capital to go to more rapidly growing industries but some existing labor and capital might be released from existing industries as a result either of slow demand growth or high productivity growth.

GDP growth is simply the aggregation of industry growth. Economic growth takes place at the industry level. The economic growth path sums the industry paths. Production (GDP in total) is the other side of the coin, the dual, to spendng (GDE in total). The value added in production is income (GDI in total). Income per capita will increase as GDP grows more rapidly than labor input due to more capital and to productivity growth.

These conditions individually are necessary for economic growth. Together they are sufficient. That is not to say that these conditions can be generated automatically or through government policy; they cannot. They have emerged in only a few countries over the past three centuries of economic growth as the core and driving features of that growth.

9.3 Pre-conditions for growth

The market system is a requirement for economic growth. The market system sends signals about where best to direct effort; market prices guide consumers in allocating their spending; market prices guide producers so as to operate efficiently; and market prices signal opportunities for productive change. Two types of productive change are crucial for economic growth – breaking through constraints on production and developing new products which consumers want. The market system signals constraints well, encouraging improvements in efficiency, encouraging productive investment, encouraging the development of new processes and encouraging the development of new resources. The market system does not directly encourage the development of new products as there are no price signals for a product which does not yet exist. However, the market system contributes to the incentives for developing new products as it provides the flexibility to try new products and the incentives to reward the introduction of new products which consumers really want. Only the market system is consistent with efficient allocation of resources and productive change.

People must be able to participate in economic life regardless of their religion, personal and social beliefs, race or class, or anything else. There is no telling where the next great idea will come from – everyone should have the opportunity to try. Conversely, there is harm in restricting people's moving their work and location to be part of new opportunities; there is harm in restricting people from adopting the latest thing; there is harm in people not being able to make use of their particular productive talents. It is important that people are free to follow their own interests including to try to improve their lot economically.

There must be freedom of thought and action. Religion is important here. Economic growth requires that the individual is the center of his/her own value system and feels free to act to advance his/her own interests, of course within a framework of behavioral beliefs and social constraints. Religions or belief systems which deny the primacy of the individual or which deny the pursuit of self-interest are antithetical to growth. Also, it is vital that education is secular rather than doctrinal and that education teaches intellectual and practical skills – literacy, numeracy and the ability to think or at least deal with practical challenges - and that education is not the rote study of religious or any other doctrine.

There must be civil and legal security so that people are able to participate fully in economic activity. This requires personal safety, the rule of law, the absence of arbitrary power by governments or aristocracy or anyone else, property rights and the enforcement of contracts; these are all essential if people are to concentrate on their work or business and pursue their chosen lines of economic activity. These also are essential to create the incentives for people to try to better themselves economically, to work hard, productively and creatively.

There must be effective incentives. Individuals and businesses must be able to work, invest, innovate and take calculated risks in the expectation that they will receive and be able to enjoy the economic and social benefits of their efforts. Effective incentives reflect a number of conditions. There must be personal physical and legal security so that people are free to pursue their own interests, can concentrate on bettering their own situation and are confident that they will be able to enjoy the fruits of their efforts. There must not be arbitrary or confiscatory taxation. The best practical conditions for creating productive incentives are to have a market economy operating within the rule of law and with limited government.

Economic growth involves change – making new products, learning new skills, producing new things in new ways, purchasing and consuming new goods and services, investing in new capital. It is essential for growth that society tolerates change. Dedication to the status quo can be sufficient to prevent change. Strict compliance with established norms and ways of behavior, for example as prescribed by some religions, could prevent change. Similarly, powerful authorities, such as governments or trade unions or trade associations, which enforce particular ways of doing things can prevent change and prevent growth from taking hold.

Finally there is the need for large markets. Growth depends on producers being able to access or create large markets. If growth is domestically driven, there must be sufficient population with sufficient discretionary income to allow the development of large markets for new products. If growth is based on exporting, there must be reasonably free international trade including access to markets in other countries.

9.4 Growth in potential output

GDP is the sum of industry GDPs so the rate of growth of constant price GDP, Y, is:

$$gr(Y) = \sum_{i=1,n} a_i \times gr(Y_i)$$

where Y_i is value added or GDP originating in industry i and a_i is the share of Yi in GDP.

The growth of Y_i can be written in terms of the growth of its inputs:

$$gr(Y_i) = gr(F_i) + gr(TFP_i)$$

where $gr(F_i)$= growth contribution of factor (capital and labor) input to i and gr(TFPi) = growth in Total Factor Productivity in industry i.

Demand conditions set the target growth in industry output. If productivity growth in the industry is given, for production to match the demand growth path requires:

$$gr(F_i) = gr(Y_i) - gr(TFP_i)$$

Over time, resources of labor and capital move into each industry to let it meet demand for its output, sustaining $gr(F_i)$. However, there are only limited amounts of labor and capital available:

$$LS >= \sum_{i=1,n} L_i$$

$$KS >= \sum_{i=1,n} K_i$$

where LS is the labor supply, L_i is use of labor in industry i, KS is capital stock and K_i is capital stock in industry i. Labor and capital are in quality-adjusted terms. Assuming that there is sufficient flexibility in the allocation of capital and labor to allow these resources to move to the industries in which they are most needed, the critical resource constraints apply at the economy-wide level rather than the industry level. The maximum production consistent with these resource constraints defines potential GDP and the corresponding potential growth rate, gr(Y). Actual GDP is the smaller of total demand and potential GDP.

9.5 Increasing productivity

Product innovation creates new markets and growth industries. Process innovation increases the efficiency of making existing products, allowing production and incomes to increase throughout the economy. Both types of innovation are essential to economic growth but it is process innovation which underlies the steady increase in incomes.

Process innovation increases productivity, allowing more output to be produced for any given level of inputs. This innovation tends to be continuous or incremental in nature, proceeding at a rate such as 1% a year. Improvements in production processes might come from operational improvements, technical improvements or managerial improvements. These improvements tend to come from established businesses as these businesses work to increase earnings by improving organizational and operating efficiencies. Occasionally, a major improvement is developed, such as a new and much more efficient production technology; this will create larger gains in productivity as it becomes widely adopted. This adoption generally follows a logistic path and adoption is relatively rapid as there is no need to establish a new market – the new process just replaces the conventional process in making established goods and services.

These process innovations underlie the TFP_i terms in the previous section. There is no rule or analytical form for their magnitude. We do know the typical magnitude of the average rate of productivity advance. Jorgenson's (2005) growth accounting for the United States over 1948 – 2002 shows that Total Factor Productivity for the economy increased at 0.7% a year. Increasing labor quality contributed 0.3% to GDP growth while increasing capital quality contributed a further 0.4%. These embodied effects may be assigned to TFP or retained within factor inputs; if they are lumped in with TFP then productivity improvements have contributed 1.4% a year to GDP growth.

9.6 Growth in total spending

It is the task of stabilization policy to keep total spending tracking in line with potential production so that the economy neither suffers lost output nor departs into inflation. In practice, this means that demands on resources do not exceed the availability of resources. Use of existing capital tends to be somewhat flexible so typically the critical target involves labor. This target for stabilization policy then becomes to keeping demand for labor, $\sum_{i=1,n} L_i$, close to the supply of labor; in practice the target typically is to keep the rate of unemployment relatively low but not so low as to lead to accelerating inflation.

Total spending needs to keep increasing if the economy is to grow. If the growth trend of potential GDP is 3.5% a year, for example, total final demand spending needs to grow at a rate of 3.5% + inflation. This rate of increase allows the growth of new industries as well as purchase of the increasing production from established industries made possible by increasing capacity.

While it is essential that spending increases it is also essential that it does not increase too rapidly. Continuing expansion in spending in excess of the growth in productive capability will lead to inflation. Inflation is inimical to growth. This is for two reasons. First, rapid inflation has the effect of redirecting activity and investment into asset trading rather than asset creation, disrupting the productive allocation of resources. Second, rapid inflation (in the modern era) leads to restrictive monetary conditions as the central bank tries to tame inflation; inflation is tamed but at the cost of a period of slow or negative growth in the volume of production. If the growth trend for potential GDP is 3.5% a year and if a tolerable rate of inflation is in the range 1 - 2%, the target growth in total spending is likely to be around 5%.

People spending out of current income will not generate this ongoing increase in spending. Injections of new spending are needed to allow this growth. The Keynesian model shows that something over and above the circular flow of production to income to spending is needed if total spending is to increase. We consider the determination of total spending in the following Keynes-style model of total economic activity. (The spending variables in this model are in current dollars.)

$C =$ $c \times (Y - T)$ for income-based spending (but excluding investment and credit-based spending) by consumers

$Y =$ total income, final demand or production; current dollar GDP

$T =$ $t \times Y$ for government tax receipts
$I_1 =$ consumer credit-based spending (mainly on durables and housing and durables but this could also include some spending on nondurables and services)
$I_2 =$ investment spending by businesses
$G =$ government purchases of goods and services
$X =$ exports
$M =$ $im \times Y$ for imports

We assume that $G = T$, government purchases equal tax revenues, so the government finances are in some sort of balance, and that $X = M$, exports equal imports, with the exchange rate adjusting to alter exports to keep foreign trade in balance.

The equilibrium current dollar GDP in this economy is:

$$Y = C + I_1 + I_2 + G + X - M$$

which implies:

$$Y = (I_1 + I_2) / ((1 - c) \times (1 - t))$$

The small letters signify parameters in the model, these are constant. The numerator in the equilibrium income equation comprises spending elements which are external to the circular spending flow and not constrained by other forces (G is constrained by a balanced government budget and X by balanced international trade). The denominator corresponds to the Keynesian multiplier.

We simplify things by assuming that business investment follows GDP growth such that I_2 grows at the same rate as GDP. This leaves one type of spending as driving GDP growth – I_1 or personal credit-based spending. The model implies:

$$gr(Y) = gr(I_1)$$

The causation runs from I_1 to Y. If monetary policy can target I_1 growth, holding it at 5% a year for example, then Y will increase at 5%. If inflation is 1.5% then GDP in constant dollars will increase at the desired rate, 3.5% in this example.

Personal consumption needs to keep increasing if GDP is to keep increasing. This requires an increasing level of personal credit. The consumer society leads people to keep borrowing and spending. This spending is principally on personal investment in housing and durables although any credit-based consumption will drive total spending upwards. Monetary policy can be effective in managing the growth in personal credit although it is essential that other aspects of government policy, including the government's fiscal situation, international trade and exchange rate policies, and competition policies are all relatively neutral so as not to destabilize the situation and impede steady growth.

This is not intended to be a predictive model; rather, it is analytical, showing that monetary policy, if it can keep credit-based consumer spending on track, is likely to be able to keep the economy growing on the target path. This target path mirrors the growth in potential GDP so that spending draws out the increase in productive capacity while inflation is kept within the target range.

This all means that monetary policy, affecting the availability and cost of credit, has a pivotal role in economic growth. Its role is to manage the growth of consumer and household credit so that total spending grows in line with potential GDP. Government policy determined by the political process focusses on the short term whereas economic growth requires that long term consequences take precedence over short term considerations. Therefore, the central bank, if it is to be able to carry out its role in securing steady growth, must be independent of the political arms of government.

9.7 Growth industries

Product innovation underlies the creation of new industries. Product innovation is the creation and introduction of new or greatly improved products which appeal to vast numbers of consumers. Modern marketing helps create this demand. Consumers then convert the desire for these new products into purchases. Consumer finance helps consumers expand their spending to buy the new products.

Product innovation by its nature is discontinuous or revolutionary. This type of innovation is not necessarily based on technology; it is necessarily based on meeting new consumer needs. This innovation is all about customers. This innovation tends to be done by individuals, people operating outside of the establishment, people looking to achieve economic success by coming up with new products for which there is a large potential market. Once a successful new type of product is launched, it generally is steadily improved and extended, further increasing the market.

A successful new product follows a logistic adoption process. Slow initial demand is followed by widening recognition and adoption, leading to rapid increases in demand until finally the market is saturated and demand levels off. This process takes decades. For a new category of product, such as the automobile, the process has taken 75 years or more - first as a mass market develops, then as consumers rush to adopt the product, then as product improvements stimulate additional and repeat purchases until finally the market is saturated and growth slows to keep pace just with population.

9.8 Mainstream industries

Mainstream industries are the established industries which cater to final demand or which make intermediate products which, ultimately, find their way into finished goods and services. These mainstream industries make up the great bulk of the economy. They increase over time as overall spending increases.

The mainstream industries are vitally important as they produce most of the goods and services purchased in consumption and other final demand, and because they generate most of the income in the economy.

Growing demand for the mainstream industries is driven by the standard forces of higher incomes, more people, and lower prices. As these are established products, their markets tend to be mature – they are past the stage of rapid adoption of new products. Instead, the key driving force is rising incomes and spending in general. However, it is likely that demand for these products rises slightly less rapidly than incomes – the income elasticity of demand is less than 1. This is because these are established products in mature markets with the more rapid increase in spending directed towards the new growth products of the time.

The mainstream industries are so large that the incomes generated in these industries in effect determine incomes in the economy as a whole. These incomes are increasing because of productivity gains, more and better capital input and more and better labor input. Income per worker increases as a result of productivity improvements, more and better capital, and better labor (improvements in labor quality associated with more human capital). Income to capital also increases, sharing the gains in productivity, capital quantity and capital quality.

9.9 Declining industries

There will be a few slow growth industries - demand for their outputs increases only slowly or even declines. There can be various reasons for this slow growth - their markets might have become saturated so volume grows only with population, they might have low income elasticities of demand or their products might have been superseded by substitutes. Once-vigorous industries might move into decline as their markets become saturated – an example is automobiles, for decades a growth leader but now growing slowly if at all. Or, substitutions might have taken away their markets as, for example, woolens were replaced by synthetic fibers. In intermediate goods, steel growth has slowed or stopped because other materials have replaced steel in many uses and as final demand has moved away from steel-intensive manufacturers to services which use little or no steel.

9.10 The vital sequence

GDP growth, on the spending side, is the aggregation of industry growth rates. Say the growth industries account for share a_1 of GDP and grow at rate $gr(Y_1)$, the mainstream industries account for share a_2 of GDP and grow at $gr(Y_2)$ and the declining industries account for share a_3 of GDP and grow at rate $gr(Y_3)$. Say demand for the mainstream industries is driven by overall income growth with an income elasticity of demand of e_2. Overall income grows at gr(Y), the rate of growth of potential GDP. The growth in demand and also production from the mainstream industries is $e_2 \times gr(Y)$. Total demand is equal to total industry output (value added) so:

$$gr(Y) \quad = \quad a_1 \times gr(Y_1) \ + \ a_2 \times gr(Y_2) \ + \ a_3 \times gr(Y_3)$$

As the shares sum to one the industry growth rates are linked by:

$$gr(Y_1) \quad = \quad ((1 - a_2 \times e_2) \times gr(Y) \ - \ a_3 \times gr(Y_3)) \ / \ (1 - a_2 - a_3)$$

This indicates one role of the growth industries – their rapid growth serves to offset the slightly lower than average growth of the mainstream industries and the much lower growth of the declining industries.

We consider a situation where growth industries make up 5% of the economy, mainstream industries make up 93% and declining industries 2%; GDP growth is 3.5% and the declining industries grow with population at 1.25%. Say the income elasticity of demand for the mainstream industries is 0.95 so these industries grow at 3.33%. Here, the growth industries must grow at 6.9% to bring total demand into line with total supply. The growth industries are doing two lots of work – they are offsetting the declining industries and also they are making up for the mainstream industries being only partially responsive to income growth.

These numbers are similar to the growth experience of the United States over the past century. It is likely that the income elasticity of demand for established goods and services is a little less than one. Consequently, continuing economic growth, on the demand side, depends on there being a succession of rapid growth industries.

Growth industries cater to final demand, primarily personal consumption. Spending on their products not only stimulates production directly but also the indirect purchases of intermediate goods and services pulls along many other industries. However, any one growth industry has a limited life cycle. This life cycle might take around 75 years of which 50 years might involve rapid growth. How can this account for economic growth which has been going on for more than 250 years?

Continuing economic growth requires a succession of growth industries. And, this is exactly what has happened in the frontier economies such as the United States. Rapid growth in a few industries has led the economy for several decades. Then, as these industries approach maturity and their growth rates slow other industries come to the fore and, moving into the rapid growth stage of their life cycle, take over the role of leading the economy upwards.

Figure 9.1 gives an illustration of the industry growth sequence. The industries and growth rates are made up although they have some foundation in what has happened.

Figure 9.1 Illustrative industry growth sequence

These industries and growth rates are made up simply to illustrate the growth process

Growth rate Industry growth	 Relative to GDP	1960 to 1970	1970 to 1980	1980 to 1990	1990 to 2000	2000 to 2010	2010 to 2020	2020 to 2030
6.5%	3.0%				Computers			
6.5%	3.0%					Internet services		
6.0%	2.5%	Vehicles						
5.5%	2.0%	Electrical appliances						
5.0%	1.5%		Telecommunications					
4.5%	1.0%		Entertainment and leisure activities					
4.5%	1.0%	Chemicals						
4.0%	0.5%				Health care			
This is the average GDP growth rate, 3.5%								
3.0%	-0.5%				Clothing			
3.0%	-0.5%			Construction				
2.5%	-1.0%				Electrical appliances			
2.5%	-1.0%				Food			
1.0%	-2.5%				Vehicles			
0.0%	-3.5%					Chemicals		
This is zero growth								
-1.0%	-4.5%					Metals		

This Figure illustrates the hierarchy of industry growth paths – leading industries growing rapidly, their supplying industries also growing more rapidly than the overall economy, mainstream income-driven industries growing in line with or a little less rapidly than the economy, then a few industries in relative or even absolute decline. Just as important, though, the Figure illustrates the succession of leading industries. The crucial feature for economic growth is that there is a succession of leading industries such that, when today's leaders slow, new industries take their place, leading spending and production upwards.

9.11 Micro foundations to growth

GDP growth from the spending side, using the notation from an earlier section, is the weighted average of industry growth rates:

$$gr(Y) = \sum_{i=1,n} a_i \times gr(Y_i)$$

These industry growth rates reflect demand forces – growth industries grow rapidly as people adopt new products, mainstream industries grow slightly less rapidly than income, and declining industries grow only slowly.

Similarly, GDP growth from the production side is:

$$gr(Y) = \sum_{i=1,n} a_i \times (gr(F_i) + gr(TFP_i))$$

The factor inputs, capital and labor (which are included within the F_i) move to the industries where they are needed to allow production to meet demand. As production restructuring is gradual, redirection of new investment and redirection of new labor generally is sufficient to allow this restructuring; it is unlikely that large scale and sudden movements of capital and labor will be needed. TFP changes at the industry level are mainly the result of incremental improvements in efficiency although sometimes there are major improvements resulting from the introduction of radically better production processes.

These simple equations give the overall rate of economic growth in terms of developments at the industry level. Industries, on both the demand side and the supply side, are where growth originates; the macro growth path is just the aggregation of industry developments. Demand and supply at the industry level are the micro foundations to growth. Demand and supply play different roles in economic growth. Demand drives growth while supply expansion, from more inputs of capital and labor and increasing productivity, sustains growth and generates income. Finally, resource mobility is an essential aspect of production at the industry level being able to match demand.

Here is an example of a growing economy:

- Demand growth. 5% of spending is on new products, from the leading industries, 93% is on purchases from mainstream industries and 2% is on the products of declining industries. The leading industries follow logistic growth paths with an average growth rate over time of 6.9% a year. The mainstream industries are driven by income with average income elasticity of demand of 0.95. The declining industries grow with population at a 1.25% rate. The growth rate of final spending in this economy is 3.5%. Monetary policy keeps spending growth at this rate which is, from the next paragraph, the growth rate in potential production.
- Supply. The growth in production capability is set by the growth in the quantity and quality of labor and capital inputs and the increase in Total Factor Productivity. Using Jorgenson's (2005) numbers in this example, factor quantities allow an increase in GDP at a 2.1% rate, factor qualities add a further 0.7% making GDP growth due to capital and labor inputs of 2.8% a year; TFP adds a further 0.7% making an overall growth in production of 3.5% a year. Inputs move from industries with slower demand growth and/or faster productivity growth to industries with faster demand growth and/or slower productivity growth so that production (supply) grows in line with demand in each industry.

This economy grows at 3.5% a year. This growth is the result of different growth patterns of different types of spending. And, it is consistent with the growth of production across the various industries. Demand and supply are in balance in each industry.

9.12 Resource mobility

Countries typically start off dominated by agriculture. Rapid productivity growth in agriculture then releases labor to other industries. Investment from the growing economy is directed to agriculture but also to new industries so that, over time, capital also shifts away from agriculture and towards the new industries. Later in the typical growth process, a similar shift of resources takes place between manufacturing and services with productivity growth in manufacturing releasing labor and, over time through new investment, capital to the growing service industries.

These are examples of resource mobility. In view of the different growth rates of different industries, movement of resources between industries is essential to growth. And, continuing restructuring of the economy is characteristic of growth.

Movement of intermediate goods is straightforward – it makes little difference to the producing industry whether it sells its output to rapidly growing or to slow growing businesses. Movement of labor and capital though is more complex. This movement might involve new investment and new entrants to the labor force going to growth industries or it might involve capital and labor moving from slow to rapid growth industries. It is further complicated by the possibility that capital and labor in existing industries have skills or features which are not needed by the growth industries.

Resource mobility takes two forms – new resources go into expanding industries and some existing resources move from established to growth industries. New workers and new investment can go into industries where they are required, this part of restructuring is relatively easy. Simultaneously, some existing labor and some existing capital can move into industries where the demand is greater. The donors might be mainstream industries where productivity growth allows them to release resources or the donors might be slow growth industries which need only modest or no increases in inputs. However, some labor and some capital might have capabilities specific to the old industry and not needed by the growth industries. This feature reduces resource mobility but does not prevent it – the growth industries might be expanding at 6 or 7% a year but are relatively small so their requirements are likely to be met from the normal increase of the labor force, from mobile workers and from new investment.

The massive restructurings inherent in economic growth take decades to become fully apparent. Growth economies have sufficient investment and sufficient expansion of the labor force, as well as some mobility in the existing capital stock and the existing labor force, that the composition of production typically will be able to change to sustain the evolving pattern of demand.

9.13 Growth accounting

There is a simple growth accounting framework for this growth process. A first order expansion of a constant returns to scale industry production function is:

$$gr(Y_i) = b_i \times gr(K_i) + (1 - b_i) \times gr(L_i) + gr(TFP_i)$$

so GDP growth, from the production side, is

$$gr(Y) = \Sigma_{i=1,n}\, a_i b_i \times gr(K_i) + \Sigma_{i=1,n}\, a_i(1\text{-}b_i) \times gr(L_i) + $$

$$+ \Sigma_{i=1,n}\, a_i \times gr(TFP_i)$$

If we denote the macro-level variables

$$gr(TFP) = \Sigma_{i=1,n}\, a_i \times gr(TFP_i)$$

$$gr(L) = \Sigma_{i=1,n}\, a_i \times gr(L_i)$$

then the GDP aggregation equation can be re-written as:

$$gr(Y/L) = \Sigma_{i=1,n}\, a_i b_i \times gr(K_i/L_i) + gr(TFP)$$

Growth in GDP per worker is the sum of the production effect of increasing capital per worker and increases in productivity. The direct benefit of economic growth is increasing GDP or income per worker; in this production sense, economic growth depends on increases in capital relative to labor and on increasing productivity.

L, L_i and K_i in this equation really should refer to inputs of capital services and labor services rather than capital stock and labor hours. If labor services (L) are split into labor quality (Lqual) and labor hours (LH) then the equation can be written:

$$gr(Y/LH) = gr(Lqual) + \Sigma_{i=1,n}\, a_i b_i \times gr(K_i/L_i) + gr(TFP) \quad (9.1)$$

Growth in GDP per hour worked depends on the rate of increase in labor quality, the rate of increase in Total Factor Productivity and the aggregation over industries of the growth in the ratios of capital services to labor services.

The changing composition of spending or production will also affect Y/LH. The differences in TFP_i across industries will affect the growth in TFP; and, as the composition of production changes, changing the a_i terms, the growth rate of TFP also will change.

9.14 Changing structure

A growing economy will be a changing economy. Spending patterns will change, the industrial structure will change, production processes will change, work practices and labor skills will change and location patterns will change. The very mechanisms which generate economic growth work through change. The only constant in economic growth is change.

Spending patterns will keep changing. At the broad level, there will be growth industries, mainstream industries and declining industries, each driven by the nature of demand for its products. Over decades, one growth industry will give way to another as one market becomes saturated and consumers move on to new goods and services. There will always be some declining industries, industries whose products are no longer in strong demand, for any of several possible reasons, and which grow only slowly or even move into decline.

Production processes will change. There will be steady, incremental changes in production organization and processes; in addition, there will be from time to time major changes in production technology as new, more productive processes are introduced and then adopted across one or more industries.

Changes in production processes are likely to involve changes in capital equipment and structures and in labor skills. Much productivity advance is embodied in capital. This will mean that new investment will be needed, embodying the new technologies, with some existing capital run down and eventually scrapped. Some capital, though, can be moved from one use to another. Labor skills similarly will evolve. Much productivity advance also is embodied in, or requires, changes in human capital. Some existing workers will need to learn new skills and new entrants to the labor force will need to have learned new knowledge and skills to find employment. Workers with skills no longer needed will have to adjust; the adjustment might be to learn new skills, shift to unskilled jobs or even leave the labor force.

There will be rigidities associated with these changes in spending and, in particular, production. Rapidly growing industries might find it difficult to obtain sufficient workers with the new types of skills required. But, over time, new education and training will solve this problem. There may be more angst on the other side – from owners of human or physical resources no longer in demand. It is not possible to prevent these changes though; these owners will have either to adapt or retire. As the Luddites found in 19th century England and the labor unions found in 1960s to 1980s Britain, it is possible to protest against change, it might even be possible to delay change but it is not possible to prevent change in a growing economy.

The location of economic activity will keep changing. Growth industries tend to be concentrated in locations which provide access to critical inputs. As these industries change, the location of rapid growth will change accordingly. In the broadest of terms, the move from agriculture to heavy manufacturing brought about a shift in activity from farms and the countryside to areas conveniently placed for access to raw materials. The shift to light manufacturing brought about a shift towards product markets – where the people were. The more recent shift to services has accentuated the shift to urban concentrations. The latest shift to internet-related industries is bringing about a shift to areas where people wish to live.

9.15 Incomes

Economic growth generates large and continuing increases in average incomes. Everyone's income will increase with economic growth.

However, not everyone's income necessarily will increase equally and certainly not everyone's income will be the same.

Absolute poverty is eliminated in the early stages of growth although relative poverty will always be present as there will always be a bottom 15 or 20% of the income distribution. For example, OECD (2009) calculates that the poverty rate in the United States is 17% where poverty is defined as household income less than 50% of the median household income. It is somewhat arbitrary and judgemental to view poverty as being income less than 50% of the median as, by definition, there will always be incomes less than 50% of the median. What is not a matter of judgement is that economic growth increases everyone's income, including those with incomes below 50% of the median.

Economic growth is associated with increasing use of capital, both physical capital and human capital. This has two likely effects. First, the share of total income going to capital rather than unskilled labor is likely to increase. Second, investing in human capital by education and training provides a route whereby individuals can gain additional income, over and above the rise in basic incomes generated by growth.

The distribution of income emerging from a market economy always will be unequal. The shape of this distribution will be log normal with a substantial number below the mean, most around the mean and a relatively small proportion with high incomes in the long upper tail of the distribution. The proportion with high incomes might increase as a result of these people leading economic change, especially in the growth industries and as income to capital increases. Those best able to lead change or cope with change and those investing in (physical or human) capital will do best. If society judges that the income distribution emerging from the market is excessively unequal, policies have been developed to redistribute income, reducing the final income of those above the average and increasing the final income of those at the lower end of the distribution. These policies, now used in all high income countries, take two forms – a "safety net" to assist the purchasing power of people at the bottom of the income distribution and redistributive taxation to take from high incomes and give, in money or in kind, to low incomes. These policies bring after-adjustment incomes closer to the mean; they reduce the dispersion of after-adjustment incomes around the mean. The mean, though, continues to increase with economic growth.

9.16 The role of government

Governments have several essential roles in helping to sustain frontier economic growth. However, this is different from causing growth - governments cannot create frontier growth. Governments can facilitate growth or they can retard or even prevent it, the choice is theirs. We do not think that governments make this choice directly but indirectly they either facilitate or retard growth by their choice of economic policies or of social policies with economic consequences. (Unfortunately, governments tend to make policy decisions unaware of the likely consequences for economic growth.)

The first government role involves the pre-conditions for growth. There must be personal security so that people can get on with their economic activities free from worry about their own safety. There must be rule of law, property rights, absence of confiscatory taxation and absence of arbitrary power, by governments or anyone else, so that people can get on with their economic activities secure in the knowledge that agreements will be respected and that they will be able to enjoy the fruits of the own efforts. And, there must be a market system to manage resource allocation as there is no opportunity for and no incentive for creative, productive change in a government-controlled economy.

Growth requires a healthy population. There must be clean water and effective waste-water systems, effective waste disposal systems, public health systems and personal health care systems. The government may provide these or private organizations may provide them or the government may contract private organizations to provide them; the essential point is that, one way or another, these services be provided. Of course, the population must be well fed. Agricultural productivity is now so high that the market will take care of providing sufficient food; all the government has to do is get out of the way.

Similarly, growth requires an educated population. Primary and secondary education is a government responsibility although there is room for private providers. Education beyond high school level must also be available. This covers technical or applied learning as well as academic learning. These education services may be produced by governments or by private institutions but it is essential that they be available and widely accessible.

Growth depends on trade and communication. Local roads and mass transit can be provided only by the government although highways, railroads, ports and airports might be provided by either government or private interests. Communications, such as telephone, radio broadcasting, television broadcasting, newspapers and the internet network, are best provided by business, not by governments. This is for two reasons – first, growth depends on the free flow of information and governments often are tempted to interfere with information flows, and second, governments cannot handle the rapid change in technology which has characterized communication media. Governments though must ensure that communication resources, such as radio spectra or cable rights of way, are available. Similarly, governments must ensure that suppliers of electricity and other forms of energy can secure access to their sources and rights of way to deliver their products.

Government standards are needed for the basic health and safety features of many activities and equipment. Performance standards are not needed for products where the customer can readily acquire the information needed for an informed decision or where purchases are small and repetitive. However, in some activities, such as residential construction or pharmaceuticals, there are fundamental information asymmetries and government-backed standards are needed to protect the customer.

Governments have a vital role in ensuring that markets are as open as possible. Internally, this means minimizing barriers to trade, barriers such as licenses, quotas, monopolies and regulations in product markets, labor markets and capital markets. Internationally, the objective should be to free up international trade so that comparative advantage in production and exchange can operate. In general, economic growth involves change; restrictions which inhibit change in spending and resource allocation are inimical to growth.

History has taught us that banking regulation is needed. This is partly to deal with information asymmetries, as small depositors lend their money to large institutions, and partly to deal with the perverse incentives in some types of lending which encourage institutions to take on too much risk in the expectation that they will not have to carry the full consequences of adverse outcomes.

There is an essential role for government macroeconomic or stabilization policy – keeping demand growth on track, not too fast (leading to excessive inflation) and not too slow (causing lost output and income). The key mechanism for macroeconomic management is monetary or credit policy where credit and financial conditions are managed so as to keep total spending growing at a moderate rate consistent with full use of the economy's productive capability. This task of the monetary authorities is made considerably easier by governments keeping their spending and revenues in line.

Government activities which try proactively to encourage growth are generally a waste of time and resources. Governments tend to focus either on preserving the past or giving preferential treatment to special interest groups or, in innovation, producing nice stuff which nobody wants. Change and innovation are central to economic growth but the innovation comes from new commercial ideas, not from science and not from governments. Governments have an important role in funding fundamental science but governments should stop there. The innovations which have driven economic growth in the past 300 years have come from commercially motivated individuals and businesses. Governments have a role in providing the foundations but not in doing the commerce.

The best policy for governments in promoting economic growth is to make sure the basics are provided and then to keep out of the way. Growth is led on the demand side by a succession of major commercial innovations and these come from highly motivated individuals operating within the market system in pursuit of fame and fortune.

Growth is sustained on the supply side by people and businesses seeking profit by improving productive efficiencies and by investment. These mechanisms do not involve the government.

9.17 Stability

Economic growth, even if it occurs, is not guaranteed to be stable. This is unlike the prediction of conventional growth theory in which the economy converges to and then grows along a steady growth path. In fact, the growth mechanisms which we have identified provide no assurance that either spending growth or the growth in productive capacity will be steady. Frontier economies have no inherent mechanism that generates growth along a steady state path.

Our growth path is determined by the interplay of several forces. Steady growth depends, on the supply side, on having steady increases in capital per worker and in total factor productivity and, on the demand side, on a succession of new, growth products and on total spending increasing steadily. These are four conditions which all have to be satisfied; there is nothing automatic which ensures that these conditions will be satisfied and continue to be satisfied.

History shows that things can go wrong and move a country away from steady growth, either temporarily or permanently. Here are some examples of instabilities over the past century.

- World War I. The United Kingdom saw rapid growth through 1918 then a slump; the average GDP growth rate from 1913 to 1921 was -1.3% a year.
- Roaring 20s. The 1920s saw a boom in the United States with GDP growth 1921 through 1929 averaging 6.0% a year.
- The Great Depression. GDP per capita in the U.S. did not surpass the 1929 level until 1940.
- World War II. The U.S. experienced rapid growth during the War; growth then slowed; GDP per capita did not pass the 1945 level until 1962, 17 years later.

- Inflation. Inflation in the U.S. in the 1970s and then getting inflation out of the system was associated with slow growth. GDP per capita growth from 1973 to 1982 was just 1.0% a year compared to the long term trend of 2.1%.

- Banking crises. There have been many banking crises in the United States and other countries, associated with rapid growth during the initial period of credit expansion and then slow growth in the subsequent clean up.

- Government interference. Extensive involvement by the government in resource allocation leads to slow growth such as the experience of Britain with the government - trade union struggle in the 1970s and the experience of New Zealand which lost 15 years of growth after 1975.

- Government ineptitude. A classic example is Argentina. This resource-rich country had a relatively high income at the turn of the 20th century, based mainly on exporting foodstuffs to the United States and Europe. But, beginning with the populist government of Juan Peron after World War II, Argentina has experienced wildly varying rates of inflation and just slow, erratic economic growth; the International Monetary Fund ranked Argentina 55th in the world in terms of GDP per capita in 2012.

Steady growth is the exception rather than the rule. The record of the United States from 1889 to 2010 indicates the level of stability or instability even for the world's leading growth country:

- Annual growth of GDP per capita was more than three standard deviations away from its trend rate of 2.1% in 94% of the years; five year growth was more than three standard deviations away 97% of the time;

- The mean relative deviation from trend growth was 1.9 for one year growth rates and 0.8 for five year growth rates.

Frontier economies grow unevenly about a growth trend; their growth has never been steady. External events and changing government policies can move growth away from the trend for several years. But, their growth generally has returned towards the trend. This is due primarily to governments eventually recognizing problems and introducing corrective economic policies. At the same time, individual prudence in managing borrowing and bank prudence in personal lending have ultimately introduced a degree of stabilization into the expansion of credit and personal spending. Individual behavior introduces a tendency to stability but corrective government policy is needed to bring the economy back from its deviations.

And, even more important, it is highly beneficial for economic growth if governments desist from pursuing the types of policies which have caused so many economic instabilities in the past.

9.18 Relationship to existing theory

The central result of conventional growth theory is that growth converges to a steady path with GDP growing at rate n + g, the population growth rate plus the rate of growth of labor effectiveness. The steady growth rate in GDP per capita is determined solely by the increase in labor effectiveness. In Solow-type models this productivity increase is the essence of growth but this "g" is given from outside of the model.

Our expression of the economic growth process can generate, as a particular case, the growth path of Solow-type models. Starting with our equation (9.1) we can arrive at a growth path with a similar, constant growth rate. If the capital/labor ratio in all industries grows at the same, constant rate "α", if the "b_i" coefficients for all industries are the same, with value "b", and if labor quality and Total Factor Productivity growth at constant rates then equation (9.1) simplifies to:

$$gr(Y/LH) \;=\; gr(Lqual) \;+\; b \times \alpha \;+\; gr(TFP)$$

This is a constant growth rate for GDP per capita. This is comparable to the growth path of conventional theory with "g", the rate of increase of labor effectiveness, replaced by three constant terms, corresponding to the three sources of increase in labor effectiveness – labor quality, capital per worker and TFP.

However, this is a special case. Our approach does not necessarily generate a steady growth rate. Solow models are completely deterministic – they are equations which cover each macroeconomic variable. One property of the solution to these equations is that growth converges to a steady path. Our approach is not completely deterministic – it does not predict every variable. As such, our approach does not generate a unique prediction about the growth path. Our approach sets out elements and mechanisms; the growth path which emerges from these depends on the specifics of these elements and we cannot predict these.

This is a basic difference between our approach and conventional growth theory. Conventional theory seeks a mathematical formulation which completely determines the growth path for GDP. The result is a precisely defined macroeconomic growth path. It is all there! We do not attempt to predict everything; our approach does not yield a completely defined growth path. Our approach is nor even fully mathematical. It is logical rather than mathematical. Our approach identifies the causes and processes of growth but we do not know precisely, numerically how these will work out in practice.

Our approach delves into the mechanisms of growth; the resulting growth path is the result of the interplay of growth in production potential, spending, new products and government macroeconomic policy. The resulting growth path for the leading country, the United States, has followed a broadly steady growth trend but with clear variations around this trend. The United States has grown in this fashion through continuing productivity improvement, continuing increases in capital per worker, a succession of major product innovations and new growth industries, and broadly effective government policies to keep spending growth within a target band. The development of a consumer society and the development of consumer credit have also been crucial in maintaining spending growth. Actual growth has reflected all these various forces and there has been nothing automatic or steady-state about the growth outcome.

We look at growth at the industry level and also introduce a demand side into industry behavior. Different industries follow different growth paths in response to their different demand characteristics. The GDP growth path is the aggregate of the industry growth paths. Figure 9.2 illustrates this. The highest line shows the growth of constant price GDP. In conventional theory, which operates at the economy-wide level, this is the direct outcome of the growth model. However, our approach builds up to GDP from the industry level. Some industries are in relative decline, growing slowly, say at 1 - 1.5%, with most industries, the mainstream industries, growing at moderate rates, say around 3 – 3.25%. A succession of rapidly growing leading industries then pulls total GDP up to its growth path of, say, 3.5%. Each leading industry grows along its own S shaped or logistic curve. As one leading industry saturates its markets and its growth slows another new industry emerges and takes over the leadership role. Meanwhile, investment and productivity advances in the mainstream industries allow these industries not only to generate rising incomes but also to make resources available to the rapid growth industries.

Figure 9.2 Composition of GDP growth

150 years of GDP growth, starting from GDP = 1

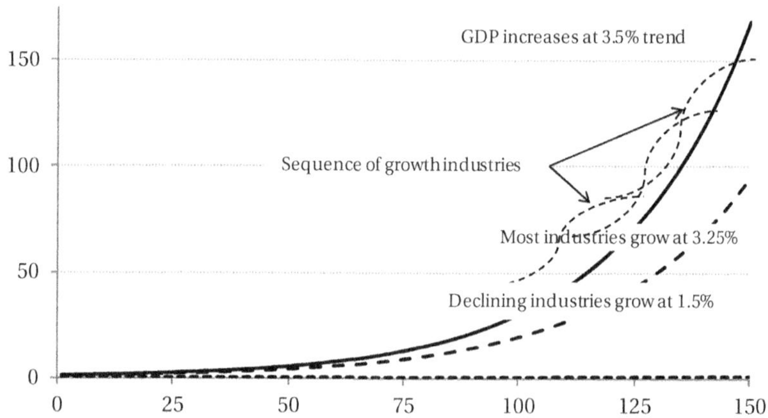

Our approach to growth, operating at the industry level and taking account of both demand and supply processes, allows us to look at the changing structure of a growth economy. This is unlike conventional theory which, operating at the economy-wide level, does not encompass structure. The different growth patterns of different industries account for much of the structural change associated with growth. As new industries emerge and old industries decline, spending patterns change, production patterns change and the location of economic activity changes. Added to these effects are the results of process innovation – improvements in the organization and processes of production. Many of these production changes are embodied in physical capital and in human capital; there are continuing changes in the demand for particular types of physical capital and for particular human skills.

Productivity improvement is vitally important in both our theory and conventional theory. Conventional theory assumes labor effectiveness or other indicators of productivity increase at a steady rate; this is frequently attributed to innovation. We separate innovation into two types – product innovation and process innovation. Product innovation operates essentially through the demand side of the economy, creating new markets and new industries; process innovation operates through the production or supply side of the economy, increasing productivity in the established industries. The nature of process innovation appears primarily to involve incremental improvements in management, operations, physical capital and labor practices which combine to increase productive efficiency. Occasionally there are step changes in production processes, usually in particular industries, which allow larger increases in production efficiency.

Conventional growth theory, although giving the impression of great precision, is not designed for forecasting. The parameters of the model and the drivers of growth are introduced by assumption so there is no independent mechanism for forecasting. But, forecasting is not the point of conventional growth theory; the objective is to try to explain past growth or at least the past set of stylized facts about growth. Our explanation of the growth process similarly is not designed for forecasting. Our objective has been to identify, clarify and explain the mechanisms of the growth process. This does not refer to stylized facts but to the actual facts of economic growth experienced by those countries which, in the past 300 years, have actually experienced sustained growth.

Chapter 10
Conclusions

10.1 What, when, where, how and why

The key to understanding anything is to answer the "w" questions – what, when, where, how and why? Understanding economic growth is the same. We have already set out a theory of economic growth in logical terms. But economic growth can be understood also in terms of the five "w"s. Here are the answers.

What is economic growth? It is the continuing increase in per capita incomes. It is typically measured on the production side (and total production equals total income as well as total final demand spending) as constant price GDP per capita. Continuing means growth sustained over a time scale not of years but of decades and even centuries.

When did it happen? Economic growth started in the early 18th century, say around 1725.

Where did it happen? The first country to commence economic growth was Britain with the Industrial Revolution. Leadership passed to the United States around the turn of the 20th century and continues with the United States to this day. Many other countries have also enjoyed economic growth either by being pulled along by the growth leaders or by using technologies developed by the growth leaders and exporting simple goods to high income countries.

How does economic growth take place? Economic growth in the leading countries such as the United States occurs through a particular interaction between growing demand and growing supply. The demand side is based on a sequence of new products (creating growth industries) and rising total consumer demand. The growth in consumer spending is based on personal attitudes and values, the consumer society, together with the availability of consumer credit. Supply expansion is based on more and better capital and labor together with rising productivity. Productivity advance takes place in the established industries, increasing incomes throughout the economy as well as releasing resources to sustain the growth industries.

Part of the "how" of economic growth is action by governments. This is not to say that everything that governments do is useful but it is to say that several types of government activity are essential for continuing growth. Maintenance of law and order, the operation of an effective legal system, and the provision of health, education and transportation infrastructure are necessary for growth. Provision of an income safety net has become an essential part of creating widespread interest in continuing, rather than opposing, the market system. Finally, the government has an essential role in ensuring that the financial system is stable and that there is an appropriate continuing expansion in the availability of credit.

Why does economic growth occur? The essence of economic growth lies in two forms of change – product innovation and process innovation. Product innovation is the introduction of a succession of new products, and the adoption of these new products by consumers, creating a succession of growth industries. Why does this happen? The flow of new products arises from the search by talented and motivated individuals for economic and social success by coming up with new products for which there are (potentially) vast markets. The adoption of new products arises from the operation of the consumer society whereby people wish to keep expanding their consumption of goods and services and also to try new goods and services. The personal attitudes and values underlying the consumer society mean that more consumption is always better; the associated increase in consumer demand keeps driving the economy upwards. At the same time there is process innovation – producing things more efficiently. Mostly, this is incremental improvement due to managerial or technical improvements; from time to time though there are step changes in managerial or production technology which result in larger improvements in productivity. The motivation for these changes also is economic – producers wish to increase incomes for themselves and for their owners.

At the heart of why economic growth continues is incentives – people want to advance their own interests. Consumers wish to keep increasing their consumption, producers wish to increase their incomes – whether labor income or capital income. The system which integrates all these incentives and actions, and allows them to work, is the market. The market system provides the signals (of shortages or opportunities) and provides the incentives (money and fame) to change, to do things more and better. Everybody then benefits from successful introduction of new products and increasing efficiency in the production of established goods and services – the innovators get rich, incomes keep increasing and consumption keeps increasing. Adam Smith's "invisible hand" translates individual incentives to economic growth.

10.2 Freedom

Personal freedom is both a cause and effect of economic growth.

A considerable degree of personal freedom is necessary for growth. This is so that people can make their own work and spending decisions and also so that people have the freedom and incentives to work, to invest and to innovate. This is so simple that it almost seems trite but it is fundamental – economic growth in a leading country depends on people being able to respond to economic incentives and opportunities, to make their own decisions and to enjoy the rewards of their efforts.

On the other side, economic growth has enhanced personal freedom - people in high income countries have an enormous range of opportunities and the ability to convert their preferences and choices into reality. These opportunities cover not just purchases and consumption of goods and services but also the use of time. One of the major benefits of economic growth has been the creation of more leisure time. Economic growth has given people leisure time together with the good health, education and purchasing power to use this time to pursue whatever their personal interests might be. We can choose what to learn, what to work at, what to consume, what to do in our leisure time, where to live, where to travel and so on. We can convert these opportunities into reality in a way unimaginable before growth.

10.3 A good thing

Economic growth is the greatest thing to have happened in the past 3,000 years. It has lifted billions of people out of abject poverty, it has allowed billions of people to live, it has improved health and extended lives, it has improved education and improved minds, it has relieved people from the drudgery of work and household chores, it has made work lives more varied and interesting, and it has made personal lives more comfortable. And, it has provided people with economic freedom.

There are, though, some downsides to growth. We know how to manage these problems and mostly have done so but there remain one or two areas where we seem to lack the collective wisdom and courage to do so.

Depletion of natural resources is not really a problem – there are a lot of resources out there and if one becomes scarce its price will go up, encouraging new supplies to be developed as well as encouraging people to switch to other forms of production and consumption. Petroleum provides a classic example of market forces working to provide continuing supply even though at the cost of rising prices.

Local environmental effects similarly are not really a problem – if these effects are perceived as being sufficiently serious people will press governments into action and force a clean-up. The economic system has shown time and again that, if pressured appropriately, it will alter production techniques and alter the mix of consumption and production to minimize new damage and even clean up old damage.

Similarly, poverty is not really a problem. Absolute poverty has been eliminated in countries which have experienced economic growth. But the market system, which is essential for growth, always generates an unequal distribution of income. Affluent societies view those at the bottom of this distribution as being poor and deserving of income protection. Modern economies have developed income redistribution systems to protect these people. Done in the right way, these redistributions provide a safety net – they ameliorate the position of those at the bottom of the distribution without seriously undermining the economic incentives and freedoms facing those in the middle or at the top, incentives and freedoms on which continuing growth depends. (Done in the wrong way, though, these redistributions destroy incentives for personal responsibility and personal improvement, and work to retard growth.)

There remains one serious cost from economic growth; this cost arises from environmental effects which transcend national boundaries. While governmental power can be brought to bear to minimize local environmental damage there is no such mechanism to handle global problems. This is a worry because we now have the capability of altering the planet in ways which we do not fully understand and which might have serious consequences for everybody on Earth. This risk can be mitigated but only if our political leaders have the foresight and courage to create effective international institutions.

10.4 Can economic growth continue?

Britain pioneered economic growth and grew steadily for more than 150 years. However, Britain then appeared to lose its spark and it fell behind, no longer serving as the growth leader. Is there anything we can learn from Britain's experience that might cast light on the ability of a country to continue as a frontier growth leader?

No-one knows for sure why Britain relinquished economic leadership. But, we can make some informed conjectures. These conjectures boil down to one adverse force – bad government. The politicians of Europe took their countries, including Britain, to war in 1914. World War I had an enormous cost in lives lost and in ongoing physical and psychological impairment. Britain lost a generation of young leaders. Britain diverted production from consumption and investment to military purposes and paid for this, in part, by selling down its world-wide assets. There followed years of instability - booms and busts, culminating in the Great Depression – until World War II repeated the trauma of the earlier war. In the hope of a brighter future, post-war Britain turned to social ownership and control of much of its industry and transportation. Then, the 1960s and 1970s saw years of industrial turmoil as organized labor tried to resist the tide of economic change while governments stood by and allowed this resistance to continue. Finally, under Prime Minister Margaret Thatcher in the 1980s, Britain returned to economic orthodoxy. These excursions into different economic and political conditions took 70 years, time when the energy and attention of Britons was directed to things other than individual economic improvement. We suspect that the reason for Britain's decline was that government actions dominated the economy and quashed individual initiative, preventing people from getting on with their own lives as they thought best.

In contrast, the United States for the past century has put together all the components needed for continuing economic growth. There have been instabilities and even periods of armed conflict abroad but, on the whole, Americans have been able to get on with their lives and with the business of economic self-improvement.

There has been a sequence of major new products. A consumer society backed up by ample credit and effective marketing has created demand for these products. Resources have shifted from older industries into growing industries. Productivity advance and investment have enabled ongoing growth in overall production and continuing increases in incomes.

The rest of the world has been pulled along by the growth of the United States. Some countries have grown by supplying raw materials and foodstuffs to the United States and other high income countries. Other countries have adopted management and technologies from the leading countries and grown by exploiting their lower costs to export manufactures to the high income countries. Growth has spread throughout the world, or at least to all countries where markets and trade are allowed to operate.

Can the United States continue to lead the growth process?

The leading industries at present, industries such as entertainment, computers/information technology and health care, still have some way to run in their life cycles. These industries have been growing strongly for only 40 – 50 years. Previous leading industries experienced rapid growth for anything from 75 years (automobiles, electricity) to 150 years (British cottons). One leading industry, telecommunications, is still going strong more than a century after it appeared.

New industries are appearing, such as internet-related services. Are information and communication technologies going to lead to rapid long-term growth? Will information technology be like the steam engine or like iron and steel and drive rapidly into uncharted waters for a century? No-one knows. But it is this sort of innovation with all manner of applications and room for development which has propelled Britain and then the United States forward for almost 300 years.

Let's look at these trends in the broadest perspective. The Industrial Revolution saw the spread of steam- (and later electricity-) powered machines. These machines expanded the power of the human body. We are now living through the Information Technology Revolution; this is expanding the power of the human mind. New products are appearing, more efficient ways of producing goods are being developed, more effective ways of managing our time are emerging, and different ways of using our time are being created. We are in the midst of these changes and do not know where they will lead. But if expanding the power of the mind is as potent as expanding the power of the body, growth has a long way still to run.

There is no reasonable argument that the world has run out of ideas or new products which people want. Charles Holland Duell, commissioner of the United States Patent and Trademark Office from 1898 to 1901, is purported to have said "everything that can be invented has been invented". This sentiment obviously has been proved completely wrong. In fact, Duell said something quite the opposite, something which has proved to be remarkably prescient: "In my opinion, all previous advances in the various lines of invention will appear totally insignificant when compared with those which the present century will witness. I almost wish that I might live my life over again to see the wonders which are at the threshold." (see Sass (1989)).

Conditions in the United States have, for more than a century now, been conducive to individuals (usually) or businesses (sometimes) coming up with "the next big thing" – a new growth product which will power ahead for the next 50 years or more. Obviously not every new product is a winner; in fact most new products either fail or just muddle along. But, one in a thousand or even one in a million innovative ideas hits on a product which resonates with customers and creates a large market with enormous growth potential. The consumer society is now ingrained in the high income countries and is spreading rapidly to other countries. It seems likely that this will provide the demand which, in the broadest sense, creates the opportunities for entrepreneurs to innovate and come up with the growth industries of tomorrow.

At the same time, growth is enabled by continuing improvements in production effectiveness. Most of these improvements are incremental increases in effectiveness in established industries; a few are leaps in production efficiency resulting from the introduction of new technologies and processes. There is no reason to think that this flow of improvements will cease. There is, on the contrary, every reason to think that production efficiencies will continue to be improved. People will continue to tinker with production processes, whether through management changes or engineering changes or materials changes or operating changes, to improve performance. The reason is simply human nature – people like the satisfaction and recognition which come from achieving something useful and, at least as important, people like the additional income which comes from successful change.

In general, conditions are promising in the United States for the emergence of new growth industries – a culture encouraging commercial innovation, rewards for successful innovation, a consumer society receptive to new products, a large market, finance for commercial innovation and for consumer spending, and the flexibility to try out new ideas and, if successful, attract the resources needed for rapid growth. At the same time, conditions are promising for continued increases in production effectiveness. Both demand and supply sides of the growth process look likely to continue.

10.5 Risks to economic growth

10.5.1 Various risks

There are, though, a variety of risks surrounding the continuation of economic growth. In the following sections we examine several of these under the headings attitudes, business, the environment and government. We have listed these in what we see as ascending order of danger to continued growth.

10.5.2 Attitudes

John Maynard Keynes (1931) speculated that people would take the fruits of economic growth in the form of increased leisure rather than increased incomes. Keynes actually raised the possibility of a 15 hour work week and speculated on what people would do to fill in all their leisure time. However, Keynes did not reckon on the consumer society.

Growth depends on the continued operation of the consumer society to provide markets for new types of goods and services. Could it be that consumers in the United States are sated? The evidence from peoples' statements and their actions is that they always want more. Only time will tell whether the consumer society continues to operate but there are no signs of its flagging. On the contrary, Figure 10.1, showing the savings rate for the United States, suggests that consumer spending is increasing – the savings rate in recent decades has actually been trending down.

Figure 10.1 Personal savings rate

Savings as % of Disposable Personal Income, United States

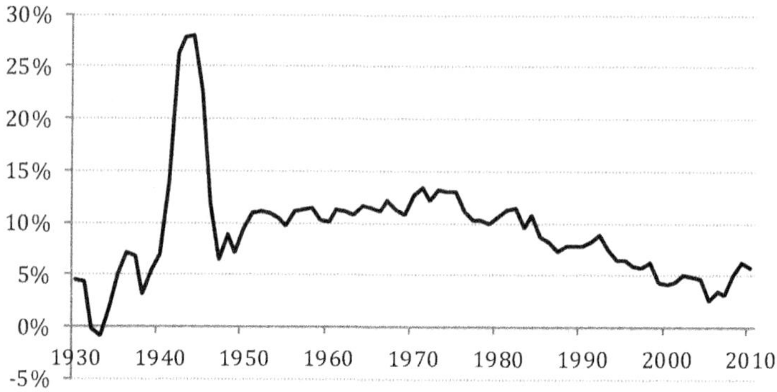

Source: Data from U.S. Bureau of Economic Analysis, National Economic Accounts.

Population aging is likely to slow future economic growth. The following analysis is for the United States although most other high income countries are experiencing similar demographic changes.

Table 10.1 shows labor force participation rates for males. (We use the rates for males in order to show the long term trend; female participation rates increased rapidly until the 2000s before beginning to decline.)

Table 10.1 Labor force participation rates, males

Civilian labor force participation rates, by age. %, United States

	20 to 24	25 to 34	35 to 44	45 to 54	55 to 64	65 on
1970	83	96	97	94	83	27
1990	84	94	94	91	68	16
2010	75	90	92	87	70	22
Rate of change 1970 - 2010	-0.3%	-0.2%	-0.1%	-0.2%	-0.4%	-0.5%

Source: Data from U.S. Bureau of Labor Statistics (2010).

Participation rates for all age groups have declined over the past 40 years. It seems likely that this trend will continue. However, the important feature is not so much the trends but the much lower participation rate for males aged 65 and over. As population growth slows and an increasing portion of the population passes age 65, the overall participation rate is likely to decline. The proportion of the U.S. resident male population aged 65 and over was 8.5% in 1970, 11.4% in 2010 and is projected (see U.S. Census Bureau (2008)) to increase to 18.5% by 2050. This huge demographic change will have a substantial effect on future participation rates. These changes are unlikely to be offset by increases in the working week; in fact, the average workweek in manufacturing declined steadily in the early 20th century but has been steady since World War II.

The consequence of these demographic changes is that labor input will grow less rapidly than population. As economic growth is measured in terms of GDP per capita, this trend will slow the rate of growth. However, this will slow but not prevent economic growth; we estimate that this will take only around 0.2% away from the annual growth rate.

10.5.3 Business

There are plenty of problems out there in the business world but we are not worried about these. The market has a way of dealing with businesses which lose touch with their customers – these businesses either reform or die. It is not unusual for a growth industry, after reaching maturity, to become sclerotic as management becomes lazy and workers extract the profits. The recent history of the automobile industry, culminating in the government rescue of General Motors, shows how a once leading industry can be hobbled by bad management, aggressive trade unions and myopic government policies. But, these inefficient businesses do not stifle economic growth – other businesses compete away their markets and consumers direct their spending elsewhere.

There are, though, some more subtle problems which could cause growth to slow.

Productivity improvements are essential to growth. We see no end to human ingenuity and the ability of producers incrementally to improve production effectiveness and from time to time come up with step changes in production effectiveness. Similarly, the development and introduction of new products are essential to growth. Again, we see no end to human ingenuity in coming up with new products. However, the introduction of new products and productivity improvements involve change. Restrictions on change limit growth. Management and workers must be prepared to do things differently, labor must be able to move from declining industries to growth industries, investment must be able to go to growth industries, and new industry must be able to locate in the most suitable places.

Change is, to many people, a most difficult challenge. Many people resist change. The modern economic and, in particular, political systems provide many opportunities to fight change. Restrictions on resource mobility, such as from labor laws, trade unions, government regulations or other government intervention can all be used for this purpose. These restrictions protect incomes today at the expense of higher incomes in the future; they are inimical to growth.

10.5.4 The environment

There appears to be little threat to continuing growth from running out of natural resources or even from local environmental effects. However, there are risks associated with global environmental effects. There is a risk to the continuing productivity of our oceans and, in particular, there is the risk of global costs and disruptions associated with climate change. These risks theoretically can be managed but our present institutions are not up to the task.

Climate change will slow future growth whether by (1) the effects of measures taken to reduce emissions of greenhouse gasses, especially to reduce the burning of hydrocarbon fuels, (2) the costs of protecting against or repairing damage caused by extreme climatic events, or (3) the costs via reduced productivity and worsened health outcomes. The Stern Review (2006) concluded that action to reduce greenhouse gas emissions to avoid what it saw as the worst effects of climate change might reduce future global GDP by 5 – 10% or even more. The Risky Business Project (2014) investigated the costs of climate change on the U.S. economy. It identified several categories of significant costs – damage to property from rising sea levels, reductions in agricultural productivity, costs from increased generation of electricity from other than hydrocarbons, adverse effects on public health and reduction in labor productivity resulting from deteriorating work conditions.

These types of studies imply that climate change will reduce but not prevent future economic growth. There are some parallels with the effects of higher oil prices in the 1970s. These energy shocks led to reductions in the use of hydrocarbon fuels while economic growth slowed but did not stop. However, today, with climate change, the world risks going into uncharted territory. There could be unforeseen effects and correspondingly unforeseen reductions in future economic growth rates. And, there is a risk, probably small but a risk nonetheless, that unchecked increases in emissions of greenhouse gasses will tip the Earth's climate into patterns never before experienced and with major or even catastrophic effects not only on our economies but also on our health and whole way of life.

10.5.5 Government

Governments today affect most aspects of economic activity. There is a real risk that government policies will retard future growth.

Restrictions on international trade in the 1930s exacerbated, although did not cause, a worldwide economic depression. New restrictions on trade could similarly hinder growth. However, the trend is for increasing trade and for, if anything, a reduction in trade barriers. Some countries are resisting efforts to reduce trade barriers but restrictions on trade serve mainly to harm the country imposing the restrictions. Other countries, led by the United States, generally favor more open trade. Our institutions here appear to be doing a reasonable job.

Taxation poses a significant risk. This risk arises not only from a high level of taxation, so governments claim a high share of incomes, but also from the resource allocation effects of the tax structure.

High tax rates on middle and high incomes pose a threat to the incentives for commercial innovation and investment. Figure 10.2 shows U.S. government spending rising apparently inexorably. The principal increase is in transfer payments. The increase in transfers will be accelerated by the pensions (social security) paid to the demographic bulge now entering its retirement years. Government spending in the long run must be matched by government revenues, essentially taxation. Will the increase in transfer payments continue? If it does, can it be taxation financed without threatening the incentives on which economic growth depends?

Figure 10.2 Spending as % GDP, United States

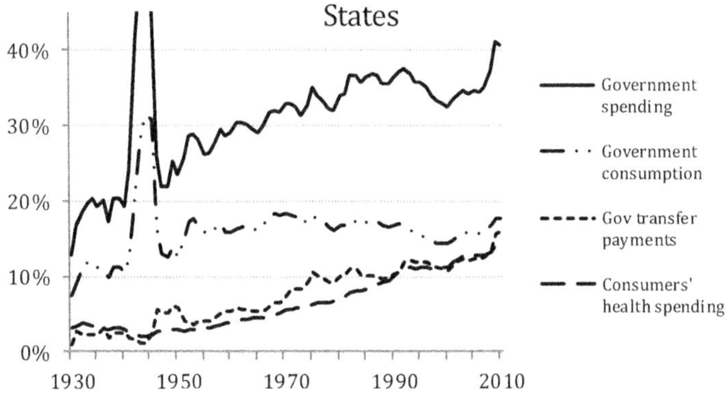

Source: Data from U.S. Bureau of Economic Analysis, National Economic Accounts.

The Figure also shows the steady increase in spending on health care. This spending already absorbs around 15% of GDP and is rising. The increase will be accelerated by recent policy moves to extend health care insurance; it also will be accelerated by the increasing proportion of the population entering the retirement years with associated increases in consumption of health care services. The economic burden is exacerbated by the reluctance of law-makers to let the market operate in health services. Will the direction of more and more spending to health care affect the ability of the economy to create and grow new industries and to increase average incomes?

A related problem concerns the U.S. tax structure. Special treatment of some expenditures, exemptions, different treatment of different forms of income and other complexities in the tax code motivate taxpayers to redirect their spending, hiring, investment and even location decisions away from an economically efficient pattern. These distortions harm productivity and slow growth. In addition, there is the economic cost associated with administering and complying with the complicated tax law.

The tax code continues to become more complex; for example, the number of pages in the CCH Standard Federal Tax Reporter increased at an average of 2.3% a year from 2004 through 2013 (see Wolters Kluwer CCH (2013)). An increasingly complex tax structure will reduce the rate of economic growth.

Arthur Laffer, Wayne Winegarden and John Childs (2011) calculate that the direct costs of administering and complying with the U.S. tax code in 2008 were $431bn, equivalent to 30% of the tax revenue collected or 2.9% of GDP. Laffer et al estimate that the income tax system reduces the U.S. annual growth rate by at least 0.45 percentage points. Richard Kneller, Michael Bleaney and Norman Gemmell (1999) use a growth model to estimate that reducing distortionary taxes by 1% of GDP can increase the annual growth rate by 0.1 to 0.2 percentage points. Conversely, the introduction of distortionary taxes might be expected to have a comparable effect in reducing the growth rate. As Federal income tax revenue is around 10% of GDP, the implication is that the tax structure is likely to be reducing growth rates significantly.

The final risk arising from government activity concerns regulation. Each regulation has an economic cost. These costs absorb labor and capital and also might force changes to production or spending processes; all of these reduce the productive potential of the economy. Each new regulation will reduce the level of potential GDP. A continuing sequence of new regulations will reduce the potential growth rate of GDP. In addition, regulations might make it more difficult to start and grow new businesses, impeding the development of the growth industries of the future.

Interest groups have worked out how to use the political process to advance their particular interests by means of regulation. The objectives might be for public interest purposes, such as health and safety, or social purposes, such as advancing the treatment or position of particular groups, or environmental purposes, such as preventing the use of particular resources, or they might be for narrow economic self-interest, such as restricting competition.

Our governmental processes appear to focus on the gross benefit of regulation, not the net benefit. Regulations typically do have a gross benefit to some (although this is not necessarily a gross benefit to society as a whole) but always have associated costs; these will be administrative and compliance costs as well as the indirect costs involved with forcing people to do things in a different and more costly way. If, as it appears to, the political process allows regulation to be pushed to the point of zero marginal gross benefit for the advocating groups, then the marginal net benefit will be negative – regulation will be extended too far, economic efficiency will be harmed.

The direct and indirect costs of regulation are only partly visible. Furthermore, these costs are dispersed and might impact any one person to only a small extent. Consequently, there typically is not strong political pressure to limit regulation – it is much easier for politicians to keep accommodating interest groups seeking new regulation. The result is that regulation keeps ratcheting up, becoming ever more extensive.

The apparently inexorable trend to more regulation must work against economic growth. Clyde Crews (2011) presents estimates that the Federal administrative cost of regulations in 2008 was $55bn while compliance costs were $1,752bn, together equivalent to 12.3% of GDP. Crews also presents page counts for the Federal Register, the journal of Federal rules, proposed rules and public notices; the trend increase in the page count is around 2.5% a year. There is no question but that government regulation imposes a large cost on the economy. If the cost of regulation, as estimated by Crews, has emerged steadily over the past 40 years, the growth rate penalty of Federal regulation would have been 0.3 percentage points. Allowing for state and local government regulation would accentuate this penalty, raising the growth penalty perhaps to 0.5 points or even more.

But, this represents a conundrum. No penalty from increasing regulation, or indeed from distortionary taxation, has shown up in the macroeconomic statistics where GDP growth has continued over the past two decades or so more or less along its prior trend (apart from the effects of the 2007-2008 financial crisis, which had separate causes).

However, it is possible that the productivity benefits of the spread of information technology might be there but have been offset by the productivity penalties of increasing regulation and distortionary taxation. This is in keeping with Solow's (1987) famous quip: "You can see the computer age everywhere but in the productivity statistics." Our conjecture about regulation is consistent with Crews' estimate of the burden of regulation, is consistent with Laffer et al's and Kneller et al's estimates of the effects of taxation, and also is consistent with the idea that the information technology revolution has had substantial and ongoing productivity benefits. If this conjecture has substance it implies that the trend to ever-increasing regulation and distortionary taxation will be real drags on future economic growth in the United States.

10.5.6 Overview of the risks

We have outlined a number of risks to continued economic growth. Each risk might lead to a small deceleration in future growth rates, such as 0.1 percentage point from one, 0.2 percentage points from another and 0.3 points from a third. Each single risk is unlikely to be overwhelming but the various possibilities together might create a substantial effect. Even though growth is likely to continue, reductions of this order of magnitude are significant when the previous trend growth rate in GDP per capita was around 2%.

10.6 Will economic growth continue?

We think that the growth mechanisms are now so ingrained that economic growth will continue unless some particularly powerful force derails it. Unfortunately, there does seem to be such a force - government.

We are worried not so much by the threat from different ideologies as we think that when (and if) the people of nations of different cultures and beliefs get a taste of higher incomes and what growth can do for personal opportunities they will be forced to embrace the market system. The east Asian countries are examples of different cultures and their governments climbing on board the growth train. And the Soviet Union and Maoist China provided convincing evidence on the other side – alternatives to the market, such as central planning, ultimately do not work.

We are more worried about the governments of the United States and other high income countries interfering with the market, resource allocation and incentive systems which generate growth. Argentina and New Zealand are two examples of once prosperous countries being derailed from their growth paths either temporarily (New Zealand) or permanently (Argentina) by poor government policies. Similarly, in Britain, a combination of poor government policies, bad management and assertive trade unions largely destroyed the manufacturing base of the once leading industrial economy.

However, there are several examples where the governments of high income countries have changed their ways when the burden of government interference came to be viewed as too great – Margaret Thatcher in the United Kingdom, Ronald Reagan in the United States, Roger Douglas in New Zealand, the reforms in Sweden in the 1990s and Gerhard Schroeder in Germany restrained leviathan and unleased new surges of economic growth.

We do not know whether the trend to big government and increased regulation in the United States can be reversed. The trend, particularly concerning regulation, is gradual, difficult to identify and difficult to resist. It generally takes a crisis to get the voting public to accept the need for bold change and follow bold leadership in overturning established policies. We do not think that the United States is yet at the tipping point in throttling growth. All we can say is that we hope that should this point be reached the American people will respond to political leadership to restrain the government and reassert the market system.

For reasons reflecting demographics and taxation and regulation and climate change we doubt that growth rates in the future will be as rapid as in the past. However, the fundamental drivers of growth are alive and, for the most part, well. We are optimistic that the stage is set for economic growth to continue long into the future.

Appendix 1
Units of Measurement

There are several different measurement systems in widespread use; the main three are the British system, the American system (based on the British system but not entirely the same) and the metric system. The principal units are:

The British or long ton: 2,240 pounds weight.

The American or short ton: 2,000 pounds weight.

The metric tonne: 1,000 kilograms.

The kilogram (kg) or 1,000 grams is the practical basis of metric weights. 1 kg is approximately 2.2 pounds weight. This means that the tonne is close to the long ton - 1 tonne is 98.4% of a long ton.

British or American distance: 1 mile is 1,760 yards or 5,280 feet. 1 yard is 3 feet or 36 inches. 1 foot is 12 inches. The relation to metric distance is that 1 metre/meter is 39.37 inches so 1 meter is close to 1 yard – 1 meter is 1.09 yards.

Longer distances in the metric system are measured in kilometers (km). 1 km is 1,000 meters. 1 km is 0.62 miles or, conversely, 1 mile is 1.61 km.

British or American area: 1 acre is 43,560 square feet or 4,840 square yards.

Metric area: 1 hectare is 10,000 square meters. 1 hectare is equivalent to 2.47 acres.

Volume – everyone is different. 1 British gallon is equivalent to 4.55 (metric) litres/liters; 1 American gallon is equivalent to 3.79 liters; 1 American gallon is equivalent to 0.83 British gallons.

Fortunately, the American, British, and metric systems all use the same measurement of time.

Power. James Watt formulated the concept of horsepower (hp) to measure the power output of his steam engines. 1 hp is equal to 746 Watts, the Watt being the metric measure of power, as it was subsequently defined. Brake horse power (bhp) is frequently used to express the power of internal combustion engines. 1 bhp is the same as 1 hp, the feature of brake horse power being simply that it is measured at the output shaft as the power needed to brake the engine.

Electrical power is generally measured in Watts, kilowatts (kW, 1,000 Watts), megawatts (MW, 1,000,000 Watts), gigawatts(GW, 1,000,000,000 Watts) and so on. Electrical energy is generally measured in kilowatt-hours (kWh), megawatt-hours (MWh) and so on.

The frequency of alternating current (AC) electricity is measured in Hertz, cycles per second.

Appendix 2
The United Kingdom

Economic growth started with the Industrial Revolution in England. England though is not a country, it is a region within what is now the United Kingdom (U.K.). The United Kingdom comprises England, Scotland, Wales and Northern Ireland.

Roman armies invaded the island of Britain and established a colony bounded on the north by Hadrian's Wall (completed in the year 128), close to the (later) boundary with Scotland. This province of Britannia was the genesis of the region which became England. Wales, to the west of England, was gradually incorporated into England with full legal integration completed in 1542. Scotland, after a series of military defeats, in 1707 entered into political union with England to create the Kingdom of Great Britain. A further Act of Union in 1800 added the Kingdom of Ireland to create the United Kingdom of Great Britain and Ireland. Ireland was partitioned in 1921 between the south, becoming the independent Republic of Ireland, and the north, Northern Ireland, which continued as part of the United Kingdom.

Any map of Britain will show the main cities. The main areas of the Industrial Revolution are the area around Manchester (cotton), Liverpool, London and Bristol (ports), Newcastle and the northeast (coal), Birmingham and Glasgow (engineering), and London again (insurance, banking and government).

Appendix 3
Sources of data

The research in this book has used data from many sources. These sources are identified in the text and in the figures and tables. There are several sources though which we have used many times. These are identified in this Appendix.

Angus Maddison has compiled the premier macroeconomic data base for more than 50 countries and going back as many as 2,000 years. Maddison calls this *The World Economy.* This work was published by the OECD in 2006; it is in two volumes. *Volume I: A Millennial Perspective* contains several essays by Madison on what he terms world development with extensive data series accompanying and fleshing out his arguments. *Volume 2: Historical Statistics* is exactly that, a huge base of GDP, population and related economic indicators covering both countries and time. The GDP and population series for the leading countries begin for the year 1CE and run through 2003. The GDP and population series are also available in electronic form as spreadsheets.

Most of the data for the United States come from U.S. Government agencies, ranging from the Department of Agriculture to the Central Intelligence Agency. There are, however, two principal sources; both are within the Department of Commerce – the U.S. Bureau of Economic Analysis and the U.S. Census Bureau.

The Bureau of Economic Analysis (BEA) compiles, among other things, the National Economic Accounts and the Industry Economic Accounts. The National Economic Accounts are the accounts for Gross Domestic Product, Gross Domestic Income and Gross Domestic Expenditure and their components. These give these economic measures in current dollars and in constant dollars, along with the associated price indexes (implicit price deflators). The Industry Economic Accounts give GDP by industry and the Input-Output accounts. The National Economic Accounts go back to 1929. BEA revised some definitions in 2013. For example, research and development expenditures were reclassified as fixed investment, the creation of entertainment, literary and artistic originals was recognized as fixed investment, and the measurement of residential fixed assets was improved. These led to relatively small changes to the accounts going back to 1929. BEA also moved the base year for measuring prices from 2005 to 2009. We had completed our investigation into U.S. growth before these changes were made. Therefore, we continued to use the previous data series which have a price base year of 2005. We have compared the constant dollar growth rates for the principal aggregates between the two data sets and find that none of our conclusions has been affected.

The Census Bureau of course carries out the census but we have made much more use of the Bureau's work in assembling information from a multitude of sources into the *Statistical Abstract of the United States.* These Abstracts have been published since 1878. We have found indispensable the *Bicentennial Edition: Historical Statistics of the United States, Colonial Times to 1970,* published in 1975. For subsequent years, we have made extensive use of the annual *Statistical Abstracts.*

Much of our historical data for England, Britain and the United Kingdom comes from statistical collections led by Phyllis Deane and Brian Mitchell. There are three core publications here – *British Economic Growth 1688 – 1959* by Phyllis Deane and W.A. Cole (first published in 1962, we use the 2nd edition, published in 1969), *Abstract of British Historical Statistics* by B.R. Mitchell and Phyllis Deane (first published in 1962, we use the 1971 edition) and *British Historical Statistics* by B.R. Mitchell (1988). We have also made extensive use of the Office for National Statistics. This Office terms itself "Publication Hub: Gateway to UK National Statistics" and it is exactly that. We have gone through this gateway for most of the more recent statistics about U.K. households and industries.

References

Abramovitz, Moses. 1986. "Catching Up, Forging Ahead, and Falling Behind". *The Journal of Economic History*, Vol. 46, No 2 (Jun.), pp 385-406.

Abramovitz, Moses, and Paul A. David. 1996. "Convergence and Deferred Catch-up: Productivity Leadership and the Waning of American Exceptionalism" in Ralph Landau, Timothy Taylor, and Gavin Wright (eds), *The Mosaic of Economic Growth*. Stanford, CA: Stanford University Press, pp 21-62.

Aghion, Philippe and Peter Howitt. 1992. "A Model of Growth through Creative Destruction". *Econometrica*, Vol. 60, No 2, pp 323-351.

Airlines for America (formerly Air Transport Association of America). *Annual Results U.S. Airlines*. Washington D.C.

Allen, Robert C. 2004. "Agriculture during the industrial revolution, 1700-1850" in Roderick Floud and Paul Johnson (eds), *The Cambridge Economic History of Modern Britain. Volume I: Industrialisation, 1700-1860*. Cambridge: Cambridge University Press, pp 96-116.

Allen, Robert C. 2009. *The British Industrial Revolution in Historical Perspective*. Cambridge: Cambridge University Press.

Arrow, Kenneth J. 1951. "An Extension of the Basic Theorems of Classical Welfare Economics" in *Proceedings of the second Berkeley symposium on mathematical statistics and probability*, Jerzy Neyman (ed.), Berkeley: University of California Press, pp 507-532.

Arrow, Kenneth J. 1962. "The Economic Implications of Learning by Doing". *The Review of Economic Studies*, Vol. 29, No 3 (Jun.), pp 155-173.

Australian Bureau of Statistics. Annual. *Australian National Accounts: National Income, Expenditure and Product*. Canberra, ACT.

Bergson, Abram. 1972. "The Comparative National Income of the USSR and the United States" in D.J. Daly (ed.), *International Comparisons of Prices and Output.* Cambridge, MA: National Bureau of Economic Research, pp 143-224.

Bliss, C.J. 1968. "On Putty-Clay". *Review of Economic Studies,* Vol. 35, No 2, pp 105-132.

Bowden, Sue and Avner Offer, 1994. "Household appliances and the use of time: the United States and Britain since the 1920s". *Economic History Review,* Vol. 47, No 4, pp 725-748.

BP. 2011. *BP Statistical Review of World Energy 2011.* www.bp.com/statisticalreview.

Bresnahan, T.F. and M. Trajtenberg. 1996. "General purpose technologies: 'engines of growth'?" *Journal of Econometrics, Annals of Econometrics,* Vol. 65, No 1, pp 83-108.

Broadberry, Stephen, Bruce M.S. Campbell and Bas van Leeuwen. 2013. "The Sectoral Distribution of the Labour Force and Labour Productivity in Britain, 1381-1851". *Explorations in Economic History,* Vol. 50, No 1, pp 16-27.

Bruland, Kristine. 2004. "Industrialisation and technological change" in Roderick Floud and Paul Johnson (eds), *The Cambridge Economic History of Modern Britain. Volume 1: Industrialisation, 1700-1860.* Cambridge: Cambridge University Press, pp 117-146.

Cardwell, V.B. 1982. "Fifty years of Minnesota corn production: sources of yield increase". *Agronomy Journal,* 74, pp 984-990.

Cass, David. 1965. "Optimum Growth in an Aggregative Model of Capital Accumulation". *Review of Economic Studies,* Vol. 32, No 3, pp 233-240.

Central Intelligence Agency. 2013. *The World Factbook 2013-14.* Washington D.C.

Chantrill, Christopher. *Spending History.* www.ukpublicspending.co.uk. Viewed 11 June 2011.

Christensen, Clayton M. 1997. *The Innovator's Dilemma.* Boston, MA: Harvard Business School Press.

Clark, Gregory. 2005. *The British Industrial Revolution, 1760 – 1860.* Course notes ECN 110B, Spring. Davis, CA: University of California.

Clark, Gregory. 2009. *The Macroeconomic Aggregates for England, 1209-2008.* WP 09-19. October. Davis, CA: University of California.

Coca-Cola Company. 2013. *Annual Report for 2012.* Form 10-K. February 27. Washington D.C.: U.S. Securities and Exchange Commission.

Costa, Dora L. 2000. "From Mill Town to Boardroom: The Rise of Women's Paid Labor". *Journal of Economic Perspectives,* Vol. 14, No 4, pp 101-122.

Court, W.H.B. 1967. *A Concise Economic History of Britain: From 1750 to Recent Times.* Cambridge: Cambridge University Press.

Crafts, N.F.R. 1985. *British Economic Growth during the Industrial Revolution.* Oxford: Clarendon Press.

Crafts, N.F.R. 2004. "Steam as a General Purpose Technology: A Growth Accounting Perspective". *Economic Journal,* Vol. 114, No 495, pp 338-351.

Crews, Clyde Wayne Jr. 2011. *Ten Thousand Commandments. An Annual Snapshot of the Federal Regulatory State.* Washington D.C.: Competitive Enterprise Institute.

Dante (Dante Alighieri). 1555. *The Divine Comedy.* This edition 2013, Allen Mandelbaum (translator). New York: Vintage Books.

Deane, Phyllis and W.A. Cole. 1969. *British Economic Growth, 1688 – 1959: Trends and Structure.* Cambridge: Cambridge University Press.

Davies and Company. 2000. *Climate Change: New Antarctic Ice Core Data.* www.daviesand/Choices/Precautionary_Planning/New_Data/.

DICE Database. 2014. *OECD Better Life Index, 2009 and 2013.* Munich: Ifo Institute.

Dickens, Charles. 1839. *Oliver Twist.* This edition 2009. London: Penguin Classics.

Department for Education and Skills. 2003. *Population of working age: by highest qualification.* London.

Easterlin, Richard A. 1973. "Does Money Buy Happiness?" *The Public Interest,* 30 (Winter), pp 3-10.

Easterlin, Richard A. 1974. "Does Economic Growth Improve the Human Lot? Some Empirical Evidence" in Paul A. David and Melvin W. Reder (eds), *Nations and Households in Economic Growth: Essays in Honor of Moses Abramovitz.* New York: Academic Press, pp 89-125.

ExxonMobil. 2011a. *Summary Annual Report.* Irving, TX: ExxonMobil Corporation.

ExxonMobil. 2011b. *Financial Statements and Supplemental Information. For the Fiscal Year Ended 31 December 2010.* Irving, TX: ExxonMobil Corporation.

Farman, J. C., B.G. Gardiner and J.D. Shanklin, 1985. "Large losses of total ozone in Antarctica reveal seasonal ClOx/NOx interaction". *Nature,* Vol. 315 (16 May), pp 207-210.

Federal Communications Commission. 2013. *Mobile Wireless Competition Report.* Washington D.C.

Federation of American Scientists. Learning Curve Calculator. www.fas.org/news/reference/calc/learn.htm. Viewed 17 May 2012.

Fernandez-Cornejo, Jorge and Margriet Caswell. 2006. *The First Decade of Genetically Engineered Crops in the United States. EIB-11.* Washington DC: Economic Research Service, U.S. Department of Agriculture.

Floud, Roderick and Donald McCloskey (eds). 1981. *The Economic History of Britain since 1700. Volume 1: 1700-1860.* Cambridge: Cambridge University Press.

Floud, Roderick and Paul Johnson (eds). 2004. *The Cambridge Economic History of Modern Britain. Volume 1: Industrialisation.* Cambridge: Cambridge University Press.

Fogel, Robert W. 1964. *Railroads and American Economic Growth: Essays in Econometric History.* Baltimore, MD: The Johns Hopkins University Press.

Fogel, Robert W. 1993. *Economic Growth, Population Theory and Physiology: The Bearing of Long-term Processes on the Making of Economic Policy.* Nobel Lecture, December 9. www.nobelprize.org/nobel_prizes/economic-sciences/laureates/1993/fogel-lecture.html.

Food and Agriculture Organization. "Atlantic cod capture 1950-2005". FAO Fishery Statistics programme (FIGIS Online). From wikipedia File:Atlantic cod capture 1950 2005.png, downloaded 28 September 2011.

Food and Agriculture Organization. 2009. "Atlantic cod capture 1950-2005". From FAO Fishery Statistics programme, FIGIS Online. Also in FAO Fisheries and Aquaculture Circular No. 1038, FIEL/C1038 (En). Rome.

Fraser, Derek. 2009. *The Evolution of the British Welfare State* (4th ed.). Basingstoke: Palgrave/Macmillan.

Friedman, Milton. 1959. *A Program for Monetary Stability.* New York: Fordham University Press.

Friedman, Milton.1962. *Capitalism and Freedom.* Chicago: Chicago University Press.

Friedman, Milton and Anna J. Schwartz. 1963. *A Monetary History of the United States, 1867–1960.* Princeton, NJ: Princeton University Press.

Friedman, Milton. 1968. "The Role of Monetary Policy." *American Economic Review,* Vol. 58, No 1, pp 1–17.

Friedman, Milton and Rose D. Friedman. 1980. *Free to Choose: A personal statement.* New York: Harcourt Brace Jovanovich.

Galbraith, John Kenneth. 1958. *The Affluent Society.* Boston, MA: Houghton Mifflin.

Government Actuary's Department. 2006. *Expectation of life at birth: by sex.* London. Office for National Statistics.

Government Actuary's Department. 2007. *National Population Projections: 2006-Based.* www.gad.gov.uk/Demography_Data/Population/.

Grossman, Gene M. and Elhanan Helpman. 1991. *Innovation and Growth in the Global Economy.* Cambridge, MA: MIT Press.

Hamilton, Earl J. 1934. *American Treasure and the Price Revolution in Spain, 1501-1650.* Cambridge, MA: Harvard University Press.

Hansen, Alvin. 1941. *Fiscal Policy and Business Cycles.* New York: Norton.

Hardin, Garrett. 1968. "The Tragedy of the Commons". *Science,* Vol. 162 no. 3859, (13 December), pp 1243-1248.

Harley, C. Knick. 1999. "Reassessing the Industrial Revolution: A Macro View" in Joel Mokyr (ed.), *The British Industrial Revolution, An Economic Perspective.* Second edition. Boulder, CO: Westview Press, pp 160-205.

Hicks, J.R. 1937. "Mr. Keynes and the 'Classics', A Suggested Interpretation". *Econometrica,* Vol. 5, Issue 2, pp 147–159.

HM Revenue & Customs. 2014. *Personal Incomes Statistics 2011-12.* London.

Ho Ping-ti. 1959. *Studies on the population of China 1368-1953.* Cambridge, MA: Harvard University Press.

Hicks, Joe and Grahame Allen. 1999. *A Century of Change: Trends in UK Statistics since 1900.* Research Paper 99/111. London: House of Commons Library.

Hudson, Edward A. and Dale W. Jorgenson. 1974. "U.S. Energy Policy and Economic Growth, 1975-2000," *Bell Journal of Economics and Management Science,* Vol. 5, No 2, pp 461-514.

Intergovernmental Panel on Climate Change (IPCC). 2001a. *Climate Change 2001: Scientific Basis.* Geneva: United Nations Environment Programme.

Intergovernmental Panel on Climate Change (IPCC). 2001b. *Climate Change 2001: Synthesis Report.* Geneva: United Nations Environment Programme.

International Panel on Climate Change (IPCC), 2007a. *IPCC Fourth Assessment Report (AR4). Climate Change 2007: The Physical Science Basis.* Geneva: United Nations Environment Programme.

Intergovernmental Panel on Climate Change (IPCC). 2007b. *IPCC Fourth Assessment Report (AR4). Climate Change 2007: Synthesis Report.* Geneva: United Nations Environment Programme.

Johansen, L. 1959. "Substitution versus Fixed Production Coefficients in the Theory of Economic Growth: A Synthesis". *Econometrica,* Vol. 27, No 2, pp 157-176.

Jorgenson, D.W. and Z. Griliches. 1967. "The Explanation of Productivity Change". *The Review of Economic Studies,* Vol. 34, No 3, pp 249-283.

Jorgenson, Dale W. 2005. "Accounting for Growth in the Information Age" in Philippe Aghion and Steven N. Durlauf (eds), *Handbook of Growth Economics. Vol. 1, Part A.* Amsterdam: Elsevier North-Holland, pp 743-815.

Jorgenson, Dale W., Mun Ho and Jon Samuels. 2010. *New Data on U.S. Productivity Growth by Industry.* Presentation to: ICT and Economic Growth Conference, Munich School of Management, LMU, November 4-6, 2010. Viewed at people.hmdc.harvard.edu/~mho/Munich.nov2010.pdf on 21 August 2012.

Jorgenson, Dale W., Mun S. Ho, and Jon Samuels. 2012. "Information Technology and U.S. Productivity Growth" in Matilde Mas and Robert Stehrer (eds), *Industrial Productivity in Europe.* Northampton, MA: Edward Elgar, pp 34-65.

Jovanovic, Boyan and Peter L. Rousseau. 2005. "General Purpose Technologies" in Philippe Aghion and Steven N. Durlauf (eds), *Handbook of Growth Economics. Vol. 1, Part B.* Amsterdam: Elsevier North-Holland, pp 1181-1224.

Kaldor, Nicholas. 1957. "A model of economic growth". *The Economic Journal,* Vol. 67, No 268, pp 591-624.

Kendrick, John W. 1961. *Productivity Trends in the United States.* Princeton, NJ: Princeton University Press for the National Bureau of Economic Research.

Kendrick, John W. 1973. *Postwar Productivity Trends in the United States, 1948 - 1969.* New York: Columbia University Press for the National Bureau of Economic Research.

Keynes, John Maynard. 1931. *Essays in Persuasion.* London: MacMillan.

Keynes, John Maynard. 1936. *The General Theory of Employment, Interest and Money.* London: MacMillan.

Killingsworth, Mark R. and James J. Heckman. 1986. "Female Labor Supply: A Survey" in Orley Ashenfelter and Richard Layard (eds), *Handbook of Labor Economics, Volume 1.* Amsterdam: Elsevier, pp 103-204.

Kneller, Richard, Michael F. Bleaney and Norman Gemmell. 1999. "Fiscal policy and growth: evidence from OECD countries". *Journal of Public Economics,* Vol. 74, Issue 2, pp 171–190.

Koopmans, Tjalling C. 1966. "On the Concept of Optimal Economic Growth" in *The Econometric Approach to Development Planning.* Amsterdam: North-Holland.

Krugman, Paul. 1979. "Increasing Returns, Monopolistic Competition, and International Trade". *Journal of International Economics,* Vol. 9, Issue 4, pp 469-479.

Krugman, Paul. 1991. "Increasing Returns and Economic Geography". *Journal of Political Economy,* Vol. 99, Issue 3, pp 483-499.

Kuznets, Simon S. 1966. *Modern Economic Growth: Rate, Structure, and Spread.* New Haven, CT: Yale University Press.

Kuznets, Simon S. 1971. *Economic Growth of Nations: Total Output and Production Structure.* Cambridge, MA: Harvard University Press.

Kuznets, Simon S. 1973. "Modern Economic Growth: Findings and Reflections". *American Economic Review,* Vol. 63, No 3, pp 247-258.

Lader, Deborah, Sandra Short and Jonathan Gershuny. 2006. *The Time Use Survey, 2005.* London: Office for National Statistics.

Laffer, Arthur B., Wayne H. Winegarden and John Childs. 2011. *The Economic Burden Caused by Tax Code Complexity.* San Francisco, CA: The Laffer Center for Supply-Side Economics.

Layard, Richard. 2005. *Happiness: Lessons from a New Science.* London: Penguin.

Lebow, Victor. 1955. "Price Competition in 1955". *Journal of Retailing,* Vol. 31, No 1, pp 5-10.

Leontief, Wassily W. 1941. *The Structure of American Economy, 1919–1929.* Cambridge, MA: Harvard University Press.

Lin, Justin Wifu, 1992. "Rural Reforms and Agricultural Growth in China". *American Economic Review,* Vol. 82, No 1, pp 34-51.

Lindert, Peter H. and Jeffrey G. Williamson. 1982. "Revising England's Social Tables, 1688-1812". *Explorations in Economic History,* Vol. 19, No 4, pp 385-408.

Lipsey, Richard G., Kenneth I. Carlaw and Clifford T. Bekar. 2005. *Economic Transformations: General Purpose Technologies and Long Term Economic Growth.* Oxford: Oxford University Press.

Lucas, Robert E., Jr. 1988. "On the Mechanics of Economic Development". *Journal of Monetary Economics,* Vol. 22, No 1, pp 3-42.

Machiavelli, Niccolo. c1513. *The Prince.* This edition 2005, Peter Bondanella (translator and editor) and Maurizio Viroli (introduction). Oxford: Oxford University Press.

Mackenzie, Debora. 1990. "Cheaper Alternatives for CFCs". *New Scientist*, Issue 1723 (30 June), pp 39-40.

Maddison, Angus. 2006a. *The World Economy, Volume 1: A Millennial Perspective*. Paris: OECD.

Maddison, Angus. 2006b. *The World Economy, Volume 2: Historical Statistics*. Paris: OECD.

Maddison, Angus. 2007. *Contours of the World Economy, 1–2030AD*. Oxford: Oxford University Press.

Malthus, Thomas. 1798. *An Essay on the Principle of Population*. This edition 1993. Oxford: Oxford University Press.

Mankiw, N. Gregory, David Romer and David N. Weil. 1992. "A Contribution to the Empirics of Economic Growth". *Quarterly Journal of Economics*, Vol. 107, No 2, pp 407-437.

Marshall, Alfred. 1890. *Principles of Economics*. London: Macmillan.

Marx, Carl. 1867. *Capital, Volume 1*. This edition 1992, Ben Fowkes (translator) and Ernest Mandel (Introduction). London: Penguin Classics.

Marx, Carl. 1863. *Theories of Surplus Value, Volume IV of Capital*. ePub version. www.marxists.org/archive/marx/works/1863/theories surplus-value/

Mathias, Peter. 1969. *The First Industrial Nation: An Economic History of Britain 1700-1914*. London: Metheun.

Meadows, Donella H., Dennis L. Meadows, Jørgen Randers and William W. Behrens III. 1972. *The Limits to Growth*. Commissioned by The Club of Rome. New York: Universe Books.

Menzies, Gavin, 2003. *1421: The Year China Discovered the World*. New York: HarperCollins.

Menzies, Gavin. 2008. *1434: The Year a Magnificent Chinese Fleet Sailed to Italy and Ignited the Renaissance*. New York: HarperCollins.

McCloskey, D.N. 1981. "The industrial revolution 1780-1860: a survey" in Roderick Floud and Donald McCloskey (eds), 1981, *The Economic History of Britain since 1700. Volume 1: 1700-1860.* Cambridge: Cambridge University Press, pp 103-127.

McKeown, Thomas. 1976. *The modern rise of population.* London: Edward Arnold.

Mitchell, B.R. 1988. *British Historical Statistics.* Cambridge: Cambridge University Press.

Mitchell, B.R. and Phyllis Deane. 1971. *Abstract of British Historical Statistics.* Cambridge: Cambridge University Press.

Mokyr, Joel. 1998. *The British Industrial Revolution: An Economic Perspective.* Second Edition. Boulder, CO: Westview Press.

Moore, Gordon E. 1965. "Cramming more components onto integrated circuits". *Electronics,* Vol. 38, No 8, (April 19), pp 114-117.

National Academy of Sciences. 1976. *Halocarbons: Effects on Stratospheric Ozone.* Washington D.C.

National Oceanic and Atmospheric Administration. 2011. *The Global Surface Temperature is Rising. Global Climate Change Indicators.* Washington D.C.: National Climatic Data Center, U.S. Department of Commerce.

National Oceanic and Atmospheric Administration. 2014. *800,000 Year Record of Carbon Dioxide (CO2) Concentrations. Global Climate Change Indicators*. Washington D.C.: National Climatic Data Center, U.S. Department of Commerce.

Nelson, L.B. 1990. *History of the U.S. Fertilizer Industry.* Muscle Shoals, AL: Tennessee Valley Authority.

OECD. 2000. *Literacy in the Information Age. Final Report of the International Adult Literacy Survey.* Paris.

OECD. 2009. *Factbook 2009: Economic, Environmental and Social Statistics.* Paris.

OECD. 2011a. *OECD Better Life Index.* ww.oecdbetterlifeindex.org. Viewed 31 May 2011.

OECD. 2011b. *Education at a Glance 2011: OECD Indicators.* Paris.

Office for National Statistics. Annual. *Gross Domestic Product by gross value added.* London.

Office for National Statistics. Annual. *U.K. National Accounts.* London.

Office for National Statistics. 2004. *Family Spending, 2003 Edition.* London.

Office for National Statistics. 2006a. *Input-Output Supply and Use Tables, 2004.* London.

Office for National Statistics. 2006b. *Focus on Consumer Prices, January 2006.* London.

Office for National Statistics. 2006c. *The Time Use Survey, 2005 (31 August 2006 Amendment).* London.

Office for National Statistics. 2009a. *Family Spending – A report on the 2002-03 Expenditure and Food Survey.* London.

Office for National Statistics. 2009b. *Report: Decennial Life Tables (2000-02).* Population Trends 136. London.

Office for National Statistics. 2009c. Labour Force Survey.

Office for National Statistics. 2010a. *Tenure of households (2001 Census).* London.

Office for National Statistics. 2010b. *General Lifestyle Survey, 2008 Report.* London.

Office for National Statistics. 2011. *Measuring National Well-being – Education and skills data tables.* Labour Force Survey. London.

Office for National Statistics. 2012a. *The Effects of Taxes and Benefits on Household Income, 2010/11.* London.

Office for National Statistics. 2012b. *Health Expectancies at Birth and at Age 65 in the United Kingdom, 2008-2010.* London.

Office for National Statistics. 2012c. *Health Expectancies in the United Kingdom, 2000-2002 to 2008-2010.* London.

Office for National Statistics. 2013. *General Lifestyle Survey, 2011.* London.

Packard, Vance. 1957. *The Hidden Persuaders.* New York: David McKay.

Parsons, Charles A. 1934. *Scientific Papers and Addresses of the Hon. Sir Charles A. Parsons.* Cambridge: Cambridge University Press.

Perkins, Dwight H. 1969. *Agricultural development in China, 1368-1968,* Chicago: Aldine.

Petit, J.R. et al. 1999. "Climate and atmospheric history of the past 420,000 years from the Vostok ice core, Antarctica". *Nature, 399* (3 June), pp 429-436.

Phelps, Edmund. S. 1962. "The New View of Investment: A Neoclassical Analysis". *Quarterly Journal of Economics,* Vol. 76, Issue 4, pp 548-567.

Ramsey, F.P. 1928."A Mathematical Theory of Saving". *Economic Journal.* Vol. 38, No 152, pp 543-539.

Ratner, Sidney, James H. Soltow and Richard Sylla. 1979. *The Evolution of the American Economy.* New York: Basic Books.

Ricardo, David. 1817. *On the Principles of Political Economy and Taxation.* London: John Murray. This edition 2004. New York: Dover.

Romer, David. 1996. *Advanced Macroeconomics.* New York: McGraw-Hill.

Romer, Paul M. 1986. "Increasing Returns and Long-Run Growth". *Journal of Political Economy,* Vol. 98, No 5, Part 2, pp S71-S102.

Romer, Paul M. 1990. "Endogenous Technological Change.". *Journal of Political Economy,* Vol. 94, No 5, pp 1002-37.

Rostow, Walt Whitman.1960. *The Stages of Economic Growth: A Non-Communist Manifesto.* Cambridge: Cambridge University Press.

Sass, Samuel. 1989. "A Patently False Patent Myth", *Skeptical Inquirer*, Vol. 13 (Spring), pp 310-313.

Schumpeter, Joseph A. 1942. *Capitalism, Socialism and Democracy.* New York: Harper.

Sloan, Alfred P. Jr. 1963. *My Years with General Motors.* New York: Doubleday.

Smith, Adam. 1776. *An Inquiry into the Nature and Causes of the Wealth of Nations.* This edition 1904,Edwin Cannan (ed.). London: Methuen.

Solow, Robert M. 1956. "A Contribution to the Theory of Economic Growth". *Quarterly Journal of Economics*, Vol. 70, No 1, pp 65 – 94.

Solow, Robert M. 1960. "Investment and Technical Progress" in Arrow, K., S. Karlin and P. Suppes (eds), *Mathematical Methods in the Social Sciences.* Stanford, CA: Stanford University Press.

Solow, Robert M. 1962. "Substitution and Fixed Proportions in the Theory of Capital". *Review of Economic Studies*, Vol. 29, No 3, pp 207-218.

Solow, Robert M. 1987. "We'd better watch out" in *New York Times Book Review.* July 12. New York: New York Times, p 36.

Statistics New Zealand. Annual. *National Accounts.* Wellington.

Stern, Nicolas. 2006. *The Stern Review of the Economics of Climate Change.* London: HM Treasury.

Stevenson, Betsey and Justin Wolpers. 2008. "Economic Growth and Subjective Well-Being: Reassessing the Easterlin Paradox". *Brookings Papers on Economic Activity*, Vol. 39, No 1, pp 1-102.

Summers, Robert and Alan Heston. 1991. "The Penn World Table (Mark 5): An Expanded Set of International Comparisons, 1950-1988". *Quarterly Journal of Economics*, Vol. 106, No 2, pp 327-368.

Szreter, Simon. 2011. Data on urbanization at www.hist.cam.ac.uk/course/szreter/urbanisation.pdf. Viewed 10 July 2011.

The Risky Business Project. 2014. *Risky Business. The Economic Risk of Climate Change in the United States.* Kate Gordon (Executive Director). riskybusiness.org/ uploads/files/RiskyBusiness_PrintedReport_FINAL_WEB_OPTIMIZED. pdf . Viewed 5 July 2014.

Tull, Jethro. 1731. *The Horse Hoeing Husbandry.* This edition 2007, Aaron Brachfeld and Mary Choate (eds). Agate, CO: Coastalfields.

U.K. Department for Transport. Annual. Aviation Statistics. *Air Traffic at U.K. Airports (AV101).* London.

U.K. Department for Transport. 2010. *National Travel Survey 2009.* London.

U.S. Bureau of Economic Analysis. Various years. *Input-Output Accounts.* Washington DC: U.S. Department of Commerce.

U.S. Bureau of Economic Analysis. Various years. *National Economic Accounts.* Washington DC: U.S. Department of Commerce.

U.S. Bureau of Labor Statistics. 2010. *Employment and Earnings Online.* January 2010 issue. Washington D.C.: U.S. Department of Labor.

U.S. Bureau of Labor Statistics. 2014. *Producer Price Index – Commodities.* Washington D.C.: U.S. Department of Labor.

U.S. Census Bureau. Annual, *Statistical Abstract of the United States.* Washington DC: U.S. Department of Commerce.

U.S. Census Bureau. 1976. *Historical Statistics of the United States. Colonial Times to 1970.* Washington DC: U.S. Department of Commerce.

U.S. Census Bureau. 2002. "Demographic Trends in the 20th Century (CENSR-4)". *Census 2000 Briefs and Special Reports.* Washington D.C.: U.S. Department of Commerce.

U.S. Census Bureau. 2008. "Table 3. (NP2008-T3)". *National Population Projections.* Washington D.C.: U.S. Department of Commerce.

U.S. Department of Agriculture. 2011a. *Farm Income and Wealth Statistics. Farm Income Data Files.* Economic Research Service. Washington D.C.

U.S. Department of Agriculture. 2011b. *Agricultural Productivity in the U.S.* Economic Research Service. Washington D.C.

U.S. Department of Transportation. Annual. *Highway Statistics.* Federal Highway Administration. Washington D.C.

U.S. Department of Transportation. Quarterly. *National Transportation Statistics.* Bureau of Transportation Statistics. Washington D.C.

U.S. Energy Information Administration. Monthly. *Monthly Energy Review.* Washington D.C.: U.S. Department of Energy.

U.S. Energy Information Administration. Annual. *Electric Power Annual.* Washington D.C.: U.S. Department of Energy.

U.S. Energy Information Administration. Annual. *Annual Energy Review.* Washington D.C.: U.S. Department of Energy.

U.S. Energy Information Administration. 2011. *Petroleum & Other Liquids: Product Supplied.* Washington D.C.: U.S. Department of Energy.

U.S. Energy Information Administration. 2012. *Cost of Finding Oil and Gas Reserves.* www.eia.gov/emeu/25opec/sld010.htm. Viewed 16 October 2012.

U.S. Environmental Protection Agency. 1998. *National Air Pollutant Emission Trends, 1900-1997. EPA 454/C-98-007.* Washington D.C.

U.S. Environmental Protection Agency. Annual. *Air Trends: Sulfur Dioxide.* Washington D.C.

U.S. Geological Survey. 2009. *Mineral Commodity Summaries.* Reston, VA.

U.S. Telecom Association. 2013. *Estimated US Internet Protocol Traffic 1990-2012.* Washington D.C.

World Bank. *World Development Indicators.* Washington D.C.

Voth, Hans-Joachim. 1997. *Time and Work in Eighteenth-Century London.* Discussion Papers in Economic and Social History. Number 21. Oxford: University of Oxford.

Von Tunzelman, G.N. 1978. *Steam Power and British Industrialization to 1860.* Oxford: Oxford University Press.

Wolters Kluwer CCH. 2013. *Federal Tax Law Keeps Piling Up.* www.cch.com/TaxLawPileUp.pdf. Viewed 3 July 2014.

Index

C

E

F

J

K

Q

R

S

T

CPSIA information can be obtained at www.ICGtesting.com
Printed in the USA
LVOW05*0536210715

447006LV00012B/62/P

9 781622 7302